WINNING
Over Pain, Fear and Worry

WINNING
Over Pain, Fear and Worry

BY JOHN HAGGAI

INSPIRATIONAL PRESS

NEW YORK

Except where otherwise indicated, all Scripture quotations
in this book are taken from the King James Version of the Bible.

Scriptures marked NKJV are from the Holy Bible, New King
James Version, Copyright © 1979, 1980, 1982 by Thomas
Nelson, Inc. Used by permission.

Previously published in three volumes:

HOW TO WIN OVER PAIN, copyright © 1987 by John Haggai.
HOW TO WIN OVER FEAR, copyright © 1987 by John Haggai.
HOW TO WIN OVER WORRY, copyright © 1959, 1987 by John Haggai.

Published in 1991 by

Inspirational Press
A division of LDAP, Inc.
386 Park Avenue South
Suite 1913
New York, NY 10016

Inspirational Press is a registered trademark of LDAP, Inc.

Published by arrangement with John Edmund Haggai.

Library of Congress Catalog Card Number: 90-86022

ISBN: 0-88486-041-8

Printed in the United States of America.

Contents

Book I

WINNING OVER
OVER
Pain

Introduction

Every Christian faces the problem of dealing with pain in his life when he has placed his faith in a God who is good and who has complete control over all His creation. It is one thing to know that the reason for pain and suffering is the present condition of our world fallen in sin (Romans 8:18-23). It is another thing to know how to trust God when evil strikes at our own lives with the full force of pain.

We have learned to distance ourselves from pain as much as possible. To a large extent we have "institutionalized" pain. Pain belongs in hospitals or other institutions for the mentally or physically handicapped, for the emotionally distressed, for the aged who can no longer care for themselves. Those who work there encounter pain as a professional in a rather impersonal manner, and leave their work to carry on with their lives. Others visit there to briefly empathize with the suffering and then leave to carry on with their lives. These institutions are good and necessary, but they can become a means of avoiding as much as possible the terrible reality of pain.

There are also those who deny the reality of pain. This denial comes in ways other than that of Christian Science. There is a theology that suggests healing is always available for those who have properly learned to exercise faith. When pain strikes our lives the appropriate response is to pray for a miracle that will take the pain away.

One of the greatest needs for the Christian faith in our contemporary society is an adequate theology of pain. We need to know how to face without avoidance or denial the suffering that will come to all of our lives. Our faith in a God who is good and all-powerful must become a strength from which we can deal with pain. We must not compromise this

9

faith in the face of pain and we cannot avoid the reality of pain that seems to challenge the faith we have.

How to Win Over Pain is a book that shows how our faith in God enables us to deal with the full intensity of suffering. It shows how Christians can face pain that seems to be most irrational and most unnecessary. It shows that Christians can not only cope with such pain but can be victorious over it. Pain must not make us bitter but must make us better. By the grace of God this can be true.

The problem of pain is one that has always caused the believer to cry out to God. This is most evident in the psalms where we often hear the lament of the trusting soul in the peril of death. One of the best-known of these is Psalm 22, the psalm quoted by our Savior in His hour of death as He said "My God, my God, why have you forsaken me?" I cannot preach from this psalm without making reference to the story of John and Chris Haggai, a story of pain and triumph. It is a story that exemplifies a life lived with an adequate theology of pain.

—Gus H. Konkel
Winnipeg Theological Seminary

1

Me Too

I'm going to start this book by telling you something personal.

My marriage to Chris has been greatly blessed, but in the first few years it carried one sadness—it seemed we could not have children. There was a miscarriage, and a false alarm, and that was all.

By the time I left Moody Bible Institute and received a call to Second Baptist Church in Lancaster, South Carolina, we had almost given up hope of a family. But it was while we were conducting evangelistic meetings with the new church that a new possibility appeared. At a church in Camden, Chris made a friend who knew a specialist. The man was apparently so good that a member of a European royal family had come over specifically to see him. And he worked quite close by, at Columbia Hospital.

"He's highly recommended by the O.B.-Gyn. Department at Johns Hopkins University," she said. "He's had unusual success helping women through difficult pregnancies."

When Chris shared the news with me I suggested going to see him as soon as the crusade was over. We were going through a hard time. We'd thought Chris was pregnant again and had just been disappointed. But we went anyway. The specialist gave Chris a full examination and said he saw no reason for her not to bear a child. It was a hymn of joy to our ears.

"And when she does become pregnant," I asked, "would it be safe for her to come to Columbia for consultations?"

"What is it," he said, "an hour's journey from your home? That shouldn't pose any problems."

This specialist was a delightful man, an urbane and engaging conversationalist. Women came from all over North America to consult him. He gave the impression of being totally competent and totally trustworthy. And from her first appointment he treated Chris like a daughter.

"I get the feeling God has a special reason for our meeting this man," Chris said to me.

"He's got a very special patient," I replied with a smile.

And so the waiting began. Months passed. We prayed and prayed. Anxiously, earnestly, importunately.

The following year Chris suspected she was with child. Of course I insisted on going to Columbia right away to make sure. The pregnancy was confirmed.

"You be careful, young lady," the specialist cautioned. "Do exactly as I tell you. To reward your efforts, in about eight months we'll have a new member in your family."

He gave her detailed instructions covering every phase of the pregnancy, and as the months went by and the chances of a second miscarriage lessened we started to anticipate our child's arrival. Chris said the baby kicked like a true preacher's son—he was practicing pounding on a pulpit. I was thrilled. Nothing pleased me more than the idea that my own son would follow me into the ministry. Not that I had much time to think about it—so many of our spare hours were taken up buying the bits and pieces needed for the new arrival.

When the day came for Chris to go into the hospital we had every detail organized. We had followed the doctor's instructions meticulously. Now all that remained was to let him see Chris through the final stages.

I got Chris's luggage into the car and phoned to notify the hospital. Then I called the doctor as arranged to tell him the baby was due.

He wasn't in.

I was perplexed, but not unduly worried. I left a message, presuming he would go to the hospital as soon as he got it. I only began to worry when we arrived and he wasn't there. He hadn't even made contact.

"There's no reason for alarm," the nurse assured us. "Doctors routinely have patients come to the hospital this way, at the first sign of labor. Then they arrive in ample time for the delivery."

"You'll keep the doctor informed?" I asked.

"Of course."

"Well, you'll have to get him on the phone first. I can't."

"I'm sure he'll be in touch with us just as soon as he can, and give us his point of contact," the nurse replied. She added coolly, "It is Sunday, you know."

Chris was taken into a room and made comfortable. The staff was very attentive. I paced up and down, praying for the doctor to come.

Eventually the nurse came in again.

"The doctor just called."

I breathed a sigh of relief. "When's he going to get here?"

"We gave him a complete report and he assured us everything was routine. He'll keep in touch with us."

"Keep in touch with us! What kind of specialist is that? He should be here!"

"That's not the way things are done."

"Look. My wife is about to have a baby . . ."

The nurse glanced at Chris.

"Has the doctor indicated anything unusual to you about the pregnancy?"

We admitted he hadn't.

"Then I'm sure he'll be here when he's needed."

We had to trust her. The evening dragged on. A new shift of nurses came on duty. Chris had been in labor for some time now and her pain was severe. At three in the morning they got her up for a walk in the corridor.

"Has the doctor called yet?"

The nurse shook her head silently and moved away. I caught her sleeve.

"Is this really routine? The way he's handling this case?"

She didn't reply, but I thought I saw a hint of concern in her eyes.

Chris is no quitter. She doesn't give in easily to pain. But that night there was no hiding it. I watched her, utterly helpless. I wanted to be able to comfort her, to tell her the doctor was on his way and everything was all right. But I could only take her hand and pray silently for the Lord's intervention.

When morning came and I was due at the office, I renewed my efforts at the telephone. The doctor's receptionist said he wasn't in yet. I was fast reaching the end of my tether and went to confront the head nurse.

"Look. This doctor is the reason we came to this hospital. I've been trying to get him since last night and he's nowhere to be found. Can you locate him for me?"

She was conciliatory. "We'll try. Go back to your wife. I'll let you know as soon as I can."

When I got back to Chris's room my heart was torn at the sight of her. I remember reaching for her hand, trying to pray. She jerked it away and clasped her face. I got right up to return to the phone and met the head nurse in the doorway.

"Did you find him?"

She nodded.

"Well?"

"I don't quite understand it. I reached the receptionist. And she said the doctor was in his office but he was too busy to come to the hospital."

I exploded. I grabbed the nearest phone and rang the doctor's number. When the receptionist answered I demanded to speak to him immediately. She said he was with a patient but promised he'd call back. He didn't.

"Is this what you call 'routine care of a patient'?" I said to the head nurse.

"Labor can be prolonged . . ."

"This prolonged?"

We returned to Chris's room to check the chart. At this point the head nurse's face registered alarm.

"The doctor delivers babies here?" I asked.

"Of course," she said nervously. "Several times a week."

"Does he always play hooky like this?"

She stood mute. Now I knew something was seriously wrong, and once again I bolted to the phone. This time I got through to the doctor himself. I was angry at him, and surprised to find his tone so detached and professional. But I wasn't going to be fobbed off with reassurances about the quality of the hospital staff.

"I want you here at the delivery. We didn't come all this way for consultations to have someone else deliver the baby. I don't want assistants, nurses, hospital staff. I want you. And I want you over here as fast as you can make it. Understand?"

"I'll be on my way shortly," he said.

"And if you're delayed, where do I call you?"

"I'm coming now."

He didn't come immediately, but he did come. Or at least a man came who had the same face and name as the specialist we'd seen. The calm geniality had vanished. Instead he breezed in with the air of a man who is late for an important engagement and has no time for pleasantries. He made a brusque examination.

"There's very little dilation," he said flatly. "I'll have an intern keep in touch with me. In the meantime we can probably send her home."

"Send her home!"

He looked faintly surprised, then patted me on the shoulder. "Relax," he said. "We've never lost a father yet."

It was a well-worn phrase delivered with conspicuous insincerity. He left.

Hours ticked by. They got Chris up again, walked her up and down the corridor, put her back to bed. I held my patience as long as I could and then went back to the head nurse.

"We're doing everything we can for your wife," she said.

I looked at my watch.

"It's been over 24 hours. Don't you think about a caesarean in cases like this?"

She gave a knowing little smile.

"Well, don't you?"

"It really does happen quite frequently that a woman experiences early labor pains with her first delivery."

"This bad? Going on for so long?"

She hesitated. At that moment I realized she didn't really know what to do. She might be right to go by the textbook, to let the labor run its course. On the other hand she might be disastrously wrong.

I made a decision and marched straight to the phone. It was after hours now. If I was going to get the specialist back to the hospital tonight I'd have to work fast. At his home no one could locate him, so I phoned his office. There was no reply. I phoned his home again.

"Look, I've got to get hold of him."

"Is this an emergency?" the voice asked.

"Yes, it is. Now can you please tell me where to reach the doctor?"

After a pause I was given a telephone number to try. The specialist was there, all right . . . at a cocktail party.

With difficulty I prevailed on him to come to the hospital immediately. It was a great relief to see him arrive, though it was plain that he'd been drinking fairly heavily. He made a swift inspection and told the nurse to get Chris into the delivery room. That was at 9:00 P.M. For an hour I paced up and down outside like a caged panther, feeling impatient and helpless. At 10:00 P.M. the doctor emerged from the delivery room. He looked at me sourly and tried to turn aside. I stood in his way.

"How's my wife? The baby?"

He bobbed his head. "Since you're a man of the cloth," he said, "I'll quote you something from Isaiah: *He shall shave with a borrowed razor.*"

He gave me a sickly smile and walked out into the night. I stared after him, confused.

For a few minutes nothing seemed to happen. No one else came out and there were no sounds from within. Finally I could contain myself no longer and I bolted into the room.

One of the nurses glanced at me as I entered, but she said nothing. There was now a second doctor in the delivery room. Someone told me later that he was a country G.P. from

Goldsboro who was coming in to see one of his patients when a nurse asked him to take over the operation. He looked busy. I went and stood next to Chris, trying to make sense of it all. She opened her eyes weakly, momentarily aware of my presence, then closed them again.

"You have a son," a nurse whispered to me.

I caught sight of him. The doctor was crossing the little fellow's arms over his waist then lifting them high over his head. The baby turned fire engine red, then pale, then blue.

"Do it again!" I called out.

The doctor glanced over his shoulder.

"I can't do it again so quickly. If I do it any more frequently I'll kill him."

"Can't he breathe?"

"Not without assistance."

"What happened?"

"It was a breech birth . . . with complications. He should never have been delivered that way."

A nurse behind me said, "I'm willing to put my entire career on the line. That was the most inexcusably bad delivery I've ever seen. If you want to sue for malpractice I'll be your prime witness."

"*Malpractice!*" I looked round at her. "Won't our son be all right?"

She said nothing.

"Please tell me. I can take it."

She lowered her eyes. "Your doctor hardly knew what he was doing. To be completely frank, he was drunk. You might as well have called for an automobile mechanic."

"My son won't be normal?"

"If he lives," the nurse replied, stressing the first word heavily, "he'll be spastic."

I stumbled out of the room, half angry, half numb. If you've had an experience like that you'll know what I mean when I say I can hardly describe the pain in words. It was the worst night of my life. At one point I even thought I was going to lose Chris. I thank God that He had put people in that hospital who could pray for us in our hour of need—a missionary nurse and a missions volunteer from Columbia Bible College had actually been in the delivery room. I knew I should be praying too. But even for a Christian, who thought he had put everything into the Lord's hands, prayer was hard. Thoughts of anger, disgust, and disillusionment came more readily to mind than prayer.

I won't go any further into the events of that night—a night that was in many ways my "baptism" into pain. But it is important for me to write about it here.

The first reason is this. I want it to be clear from the beginning that I am not writing about pain from any religious ivory tower. I've been there. I know what it's like. Whatever I say about it in the pages that follow you can know the words have been beaten out on the anvil of experience. You will have different pains than I have. No two people have the same pains, or experience them in the same way. But if a Geiger counter is ever invented for measuring the amount of pain a person has had I can tell you I'll score pretty high. Otherwise I wouldn't have the audacity to write a book about it.

If you are a person in pain—and you almost certainly are—I want you to know right now that there is a way through it. *You can win over pain.*

My second purpose in giving my own experience here is to introduce you to Johnny. However much pain I have suffered in my life I know that in his 24 years my only son, Johnny, whose birth I have just described, suffered much more. At birth he underwent cerebral hemorrhages that caused extensive brain damage. His jaw was badly injured and both collar bones broken. His right leg was pulled apart at the growing center.

That's some way to start out in life, and it didn't get any easier. The nurse was quite right in her prediction. Ironically, so was the specialist, for Johnny never was able to shave himself. He always had to "borrow" his razor. And yet Chris's life and my life have been marvelously enriched by the privilege of having such a son as Johnny. He might not have been the pulpit thumper I'd expected—though I know he'd have loved to if he could—yet he taught us things we would never have learned and inspired us to do things we'd never have done under more normal circumstances.

In many ways this book should have his name on it, and not mine. I know you can win over pain, because Johnny proved it to me.

2

The Easy Way Out

The first thing we learn about pain is that it's unpleasant. We learn that as children the first time we touch a hot kettle or get smacked for doing wrong. We learn it so early in fact that it seems like we've always known it.

This quality of pain goes a long way to determining our reaction to it. When a building is on fire the first thing we want to know is—*Where's the way out?* The fiercer the blaze the more urgently we desire to find the exit. So it is with pain. No one likes being hurt, physically or otherwise. When we have a pain the first and most natural thing to do is to seek an escape from it.

Of course providing "exits" from pain is big business. Just look around the drugstore the next time you're in. There's no end to remedies for flu, colds, sore throats, coughs, headaches, hangovers and all the other day-to-day pains people suffer in the modern world.

The crucial factor with these pharmaceutical exits is what we might call "speed of deployment." In a market economy manufacturers supply what the population wants, and that means supplying effective ways of suppressing pain. But people want more than that. They want instant solutions in the form of products that will remove pain in the shortest possible time. No one, after all, wants to stay in a burning building longer than he has to.

Naturally, it is a marvelous thing to have drugs capable of relieving the symptoms of illness. But they have a side effect on society as a whole. We have come to assume that pain always has a solution. We tend to think that if only we could find the right drug, or possibly the right technique or therapy, all the pain and discomfort in our lives could be ironed out.

21

The Healing Fallacy

There is a similar belief at large in the church, though it may not be related directly.

Those who espouse this view take God's promises in the Bible concerning healing very seriously. To the Christian, they argue, all the resources of God's healing are instantly available. All you have to do to overcome the pains arising from illness is to *claim that healing*. Consequently from this point of view a sick Christian is a contradiction in terms, because no Christian who is living in obedience to God can fail to enjoy full health and vigor. If a man is going to give his best for God he can hardly do it sitting in a wheelchair. Any such disability or pain will only inhibit his ministry.

Now that makes sense—until you scrutinize it.

I'll give you the clearest example I can think of—Johnny. You can imagine the dilemma I was in as a young pastor. I'd been telling people on my staff that I wanted not a 40-hour week, but a 40-hour day. I was leading a big church and I was stretched to the limit already. And now my wife would have to care for a chronically sick child. At this of all times I could least afford to be working long hours out of the house. Yet if I cut back to a normal workweek the momentum of my ministry would dissipate and the church would suffer.

I didn't want to choose between Johnny and the church. I wanted both. So I began thinking to myself: Since God is so obviously blessing my ministry at the moment, isn't it His will that Johnny be healed, so that my wife and my son can be released from this situation and become part of the work? Isn't Johnny's sickness binding up my wife's considerable gifts in public ministry and preventing her from serving as effectively as she might? Isn't it closing in some fabulous, unexpressed abilities in Johnny himself?

Evidently I wasn't the first to think along these lines. One person who believed implicitly in God's readiness to heal had already begun to ask why Johnny was still sick. Now if you believe God will heal "on demand," yet has so far failed to do so, there is only one conclusion to be drawn.

Our friend didn't pull his punches.

"You've got unconfessed sin in your life," he told us. "If everything is right with you and God, you can ask for the healing of your son and it will happen immediately."

God knows—if there were any unconfessed sins lying around in my life I'd have dug them out. And if healing depended on the power of prayer alone Johnny wouldn't just be alive and healed today, he'd have won 20 Olympic golds. But the plain fact is that Johnny never did get healed. Not comprehensively. Not satisfactorily. Johnny suffered sickness, deformity, and pain on a grand scale for the rest of his life. Looked at from the outside it might seem that prayer had failed.

So I am not going to pretend that winning over pain will always be a simple matter of "snapping the fingers" in prayer.

Healing for Real

At the same time I want to make it clear that I believe in divine healing. The Great Physician does reach down to touch us and set us free, just as He did to the lame man at the temple gate in Acts 3. I've experienced it in my life.

When I was a child I fell victim to cholera and hemorrhaged for three days. The doctors had all but given up on me—in fact they told my parents I couldn't possibly live. But God had a different plan for John Haggai. My parents had committed me to the Lord at birth and during that illness they prayed earnestly for the divine touch on my body. They asked for God's will to be done. And God performed His will.

The day after Christmas 1940 I was riding with a friend in an old Model A Ford. We were on a back road. There had been a heavy freeze for several weeks. The sun had come out and melted the surface ice; what we didn't know was that there was more ice under the gravel. Suddenly the car went out of control and turned over. The windshield gashed my leg.

As I was recuperating, streptococcus infection set in. The doctor said the hole in my leg was the size of half an orange. A blood clot formed and began moving towards my heart.

"1 think we'll have to amputate," one of the doctors told my parents.

But my father was a man of dauntless faith. He asked the doctors to wait just a little while longer and urged all our friends to pray. A few days later I was clearly on the mend.

The physician, who was an avowed atheist, was at a loss to explain it, "unless, like you say, some power other than human intervened."

So I believe in divine healing. I believe that God will step into any medical situation and heal directly, according to His will. That is the teaching of the Bible and the testimony of my own personal experience. God can be relied upon to stand by the Scriptural promises.

But while I affirm wholeheartedly that God heals I still take exception to the cut-and-dried view of healing offered to me over Johnny.

I wish I had been able to find my "unconfessed sin"; I wish I had been able to pray in complete confidence that faith would assure him the sort of life I had envisaged before his birth. I would like to have saved him all the pain he had to endure. Like any father I craved for my son that his life might be as near as possible to heaven on earth.

But life isn't that simple, and neither is healing.

Exactly why it isn't simple will become clear later in the book. However, the explanation begins at the same point as this chapter, with our relationship to pain. So it is important to understand, from a biblical point of view, the role pain plays in human life as a whole.

3

Understanding Pain

Ask the average Christian where pain comes from and he will probably say, "From the Fall."

This is the truth, but it's not the whole truth.

It is the truth because as far as we can tell from Scripture man in his pre-fallen state did not know pain. It is possible of course that Adam got a sore stomach from eating green apples or cut himself falling over a tree stump. But there is no indication that this happened. Adam and Eve seemed to live in a state of undisturbed harmony with each other, with the environment, and with God. In such a situation pain had no function.

But that is not the same as saying that pain did not exist as a *possibility*. Adam and Eve were in the physiological sense exactly the same as any man or woman alive today. They could touch, feel, smell, hear, and see. And everything they encountered with these senses told them what God had already thought of His new world—"Behold, it was very good" (Genesis 1:31).

If Adam had ever snagged his thumb on a rose prickle or stubbed his toe on a stone, his senses would have told him something else too: It hurts. He already carried in his body all the neurological apparatus that conveys to the mind what is potentially harmful. He could have caused himself pain, and caused pain to Eve and to the animals he'd been given charge of, if he'd wanted.

That "if" is the crux of the whole matter.

You see, after making a creature with a body like Adam's God could have done one of two things with regard to pain. He could have regulated pain by stripping man of one or more of his faculties. If He'd eliminated part of the nervous

25

system, for instance, man could have had a foolproof guarantee against pain. Adam could have stubbed his toe as often as he liked and never felt a twinge. Or God could have deprived man of his freedom—protected Adam's toe, as it were, by running him like a remotely controlled automated toy, so that he never went near a tree stump. Both these methods would have resolved the problem of pain simply by making pain impossible.

But God didn't do that. Instead He opted to give man informed freedom of choice.

I say "informed" because freedom is available by degrees. It was Newell Dwight Hillis who pointed out that freedom increases in proportion to the number of laws one obeys. A stone, obeying only the law of gravity, sits motionless on the ground. A worm, obeying the laws of gravity and motion, has the freedom of movement. A bird obeys three laws: gravity, motion, and aerodynamics, so it can perch, walk, or fly. Of course, not obeying the laws that govern you reduces your effectiveness. Only the river that stays within the confines of the river banks is able to perform the useful work of generating electricity at a turbine.

Man's freedom engaged the highest law—the moral law. Obedience to that law opened to him the finest and purest form of existence, that of communion with God. That was really God's purpose in creating man. The fact that obedience to this law brought freedom from pain was a mere side effect. Nonetheless the possibility of pain if the law were disobeyed was what gave the law its cutting edge. Little was at stake in Adam's other freedoms. If he had decided to call a giraffe a banana and vice versa we would be none the worse for it. As it was:

> The Lord God commanded the man, saying, Of every tree of the garden thou mayest freely eat: But of the tree of the knowledge of good and evil, thou shalt not eat of it: For in the day that thou eatest thereof thou shalt surely die (Genesis 2:16,17).

This is real freedom—to do right or wrong.

Note that God does not say to Adam, "Of the tree of the knowledge of good and evil *thou shalt not be able to eat.*" The tree of knowledge presumably looked much like any other fruit tree. It wasn't hedged about with barbed wire and warning signs. All that stood between Adam and Eve and eating the fruit of that tree, were God's command and a frank summary of the consequence if they disobeyed.

In other words God was appealing to their free will. As long as they used that free will correctly, as long as they honored their relationship with God by obeying His command, their lives remained harmonious and free from pain. There was no occurrence of sickness or injury, and in our modern jargon we would say that socially they were totally fulfilled. Disobedience and its cargo of pain and death were what they were always intended to be—possibilities forever unexplored.

Well, you don't need me to tell you what happened next. It is quite literally "history," the keynote of all that followed.

But once again be clear about the details. When pain entered human experience at the Fall it wasn't an act of retribution on God's part. He hadn't said to Adam, "If you eat of this tree I will kill you," The "Thou shalt surely die" was a statement of fact. I speak in the same way if I say, "As soon as I step out of my front door I shall be outside." As soon as the first happens the second is automatically true. I don't decide to be outside after I've closed the front door behind me: The act of leaving the house has brought me outside whether I like it or not.

You can see this effect working in Genesis. When Eve takes that first bite it's as if someone switched on a stage light. The whole scene seems to change color. Even her seeing that the tree is "to be desired to make one wise" is in contrast to her previous state of innocent, voluntary surrender to God. Suddenly she is self-oriented.

When she gives some of the fruit to Adam the first thing that happens is that their relationship is broken. In the place of carefree happiness, they now experience shame at their bodies and want to hide from one another. And when God comes walking in the garden they want to hide from Him too. In a single act of disobedience the entire delicate structure of their freedom is brought crashing down. Pain has entered Paradise, though they have not yet learned to name it.

And the consequences spread. In this first act of self-assertion man not only ruins his relationship with God, he also ruins his relationship with the natural world. "In sorrow thou shalt bring forth children," God says to Eve; and to Adam, "Cursed is the ground for thy sake . . . in the sweat of thy face shalt thou eat bread" (Genesis 3:16,17,19).

Everything in man's life, from his worship of God to his eating and childbearing, is suddenly and disastrously transformed. The being who so coveted his own wisdom now has to do his own work by the sweat of his brow. He can't expect the elements to cooperate with him, either. He faces hardship, and in hardship the constant likelihood of pain. Far from being a mere possibility or a matter of theory, pain becomes what it has remained to this day—part of the human condition.

You may have a broken marriage. You may have cancer. You may have gone through the windshield of your car. You may suffer from anxiety or insecurity. You may have lost a loved one, or be enduring the privations of old age. Whatever your particular pain or pains, self-assertion is the root. Pain pervades human society. It dogs every man and woman from the cradle to the grave. None of us escapes it entirely. Even in the prosperous western world pain keeps intruding into our lives.

To be alive is to know pain.

One obvious reason for this is the paradox involved in man having disobeyed God in the first place to get something he wanted for himself, and then forever after being frustrated in his attempts at self-fulfillment. It is, almost by definition, no longer possible for man in his natural state to find contentment and satisfaction. Life continually presents us with situations and experiences that we don't like, and this is the essence of pain.

Pain, then, can be defined as *disagreeable experience*.

Whether I've just broken my leg or lost an important business deal, I am still suffering pain. Pain can be physical or mental. It can be acute or barely perceptible. It can be drawn out over years or be over in a minute. All that matters is that while I experience it I find it unpleasant; otherwise it is not truly pain. Correspondingly it may be that the same thing experienced by two separate individuals is pain to one and neutral—maybe even pleasurable—to the other. If you don't believe me, think back to the first "grown-up" function you were made to attend in childhood as a matter of duty!

Why Me?

Many of the pains we suffer are inconsequential. But for every one of us a few pains are serious, perhaps debilitating, and when they come, we ask urgent questions.

A very common one is: *Why me?* or possibly: *Why am I being punished like this?*

The biblical answer is that no one gets singled out for punishment. In a sense we are all Adam, we are all Eve. We share their guilt and compound it by our own sins, with the result that we share their death. The types of pain preceding that death vary from one person to another. Some seem to get off lightly. Conversely, some who lead apparently good lives nonetheless suffer a lot of pain.

Forty-three years ago a dear friend of mine, who later became a prominent platform artist, accompanied me to my little church in Ainsworth, Indiana.

During the train trip from Chicago he was in tears practically all the way. His body shook with emotion. Since this was very unlike him I asked what the problem was, and he told me his story. He was in love with a beautiful young coed, a fine Christian whom he wanted to marry. The trouble was that although they got along very well, she kept putting him off. It took him weeks to persuade her to tell him the truth. Amid her sobs she said that her father had lived recklessly in his youth and had passed down to her a congenital disease which, if she married, would certainly be passed on to her children. That she refused to do.

There, surely, were two people for whom the question of personal guilt had little relevance. Of course they were sinners, saved only by grace. We all are. But neither of them was deserving of a specific and cruel punishment like that, and to say they were is to have a very vindictive picture of God. The fact is; original sin is about as discriminating in its effect as nuclear fallout. People get hit who are miles away from the explosion.

But then maybe we question our consciences when we feel pain in the hope that our consciences contain a solution to it. It's a little like finding the bullet in a wound. Certainly "Why me?" was a question we asked on Johnny's behalf.

In the weeks after his birth he had to be treated in an intensive care unit. Occasionally we got reports from the nurses about his progress, but I had seen him only at birth, and Chris, who was very weak, hadn't seen him at all. The doctors had avoided telling her the truth about his condition for fear of causing her distress.

Those days remain a blur in my mind. I had to get back to church, and to the responsibilities of preparing sermons and Bible studies, taking phone calls, and answering correspondence. I did it all like an automaton. But I also affirm that the promises of God stand firm. "My grace is sufficient for thee" was as true for Chris and me as it was for the apostle Paul.

One of the toughest milestones was deciding on a name. Names are very meaningful to me, and we had agreed during the pregnancy that if we had a son he would be called John Edmund Haggai, Jr. But now I began to have doubts. What if this poor spastic baby turned out to be little more than a vegetable? Wouldn't it be better to save the name for a baby who was normal? Chris was also cautious.

"Shouldn't we wait to see if he lives?" she said on one of my visits to the hospital.

"People at the church are going to ask me. And we agreed to name the baby after me if it was a boy . . ."

"Only then we hadn't realized what the situation would be."

We left the matter unresolved. That night I had to attend the choir practice and was obliged to give a report on the baby. The inevitable question came up.

"Have you named the child yet?" asked one of the women.

I was surprised at my own answer.

"We have. He's John Edmund Haggai, Jr."

The choir broke into applause. The next night I was back at the hospital to tell Chris.

"I'm so pleased," she said. "But . . ." her face clouded. "I'm also troubled."

"About what?"

She hesitated. "I've just been lying here today thinking: Why has it happened to him? I wondered if there's something in my life that isn't pleasing to the Lord."

I nodded.

"Yes, something like that has occurred to me, too." I took her hand. "You know that story in the Gospels about the man born blind, and how the disciples asked whether it was he or his parents who had sinned? I guess they assumed it was some sort of punishment for something God wasn't pleased with. But Jesus had a different answer. He said, 'Neither hath this man sinned, nor his parents: but that the works of God should be made manifest in him' " (John 9:3).

We had both searched our hearts and to the best of our knowledge there was nothing we were holding back. Right then we dedicated our Johnny to God.

"We place him by faith on Your altar," I prayed. "If it's Your will that he die, take him. But if possible, in Your sovereign will, we ask You to heal him. If he lives, whatever the circumstances, we trust You to show us Your plan for his life."

If I hadn't been brought up to trust God implicitly, that would have been a tough prayer to pray. But I've never, not even with Johnny, found myself demanding to know from God what He thinks He's up to.

Yet, if we have a concept of God as all-powerful and all-loving, it is natural to ask a second question about pain: *Why does God allow it?* or maybe: *Why doesn't He stop it?*

Is Pain God's Fault?

In brief, the answer to these questions is probably that God allows it because He cannot stop it—not at least in the way most people imagine.

Pain is not a sort of plague. A plague has nothing to do with human beings except for the fact that it kills them. Pain on the other hand is something human beings collectively have *chosen* to take on board. Adam and Eve may not have known it, but when they ate of the fruit they chose to endure pain just as surely as, on a rainy day, I "choose" a rainstorm when I step out my front door. Once I'm outside I may regret my decision. But the fact is that I can avoid the rain only by turning around and going back into the house. On a rainy day there is no such thing as being outside and not being rained on.

In exactly the same way there is no such thing as being sinful and staying out of pain.

In Adam we all chose to disobey God, and, Christian or not, to our dying day we will be suffering the consequences. When man asks to have his pain removed, he is really asking to be readmitted to Eden. But what does that mean? It means being restored to a proper relationship with God. And how will he do that? By repenting of his sins and believing in the Lord Jesus Christ. In other words, the only one who can do anything about pain is man himself, and not man collectively but each individual man and woman. Each one of us individually makes the decision to turn about and go back in that gate.

And it has to be said, even this does not free us from pain until we die and go to be with the Lord. The Christian takes his place with the rest of humanity in the realm of pain. It has to be that way because pain is such that it accumulates and leaves scars and memories, and these will not be erased until in the resurrection "all things are made new" (Revelation 21:5).

We read in the Old Testament how David had to live with the memory of his dead child and his adultery with Bathsheba. Similarly, an executive I know from one of the major spark plug manufacturing companies, though he now lives for the Lord, still grieves that he disobeyed God's call to preach as a young man.

Solving what C.S. Lewis calls the "problem of pain," then, is a matter of changing not just the experience, but the complete spiritual condition of man. And there the ball is in our court. A relationship that we have voluntarily broken cannot be restored by force. Remember, freedom to obey or disobey the moral law, to live under God or without Him, is that highest and unique freedom granted to us at creation. Our pain is the price we pay for having God honor our choice.

God's Attitude Toward Pain

That said, there are two other reasons why God might choose to leave the human race with its pain.

The first is that in spiritual terms pain actually performs the very useful function of bringing us down to earth. If Adam had been allowed to leave Eden to enjoy a fallen, yet blissfully pain-free existence elsewhere, he would have had no motive to reform. His coup would have been successful, and he would have become master of a world in which man claimed all the privileges of heaven while sinking steadily into spiritual degeneracy.

Even if it were possible, which is doubtful, this state of affairs would be to nobody's benefit, least of all ours. It would probably have the effect of spoiling us, just as loading children with an excess of material goods can turn them into perfect brats. In this sense, to have pain in our world is good for us. C.S. Lewis describes it as "God's megaphone, to rouse a deaf world . . . planting the flag of truth within the fortress of the rebel soul."

Pain shatters the very illusion the devil used to dupe Eve in the first place—that "ye shall be as gods" (Genesis 3:5). What better way to remind the would-be "god" of his need for the real Creator than a dose of pain? It was because the prodigal son "fain would have filled his belly with the husks the swine did eat" (Luke 15:16) that he thought of returning to his father.

That doesn't make pain good. Anyone who's tried eating pig swill can testify to that. Pain is an evil that should never have come into the world. No one knows that more acutely than I do. I also know how easily it can lead to anger and bitterness, instead of repentance and reality.

There was the first time I saw Johnny after the delivery room experience.

Right after Chris and I had committed him to the Lord in prayer, Chris leaned back on the pillows and said, "I wish I could see him."

I knew the nurses wanted to shield her from disappointment, so I began to explain, "They can't bring him. He needs constant care."

She nodded. "I understand."

But as I pondered I couldn't find any reason for me not to go to him, so I went to the floor supervisor.

She wasn't very cooperative.

"That's not possible," she said, then added condescendingly, "You need to spend all the time you can with your wife. Frankly, Mr. Haggai, if she doesn't have a real good cry she's going to crack up."

"My wife is undergirded by the strength and peace only Christ can give," I replied.

The woman shrugged and turned back to her desk.

"So when can I see the baby?"

She looked up. "I told you—"

But this time I interrupted. "Look. I'm a clergyman. If you can't let me see him as his father, then you must let me see him as his pastor."

This seemed to catch her off guard.

"I want to offer a prayer for the child," I said.

That clinched it. The nurse supervisor, Sudy Waters, was summoned and I was issued a sterilized coat and mask. We went together into the ward.

I think Sudy said something like, "He's such a dear baby." But that wasn't what I saw. In front of me was a helpless infant, struggling for breath, the marks of injury plain on his body. I'm not sure whether in that moment I wished to see him dead or alive. Across my mind flashed the face of the specialist, the man who had robbed my son of his rightful start in life, and I began to feel angry.

It was a sensation made worse by other frustrating experiences I'd had at the hospital. Sometimes it seems as if the doctors knew what had happened and were closing ranks. One told me, "Your son wasn't injured at birth. He simply suffered a maldevelopmental midline defect." This was so much pseudo-scientific baloney. The greenest medical student could have seen that Johnny's injuries were the result of ineptitude on the part of the obstetrician.

It was also very hard to get information. The only person who gave us reliable progress reports on Johnny was Sudy. The rest adopted the practice, all too common in medical circles 30 years ago, of withholding the whole truth. At first we were given to believe Johnny would live a few months, a few years at most, and then only in a comatose state: blind, deaf, and unable to recognize us. The prospect was heart-rending. And yet the thought of opening a malpractice suit (much as I was urged to do it) seemed wrong. Johnny had nothing to gain by it. I would be acting purely out of revenge. And after all, this specialist was still a world-famous physician who had helped hundreds of people.

Significantly, I learned later we were the victims not of his deliberate negligence and cruelty, but of his pain. His only son, a Navy pilot, had been shot down and killed in the Korean War. The man had tried to put on a brave face, but inside he was broken. It just so happened we were on the scene when he couldn't hide it anymore, and was turning to drink.

The sudden arrival of pain in our own lives left us with no doubt that pain is an evil thing. But we learned to look on this evil in a very particular way.

It was six weeks before we were able to take Johnny home. To compensate for the paralysis of his throat muscles he had to be force-fed with a Brecht feeder—a kind of baby bottle with a nipple at one end and a plunger at the other.

"Will I ever be able to master it?" asked Chris, stepping a little closer.

"Of course you will," said Sudy. "It does take some skill not to give him too much milk, or you'll strangle him. And not too little, or he'll take in air. But you'll catch on to it."

Chris was ready to give her utmost for Johnny. Her determination and commitment were tremendous.

She leaned over the cot to get a better look at our baby.

"He's handsome, John," she said, grinning. "He looks just like you."

I admit I winced. But as we stood looking at our son we did not feel anything like despair, even though we knew the chances were one in a million that he would have a normal life. We accepted him. We wanted him. He was God's gift.

The late Dr. Harold John Ockenga said to an audience at the First Presbyterian Church in Chattanooga in 1951, "I don't believe God ever used anyone in a powerful way who had not first suffered."

At the time, as a 27-year-old clergyman, I thought the statement rash. Over the years that followed I have become convinced that Ockenga was right.

4

Labeling the Bag

So far we've collected all of our pains, put them in a big bag, and tied it with a label saying *disagreeable experience*.

That tells us what all kinds of pain have in common, at least at the most obvious level. It's a definition. It tells us how to recognize pain when we see it.

But that's not the only label we could put on the bag. A second label might read: *warning signs*.

Pain as Warning

We've already seen the warning effect of pain in a spiritual sense; in other words, that the existence of pain in general serves to alert us to our fallen state. On a spiritual level, pain is the symptom confirming the human disorder of rebellion against God (not, I stress again, on an individual basis, but in the area of mankind's relationship with the Creator as typified by the story of Adam and Eve).

If you develop a peptic ulcer it is extremely unlikely that God is visiting on you the punishment for sins committed by you or your forebears. More likely you've been working too hard or eating too much spicy food. But the ulcer, like every other pain in your life, nonetheless acts as a reminder of your need for God.

While pain generally warns us of our spiritual deficiency, pain in specific cases warns people that something is wrong in their body, mind, or situation.

The most obvious example is physical pain.

Let's say I stick my finger in some hot water. My nervous system is preprogramed to cope with this emergency, so a message is immediately relayed to my brain which, if you could translate it into words, would say something like: "If you don't get your finger out of there you'll be serving it up as a hot dog." Of course it is never translated into words. Usually some circuit lower down in my nervous system is activated and my arm is jerked backwards before I've had time to think about it.

Most of us have thought at some time that it would.be nice not to have physical pain. But pain performs an essential function. Left in the hot water my finger would suffer injury, so it's vital that I remove it fast. The body in effect declares a red alert and "cranks up the siren." The siren may make a loud and unpleasant sort of noise, but at least it makes me listen.

To see how important pain is you only have to look at people who are without it.

Much of the damage sustained by the limbs of a leper, for instance, results not from the disease itself, but from the fact that leprosy destroys the nerves. A leper who has a job cutting bamboo with a machete can sever his thumb and not know it until he sees the blood. In fact he will be more likely to injure himself in this way because the lack of sensation in his hand will encourage him to treat it like an inanimate object or a tool.

So given that we occupy a material world where it is possible to suffer injury, pain is more of an asset than a liability.

The real problem with physical pain comes when it is protracted. Cancer, arthritis, burns—and for that matter flus and colds—can all cause varying degrees of prolonged pain.

I know that only too well from living with Johnny. As he grew up his body looked like a sapling struggling to survive in a cold wilderness. It was bent and gnarled. I will never know just how much pain he had to endure, but I know it was severe. We could see it in his face. Often he had to spend most of his day lying down because it was the least taxing position for him; if he sat up for too long he'd get a fit of vomiting. And because the trap at the bottom of his esophagus wouldn't close properly, he always had to be elevated slightly to keep acids from the stomach from moving up and causing burning and irritation. Eating, sleeping, bathing, even just sitting—in every part of his life Johnny experienced pain. How he rose above it is a mystery to me.

Physical pain like this is no longer useful. It's sending the same message over and over again, that there is injury, deformity, malfunction.

Consequently one of the main ways of dealing with physical pain is by "killing" it; that is, by trying to turn the volume down on the siren, and maybe stop it altogether. And if drugs are ineffective in this, there are other ways of drowning the siren. Biofeedback or self-hypnosis, for example.

I've talked about physical pain at some length here, though it is not the major focus of this book, because of its importance. Physical pain *per se* can often be controlled by modern medicine, and to that extent it is a special sort of pain, with specialized solutions.

However, medicine cannot control every physical pain. In addition, painkilling drugs frequently have destructive side effects. Most important, there are few conditions causing physical pain that do not at the same time cause pain of other kinds. AIDS, to take a recent example, debilitates as much by the sense of isolation it imposes on the victim as it does by physical suffering.

This other region of pain, broadly termed "mental" pain is if anything more pervasive and complex, and certainly harder to control.

But mental pain too is a warning sign.

In the first months of Johnny's life Chris worked unceasingly to nurse him. She had some much-valued assistance from her mother, Mother Barker, who made a point of treating Johnny like a completely normal grandchild. But as time went on and the doctors insisted Johnny was showing no signs of mental growth, the advice they so often gave us, to put him in an institution, began to weigh heavily on our minds.

"What do you think we should do?" I asked Chris one day.

She knew what I had been pondering.

"If we put him in an institution he'll die in a very short time."

"Looking after him is a very heavy commitment."

"I know. But I want to keep this baby right here at home."

"It'll mean constant care."

"I'm prepared to give him constant care."

"Day and night?"

"Day and night."

That was when we finally passed the point of no return. I have to admit it was Chris who showed the most confidence and courage. Somehow she'd caught the conviction that God was absolutely, unquestionably right when He gave us Johnny, and that we must keep him at all costs.

A few months later, I transferred to a pastorate in Chattanooga, where there was an excellent specialist to care for Johnny. There Johnny began to show the first small signs of alertness. He would follow Chris's finger as she moved it in front of his face, and he responded to my voice. We were delighted.

But at the same time I was under great pressure in my new position. It proved so hard to change things in the church that I almost regretted leaving Lancaster. To compensate I threw myself into a radio ministry. I wanted to reach successful, goal-oriented people and challenge them to put God first. It was only a small 5,000-watt station, but by taking the early slot at 5:45 A.M. I could be heard 750 miles away in Binghampton, New York.

Working early in the morning, though, brought extra problems. I frequently had special committee meetings in the evenings, so more often than not I'd be out till midnight and up the next morning before Chris was awake. She hardly ever saw me. And unless I took the most extravagant precautions my foot would always make a squeak on the stair at five o'clock and wake Johnny. His strange, plaintive cry would sound, and Chris—who for the first few years with Johnny never had more than two hours of uninterrupted sleep— would have to get up and see to him.

Chris became more and more weary. Some days she performed her chores like a robot.

I felt wretched about it. "I would have to take the most difficult pastorate in the South," I lamented, "right when I need to be helping you."

"I'm managing," she replied.

That courage made me proud of her. But one evening when I returned home from a meeting I slipped quietly into the house to find her weeping.

For a moment I was at a loss for words.

"I know it's rough on you," I said eventually.

But she shook her head.

"It's not me." She pointed to the bed where Johnny was lying fitfully asleep. "He's had such a bad day. Oh, John, to see him suffer so!"

Here were three instances of mental pain going on at the same moment. My pain over the church, Chris's pain over Johnny, and our pain over one another. Each one spoke its own warning about a particular stress in our lives. Looking back I could have acted on those warnings more swiftly. I knew that my work schedule put a strain on Chris. I confessed it to her frequently. There were times when she wanted to tell me something important and because I had so much to cope with I blocked her out, appearing to listen while my mind was elsewhere. And there were also times when I tried to encourage Chris to get out of the house—to sing, for example—and she wasn't able to respond. In all of these cases the pain we felt was a form of protection.

This protective function of mental pain can also operate in a spiritual context.

I remember the story of a young man who was tempted once to go into a Parisian brothel. It was winter, and he was just removing his wallet when he slipped on the ice and his wallet fell onto the pavement, opening to reveal a photograph. He picked it up and looked at it. Staring at him was a photograph of his mother. Immediately he felt a pang of shame and remorse. It was that disagreeable experience, that pain, that saved him from going into the brothel and sent him home.

So now our "bag of pains" can be labeled as *disagreeable experience* and also as *warning signs*.

But there is a third label we can put on the bag, the label of *limitation*.

Pain as Limitation

It may seem crazy to ask a question like "Why does pain hurt?" As we've said before, that a pain hurts is what makes it a pain in the first place. Yet as soon as you get away from physical pain, which hurts in the most literal sense, it is often less clear why a so-called pain is unpleasant to us.

I believe one of the commonest answers is that pain *limits* us.

Take the example of a woman who has just been abandoned by her husband. He's vanished. She's left with the bills, an apartment, and a couple of preschool children. Limitation will cause much of her pain. That may mean the physical limitation of not having anyone to help look after the children, or not having enough income to provide as she'd done before. But limitation will strike her in many other ways as well. She will be limited by the removal of her partner's love, presence, and support. All the joys and opportunities of married love will be stolen away from her.

In every hurt there is an unfulfilled desire for a better situation, one which the person can imagine would have been possible had he not been in his present circumstances. This better, fuller, freer, richer life may have been his until the hurtful experience deprived him of it. It may be one other people are leading which he has never been able to attain. Either way he will feel something he values has been taken away from him, that he has been limited.

The most obvious example of the pain of limitation is the prisoner, the person whose confinement is literal. But limitation occurs in almost every pain.

The bereaved mother is limited by the loss of her child. She will miss not just the physical presence of the child, but the time spent together, the entire future of joy and happiness that cannot be regained. She may have another child, several other children. But she will never be able to experience the pleasure and opportunity of that particular child's life. It will always be a locked door.

Similarly a couple moving overseas will often experience the pain of limitation. They are far away from family and old friends, all the people who give them stability and reassurance. They may be limited by their poor knowledge of the new language, their unfamiliarity with the social customs of the people they now have as neighbors.

Johnny was limited.

As he grew up it was clear to us that there was nothing wrong with his mind. He was just trapped in a broken body.

We took Johnny to the Institute for the Development of Human Potential in Philadelphia. There he had a session with the head of the University of Pennsylvania medical school's Department of Neurosurgery, Dr. Eugene Spitz.

"Your son has an exceptionally fine mind," he said. "Unfortunately, we have no methods devised for giving an IQ test to someone in his situation—his communication is so severely limited. But were we able to conduct such a test, I have no question but that he would have a rating in the junior-genius or the genius class."

But not only could Johnny not take intelligence tests, we couldn't even find him the kind of toys that would provide him with a proper education.

We did have one asset in the form of a great next-door neighbor, Mr. Merchant. Mr. Merchant took special pains to entertain Johnny, and it didn't take long for the mowing of Mr. Merchant's lawn on a Saturday afternoon to turn into a spectator sport. As soon as she heard the lawnmower Chris would wheel Johnny out and place him in the little unmown patch of grass Mr. Merchant left in the shade of a tree. I think he purposely let the machine run out of fuel just so Johnny could watch him refilling it.

I'm sure Johnny would have given anything to pull that starter cord himself. He loved anything mechanical and noisy.

Gasoline pumps fascinated him. When a mechanic came to work on the car we arranged for Johnny to watch if we possibly could. If that boy had had just one steady hand capable of holding a screwdriver or a pair of pliers I suppose he'd have tried to take apart and reassemble every gadget in the house.

We spent a long time trying to teach him something most children pick up naturally in the first few years of life—the gift of language.

I'm sure it was all there in his mind. There was never any doubt that he could understand what we were saying to him, and when he tried to reply the sounds he made always had the correct number and arrangement of syllables. But understanding him was like listening to a distant radio station in an electric storm. Hard as he tried, nothing was intelligible.

He did master two words: "yeah," meaning "yes," and "umn," meaning "no." And with those two he managed to do a lot of communicating.

There was an afternoon just after we moved to Atlanta when I took Johnny in the car on an errand. We got there all right, but on the way back I lost my way completely.

I didn't know Johnny had noticed until he told me.

"Umn!" he said, all of a sudden.

"What's the matter, Buddy? Did I turn the wrong way?"

"Yeah," Johnny said.

So I circled around the block till we came back to the street we'd been on before.

"Is this the street we turn on, up ahead?" I said.

"Yeah."

I really didn't know whether it was or not, but I took it anyway. We rolled on for three or four more blocks, and then Johnny said loudly, "Yeah!"

We'd hit the main street we'd been looking for.

"Do we go left?" I said.

"Umn!"

When I reached the intersection I turned right, and soon recognized the road we'd taken coming out. Frankly, I would never have found it again by myself.

"Yeah," said Johnny as we turned. I don't know, but I'm convinced I heard a note of dry humor in his voice, a sort of friendly reproach for being dumb enough to need directions.

For me Johnny's limitation provides a scale for measuring everyone else's. There wasn't much in Johnny's life—in fact I can't think of anything—that wasn't subject to the pain of limitation. He didn't even have any real childhood friends. His disabilities made such friendships impossible to sustain.

It is because limitation of the kind Johnny suffered is so obvious that we often put people like him in a special mental compartment. We call them "handicapped" or "disabled," and their disability will probably color the way we relate to them. But inside Johnny was a normal person just like the rest of us. He knew the same joy and hunger for life, and it distressed him—as it distresses any disabled person—to be treated differently from others.

Really, it is ironic that "normal" people set themselves apart in this way, because in one sense we all have a limitation far more severe than Johnny's. It is pictured in Jesus's visit to the pool of Bethesda:

> And a certain man was there, which had an infirmity thirty and eight years. When Jesus saw him lie, and knew that he had been now a long time in that case, he saith unto him, Wilt thou be made whole?
>
> The impotent man answered him, Sir, I have no man, when the water is troubled, to put me into the pool; but while I am coming, another steppeth down before me.
>
> Jesus said to him, Rise, take up thy bed, and walk. And immediately the man was made whole (John 5:5-9).

The Fall left us with physical and mental limitations. It also left us with spiritual limitations. Just as the impotent man was unable to make good on the angel's visit to the pool, even when he knew it had occurred, we too are naturally unable to respond to God. We have a spiritual limitation that can be overcome only by the quickening of the Holy Spirit.

In effect this is the baseline from which we all begin. Whatever limitations pain places on you, your spiritual limitation will be the severest. If you haven't noticed that, and many haven't, it just goes to prove how powerful a limitation you are under.

This book will help you only if you recognize your spiritual limitation. And not just recognize it, but take it to God in repentance, so that you can begin a new life of spiritual wholeness, as the impotent man began a new life of physical wholeness. The two go together. No one can build a house without first laying a foundation.

Let me summarize.

I've said that pain is anything we can put in a bag labeled *disagreeable experience*. I've also said that we can label the bag in at least two other ways, because pain generally functions as a *warning sign*, and imposes *limitations*.

But that's all very general.

If we want to start learning how to win over pain, we'll have to slit open that bag and see what's inside.

5

Where Does It Hurt?

Just before I started this chapter I developed a physical pain. It wouldn't go away, so I went for a checkup to make sure I wasn't in the running for a serious illness.

Nowadays there are all kinds of fancy machines doctors use to diagnose a patient. Machines that monitor your heart-rate, machines that photograph your insides through optical fiber. Machines that electronically slice you up like a meat slicer and pop your cross section on a TV screen.

But a doctor doesn't start using his medical box of tricks until he's asked the very simple questions doctors have asked since the days of Hippocrates.

The simplest question is one you have been asked yourself: *Where does it hurt?*

A doctor will ask this because, as we noted in the last chapter, pain acts as a warning sign. Pain is the doctor's indication that something is wrong. Exactly where the pain is located tells him—or may give him a clue—what is causing it. A man complaining of an acute pain in his lower right abdomen, for instance, is likely to be suffering from an inflamed appendix, and not from tennis elbow.

Even if the doctor doesn't have enough information to make a temporary diagnosis at this stage, he will at least be looking in the right place. He can use the appropriate technology to look at the area of pain more closely. He may take blood samples, or use an X-ray. If all else fails, he may opt for an exploratory operation.

Whatever he does he will now be asking a second question. Not *Where does it hurt?*, but *Why?* If he can answer this with sufficient certainty he will have made his diagnosis.

The answer may confirm or contradict his original suspicions. The man with an acute stomach pain may turn out not to be suffering from appendicitis after all, but from some completely different condition that has produced very similar symptoms. This is extremely important, because the *Why?* of a pain determines how it will be treated. The whole practice of medicine hangs on discovering the correct cause in order to alleviate the correct problem. Get the wrong cause and the treatment will be ineffective—taking out the man's appendix isn't going to cure him if his real problem is a hernia. Worse still, if you get the wrong cause you may inflict unnecessary damage; for example, by carrying out a mastectomy when the growth in a woman's breast is benign.

In short, it is vital to the welfare of the patient that the doctor answer the question *Why?* correctly.

I'm oversimplifying things a little. In a good many cases the answer to the first question is vague, a general feeling of ill-health, or of being run-down. Here a doctor may get as much information from the nature of the pain as from its source. Of course the pain may be much more a "disagreeable experience" than an actual physical pain (blurred vision rather than stomachache). It doesn't matter. In general the doctor still moves from the first question to the second—from *Where?* to *Why?*—in order to identify the cause of the disorder and decide on its treatment.

The same is true of emotional pains. If you have a pain it's no good saying, "I'm hurting, I'm hung up, I'm miserable." You've got to locate that pain. When a doctor asks, "Where does it hurt?" and the pain's in your ankle, you don't say to him, "All over—I'm just in pain." You let him know where the pain is. Treatment, and winning over pain, begins with answering the question *Where?*

You may know the answer to that as clearly as if you had an earache or a cut finger. "This pain's in my marriage," you might reply. Or, "This pain's in my relationships at work."

On the other hand, the pain may be harder to track down. You may feel a pain—say, a vague sense of insecurity—whenever you are in a social situation with other people. You may feel a desire to be a better person, without knowing in what way. Your whole life may be dogged by emotional lethargy and appear lackluster and frustrating.

If that's true, then, like the doctor, you will have to do some hard thinking.

But you have one big advantage over the doctor. He cannot see inside the patient. What he knows about the patient is what he observes, what his equipment can find out, and what the patient tells him. Those communication bridges aren't necessary for you. You are the patient. You know your life and situation more intimately than any other individual on this planet. Sure, it may help to talk it out with someone else. But if anyone's going to find where that pain comes from, it'll be you.

There's another consideration too.

When the Israelites arrived on the borders of the Canaan they didn't know what was ahead of them. They'd heard rumors, but that was all. So they started on a bit of reconnaissance work, and sent in 12 spies to tell them as accurately as possible what was in the land God had promised to them.

All of those spies saw exactly the same thing. They saw land and crops and fortified cities and giants. But for ten of them the picture was confusing and they came back with reports of unremitting gloom: "We are not able to go up against the people; for they are stronger than we" (Numbers 13:31).

Only Joshua and Caleb saw the place as it really was—as God had shown it to them. For these two men,

> The land, which we passed through to search it,
> is an exceeding good land. If the Lord delight in us,
> then he will bring us into this land, and give it us; a
> land which floweth with milk and honey (Numbers 14:7,8)

The message is clear: Our thinking, when committed to God and done in His strength, will be clear and true. The reason? Because the man who sees in this way is seeing with the eyes of the Spirit. As Jesus promised, "The Spirit of truth . . . will guide you into all truth" (John 16:13).

So as you answer the question, "Where does it hurt?" be aware that you can rely on God's resources as well as your own.

For my part, I am simply going to provide a framework to help you see where your particular pain fits in. The structure of this framework will be rather like a medical textbook in that I will mention, and comment on, many different types of pain. But it will not be nearly as complicated as a medical textbook. Nor do I claim that it's comprehensive. I am sure you can have emotional pain in more places than you can have physical pain, and I make no claims to cover them all.

The purpose of the framework is exactly the same as the doctor's first question. It brings you to the point where you can stop asking *Where?* and start asking *Why?*

This leads us to a problem. In both the physical and emotional areas the reason for a pain can differ with each individual. In the physical realm there are common sources of pain; we all may suffer from the same sort of flu, for instance. But especially with emotional pains the situations that give rise to the pain, and to our response, are never quite the same.

Two women are undergoing marital breakdown. One is a pregnant teenager from a broken home, the other a wealthy 45-year-old with a job that takes her away from her husband and family. For both the *Where?* is the same. The pain is located in their marital relationship. But in the *Why?* they are probably completely different.

That doesn't mean you're doomed to failure. It does mean you'll have to be careful and honest. Careful because, as we said before, the right treatment of your pain depends very much on understanding what is causing it. Honest because you may be tempted to lie to yourself. I stress that because there is such a thing as self-induced pain. In other words, there is a kind of pain that arises out of a situation for which the sufferer is responsible.

I know a man who used to head a massive Christian organization. I don't think there is a single American in the twentieth century who has had the same impact for Christ. I still admire his dynamism and his outstanding leadership qualities. But he was a loner, and because of that he was always at odds with his executive staff or his board.

His way of resolving these disagreements was unusual. He resigned. And because he was so indispensable, as soon as he resigned everyone rallied round and asked him to reconsider. Things went on this way for years and years. But it was like the boy in Aesop's fable who kept on crying wolf; it couldn't work forever. One day, when this man resigned in a pique, the board accepted his resignation.

This resulted in pain for him, for the board, and for the organization. But it would be unfair to say the pain had been imposed on him by others. He had brought it on himself.

What this means in terms of winning over pain I shall return to later. For now it is important only to recognize it if it's there, and not to try and hide it. Remember, just as in physical pain, winning over it depends on answering the two questions correctly. The difference is that with emotional pain there is no doctor to do it for you. When the rubber hits the road, it's in your hands.

To begin with, our framework divides emotional pains into two groups: people pains and situation pains. Nearly all the causes of emotional pain have to do with the people we relate to (or do not relate to, as the case may be), and the situations in which we find ourselves. Each covers a good many different pains, so in the chapters that follow each is subdivided. They are followed by some general comments relating to the way we experience these pains.

Now that we have finally reached the point where we can get out the knife and slit that bag open, do you still want to win over pain?

If so, here goes . . .

6

People Pain:
Tweedledee and Tweedledum

Unless we are hermits we spend most of our time with other people. We all belong to a social group of some sort—a marriage, a family, a company, a sports club, or a community—even if we do not acknowledge it or have much face-to-face contact with the other members. The most determined loner practices his togetherness with the national "group" just by switching on his radio or TV.

It is our membership in social groups that gives us much of the pleasure and satisfaction in our lives.

Think of the good times you've had sharing a beach barbecue with your folks, camping with friends from college, or working with colleagues on some business project. Now think of those activities without the other people. It's not the same, is it? Our sense of well-being, our joy and fulfillment, come from being together with others, playing our part in a group. And that group can be as small in number as a marriage or as large as the church universal.

But the formula isn't as simple as: *Person plus Person equals Mutual Joy and Satisfaction.*

It would have been in the garden of Eden. Adam and Eve had a natural sensitivity for one another's feelings, an intuitive harmony with their environment both social and physical. They had separate wills, but those wills worked together like instruments in an orchestra, to make something beautiful and rewarding to them both.

In our fallen world, the picture is different.

To have separate wills is to have conflicting wills, no matter how hard you try. The most ideally suited people with the most placid temperaments will fall out over something at some time. And if they don't actually reach open conflict they will certainly experience emotional pain.

We've all had the experience as kids of being told "not to do that because . . ." It was incredibly frustrating. Yet now that we're adults we say exactly the same thing to our own children, the reason being that it is fair preparation for the give-and-take of adult life. We cannot get what we want all of the time, and this restriction, this limitation, will often be painful to us.

That's not to say our relationships will constantly be marked by frustration and bitterness. We tend to swing back and forth, finding the company of others alternately pleasurable and problematic. We're all a little like Tweedledum and Tweedledee in Lewis Carroll's *Through the Looking Glass*, who fell out over a rattle:

> "We must have a bit of a fight, but I don't care about going on too long," said Tweedledum. "What's the time now?"
>
> Tweedledee looked at his watch, and said, "Half past four."
>
> "Let's fight till six, and then have dinner," said Tweedledum.
>
> "Very well," the other said, rather sadly. "And *she* can watch us—only you'd better not come too close," he added: "I generally hit everything I can see—when I get really excited."
>
> "And *I* hit everything within reach," cried Tweedledum, "whether I can see it or not!"
>
> Alice laughed. "You must hit the trees pretty often I should think," she said.
>
> Tweedledum looked round him with a satisfied smile. "I don't suppose," he said, "there'll be a tree left standing, for ever so far round, by the time we've finished!"
>
> "And all about a rattle," said Alice, still hoping to make them a *little* ashamed of fighting for such a trifle.
>
> "I shouldn't have minded so much," said Tweedledum, "if it hadn't been a new one."

"I wish the monstrous crow would come!" thought
Alice.

The point is that Tweedledee and Tweedledum are the best
of friends. When Alice comes across them in the wood they
are pleased as punch, like a couple of kids touring Disney-
land. It's only when one thinks the other has stolen his new
rattle that they start to squabble.

Lewis Carroll is highlighting something we learn daily
from reading the Bible and observing the world around us.
We know we need other people; we surround ourselves with
them and enjoy their company. But every so often we are
hurt—we have our rattle stolen, so to speak—and then we put
on any piece of armor we can find and rush into battle. The
fact is, our companions pain us and please us almost at the
same time.

And yet we wouldn't be separated from them. Tweedledee
and Tweedledum might have been at war every other day, but
separation or loss would have caused them every bit as much
pain as their arguments. Probably more.

Ironically, even if a relationship isn't wholly to our liking, it
still fulfills a basic need for companionship, and we would
miss it if it were gone. David, for instance who had every
reason to detest his ungrateful child, Absalom, is instead
shattered by the news of his death:

> And the king said unto Cushi, Is the young man
> Absalom safe? And Cushi answered, The enemies
> of my lord the king, and all that rise against thee to
> do thee hurt, be as that young man is.
>
> And the king was much moved, and went up to
> the chamber over the gate, and wept: and as he
> went thus he said, O my son Absalom, my son, my
> son Absalom! Would God I had died for thee, O
> Absalom, my son, my son! (2 Samuel 18:32,33).

People pain arises from broken relationships.
Much of the time this brokenness is a temporary phase,

maybe an interlude of a few minutes in a basically stable relationship, as in the celebrated "lovers' tiff." It is over as soon as it has begun, and both partners quickly try to heal the rift because they value the relationship and don't want to see it spoiled.

On other occasions, though, brokenness becomes a progression. The tiff happens again and again until trust and love are undermined and the people drift apart. The outward expression of this may be a broken engagement or a divorce. But it would be a mistake to blame the pain here on the situation. The man and woman who divorce are not in emotional pain because of the divorce as such. The problem lies within, in the accumulation of positive and negative contacts that made their relationship first of all sweet, and finally sour. It is a broken relationship. *People pain.*

That's one example. There are as many varieties of people pain as there are shades of relationship between people or groups of people. But generally relationships are broken in one or more of the following ways. Thus *people pain* can arise through:

    a. rejection by a person or a group of people;
    b. discipline or punishment by a person or a group
       of people;
    c. the absence or loss of a person or a group of
       people.

David's pain over Absalom came in the first and last ways. He was rejected by Absalom both as a father and as a king, and finally separated from him because his men disobeyed explicit instructions to restore his son alive. Rejection and loss both broke the relationship. Both caused *people pain.*

The middle way, discipline, is not illustrated directly in the story of David and Absalom, though it is present in the trials of Jeremiah and Paul. Discipline is rather like rejection in that someone who is being punished by society at large; for instance, by imprisonment, is in a sense being rejected. The difference lies in the fact that the pain inflicted, whether or not it is inflicted justly, is the official decision of a presiding government or authority.

It is what finally ended the quarrel over Tweedledum's rattle:

> It was getting dark so suddenly that Alice thought there must be a thunderstorm coming on. "What a thick black cloud that is!" she said, "And how fast it comes! Why, I do believe it's got wings!"
>
> "It's the crow!" Tweedledum cried out in a shrill voice of alarm: and the two brothers took to their heels and were out of sight in a moment.

The way to find which category your own pain belongs in is to ask yourself a simple question: *Which particular relationship in my life would need to be altered to take away my pain and restore me to tranquility and happiness?*

I admit it's a loaded question, because total happiness, in the way we dream of it, is unlikely to be the result of winning over pain.

Imagine you're a father with an estranged son. You've never understood one another. Now he's walked out of the house. You know the relationship is going to take a lot of work to put back together. It will be hard enough just to do something straightforward with him, like share a meal. Things may never be the way they were before, or the way you dreamed they would be. Nonetheless, the fact that you have those dreams, the fact that you wish so hard for an apparently impossible thing, shows you where your pain is just as surely as if there was a flag marking the spot.

And finding the pain is the first stage in doing something about it.

PAIN FROM REJECTION

1. *Marital Breakdown*

I'd guess that most of the pain suffered through rejection

occurs in the marriage relationship.

All marriages have their tensions. That was the first thing that happened to Adam and Eve when their sin was found out. As God said to Eve, ". . . thy desire shall be to thy husband, and he shall rule over thee" (Genesis 3:16).

This is no different from what happened to all human relations after the Fall. They were disrupted, and made difficult, at every level.

I'm not saying there's no such thing as a happy marriage. But as a former pastor, I would be foolish not to warn young couples that they may face some pretty trying times. You can't tie two human wills together like you do in marriage without producing some friction, and that is true of Christian marriages just as much as non-Christian marriages, though Christians have the special grace of the Holy Spirit in resolving these frictions.

Tension in a marriage results from a variety of factors: the personalities of the married partners, the state of their work and finances, their children, how they use their time, and so on. Tension isn't always proportional to external pressure, either. Some people with apparently carefree lives seem to make their marriages miserable. Others with heavy commitments and responsibilities somehow soak up the pressure and nurture and support one another in the most difficult circumstances.

What makes or breaks a marriage, though, is the degree of *fidelity*.

This is an old word, and when most people hear it they immediately think of sexual fidelity. But there are more ways of breaking faith in a marriage than taking a lover. In one way, the man who spends his weekends propping up a bar is being just as unfaithful as the one who spends them in bed with his mistress. Both of them are regarding some extraneous concern as more important than the marriage itself, and are squandering energy and time on it that should be going toward fostering the marriage relationship.

The act of unfaithfulness may not be the first tension in a

marriage. Usually a lot has to happen to provide the motivation for infidelity. But once one or both of the partners have reached the stage of indulging in some sort of infidelity the marriage is on the skids, and they may begin the slow, painful spiral down that often ends in separation and divorce.

That spiral leads to many other pains, from loneliness to physical violence. You may feel, as many do, that things are so bad in your marriage that divorce is actually the solution to your problems. But be warned. A relationship doesn't end just because you sign a piece of paper. If you're in Memphis and your partner is in New York, that doesn't mean you don't have a relationship. If your partner dies you still have a relationship. Once it's begun a relationship only changes in its state. You can go on feeling pain for years after a marriage has been legally dissolved, like the man with an amputated hand who still "feels" his fingers. Divorce is no panacea.

Take the example of a young woman my wife and I knew in the first church I took charge of.

I'll call her Mary, though that isn't her real name.

Mary was a Christian who from a very early age had dedicated her life to be a foreign missionary. However, the Second World War intervened and things didn't work out for her. Her hopes weren't completely dashed, though, because during the war she fell in love with, and married, a young army chaplain. She consoled herself with the thought that even if she never got overseas herself, she would at least be able to serve the Lord as a pastor's wife when her husband's tour of duty was finished.

The war didn't give them much time to enjoy their marriage. She became pregnant shortly before he was called away to Atlanta, Georgia, in preparation for service abroad. She visited him for a few days at his hotel just before he was to ship out. He seemed very busy, and when the day came for her to go home they parted in the hotel lobby because he said he had an appointment and couldn't take her to the bus station.

She left happy. There was only one hitch. She got to the station only to find she'd left one of her bags behind. But since she had plenty of time she walked back to the hotel and explained the problem to the desk clerk, who gave her the key she'd just turned in and told her to go and search the room.

When she opened that door, though, she found something she'd never dreamed of.

Her new husband was in bed with another woman.

There was a divorce. But divorce couldn't take away the pain of his infidelity. Ask anyone who's been through divorce—the pain stays with you. You live it again every time someone asks your child about the mommy or daddy they don't have, and every time you're excluded from a social function that's for couples only. Rejection by the partner who's left you is duplicated in the attitude of friends and acquaintances to whom you are now an anomaly, an outsider. For Mary, even though she chose to stay unmarried from then on in order to give her daughter the best possible upbringing, the pain of rejection stayed fresh for 30 years.

Mary's case is a relatively simple one. It was her husband who broke the marriage. She was an innocent. Yet in the vast majority of broken marriages it's hard to apportion blame to one partner alone.

A wife who has a lover will probably claim she was driven to it by her husband's inattention, and while that is an excuse it is usually not without a grain of truth. Infidelity often follows from a person's desire for the fulfillment that the marriage is failing to supply. If that is true, infidelity is as much the result as the cause of relationship breakdown. But even if it is not, infidelity can soon incite a cross fire of retaliatory hurting, in which the question of who started the breakdown matters little if at all. Once this stage is reached the exchanges of pain have become extremely complex.

And there is one more pain too. It's easy to imagine the rejected partner experiencing pain. Less often acknowledged is the pain borne by the one who rejects, especially when he or she desires to make amends and start over.

It is a kind of self-rejection. I have a friend who is dying from an ulcerated condition that had its source in a moment of betrayal to his wife and family. His wife has forgiven him. His family has forgiven him. His church has forgiven him. The relationship should be restored.

But he won't forgive himself.

The consequences of this are serious. As his physician says, "His inability to accept the forgiveness of his loved ones and, above all, the forgiveness of God, is wrecking his life and assigning him to a premature grave."

2. *Parent-Child Rejection*

Children are nearly always the worst victims in marital breakdown and divorce.

Even in a home where the parents stay together for the sake of the children, conflict will communicate itself to the kids. They know what's going on, even if they're too young to understand it. And the impression made on them by a world in which the two most significant people in their lives are at loggerheads will stay with them for the rest of their lives.

Divorce isn't the only situation to inflict emotional damage on children. They are vulnerable to every influence, good or bad, and just like saplings they require careful tending if they're going to grow up well. They can be hurt by neglect— for instance by lack of parental love—as well as by actual mistreatment.

But if a child can be hurt by a parent, a parent can also be hurt by a child. Growing up necessarily involves the development of independence, and the parents may sometimes react to this natural process as if it were rejection.

If you don't believe that, just give it a moment's thought. As a child you start off knowing nothing about the world. You don't know what's right and what's wrong, and as often as not you find out by experience—trying something dad's told you not to do and suffering the consequences. When you get to be a teenager you may start trying these forbidden forms of behavior in earnest. But rocking the parental boat to insure you can stand up in the adult world you're about to join isn't the same as rejecting your parents, much as it may look that way to them. It's the reverberation sent out by a helpless infant changing into an independent adult, which is, after all, what the parent desires to happen.

If the process of growing up goes wrong, pain can arise on both sides. The child can feel rejected (unwanted, unloved, disapproved) by the parents, and the parents can feel rejected (unappreciated, neglected, resented) by the child.

Of the two, the worse effect is likely to be felt by a child, simply because his or her personality is more impressionable. We've all been children. We've all had to pass down that risky road of adolescence. It is quite likely therefore that some of the pains we still feel as adults have their root in relationships begun in our early years.

The apostle Paul knew that the key to right relationships between parents and children, as between adults, is love. It is the loved child who is most able to love.

"And, ye fathers," he writes in Ephesians 6:4, "provoke not your children to wrath; but bring them up in the nurture and admonition of the Lord."

3. *General Rejection*

Any human relationship carries the potential of pain because any human relationship can come to grief.

I could extend this chapter indefinitely by writing about brother rejection, sister rejection, uncle rejection, friend rejection, boss rejection, and so on. But that is unnecessary because much of what has been said about the breakdown of marriage, the supreme human relationship, is also true to some extent when rejection occurs in other contexts.

Instead, I am going to make a few general comments about the way in which relationships break down.

As I said at the beginning of this chapter, it is important to remember that you have a relationship not just with certain individuals in society, but with groups, and with society as a whole. And those group relationships can go wrong just like the individual ones.

If you were a member of a high school class you know there is a dynamic between the individual and the group. You can be "out" or "in" with particular sets of friends depending on which individuals you're buddies with. As a result, a friend-relationship is more likely to exist in the context of a group than a marriage relationship is. In marriage the inside ties are stronger, the outside ties weaker.

Which brings us to another dimension of rejection.

A minister friend of mine who died some years ago once took a pastorate where some troublemakers fabricated the story that he was guilty of loose relations with a woman in the church. What made this especially hurtful was the fact that a close associate, a man whom he had befriended and who had assisted him on many preaching missions, pressed the allegations and incited the congregation to drive him out.

He took on a tough missionary post in a nondescript area of a distant state, and died before his time.

The event triggered a complex of pains. He suffered rejection by his former friend, as Jesus did from Judas. But added to that was the pain of rejection by his church, the group of people closest to him. And not simply rejection, but humiliation, the spoiling of his good name. He would have survived the accusations of one man; he could not survive the rejection of the group.

But if the memory dogged him for the rest of his life, at least he was able to escape the painful *situation*. There are plenty of instances of rejection where the victim is made to feel rejected by the group and yet is stuck within it.

The new kid at school experiences this; in a more permanent way so does the man trapped in a crummy job where none of his workmates like him. He'd love to get out, but he's got a family to feed. He is forced to live with the rejection and the pain it carries.

Of course the unpopular individual may be part of an unpopular minority. He may be black in a block occupied by whites. He may be a Christian in a country full of revolutionary Marxists. Whether it's his own characteristics others find distasteful, or those he bears on behalf of his group, he will still be rejected.

I don't mean to imply that your experience has to be extreme to qualify as a pain. Take the example of sexual discrimination. Here the pain often builds up in an accumulation of small snubs and condescensions. But having your opinion dismissed in a meeting because you're a woman is just as insulting as having a male colleague make a pass at you. In both cases the message communicated is "You don't really matter," or at best, "You only matter because I happen to find you physically attractive." The fact is, as a whole person a woman is often rejected.

4. *Noncommunication*

I add this fourth section under the title of rejection because it is possible to feel something akin to rejection without actually being rejected.

This happens when a person wants to establish a relationship, either with an individual or with a group, but is prevented from doing so by shyness or lack of confidence. It's not every Romeo who can make it as far as Juliet's balcony. It's not every man and woman who finds it easy to attend church meetings—some deliberately stay away because they are embarrassed at having to socialize.

This has nothing to do with actual situations (most Juliets I know are delighted to meet a Romeo) but with the person's state of mind.

The relationship isn't broken, only unestablished. Yet the effect is much the same—a bicycle without a chain is of no more use than one just run over by a truck. And the shy person may well respond as if he had been rejected, and feel distraught or think himself a failure, thus developing a broken relationship with the self as well as an unestablished relationship with other individuals.

It is this reaction which defines shyness, diffidence, or a sense of inferiority as a pain of rejection. As with a broken marriage, pain is caused by a *quality* of relationship. Only in this case the quality is nonexistence.

PAIN FROM DISCIPLINE

1. *Home Discipline*

I've said already that the correction of our elders and betters is likely to be one of our earliest experiences of pain.

That may be because our elders and betters don't do the job very well. Lewis Carroll's *Alice in Wonderland* provides a good illustration of this, in the shape of the Duchess. The Duchess is nursing a baby in a small kitchen where a cook is preparing an extremely peppery soup. The child howls and sneezes by turns. In the middle of all this the Duchess expresses her entire philosophy of child education in the following four lines:

> Speak roughly to your little boy,
>   And beat him when he sneezes:
> He only does it to annoy,
>   Because he knows it teases.

The baby never stands a chance. He howls because of his home environment, and the Duchess beats him, not to teach him anything, but simply because he's howling. Which probably makes the kid howl even more. The situation is a perfect circle.

This sort of discipline, issued without reference to any system of values, is quite common, and very likely to damage the child. It is emotionally testing, intellectually confusing, and the cause of a fair amount of confusion and pain, not to mention social maladjustment, in adulthood. Lewis Carroll probably didn't have his tongue pushed too far into his cheek when he described the Duchess's baby turning into a pig as soon as he got out of the house!

But not providing any discipline is just as harmful as providing too much, or too much of the wrong sort. Discipline isn't about inflicting pain. Discipline is about education. It prepares children for freedom by teaching them the language of responsibility. Refusing to discipline a child isn't being humanitarian; it's depriving him of a vital and basic part of his education.

The lessons may sometimes be painful for parents as well as children. I remember how hard it was for me to be firm with Johnny. How do you discipline a son who's so helpless? But I knew I had to do it for his own good, so one day when he was kicking up a fuss at not being allowed to go swimming I put him over my knew and gave him a lively spanking. He was a model child for the rest of the day!

2. *State Discipline*

Just as it is the duty of the father in a Christian home to impose discipline in the interest of both the home and the child, so also is the state duty-bound to impose discipline on its citizens.

I don't mean Big Brother. State terrorism isn't real discipline any more than it would be real discipline if I ruled my children by brutalizing them indiscriminately with a baseball bat. Discipline is the upholding of justice. Parents use it in the home because they want their children to grow up knowing the difference between right and wrong. The state uses it to protect its citizens against those who are trying to exploit them.

In both cases the cutting edge of discipline is pain. What deters the criminal and the disobedient child alike is that knowledge that wrongdoing is punished and that they themselves are likely to suffer pain. All punishment, from the life sentence down to the verbal reprimand, is pain in the sense that it involves "disagreeable experience." Allied to justice, pain is made to exercise its disagreeable and limiting function in order to act as a warning sign to the offender and society in general, that evil is not to be tolerated.

Unfortunately pain does not have to be allied to justice. Linked to something else, like totalitarianism, it will work in exactly the same way to communicate a different message— that disobedience to the state is not to be tolerated.

The problem is that when you unhitch pain from justice you unhitch it completely. You may say your state's discipline is just, but because it is controlled by the interests of the state and not by the absolute morality of right and wrong, the discipline easily slips into excess and becomes victimization—in other words, injustice. Witness some countries in West Asia and Eastern Europe, and the so-called Christian Inquisition of the Middle Ages.

In the 1940's my father met Dr. I.V. Neprash, who for his uncompromising witness for the gospel in Soviet Russia had been sent to Siberia. When my father asked him what it was like, he winced. He said he had been incarcerated at first in a cell smaller than a public telephone booth. He couldn't sit down. He wasn't let out to relieve himself. His food supply consisted of some soggy bread and a limited quantity of water. Besides all this a light was left on day and night just at his line of vision, preventing him from sleeping.

After three days a hole at the top of the booth was opened and a prison guard poured lice over him. The booth being so small, he was unable to reach any part of his body with his hands except his legs and lower abdomen, and had to overcome the irritation by rubbing himself against the sides of the booth, soon rupturing the skin in several places.

After 48 hours the guard opened the hole again and drenched him in turpentine.

When my father remarked on the cruelty of this treatment Dr. Neprash told him it was only the beginning. There had been a further 14 torments, each worse than the one before it. Understandably he declined to talk about them. He didn't want to relive that pain even in his memory.

Letting the punishment fit the crime is more than a theme for a Gilbert and Sullivan opera; it is a principle of proportionality that governs the just use of state discipline. To suffer for wrongdoing is biblical, and the sufferer has no grounds for complaint. As Peter says, "For what glory is it, if, when ye be buffeted for your faults, ye shall take it patiently?" (1 Peter 2:20).

If on the other hand you suffer pain in excess of your faults, or without having committed any faults, the physical restriction and discomfort are compounded by the pain of rejection by the society in which you live, expressed in persecution by its authorities.

PAIN FROM LOSS

1. *Separation*

When the infamous wall was built across Berlin in 1961 it cut a city in two and divided a community. Families who lived only a short distance apart suddenly found themselves on opposite sides of an international border whose effective width was boundless. They could see one another from the buildings, even wave to one another. But a political division had separated them.

Just how important proximity is to human relationships is demonstrated by the ingenuity with which the Berlin wall has been scaled, penetrated, and tunneled under. Separation from loved ones—wife, husband, children, friends—causes such severe emotional pain that you wonder how anyone allows it to happen. Yet happen it does, again and again.

The starkest examples derive, like the Berlin wall, from great political or economic upheavals. The twentieth century abounds with them. Wars in Europe and Indo-China, geo-political movements like the creation of Pakistan from India, famines in sub-Saharan Africa. All produced waves of refugees, individuals or broken fragments of families torn by their separation from loved ones and by the bleak hostility of their new surroundings.

But it doesn't require a cataclysm to produce separation. For many separation is an aspect of daily life, something families have learned to live with. Migrant workers in Europe cross international boundaries for six months at a time to earn money by working in factories overseas. The only contact their wives have with them is the occasional letter or phone call, and the checks they send home to pay the bills.

Even in wealthy countries many men in the armed forces, as well as many businessmen, are likely to spend long periods away from home. I know that because my own work involves extensive travel. I spend so much time in international airports, I sometimes think I live in one.

Separation can make itself felt in something as simple as taking a job or a house in a new area, leaving home for the first time, or retiring from the work you've done for 30 years. It's not unusual, and never has been. In biblical times Jacob, Joseph, Ruth, and David all knew the pain of separation from the ones they loved. It's a common human experience, and it's a real source of pain.

Incidentally, you can be separated from someone by more than geographical distance.

In Berlin, political factors cause the separation. But separation can arise just as easily from social or cultural factors. I've already mentioned all those aspiring Romeos. If you read Shakespeare's original play you'll realize how complete a separation can be achieved by tradition and sectarianism. You can see race doing the same thing today in many nations. Not so long ago it did it right here where I'm writing, in the United States. And if that doesn't convince you, look at the Indian caste system, the long and tragic history of sectarian violence in Northern Ireland, or the persistent denial of human rights in countries like Ethiopia, Cuba, North Korea, and the Soviet Union.

You can also suffer separation in illness, especially if it produced personality changes in the person who's sick. Senile dementia is a good example. The aging parent, whose memory is failing and who perhaps now fails to recognize you, is not the person you once knew. You don't love them any less because of that, but adjusting to the change in personality will inevitably bring with it a sense of loss.

Which brings us to the last sort of *people pain*.

2. *Bereavement*

I know a minister at the Mount Paran Church of God in Atlanta called Dr. Paul Walker.

He is a celebrated clergyman. But fame will never protect you from tragedy. At holiday time not long ago the Walkers had a visit from their 24-year-old son and his wife, who lived in Augusta. On the way back a drunk driver pulled out in front of them. There was nothing the son could do to avert an accident. It was a head-on collision. Both he and his wife died instantly.

It was an event no one would hesitate to label a tragedy. Here were two young people in the prime of life who could have achieved much for God, and they were wiped out.

The fact that we feel they didn't "deserve" to die underlines the arbitrariness and gruesome efficiency of death. God's warning about the tree of knowledge was accurate; death became a reality that none of Adam's children would escape. It became real in the sense that a new rule of mortality was written into creation by human disobedience: Adam and Eve would one day grow old and die. The releasing of human freedom from the shackles of natural goodness also meant death could be inflicted as a form of pain. Abel not only died—he was killed. He died before his time.

This sort of death, death before you have gotten to be old and full of years, fills the pages of the Bible as well as those of daily newspapers. It doesn't occur only through the infliction of human cruelty. The young also die of cancer, of AIDS, of accidents, of suicide.

The pains of death, premature or otherwise, don't need any emphasis here. But you'll often hear it said, "It's worse for the ones who are left." Dying at least has an end point, even if the road between the signpost and the grave is a long and hard one.

But with bereavement we can often see no light at the end of the tunnel, no prospect of relief. The experience changes, gradually becoming less severe. We adjust. But it's never quite over.

I can say that from personal experience. There are moments today, 12 years after Johnny's death, when I still miss him intensely.

It's not hard to see why. To be bereaved you have to have been close to someone. We are not bereaved by the death of the cancer patient we hear about on the news, however much we may sympathize. The key is closeness. And being close to someone means that your life is molded around theirs. Your time, your work, your meals, your relaxation, even your personality, is shaped by close proximity to another person. Think how your own behavior reflects that of your father, mother, brother, or sister. So important are some other individuals that you sometimes say they are "part of you."

Consequently, when that person dies it's like the side of your house fell in. You feel exposed, vulnerable, and unprotected. There are loose ends flying around that the other person was holding on to.

If the death happens without warning the shock may be so great you literally can't believe it. When a wife whose husband was killed in an industrial accident was told the news, she fainted. She came to, and wanted to know what had happened. When she was told, she fainted again. She fainted five times before she was able to soak up the blow of his death without passing out.

To the nonbeliever news like that is unutterably painful, because a loved one separated by death is separated completely. By contrast a Christian knows that death is only a temporary separation. The person death has taken from us will be restored in the resurrection. Because of this, a lot of people think a Christian should not experience the pain of bereavement. But the consolation of faith, and it is a great consolation, will not stop the bereavement caused by separation. To say a Christian should be immune to it is to say that a wife whose husband goes to spend the rest of his life in another country should not miss him. The apostle Paul said that though we sorrow, we sorrow not as those without hope (1 Thessalonians 4:13).

Also, we all suffer bereavement differently. How we react depends on who we are, what our relationship was with the dead person, whether or not the relationship was active at the time of death, and so on. In my own case, the period after Johnny's death was comparatively easy to bear. But I admit I had three things working in my favor.

First, I only had one death to cope with.

I sometimes tell the story my father told me, of a minister he met in Pittsburgh, Pennsylvania, a Dr. Blair. This man knew what it was to be acquainted with grief. It had begun for him early in his marriage when his wife gave birth to a handicapped child. But in spite of the burden this laid on them they pursued their commitment to go as missionaries to India, and it was here that Dr. Blair developed a severe eye disorder. One of his eyes literally popped out. He was told by a doctor that pressure building up behind the other eye would make that one fall out as well, which happened shortly after they returned to the States on a well-deserved furlough.

Blindness and a disabled daughter would be more than enough for most men to bear. But Dr. Blair's troubles had only started.

Just months after he went completely blind he lost his wife. Then one of his sons came into contact with a deadly poison as he brushed through some bushes on a cross-country run, and he also died. Finally his Seeing-Eye dog was injured when a car streaked out of nowhere, hitting the dog and narrowly missing Dr. Blair's other son.

The night after this last accident Dr. Blair listened to the dog whining in pain beneath his bed. "Oh God," he cried, "can't I even have my dog?"

But the dog died. Dr. Blair arranged the funeral. The text was: "The Lord gave, and the Lord hath taken away; blessed be the name of the Lord" (Job 1:21). It was very moving. And in all this immense suffering Dr. Blair remained a radiant man. My father said people at the church would compete for the chance to talk to him after the service because of the uplift they received from just a few moments in his presence.

So when I am tempted to feel down about my own bereavement I remember Dr. Blair, and I am glad that I lost only Johnny.

The second factor in my favor is that I know Johnny is dead. That may sound strange, but the importance of this simple assurance is clear when you look at people for whom the death of a loved one is only a statistical probability.

The rule of the military junta in Argentina during the 1970's was marked by numerous "disappearances." Tens of thousands of young men and women suspected of subversive activities were seized by the security forces and never seen again. Eyewitness evidence and the discovery of mass graves tell the tale clearly enough—usually victims were killed after hours of senseless and inhuman torture.

Until modern forensic techniques were developed to identify the buried remains, the death of particular individuals could not be proved. For their wives, husbands, and parents they were "missing, presumed killed." And that "presumed" was the tiny ray of hope that undermined the bereavement. Instead of receding into the past, the death stayed forever in the present, always about to be confirmed but never quite a certainty. It was the same for families of men missing in Vietnam. A pain that should have worn down with the years stayed as fresh as the day it began.

The third and final factor in my favor is that Chris and I had anticipated Johnny's death.

In one sense I lived with the possibility of his death from the moment of his birth, when I watched that doctor resuscitating him in the delivery room. But there is a difference between knowing the odds are stacked against you, and knowing that you're losing. It was the second situation, in the last year of Johnny's life, that really prepared us for his death.

When I say prepared, I really mean that we were going through much of the pain of bereavement before he actually died. It wasn't a conscious decision any more than the healing of a physical wound is a conscious decision; it's something the body and mind do to protect themselves. As a result, when that final night came and Johnny slipped away from us, we were ready, in our sadness, to give thanks to God both for his life and his release from its pains.

I'm not sure if seeing death coming reduced the overall degree of pain. In one way it made it worse because the pain contained an element of anticipation. At the same time it took this worst of *people pains* and spread it out a bit. There was no shock, no unexpectedness. Just the blunt fact of death.

7

Situation Pain:
Doors and Bottles

If we're going to learn how to win over pain we need to know about the second kind of pain—not *people pain*, but *situation pain*.

Here again Lewis Carroll's Alice provides a useful illustration. In her first adventure in Wonderland, she pursues the White Rabbit down the rabbit hole and suddenly finds herself standing in a long low hall:

> There were doors all round the hall, but they were all locked; and when Alice had been all the way down one side and up the other, trying every door, she walked sadly down the middle, wondering how she was ever to get out again.
>
> Suddenly she came upon a little three-legged table all made of solid glass; there was nothing on it except a tiny golden key, and Alice's first thought was that it might belong to one of the doors of the hall; but, alas! either the locks were too large, or the key was too small, but at any rate it would not open any of them.
>
> However, the second time round, she came upon a low curtain she had not noticed before, and behind it was a little door about fifteen inches high: she tried the little golden key in the lock, and to her great delight it fitted!
>
> Alice opened the door and found that it led into a small passage, not much larger than a rat hole: she knelt down and looked along the passage into the loveliest garden you ever saw. How she longed to get out of that dark hall, and wander among those beds of bright flowers and those cool fountains, but

she could not even get her head through the door-way; "and even if my head would go through," thought poor Alice, "it would be very little use without my shoulders. Oh, how I wish I could shut up like a telescope . . ."

It is then that she returns to the little table to find a bottle with a large paper label on it saying "DRINK ME."

. . . Alice ventured to taste it, and finding it very nice (it had, in fact, a sort of mixed flavour of cherry-tart, custard, pine-apple, roast turkey, toffee, and hot buttered toast), she very soon finished it off.

She wonders if it is having the desired effect.

And so it was indeed: she was now only ten inches high, and her face brightened up at the thought that she was now the right size for going through the little door into that lovely garden. First, however, she waited for a few minutes to see if she was going to shrink any further: she felt a little nervous about this; "for it might end, you know," Alice said to herself, "in my going out altogether, like a candle. I wonder what I should be like then?"

After a while, finding that nothing more happened, she decided on going into the garden at once; but alas for poor Alice! when she got to the door, she found she had forgotten the little golden key, and when she went back to the table for it, she found she could not possibly reach it: she could see it quite plainly through the glass, and she tried her best to climb up one of the table-legs, but it was too slippery; and when she had tired herself out with trying, the poor little thing sat down and cried.

I doubt if he meant to do it, but Lewis Carroll gave us a perfect parable of *situation pain*.

Situation pain differs from *people pain* because it has nothing directly to do with people. It is pain that comes to us through our circumstances.

By the time we find Alice here, the White Rabbit has vanished in a flurry of anxiety over the Duchess. Alice is alone in the hall with its rows of closed doors. But it is not the White Rabbit's absence that causes her pain; she soon forgets about him. She is trapped, limited, by her situation. And the discomfort of being stuck in a gloomy hallway is only added to by her view of the garden through the tiny door. It emphasizes her powerlessness by showing the way it might have been.

Alice's response is the one we all make: "Oh how I wish . . ." And as with *people pains* it is what we wish for that identifies our problem. For Alice, shutting up like a telescope was the only conceivable way of getting what she most wanted to have. For another person the wish may be a promotion at work. For another it may be the restoration of youth. What we wish for is what we think will cure our particular problem.

This makes us vulnerable. We want our wishes fulfilled so badly that when someone comes along claiming to be able to fulfill them, we are half inclined to believe him. That's why the traveling medicine man made such a financial killing. Today's medicine man, of course, is apt to fall foul of the law, because a product for sale to the public has to do what it says it will do. But we're still not entirely safe. Take, for example, the British lottery organization that recently advertised itself with a picture of a man trying to pay his bills. It's undoubtedly true that if you win a million dollars, your worries over household finances will be a thing of the past. And there is nothing illegal about the use of such an image on such an advertisement. But is not the public's wish for freedom from the pain of financial difficulty still being exploited?

And advertising doesn't stop at suggesting a product will cure more pains than it is actually capable of curing. It works hard to persuade us that we have hitherto unrecognized pains in dire need of being cured. In other words it sets out, not to publicize a product, but to manipulate people's tastes.

By this process the man with a hundred-dollar suit, a small house, and a secondhand car is made to feel he needs a two-hundred-dollar suit, a bigger house, and a new car. He doesn't. His suit looks smart, he's already rattling around in the house he's got, and the car, while it's secondhand gets him around just fine. But he is persuaded to feel these circumstances not as a privilege (after all, a secondhand car is better than none at all) but as a pain, a limitation.

The change is not in his circumstances but in his perception. His actual needs are the same as they ever were and they have been completely satisfied. What has happened is that his threshold of pain has been reduced.

As an average American he would once have been severely limited without the use of a car. But now that he has a car—say, an old Ford—he feels severely limited without the use of a Porsche. If he thought about it he would probably admit that intrinsically the Porsche is of no more use to him than the Ford. Yet he feels a pain of limitation just the same.

To such artificial needs the consumer industries have every possible answer. Like Alice's bottle, they all come with a little label saying "DRINK ME," and they all suggest to us that they are the perfect solution to our pains. They're not. Like Alice's bottle, you get them only to find you've moved from one *situation pain* to another. The pain threshhold simply goes down a bit further.

I dwell on this because this kind of pain, which we normally describe as frustration or discontent, is pervasive in western society. We're not all like the millionaire who couldn't bear the thought of life without owning Paris, but there's a bit of him in every one of us, and it's important to see our pains, and our wishes, in realistic perspective. The warning sign in our *situation pain* may be alerting us to our damaged values as much as to our straitened circumstances.

You'll also find it helpful to remember that *situation pain* is often found alongside *people pain*.

This is true of the advertisement-induced pain we've just been talking about. Part of the pressure to buy a certain car or style of clothing often comes via the social group—all the people you admire who've already bought it. If you don't make the purchase, you're left with a vague sense of inferiority, a feeling that your friends will look down on you or reject you. The pain consequent on this is still essentially situational, but it has a clear social dimension.

Imagine you've recently moved from Colorado to New York. The adjustment to your new situation may well involve pain. It's stressful adapting to new work and finding new accommodations. The physical surroundings are strange to you. You may feel homesick for the landscape and atmosphere of your old haunts, but it will be hard to divorce that homesickness from your loneliness for old friends. People are a big part of place. You miss the group you went camping with as much as you miss the mountains.

This sort of *situation pain* makes up half of the whole. "Situation" in this case means the external situation—what we might call our environment. The second sort covers those pains that come from our internal situation—the state of our own body and mind.

Let's look at them in more detail.

PAIN FROM ENVIRONMENT

1. *Displacement*

"By the rivers of Babylon, there we sat down, yea, we wept, when we remembered Zion. . . . How shall we sing the Lord's song in a strange land?" (Psalm 137:1,4).

Those lines from the psalmist sum up the pain of displacement.

As a nation Israel knew very well what it was like to suffer by having to live away from the place where they belonged. That suffering has remained the keynote of the subsequent history of the Jews and provided the springboard for the formation of the State of Israel after the Second World War.

It's not hard to find examples of this sort of major displacement in today's world. It may be a literal removal of people by a government from one area to another. On a wide scale this has occurred in Ethiopia in the 1980's as a way of dispersing the forces in opposition to the Marxist regime. It has occurred on an individual basis in the Soviet Union, Cuba, Argentina, and the Philippines—anywhere that dissent from the ruling ideology has not been tolerated.

Of course it doesn't require a government directive for people to be forced to move. War and famine have done the job just as effectively over most of Africa, creating a new class of landless refugees. Political upheaval in Vietnam produced the boat people. White settlement of North America dispossessed the Indians and confined them to reservations.

Few of us who have the means to come by a book like this will ever experience displacement on such a scale. But we have our own displacements which in their own context can cause severe pain.

These arise mostly from economic factors. We move not because of a war or a shortage of food, but to find work. For instance, under recent legislation passed by one European government, people under the age of 26 in search of jobs are obliged to change their area of residence an average of once every four weeks if they wish to continue receiving state benefits for their board and lodging. There are sound reasons for this as far as the government is concerned, but for the young people it is often a real source of stress.

2. *Impoverishment*

A bigger problem for many in the West is their personal state of affairs in the places they already live.

I call this kind of pain impoverishment because it reduces the overall quality of life. But once again—since the quality of our general environment depends to a large extent on our ability to pay for what we desire—the governing factors are economic.

Probably the most obtrusive sympton of impoverishment in the West is unemployment.

In Britain, where the unemployment level is over three million in a total population of around 56 million, it is a major political issue. World recession isn't the only cause of this unemployment. The shift toward greater efficiency and auto mation in developed countries means that few jobs are avail-- able in the manufacturing industry. In Britain this change has not yet been compensated for by an expansion in the service sector.

The financial consequences of layoffs are clear enough: Losing your income won't help you keep up the mortgage payments. Lack of money is the pain of limitation writ large. No vacation, no car, no dental care, maybe no heat. And this often sets in motion a whole train of secondary effects, such as demoralization, listlessness, or loss of self-esteem, which feed back into the situation and make it worse.

The result is pain.

The pain of not being able to afford presents for your children. The pain of living in cramped, cold conditions. The pain of not having a place to call your own. The pain of missing out on all the entertainments and facilities available to those with cash. The pain of being dependent on welfare.

At least in the West welfare is the bottom line of impover- ishment, because society as a whole is wealthy enough to support its poorer members.

You don't have to go far, however, to find countries where the majority of the population lives below what we in Amer- ica and Europe would call the poverty line. For people like that, inadequate housing means a hole in the ground with a cardboard roof. No health care means half of the children sick or dying. Poor diet means anything from a bowl of rice to starvation.

That kind of *situation pain* needs no further comment from me.

PAIN FROM INCAPACITY

1. *Injury*

I'm not going to insult your intelligence by telling you that injury hurts!

But injury often hurts more by the limitations it imposes than by the physical pain it causes. We all know what it's like to get a visit from friends when we're in the hospital after an operation. We're grateful they came, but it hurts that they can walk out of the ward while we have to stay, or that they can stand or sit or lean against the wall while we can only lie in bed.

For most of us the limitation of injury is temporary, at least while we're young. Later on we're more likely to wear glasses, or to have a doctor tell us to take it easy because of a heart condition. But in our youth we take health for granted—unless we begin life in an injured condition.

I'm sure that was one of the most hurtful things for Johnny.

He couldn't manage even the simple things in life—the things we all do so naturally we don't even think of them. When was the last time you vomited after a meal? Probably months ago, maybe years. But Johnny did it every day. Often he'd lose his entire meal. And that hurt him. He knew other people could keep their food down, and whenever he failed, you could see the pain and disappointment in his eyes.

Mother Barker, particularly, was wonderful when it came to coping with those situations. She'd quietly wipe away the mess, take off Johnny's soiled clothes, and clean him up again, all the time chatting to him to take his mind off the frustration. I don't know how many times I heard her say, "There now, Johnny, just don't you worry. We'll take care of it."

Her approach encouraged me to minimize Johnny's isolation from the world as much as I could.

In the days of my evangelistic ministry, after I resigned from the church in Louisville, I had some marvelous experiences. But inevitably the highlight of my day when I was in town was returning home to Chris and Johnny.

As time went on I came to realize how devotedly Johnny loved me, and how interested he was in my work. So I began to talk to him about the events of the day. It was awkward at first—after all, Johnny could hardly converse with me in the normal way—but I soon found myself sharing with him frankly and fully. That helped me. And I know it helped Johnny too, because as the years went by his enthusiasm for my work grew by leaps and bounds.

That's why when he got older I suggested to Chris that she and Johnny accompany me on some of the crusades. To have them with me everywhere just wasn't possible because of the logistical problems of looking after Johnny while we traveled. But when a suitable opportunity came up, Chris performed a miracle of organization and made it happen. I was glad. It opened up Johnny's horizons, and it made a real difference to me to have my wife and son around when I was working.

The pain of Johnny's incapacity was eased by those who, like newscaster Paul Harvey, and founder of World Vision Bob Pierce, made an effort to talk to him naturally. I remember Bob approaching Johnny one day and saying, "Hey, Buddy, I'm counting on you to pray for me when I go to Korea next month." Johnny loved that. He could have listened to Bob all day.

Conversely, his pain was intensified by people who couldn't handle his disability.

When we went to Honolulu we took Johnny with us to an outdoor restaurant where a group of Hawaiin singers was performing by torchlight. We didn't notice what an irritation our presence was to one poor woman until she leapt to her feet and stormed toward us.

"Haven't you got a nerve," she thundered, "bringing that miserable child out in public when some of us are trying to have a decent meal!"

That type of incident was unnecessary and hurtful. Looking back on it I wonder what sort of life that poor woman must have led for her to find Johnny's presence a pain. We felt sorry for her.

I could say a lot about Johnny's pain of incapacity, and about the fantastic way he managed to overcome it, but there isn't space enough in this book to do it justice.

However, I will say one thing in tribute to Johnny. He usually came through encounters like the one in the restaurant with great humor and dignity. I doubt if there are many men and women more restricted than he was. His incapacity was a supreme challenge. And yet in dealing with his own pain he won in a way that puts us all to shame.

2. *Old Age*

For most of us getting older means getting sicker. The more years you have behind you, the better your chances of having some physiological disorder that restricts you, causing you pain through incapacity. The writer of Ecclesiastes gives us a picture of some of those pains:

> . . . The keepers of the house shall tremble, and the strong men shall bow themselves, and the grinders cease because they are few, and those that look out of the windows be darkened (Ecclesiastes 12:3).

Metaphors like these come easily to mind when you know what it's like to have the soul of a 20-year-old and be trapped in a decaying body.

At 80 years of age John Quincy Adams met an old friend in the streets of Boston. The man grasped Adams' trembling hand and shook it firmly.

"Good morning," he said. "And how is John Quincy Adams today?"

The ex-President of the United States looked him in the eye.

"John Quincy Adams is well, Sir; quite well, I thank you. The house in which he lives is becoming quite dilapidated. It's tottering upon its foundation. Time has nearly destroyed it. Its roof is pretty well worn out. Its walls are much shattered, and it trembles with every wind. The old tenement is becoming almost unfit to live in, and I think John Quincy Adams will have to move out of it soon. But John Quincy Adams himself, thank you, is quite well, Sir. Thank you, quite well."

And with that the sixth President of the United States proceeded slowly down the street with his cane.

Dying not long afterwards in Washington he is reported to have said, "This is the last of the earth. I am content." That's a good way to go! Too many people reach their final years in discontent, regretting their misspent years, angry that they have drifted out of life's main shipping lanes into the backwaters of obscurity.

Even Christians can feel like that.

At Louisville one man who faithfully attended my church was the late Dr. Mordecai Ham. He told me about attending a meeting in North Carolina led by one of his converts—Billy Graham. He complained to Billy afterwards that he felt redundant. Dr. Ham said that although he had the same passion for God's work that he had as a young man, and although he could still get around, there didn't seem to be much demand for an 83-year-old preacher at public rallies.

Apparently Billy Graham replied, "Dr. Ham, think how God has used you. This very meeting tonight never would have been a reality had it not been for God's using you to bring me to Christ."

But Dr. Ham wasn't impressed.

"Billy," he said, "if the Lord lets you live long enough you'll remember this day, and you'll know my heart, and you'll understand my words. For the day will come when, as far as great rallies are concerned, you too will be laid on the shelf."

When he returned to his home in Louisville, Dr. Ham couldn't sleep. He prayed, asking the Lord why he was being put aside when he was willing to spend and be spent.

He got no answer.

Finally, at three o'clock in the morning, out of desperation, he went into his study and plucked a volume of Spurgeon at random from the shelf. It opened to a sermon from Luke 10 with the title "Stop Rejoicing." The disciples, it said, were told by Jesus to rejoice not that they could trample on serpents and scorpions, but simply that their names were written in heaven.

After reading that, Dr. Ham went back to bed and slept like a baby. He rejoiced that his name was written down in heaven. The experience didn't obliterate his pain. He felt a pang every time he went to a rally and listened to a great preacher. But he was able to live with it.

I don't mean to imply that old age is necessarily a period of relentless misery and privation. It's not. I know many old people, some of whom are in pretty poor shape physically, who are still happy and content. Nonetheless, old age is a *situation pain* likely to bring its own distinctive problems mental weakness, physical frailty, and so on—as well asother, more general pains like bereavement and loneliness.

Unless like Johnny we are called to glory before we get on in years, old age is something we will have to face. Many people dread it. Certainly it can be the "winter" of life's seasons, the "valley of the shadow" to be passed through on the way to eternity.

But I want to make this quite clear—in one important way old age is no different from other pains.

You can win over it.

8

Jam Yesterday, Today, and Tomorrow

We've looked at the two major types of pain in some detail. I hope it has helped you understand your pain and helped you define it more accurately. But before we look at solutions to pain we need to realize that pain of any sort can affect us in more than one way.

Back to Alice.

Shortly after leaving Tweedledum and Tweedledee in *Through the Looking Glass* Alice meets the White Queen, who promptly offers her a job as a lady's maid. The wages are generous to a fault:

> "Twopence a week, and jam every other day."
>
> Alice couldn't help laughing as she said, "I don't want you to hire me—and I don't care for jam."
>
> "It's very good jam," said the Queen.
>
> "Well, I don't want jam today, at any rate."
>
> "You couldn't have it if you *did* want it," the Queen said. "The rule is jam tomorrow and jam yesterday—but never jam today."
>
> "It must come sometimes to 'jam today'," Alice objected.
>
> "No, it can't," said the Queen. "It's jam every *other* day: today isn't any *other* day, you know."
>
> "I don't understand you," said Alice. "It's dreadfully confusing!"

"Dreadfully confusing" is a phrase we could aptly apply to pain.

To be in pain—*people pain* or *situational pain*—is distressing and disorienting in itself. But on top of that we have to cope with the *time* dimension of pain.

It is possible for there to be nothing in a person's present circumstances that causes him pain. If I'm not taking liberties by using the White Queen's jam as a symbol for pain, we can say that in such cases there may be no "jam today." But even if that is true there will certainly be "jam tomorrow and jam yesterday." Pain exists in our past and our future, even if it doesn't exist for us right here and now. And if it exists, it is able to affect us. In other words, we can suffer pain rooted in times other than the present.

Take for example a woman whose husband abandoned her two years ago. The actual experience of that event is past; it's over and done with. But although she's over the shock, the memory of it stays fresh. She will find herself reflecting on the arguments, wondering how a good relationship turned bad, wishing she'd said this or not said that. If the parting was acrimonious or traumatic—as it was for the wife who found her husband in bed with another woman—particular moments may lodge in her mind and be vividly relived years after they happened.

Like a river at a delta, past pain splits into many different channels.

A common channel for past pain is *guilt*. A family bereft of an elderly parent can be dogged by the feeling they didn't do enough. They didn't have their mother or father over for supper as often as they could have. They didn't set the record straight on past disagreements. Maybe they pushed the parent into a nursing home rather than finding a room in their own house. Possibly they didn't do anything at all that circumstances didn't force them to, and they feel guilty when it's too late to say they're sorry or to do more.

A rape victim, on the other hand, is more likely to suffer pain through the channel of *fear*. This is true whenever someone has had a painful experience associated with certain surroundings. The woman who has been raped may be afraid of walking through the park alone at night. The elderly person who has fallen may be afraid of ice. A child once bitten by a dog may be terrified to go near one.

Pain in these cases arises when the person is placed in surroundings they associate with past distress. It may arise even without that stimulant—for instance, the rape victim may experience fear in general, and not just when she is in an environment that reminds her of the one in which the rape took place.

Either way, as with guilt, the pain of fear comes from a link between past and present.

But pain through fear also carries a strong element of *anticipation*.

Until I reached my mid-teens I was the sickliest kid in the school. I was the runt in every class—inches shorter than the shortest girl and no match for anyone in athletics. I was pushed around, bullied, and made fun of. And not surprisingly I began to be afraid. But although my fear was based on my present situation— in other words, on the environment that I had learned to associate with bad experiences—I was also afraid because of what I thought was *about to happen to me*.

The effect of anticipated pain can be paralyzing, especially when its advent is unknown. Past pain is at least a devil you know. The bully is someone you've seen before, with fists no bigger than regulation size. But the future is *terra incognita*, and consequently the anxious person imagines it to be populated with monsters. That is why it's said the coward dies a thousand deaths and the brave man only one. The brave man sees death clearly enough not to hallucinate about it.

Not that you have to be a coward to suffer pain from anticipation of the future. It is at the core of Christ's prayer in the garden of Gethsemane:

> He was withdrawn from them about a stone's cast, and kneeled down, and prayed, saying, Father, if thou be willing, remove this cup from me: nevertheless not my will, but thine, be done.
> And there appeared an angel unto him from heaven, strengthening him. And being in an agony

he prayed more earnestly: and his sweat was as it were great drops of blood falling down to the ground (Luke 22:41-44).

The crowd with its cudgels had not yet come within earshot. Christ prayed with hands and feet unpierced, His head as yet unbruised by the spears of the soldiers. Yet He was in pain as He contemplated the hours immediately before Him in the Garden. He was in pain while He received the comfort of the angel. He was in pain at the possibility Satan might controvert His plan for world redemption.

That's the way future pain is. The anticipation of unpleasantness is as bad as, often worse than unpleasantness itself. It can exist on its own, too. All you need in order to suffer from it is a firm *conviction* that something unpleasant is going to happen to you. The conviction alone does the work. If you don't believe that think about the time when you suffered for a whole week, dreading a visit to the dentist, only to find on the morning of the ordeal that your appointment had been canceled!

Ironically, this kind of pain also works in reverse. It stands to reason that pain anticipated is suffered in advance. But pain also occurs when pleasure or achievement anticipated is snatched without warning from your grasp.

In the very early days of what has now become the Haggai Institute (a ministry designed to evangelize the Third World by providing its leaders with advanced training in evangelism) we were sure that Switzerland was the ideal venue for our training program. Switzerland was neutral. It had no strong political associations. And besides that it was the home of reputable international organizations like the Red Cross and the International YMCA.

I remember how we searched to find a location and sacrificed to scrape together funds to pay for it. We finally chose a three-story chalet on Lake Brienz, near Interlaken. The seller gave us a letter of intent. To make sure things were kept in order, several of our staff—and one of our leading board members, Gay Juban, who had spent a lifetime in finance and real estate—went out to make arrangements.

But just when it looked like the ministry was going to take off, the seller reneged.

I can hardly tell you how I felt at that moment. All the planning, all the prayer, all the hope and enthusiasm went up in smoke. We were nearly bankrupt. We felt certain the training program would have to be scuttled. It seemed like the ministry we'd spent so long putting together was falling flat on its face.

By a miracle it didn't. Through that disaster God was redirecting us to the far more suitable location of Singapore. I'd love to relate that story here, but if I did I'd be wandering off the point. I just want to show you what it's like to suffer disappointment in a big way.

So to summarize: Pain doesn't only affect us at the time we feel it. We can suffer beforehand through our anticipation of it, and afterwards through the memory of it.

The River of Pain

It would be misleading to talk about pains as though they existed in isolation, even if they do cast their shadows backwards and forwards in time. In fact, as I suggested earlier in this chapter, they act like channels in a river. Some channels can braid, splitting into numerous distributary streams. Other channels flow together into one larger one and so become indistinguishable. The whole pattern swings and wanders and increases in complexity.

That's only to be expected. After all, life is complex. It only means that we have to take care in identifying the ultimate sources of our pain—finding, as it were, the places where the streams rise. If you feel you have a pain that's as big and overwhelming as the Mississippi, the chances are it springs from many different places, and that some apparent causes of pain are not causes at all, but points where pain is transformed from one type into another.

I'll give you the best example I can think of.

My wife Chris is a marvelous singer. She loves it. But for reasons you know by now, she had to give up professional singing almost entirely for the first seven years of Johnny's life. She was confined. She had no opportunity to serve the Lord in public. She couldn't attend church regularly. While Johnny was very young she couldn't even relieve the frustration by singing at home, because Johnny would be distressed if he heard her in another room. On a bad day Chris would be on her feet from dawn till dusk. There were times when she would sit down sobbing with the strain, realizing at the same time that she had to keep going because there was no one else to keep Johnny alive.

Contrast that with my own lifestyle. I tried to be sensitive to Chris's situation, but at the same time I was driven relentlessly by a divine call I had publicly acknowledged in 1934. I was determined not to yield to the "menace of mediocrity." If the congregation reached five hundred, I wanted it to be a thousand. If it was a thousand, I wanted it to be two thousand. I gave myself with unspeakable devotion to my calling, and the growth of the ministry gradually increased the drains on my time and energy.

Tensions appeared.

Not explicit tensions, but things happening below the surface in our marriage that we couldn't resolve. We didn't have time to resolve them. I was fully committed to a church and a fledgling evangelistic ministry, and Chris was fully committed to looking after Johnny. We knew we should be seeing more of one another. I felt guilty that Chris was underwriting my success as a pastor and evangelist with an almost total sacrifice of her own creative abilities. Maybe it was because she had the strength to get on with the job without complaining that I failed to acknowledge the pressure she was under.

It cracked when I was working flat out in Louisville and Chris had had a particularly bad day with Johnny.

"It looks to me like you care an awful lot more for your work than you care for your own wife and son!" She looked at me, her face white and tense. "It's exciting, isn't it, meeting people and having them praise what you're doing?"

I went to the telephone and began to dial.

"What are you doing?"

"Calling to cancel a committee meeting I had for tonight!" I snapped at her.

Chris wrested the phone from my hand.

"Speaking of the telephone," she said, "You got a call from that woman who phoned you last week, reminding you you're having Sunday dinner with her family. She told me how sorry she was I couldn't join you because of Johnny."

I stayed at home that evening, but we scarcely spoke to one another. It was clear to me then how much Chris was hurting. What I failed to realize was how much of my own pain I was holding back from her, and that this actually added to hers.

In the end it was she who took the initiative in breaking down the barrier.

Things had been pretty tough at the church for some time. But one day I came home to find the dinner table spread for a king.

"Whose birthday?" I asked.

Chris smiled, and hurried me upstairs to wash. We had a marvelous meal, after which Mother Barker, who was living with us by then, quietly cleared away the dishes and retreated into the kitchen.

Chris's expression had turned serious, and I asked if there was anything wrong.

"There has been," she said. "But I want to help you make things right."

"What do you mean?"

"I've been getting telephone calls."

"What kind of telephone calls?"

"A woman phoned last week. She didn't give her name. I think her exact words were, 'Do you think it's right for you people to raise a cripple and still try to serve a church?' "

"What?"

"She's not the only one. There was a second woman who said, 'You know you could so easily get someone to care for that child. But you live on sympathy. Well, don't expect to get any from me!' There have been other calls too, about you. One man shouted at me that you were tearing up his church. Another one accused you of building a bunch of supporters against the people who've been faithful from the beginning. His advice was, 'Why don't you take that kid and get out of town?' "

I was stunned. But before I could speak, Chris went on, "I didn't realize what you were going through. Why didn't you tell me?"

"And put a bigger load on your shoulders?"

"It'll be easier for me," she said, "If I know I'm sharing all your experiences. You want to know everything that's happening to Johnny, and he adores you for it. I want to know what's happening with you."

We embraced.

She was right. I'd been keeping my pain to myself, and that had helped it to multiply. Pain in Chris's and my separate situations had spilled over into our relationship because I, particularly, had tried to keep mine hidden. I wanted to protect Chris from my pain, thinking that she had enough to bear already. And she had done the same.

By exposing our feelings, by being honest about our hurts, we had learned the first important lesson in winning over pain.

You can't do anything about pain while you're trying to hide it, even for the best reasons. Pain forces you to look for a solution somewhere outside of yourself. That means you've got to be willing to open up and be totally honest with yourself about the identity, source, and nature of your pain and how much it's hurting you. If I'd refused to admit I was in pain about my rejection by some members of the church I'd have been no nearer to resolving it. And Chris would have gone on hurting too.

I'm not telling you to become a chronic complainer. In that way I was right—I could have made Chris's life miserable by coming home at the end of the day and venting my self-pity on her. Pouring your troubles indiscriminately over others is just as bad as keeping them bottled up, and will probably lose you more friends!

Jesus said no man builds a tower without first making sure he has the money to do it. No leader goes to war without a reasonable assurance of victory. Winning over pain is like that. There's no use looking for an answer to your pain if you're not willing to put some spadework in yourself. And that begins with openness.

9

God's First Answer to Pain

Probably at this stage you want to say something like: "Okay. I understand a bit about what pain is and where it comes from. I know a bit about my own pain and what gave rise to it. Now—*what am I going to do about it?*"

Well, here goes.

First of all I want you to remember a simple formula. Wherever you stand in relation to pain, this formula is the key to your progress. So commit it to memory. Say it over to yourself at every opportunity. Speak it into your consciousness and your subconsciousness.

It goes like this:

I WIN OVER PAIN
WITH PRAYER, PURPOSE, AND PERSISTENCE.

Got that? Okay. Now let me unpack it for you.

You may be familiar with the story of Nehemiah, the Jewish leader who brought the Israelites back from the Exile. Nehemiah had a pretty respectable job as cupbearer for King Artaxerxes. He was comfortably off. He had no particular reason to be unhappy. But one day he met some Judeans who told him what was happening to the Jews left behind after the invasion, and how Jerusalem, the city of his fathers, lay in ruins.

A pain grasped Nehemiah's heart that he could not shake off.

> And it came to pass, when I heard these words, that I sat down and wept, and mourned certain days, and fasted, and prayed before the God of heaven, and said, I beseech thee, O Lord God of heaven, the great and terrible God, that keepeth

97

covenant and mercy for them that love him and observe his commandments: Let thine ear now be attentive, and thine eyes open, that thou mayest hear the prayer of thy servant, which I pray before thee now . . . (Nehemiah 1:4-6).

Take note of that. What Nehemiah did was what God's people have done down through the ages when they are in pain—they pray and seek God's help. Moses did it in the wilderness; Joshua did it in the Promised Land; Gideon did it; David did it; Jeremiah did it. Time and time again we read in the Old Testament how pain produced prayer. Prayer is the first and most essential response to pain. It takes first position in the formula, and without it the rest is useless.

As we noted earlier, it is the fact that pain drives us to prayer that makes it a useful tool in God's hands. If everything had been fine and dandy for Moses and the Israelites in Egypt they would never have cried to the Lord. But they were in trouble. The Egyptians "made their lives bitter with hard bondage" (Exodus 1:14). And that provided strong motivation for them to follow Moses into the desert. In fact pain was so strong a motive that it almost turned them back again at the Red Sea when they considered what punishment they might suffer at the hands of Pharaoh's pursuing army. "For it had been better for us to serve the Egyptians, than that we should die in the wilderness" (Exodus 14:12).

Similarly, if Nehemiah had been so satisfied with his position in exile that the ruin of Jerusalem meant nothing to him, the return would never have occurred and Jewish history would have been very different. It was pain that forced Nehemiah to turn to God. Pain that told him there was something so amiss in the present state of things that action had to be taken.

With Moses and Nehemiah the issues were political. They did have personal motivation—Moses had to flee his home country as a homicide before he met God in the burning bush—but in the end the pain and its rectification involved whole peoples. God was bringing the entire nation into obedience, not only individual citizens.

And yet there is plenty of evidence in the Old Testament that the tool of pain worked to call the individual man or woman back into a realistic relationship with God.

The Psalms are full of references to it:

> O my God, my soul is cast down within me: therefore will I remember thee from the land of Jordan, and of the Hermonites, from the hill Mizar (Psalm 42:6).

> Give ear to my prayer, O God, and hide not thyself from my supplication. Attend unto me, and hear me: I mourn in my complaint . . . (Psalm 55:1,2).

> Before I was afflicted I went astray: but now have I kept thy word (Psalm 119:67).

Many people have had such an experience of pain. I've had one myself.

I knew God had called me to preach when I was six years old. I didn't hear voices speaking to me from bedposts, or see flashing illuminated signs in the sky. It was just a quiet, deep, persisting impression that God wanted me to preach.

In 1937, though, my school started giving aptitude tests, and mine happened to show that I would do exceptionally well in business. Unfortunately this coincided with a period when I was exasperated with the financial arrangements of the ministry. I knew that my father, a man of deep faith and outstanding intelligence, who toiled in the service of the gospel, received an income of only $30 a week. That was total. No extra allowances, no perks, no accommodations.

I knew better than to complain openly in front of my parents, but inside I was simmering with anger at what I perceived to be an outrageous injustice. The school aptitude test provided me with a way of expressing my feelings. I determined I would use the aptitudes I was supposed to have, go into business, and make a pile of money to support Christian work around the world. Consequently, at the age of 16 I persuaded my mother to sign for my purchase of a Lincoln Zephyr V-12 automobile and became a salesman of books and magazines for a large company with headquarters in Boston.

This should have been a story of astounding success. My selling opportunities defied limitation. But noble though my ambitions were, they weren't the right ones for me, and God soon set about redirecting me. It wasn't long before I was in financial trouble. My uneasiness grew. I knew in my heart that God had set me apart for the ministry, and whatever good reason I came up with for my business venture, it was really a cheap cop-out. Still I went on with it.

Then, on the day after Christmas 1940, came the automobile accident I mentioned earlier in the book. Along with a severe leg laceration and thrombosis in the hip I suffered a streptococcus infection of the wound, and I was either off my leg or on crutches for months.

The message was clear. I resisted until finally, nine months after the accident, I came around. Sitting defiantly in my car outside the auditorium at a summer Bible conference in Rumney, New Hampshire, I told the Lord I would go into Christian work. At first I added the condition that it had to be Christian *music*, but in another year God had brought me full circle, and I began preparation for the ministry.

I think I can honestly say that those pains—first the embarrassment and stress of failure in business, and then the physical pain of the accident—were responsible for my entering the ministry. God used the pain to redirect me, and without it the Haggai Institute for Advanced Leadership Training, with its work in over 100 nations, would never have been born.

Dr. Kyung-Chik Han has found pain an asset in the same way. Dr. Han is the celebrated pastor emeritus of the 63,000 strong Young Nak Presbyterian Church in Seoul, Korea. In my book *Lead On!* I described him as the greatest leader I've ever known. I have no reason to revise that assessment. After the Japanese had signed the surrender papers on board the *U.S.S. Missouri*, the leaders of Korea asked Dr. Han to become the head of State. He declined because he said he had a higher calling.

But this man, who has founded schools, established orphanages and built churches, was once the victim of a severe tubercular condition. When he finished his studies at Princeton Seminary, friends advised him to go to the more advantageous climate of New Mexico. But there he showed no improvement. He knew God was calling him to be a pastor in Korea, but his health was holding him back.

During his convalescence he thought a great deal, read his Bible, and prayed fervently. He had been married at the age of 12 to a girl three years older than himself. It was an arranged marriage, and he had never loved the girl. Now, he realized, the thought of returning after 20 years to embark on a normal married life filled him with horror.

I met Dr. Han when he was in his seventies. I could still see the emotion when he described to me the day he realized the link between his illness and his marriage. He had been unwilling to obey God because he knew it meant returning to join his wife, and being a Christian husband to her. Yet he did obey, and when I was with them—every day for three weeks—his solicitude for her and her care of him were exemplary. She was truly a "mother in Israel." God used the tuberculosis to push Dr. Han into a total commitment of life and service. And in the end he not only became Korea's premier citizen, but a happily married man as well.

If you still don't believe that God uses pain, let me give you one more example.

Dr. Chandu Ray was born into a wealthy family in India. As a warrior caste intellectual he had studied every major religion, and with his mother had visited many of the holy places in the subcontinent of Asia. But he never found the answers he was looking for until one afternoon he heard that a very close friend was to go into the hospital for an operation. The man's eyesight was endangered, and the only way the doctors had of saving the sight of one eye was to remove the other. A compassionate man, Chandu immediately altered his schedule to visit his friend.

When he walked into the room he was surprised to find his friend reading a large book.

"What's that you're reading?" Chandu asked.

"The Bible."

"May I see it?"

His friend handed it to him. It was open at John 14. Chandu's eyes fell on the page and read the amazing words:

> Let not your heart be troubled: ye believe in God, believe also in me.
>
> In my Father's house are many mansions: if it were not so, I would have told you. I go to prepare a place for you. And if I go and prepare a place for you, I will come again, and receive you unto myself; that where I am, there ye may be also. And whither I go ye know, and the way ye know.
>
> Thomas saith unto him, Lord, we know not whither thou goest; and how can we know the way? Jesus saith unto him, I am the way, the truth, and the life: no man cometh unto the Father, but by me. If ye had known me, ye should have known my Father also: and from henceforth ye know him, and have seen him.
>
> Philip saith unto him, Lord, shew us the Father, and it sufficeth us.
>
> Jesus saith unto him, Have I been so long time with you, and yet hast thou not known me, Philip? He that hath seen me hath seen the Father; and how sayest thou then, Shew us the Father? Believest thou not that I am in the Father, and the Father in me? The words that I speak unto you I speak not of myself: but the Father that dwelleth in me, he doeth the works. Believe me that I am in the Father, and the Father in me: or else believe me for the very works' sake. Verily, verily, I say unto you, he that

believeth on me, the works that I do shall he do also; and greater works than these shall he do; because I go unto my Father.

And whatsoever ye shall ask in my name, that will I do, that the Father may be glorified in the Son. If ye shall ask any thing in my name, I will do it (John 14:1-14).

"Do you really believe this?" Chandu asked his friend.
"Of course."
"Then why don't we pray?"
"Do you think God will restore my eye?"
"Well, that's what your Bible says."
They got on their knees and prayed from late afternoon until nearly daybreak the next morning. Then they prepared to go to the hospital.

Chandu said, "When you come back from the hospital seeing, I shall accept Jesus as my Saviour."

"Do you really think," his friend said again, "that I will come back with both eyes restored?"

"Well, that's what your Bible says, and we did what we were told."

Later in the day Chandu's friend was taken to the operating room. Because the door was left ajar, Chandu was able to see the doctor measure the pressure in the eyeball. He saw an expression of surprise come over the doctor's face as he read the instrument, and heard him dispatch a nurse to get it replaced. A few minutes later the doctor came out.

"Have you been here long?" he asked Chandu.

"Since you first undertook to measure the pressure in my friend's eye."

"Well the pressure's disappeared."

"That's a miracle!"

But the doctor wasn't so easily convinced. He looked at Chandu benignly and said, "We doctors don't believe in miracles. The pressure will return, and when it returns your friend will come back here and we will remove the eye. By the way, what did you do last night? Did you put anything in his eyes?"

"No. We simply prayed to Jesus."

"Were any tears shed?"

"Yes. We were very conscious of the presence of God."

"I thought so. Probably the tears reduced the pressure. In that case it will return."

Whenever Chandu Ray related this story he would beam as he told about his commitment to Christ and subsequent training for the ministry. He was the first Asian to be consecrated an Anglican bishop. Then, with an almost mischievous smile, he would add, "I went on to be the Bishop of Karachi. My friend, who sees today as well as I do, went on to become the Bishop of Birmingham in England!"

Chandu Ray, Dr. Han, and I have all been directed through pain. James affirms this function of pain as "God's megaphone" when he calls upon his readers to "count it all joy when ye fall into divers temptations; knowing this, that the trying of your faith worketh patience" (James 1:2,3). Later he tells the sick man to "call for the elders of the church," who will then "pray over him, anointing him in the name of the Lord" (James 5:14).

He goes on:

> And the prayer of faith shall save the sick, and the Lord shall raise him up; and if he have committed sins, they shall be forgiven him (James 5:15).

Which brings us to the fact that while pains (or trials, or temptations, or afflictions) are made to be agents of God's purpose, they are nonetheless *intrinsically evil*.

The Dark Side of Pain

There is a dangerous, double-edged nature to pain. Like an ambulance siren it has to be loud and unpleasant, or no one would take any notice of it—that is inevitable if it is going to be an effective warning sign. But this has a spin-off. Because pain by its very nature drives the sufferer into an extreme state there is always a possibility that he will react the wrong way.

This is illustrated well in the book of Job.

The first chapter pictures God and Satan in an earnest conversation about the earth. Satan, who has spent a good deal of time "walking up and down in it," doesn't seem much impressed. So God pushes Job forward as a paragon of virtue, a man "that feareth God, and escheweth evil." He eschews it so much, in fact, that he is continually offering sacrifices in case his sons have inadvertently cursed God in their hearts and sinned.

> Then Satan answered the Lord, and said, Doth Job fear God for nought? Hast not thou made an hedge about him, and about his house, and about all that he hath on every side? Thou hast blessed the work of his hands, and his substance is increased in the land. But put forth thy hand now, and touch all that he hath, and he will curse thee to thy face (Job 1:9-11).

Satan's accusation is that Job is devout only because God treats him like a Ming vase. Introduce him to pain, he says, and Job will be corrupted faster than milk turns sour.

So God gives Satan permission to subject Job to pain. Job is promptly reduced to poverty and bereaved of his beloved family. But he does not curse God. Pain in this instance has the right effect: "Then Job arose, and rent his mantle, and shaved his head, and fell down upon the ground, and worshipped" (Job 1:20).

> And the Lord said unto Satan, Hast thou considered my servant Job, that . . . still he holdeth fast his integrity, although thou movedst me against him, to destroy him without cause.
> And Satan answered the Lord, and said, Skin for skin, yea, all that a man hath will he give for his life.

> But put forth thine hand now, and touch his bone
> and his flesh, and he will curse thee to thy face
> (Job 2:3-5).

God then lets Satan bring pain to Job not merely in his circumstances, but in his body. He is smitten with boils, and sits in ashes scraping himself with a potsherd.

This time Job very nearly gives way. For the following 40 chapters of the book he is really asking himself a question we all tend to ask when we're in pain—"What have *I* done to deserve this?" And of course there is no answer. As we discovered earlier, pain isn't the result of God's judgment on us as individuals. It's very unlikely, too, that we are a test case in the way Job was—we're not virtuous enough! Pain is just part of the avalanche of the Fall.

There is a lot in Job about pain that we haven't time to investigate here. But note two things.

First, Satan's intention in subjecting Job to pain was to separate him from God. If pain can make us curse God—if it causes us to do exactly the opposite of the great men of faith in the Bible—then pain has backfired and the purposes of Satan have been achieved.

I have experienced the force of pain in my own family. God sustained us. He sustained Johnny in the inner pain that Chris and I could do nothing to alleviate. But we lived with pain for long enough to realize that it could break a person's normal poise and throw him on a downward spiral into chronic guilt, anger, remorse, bitterness, depression, and miserable, self-pitying loneliness. At that stage pain is no longer a tool in God's hand. It is merely destructive. It leaves lines on the face and scars on the heart. The sufferer's whole life is dominated by it.

Nonetheless—and this is the second point to come from the story of Job—it is important to distinguish pain from its causes and effects.

Without a doubt pain is evil. But when I say that pain is evil I don't mean evil in quite the same way as lying, murder, or adultery is evil. Take the example of a man who is cheating on his income tax, and who is at the same time experiencing the pain of mental stress. His dishonesty and his stress are both evils; neither would have existed but for the Fall. But his dishonesty is also evil because it is a sin—he is willfully disobeying God's law. This is not true of the stress, or of any other pain. The evil of pain does not derive its power from disobedience. Even if the man's stress results directly from his sin, it is still only the sin of which he is guilty.

I labor this point because I occasionally hear it said that being in pain is a sin *in itself*.

It's not. Sin and pain are both evils, but they are evils of different kinds. I saw this in a young man I met as a student. He was tall, handsome enough to be a male model, brilliant, articulate, and charming beyond description. I have no doubt whatever that when it came to talent and potential this young man topped the whole class. But behind the engaging personality lay concealed a snakepit of psychological problems. There were times even in his student days when he thought he was losing his mind, and had to be confined. His life has been a shambles. Looking back on it now he has an almost psychotic obsession with his shortcomings and mistakes. Time and again he has confessed his sins, yet he cannot accept God's forgiveness. Consequently the pain of a tortured conscience, which is not sinful in itself, has in his mind become part and parcel of his ruined, sinful life. No amount of counsel, no repetition of encouragement, no reiteration of God's grace can persuade him to distinguish between his sins (which are forgiven anyway) and his pain, which to a large extent is now self-induced.

That pain is not sin in itself is clearly illustrated in the case of the rich man and Lazarus in Luke 16. The rich man dies and goes to Hades. But the evils of poverty and destitution suffered by Lazarus do not result in his condemnation—they are left behind as he is taken into Abraham's bosom. Being in pain does not make a person guilty. If pain was a sin, Lazarus would have been thrown into the flames along with his rich neighbor.

So why was the rich man condemned? Because he "was clothed in purple and fine linen and feasted sumptuously every day"? No. He was condemned because he was wealthy and did nothing to help the poor. He was condemned because he would not use his resources to combat the evil of pain. In Matthew 25 Jesus goes even further. At the end of time, He says, mankind will be divided into two groups, the sheep and the goats. What is it that distinguishes the righteous from the unrighteous? It is not that the righteous got through life untainted with the evil of pain, but rather that they treated suffering people with compassion.

> I was an hungered, and ye gave me meat: I was thirsty, and ye gave me drink: I was a stranger, and ye took me in: naked, and ye clothed me: I was sick, and ye visited me: I was in prison, and ye came unto me (Matthew 25:35,36).

The message is clear. Jesus is telling His disciples to follow in His own footsteps. For while He was the uniquely divine Savior of the world, Jesus was also concerned to relieve present human suffering. It wasn't any rarified spiritual proof of His divinity that He sent back to John when asked by John's disciples if He was the Messiah, but news that "the blind see, the lame walk, the lepers are cleansed, the deaf hear, the dead are raised, to the poor the gospel is preached" (Luke 7:22). It was this aspect of His ministry that must have struck Peter, for his first remark about Jesus to the gentile Cornelius in Acts 10:38 is that "Jesus of Nazareth . . . went about doing good and healing all who were oppressed of the devil; for God was with him."

Attacking the evil of pain, in the widest possible sense, characterizes Jesus' ministry as He described it Himself at the synagogue in Nazareth:

> The Spirit of the Lord is upon me, because he hath anointed me to preach the gospel to the poor; he hath sent me to heal the broken hearted, to

preach deliverance to the captives, and recovering
of sight to the blind, to set at liberty them that are
bruised, to preach the acceptable year of the Lord
(Luke 4:18,19).

Fighting Pain

I have a good friend in Palm Beach, Florida, by the name of
Madge Yoakley. Madge is the wife of a prominent lawyer. She
and her husband move with ease in any level of society. They
could very easily devote themselves to their own work, and to
their own social circle, and feel that they had done their bit in
contributing to the work of the church. But Madge has for
many years made a point of visiting the local hospital every
day to talk to, encourage, and pray with the sick. She feels it is
part of her duty and privilege as a Christian.

I want to affirm that this often time-consuming and unspec-
tacular ministry is an important part of "preaching the gospel
to the poor." Remember, sickness can make a "poor man" out
of the richest resident, even of Palm Beach.

In trying to relieve the pain of the world Christians too
often go for the high-profile approach. That's not wrong in
itself. Far from it. When Peter and John met the lame man at
the Temple in Acts 3 they didn't just sit down for a chat with
him, though that in itself would have been perfectly good and
Christian, they reached out to him in the power of God and
bade him rise and walk.

Now I'm all for that.

God heals. Miraculously.

But I am not betraying the gospel by encouraging you as a
brother or sister in Christ to relieve another's pain with a
word, a smile, a gift, or a visit. That's not second best. James
actually calls the visiting of orphans and widows in their
distress "pure religion and undefiled" (James 1:27). Paul instructs the Romans to "rejoice with them that do rejoice, and
weep with them that weep" (Romans 12:15). And when he
says to the Galatians: "Bear ye one another's burdens, and so

fulfill the law of Christ" (Galatians 6:2), he implies that one good solution to pain is not to eradicate it, but to share it.

For the record, that is why my definition of divine healing doesn't stop with prayer and the laying on of hands. God has provided at least three more ways of bringing comfort, relief, and healing to those who suffer the pains of illness than what we generally call the ministry of healing.

1. *The use of prescription drugs and natural medicines.*

James says quite clearly, "Every good gift and every perfect gift is from above, and cometh down from the Father of lights, with whom is no variableness, neither shadow of turning" (James 1:17).

Every natural substance in this world was created by God. Long before any pharmacists were around to identify or dispense them, all the ingredients of the aspirin tablet were present. We have only combined them to maximize their effect. So if you've got a headache, take an aspirin tablet and thank God for His providence!

Someone will probably point out that if God made the ingredients for aspirin He must also be responsible for thalidomide and napalm.

That is true in the sense that by producing these substances man has created nothing that was notalready theoretically possible in the scheme of God's creation. The same can be said of anything man has made, from the first flint knife to the thermonuclear bomb. If I wanted to I could kill someone by hitting him with my Bible! Everything given to us has a potential for good or evil, and drugs, like anything else, can be used for evil. But if human ingenuity combines materials for a good purpose, then the unseen hand of God is at work.

2. *The instrumentality of doctors.*

In the course of history it is only comparatively recently that medicine as a science has achieved a reasonable degree of accuracy and reliability. The physician of the European Middle Ages may have been a good man, but he was ill-equipped to be a good doctor. Twentieth century medicine—thank goodness!—has taken surgery out of the barbershop and into the operating room. It has developed microsurgery, body scanning, heart and lung replacement, and a host of other lifesaving and life-enhancing skills.

Yet it would be a mistake to think that this knowledge exists apart from the grace of God. Somebody said to me the other day, "I have a great doctor. He healed me." That's not true. The doctor's skill is a potential in God's creation that is revealed by the providence of the Creator. And even this is not *directly* responsible for healing. The surgeon may remove an obstruction or introduce a new length of artery, but the body obeys laws of healing that God has already built into it.

3. *The relief of psychosomatic symptoms caused by stress.*

It is widely accepted now that stress can be a decisive factor in blood-pressure conditions, irrational phobias, peptic and duodenal ulcers, and headaches. These symptoms very often disappear when the sufferer progresses in the Lord and learns to rejoice instead of worrying and feeling fraught. And that is not a mere by-product of conversion—it is the grace of God active in healing and release from pain.

Just moments before writing this I was talking to evangelist Eddie Lieberman. He told me about a letter he'd received. The woman who wrote it—whom he didn't know—had recently tried to commit suicide. Her husband had turned their home into a living hell shortly after their marriage, and had abused and mistreated her for years. The emotional trauma and mental pressures did their work: She became crippled, and felt she had nothing left to live for.

As she went to the bathroom to take her own life she saw a book called *The Whirlwinds of Life*. The title fascinated her, and she picked it up and began reading. Consequently she was converted. She committed her life to the Lord, and was soon freed from her psychosomatic condition. While her husband, who ran out on her, has not returned and is presumably still living his life of wanton debauchery, she is a renewed, joyful, and productive person.

Such is the power of the Spirit to untie the emotional knots of the human body. Another lady who found release from psychosomatic illness through coming to Christ said to me, "Mr. Haggai, there is a lot of difference between being tranquilized and having the peace Christ gives. No tranquilizer can heal the pain of the soul."

Implicit in all these routes to healing is our personal initiative. God won't answer your prayer if you don't make use of the solution He has put before you. That would be like a hungry man sitting behind a plateful of food and complaining that he's not being fed, just because he has to lift the spoon himself!

I've illustrated this with the healing of physical disorders. But the same point can be made about any form of pain. If I am unhappy with my job, for instance, there is nothing wrong with my resigning my post and looking for something else. I am perfectly free to do that, and if the job is a source of pain then resignation is one very clear solution to it. Two things should be borne in mind, however.

First, I am only justified in resigning if I am not betraying any responsibilities in the process. I can give my notice at work, but I can't leave a letter of resignation on the kitchen table to tell my wife I'm divorcing her. Marriage has more extensive and complex commitments than employment, and I cannot simply withdraw from it as soon as it causes me pain.

Second, for my own sake I will be well advised to think through my reasons before I make my move. That is why I've spent so much time looking at the precise nature of pain. If the real cause of my unhappiness at work is my aggressive personality, which drives others away and makes me feel isolated, I am not doing myself a favor by resigning. I will carry the root of the problem around with me, and it will grow and bloom in whatever social situation I enter. I don't need to change my job—I'd be better off taking a long hard look at my own behavior.

I have in mind one highly paid professional man who worked hard, read widely, and served generously both in his community and in his local church. He had superb acumen. On several occasions I heard men and women, his seniors in age and experience, rhapsodize over the brilliance of his insights. Yet the better they got to know him, the less they liked him.

Brilliant he might have been, but he had almost no competence in handling relationships. He talked to his beautiful and talented wife like a ruthless tyrant would talk to a prisoner of war. He laid out an almost inhuman regimen for his children. In business his relationships always seemed to follow a set pattern of deterioration. For the first few meetings he would be admired, and other leaders would voluntarily take a backseat to make room for his recognizably superior talent. But sooner or later they grew resentful at his dictatorial style and his habit of short-circuiting the principles of democratic leadership. Some saw him as an egomaniac. Others just dropped out and no longer came to meetings. "With Sam," they said, "it's either rule or ruin."

As it happened, for this young man it turned out to be both rule and ruin. He lost credibility within his own professional fraternity. His finances took a beating. He saw the dreams he had striven for crumbling to dust. At first he solved his problems by moving to a new place, but by the time he reached his fifties there was simply nowhere left for him to go. One of his longtime friends and colleagues said, "I don't think he ever grasped the fact that his problem was himself. He was generous to a fault with his money. But he insisted on tying everything he did to the impossible conditions he imposed on others. He doesn't know the meaning of the Golden Rule—'Whatever you want men to do to you, do also to them.' "

Let's pull a few threads together.

The Bible teaches us clearly that our response to pain should be to take it to God in faithful prayer. That is the first and essential part of the formula for winning over pain.

It also teaches us that God's first answer to pain—any kind of pain—is "Arise, and take up thy bed, and go thy way . . ."

(Mark 2:11). In other words God's first answer to pain is to remove it at the source, either by direct intervention, as we see Jesus doing time and again in the Gospels, or indirectly through prayer, through the ministry of God's people, through drugs, medical treatment, natural medicines, or any of the numerous other means by which the grace of God can reach us.

The removal of that pain may be rapid, or it may take days, weeks, and sometimes even years.

It may require a lot of careful thought about your situation, and some honesty if you've been in a difficult relationship where you've given hurt as well as received it.

It may require the assistance of trustworthy and skilled friends or counselors to help you sort things out.

But whatever means God in His infinite wisdom chooses for the removal of your pain, remember, it is the Lord who heals. The key lies in your sincere and trusting approach to the throne of grace. God heals. He gives relief in suffering even when the pain is still there. In a score of different ways He will help you to win over your pain perhaps by reducing or removing it altogether. He will faithfully see you through if you trust Him.

And before I finish this chapter let me drop a little trailer to the next one.

I know there will be a lot of people reading this book who agree heartily with everything I've said so far. Their only objection will run something like this:

"I do believe in God's power to heal, through many different means. I do trust in Him to relieve my pain. I've received ministry, I've been to many doctors, talked to many specialists, prayed, and made every effort with God's assistance to overcome my pain. The problem is—I'm still hurting!"

Well, that's why the formula for winning over pain doesn't stop at prayer. So, if you're still hurting, read on.

10

Through the Looking Glass

I once asked a leading exponent of divine healing, a man who believes that God will heal anyone who comes to Him in faith and purity of heart, why it was he wore glasses.

He never gave me a satisfactory answer. I don't believe that he could—not because he isn't an intelligent, thinking man, but because his theology had him backed into a corner.

I'll explain.

Suppose I was writing this book using a theology that claimed it was always God's will to bring miraculous healing, always His will to bring immediate release from pain. You read the book, and then attend the next healing crusade you can get to so you can have the laying on of hands for your pain. You're full of faith. I have done such a good job of persuading you that it's God's will for your pain to be removed that failure is no longer in your vocabulary. You go forward at the meeting. The minister lays his hands on your head and prays in the name of Jesus Christ for your pain to be healed.

Nothing happens.

You wait a week and still nothing happens. You wait a month, a year, two years, and still nothing happens. Finally you pick up the book again and turn to an appendix entitled something like: "Reasons Why You May Not Be Healed."

It presents you with an argument we can break down as follows:

> FIRST PREMISE: It is God's will for you to be free from pain.
>
> SECOND PREMISE: If you have not been healed it is because either you or the person who prayed for you lacked faith or is living in disobedience to God.

THIRD PREMISE: Since the person who prayed for you is up there on stage and you're down in the cheap seats, you're more likely to be the culprit.

CONCLUSION: The fact that you're still in pain is like a big neon sign telling the world what God thinks of you.

I'm sorry if that sounds cynical, but that's what failed healing looks like from the worm's-eye view.

Not only does the pain remain, but the sufferer is saddled with the stigma of implied personal sin. I know that from my own experience. When Johnny wasn't healed the conclusion drawn by some was that "John Haggai must be holding out against God over something." In one short step Christian ministry turns into moral judgment.

I am not saying the argument is completely invalid. Harbored sin *can* be an impediment to healing. To take a very obvious example, the person nursing bitter feelings over a broken relationship can hardly expect God to put it right for him. The solution lies to a large degree in himself.

Harbored sin can also explain physical pains. A leading member of a church in Roanoke Rapids, North Carolina, told me the story of a heart condition that had baffled four doctors. None of them could explain it, but this man had suffered a series of heart attacks, and lived in stark terror lest he die from one.

He readily admitted to having sins in his life. But there was one sin, an anchor sin, that seemed to torment him. He couldn't shake it. One night he attended an evangelistic service and heard the gospel preached. That night he turned his back on all of his sins, got up to confess Christ, and went to the front to announce his decision. When he went home afterwards he discussed the personal situation that had plagued him so long with his wife, and then slept like a baby. He lived for another 14 years, free from any cardiac irregularities, and died a natural death. "Until I knew for sure that my sins were all forgiven, including that sin that had tormented me for years, I not only suffered mental anguish, but physical ailments," he said.

So the preachers who blame sin for illness and pain aren't always wrong. But there are four reasons why I am convinced that lack of faith and/or personal guilt are not *general* causes of persistent pain:

One—*Jesus did not associate pains suffered by individuals with sins committed by them or by their families.*

"Who did sin, this man, or his parents," the disciples asked Jesus, "that he was born blind?" (John 9:2). But Jesus is emphatic in his reply:

> . . . Neither hath this man sinned, nor his parents: but that the works of God should be made manifest in him (John 9:3).

The man's pain was part of the random fallout from the Fall—it did not stem from God's judgment of specific sins. He could no doubt have made his pain worse by sinning, as the Samaritan woman in John 4 had done by her reckless adultery. But at base both of these were simply ordinary sinners like you and me. God was not directing their pain.

Jesus makes a similar point when somebody asks him about the Galileans who had come to a grim end at the hands of Pontius Pilate:

> Jesus answering said unto them, Suppose ye that these Galileans were sinners above all the Galileans, because they suffered such things? I tell you, Nay: but, except ye repent, ye shall all likewise perish (Luke 13:2,3).

The moral is not so much that those who suffer pain are especially bad, but that none of us are especially good.

By that reckoning, if healing depended on our ability to keep a sparkling clean conscience we'd all be in big trouble. The best of us are far from perfect. Like David we all have sins—"secret faults" as Psalm 19:12 calls them—that we have to ask the Holy Spirit to reveal because they are so well hidden we cannot find them.

> Search me, O God, and know my heart: try me, and know my thoughts: And see if there be any wicked way in me, and lead me in the way everlasting (Psalm 139:23,24).

Really the best we can do is to try our utmost to be honest with God, as I believe Chris and I were when we first prayed over Johnny's pain. We can rely on God to reveal our hidden faults to us if we ask Him to. But to treat our failed healing as a command to ferret out some monster "unconfessed sin" will probably cause us, like the early astronomers who studied Mars, to see canals and cities where there are really only craters and dust. That will move us further away from healing and not closer to it.

For the record let me give you some more details of the talk I had with that exponent of faith healing. Naturally I won't use his real name. But I will say I met him for three hours in a hotel room in 1966—a time when Johnny's illness was causing me much distress.

I remember he urged me to find some hidden sin. When I demurred he asked if I didn't believe that all sickness was the result of sin.

"I do," I replied. "But I don't believe all sickness is the result of personal guilt. The Bible teaches that sin is the result of Adam's rebellion against God. But to say that all sickness and disease comes from personal guilt can't be substantiated from the Scriptures as I understand them. Johnny was brutalized by an intoxicated doctor before he had one conscious thought of rebellion. How does Johnny's own sin fit into that?"

I paused, then went on. "Look, Andy, if I believed what you profess I'd gladly fall on my hands and knees and crawl on broken glass all the way to Boston to have you pray for Johnny."

"Don't you believe God can heal?"

"Absolutely. The atheistic doctor who operated on my leg after that accident in 1940 said my recovery couldn't be explained in normal medical terms. I should have lost my leg, probably my life. He had to prescribe so much sulfanilamide I was warned I'd probably die soon enough of leukemia. Well, here I am at 42 years of age and enjoying robust health. So absolutely—I believe God heals. However, it's not always His way of dealing with the situation. More people have prayed for Johnny than for all the rest of the family combined. I know for a fact that people in more than a 150 countries have prayed."

We had a serious discussion. I testify to my unshakable conviction that this man is as sincere, as dedicated, as compassionate as any man I've known. But I wasn't going to let him imply that Johnny's paralysis was the result of personal guilt. I quoted a few passages in the New Testament where Christians didn't seem to be healed, and stressed the fact that since everything possible had been done to heal Johnny, he really *ought* to be healed. Eventually I got my friend to admit that Johnny's illness was not the result of unconfessed sin.

"But isn't that exactly what your whole theology of sin, sickness, and healing shouts out?" I asked him.

And there lay the contradiction. My friend could construct a theology of healing that implied personal guilt, but he couldn't make it work satisfactorily in practice. It didn't pan out with Johnny. It didn't even pan out with him—which was why I smiled warmly and asked him why, in private, he wore glasses. Why hadn't his eyes been healed? Presumably for the same reason that Paul's weren't. Which brings me to the next point.

Two—*I can find no evidence that the New Testament Christians expected healing to "work" every time, or that they blamed unconfessed sin or lack of faith in the cases where healing "failed."*

Had they done so, Paul would surely have taken a different view of Timothy's "often infirmities" (1 Timothy 5:23). But Paul never even suggests that Timothy's condition, which was clearly a great nuisance to him, might be changed by a flick through his catalog of secret sins. And if Timothy lacked boldness, he is nonetheless commended for his "unfeigned faith" (2 Timothy 1:5). The epistles addressed to him contain no urgings to greater personal holiness. Rather the advice is for Timothy to be a little easier on himself, to drink some wine as well as water.

This wasn't exceptional in Paul's approach. He adopted a similar attitude in other places, as when he remarked very matter-of-factly to Timothy that he had to leave the ailing Trophimus behind in Miletum.

Paul knew in himself that direct, "interventionist" healing of pain wasn't always God's answer. It's pretty well agreed among commentators that when he said to the Galatians, "Ye see how large a letter I have written unto you with mine own hand" (Galatians 6:11), he meant the writing must be his because anyone else would see well enough to write small.

If ever anyone had a claim to God's perfect health it must have been Paul. He didn't get it. And how many unconfessed sins did Paul have?

Three—*Those who advocate this view of healing do not apply it consistently.*

Here I'm back with my friend and his glasses.

No minister can demand standards of others he is not willing to apply to himself. He has to demonstrate the truth as well as preach it. So if you say God always heals when faith and personal holiness combine, you've got to be a living example of it.

No one in his right mind is going to pay attention to a preacher who says from the platform, "I know God can heal you," then limps down from the podium and breaks out in a fit of consumptive coughing. How healthy does a man have to be before he is credible? Can he have a cold? Is he allowed to have pulled a muscle jogging? I know for a fact that some people with a healing ministry wear dentures, none of them seem to have an answer for baldness, and ultimately they all die!

To be fair, I'm not waiting for someone to prove he's immortal before I let him pray for me. But I do want to know he's applying the same standard to himself as he is to me when he tells me it's my fault I'm still in pain.

Four—*Christians who suffer the most awful pain nonetheless seem to accomplish great things for God.*

This isn't what you'd expect. Someone sitting on a secret sin isn't likely to be one of those seeds of the Kingdom that yields a hundredfold. Yet, as far as we are able to judge, God has accomplished some fantastic spiritual victories through some very sick Christians.

The writer of *Paradise Lost,* John Milton, was blind. So too was Fanny Crosby, but she still wrote over eight thousand songs and poems, which have brought blessings to millions. William Cowper wrote some of his finest hymns from the pain of depression. Johnny overcame his pain to be a powerful influence in the formation of the Haggai Institute.

These are the observations that lead me to believe healing and relief from pain aren't, as I said earlier, just a matter of "snapping the fingers in prayer" and producing perfect physical, mental, and emotional fitness.

They also lead me to believe that "failure" in prayer for healing or relief from pain is not always the fault of the person in pain. It's not because he hasn't learned the technique of finger-snapping that he still hurts.

I am convinced the reason pain survives our most heartfelt prayer is that God has *two* answers to our prayer, and not just one. Hold tight—we're now going to change the approach we've been taking for most of the book and move in a completely new direction. Like Alice we're going to step "through the looking glass" to a place where things are back to front, almost the reverse of what they were before. Off we go.

Looking Glass Pain

So far we've made an assumption about pain that's really quite unjustified.

Pain is a disagreeable experience, yes. It is a warning sign and a limitation. But without actually saying so we have also assumed that it is something *imposed on us against our will*. The reason for this is simple—to have something forced on us is a limitation of our freedom and therefore automatically a pain. But during the course of our lives we tolerate a good many pains because we ourselves have chosen them.

Let me descend for a moment from the sublime to the ridiculous and tell you how I learned to ski.

I'd wanted to learn downhill skiing for years, but I'd never had the time, and originally hadn't even had the money. Finally I set aside two weeks to go to Austria to ski. Unfortunately, on the third day I got in the way of some more advanced skiers, crossed my skis and fell into a guardrail. I cracked my collarbone. The pain was severe; each night I suffered agony. But though the pain deprived me of sleep I braved out the two-week course and finally had the joy of skiing the steepest slopes from the top of the mountain at Hopfgarten.

I was willing to put up with physical pain in order to achieve what I considered to be a higher goal. But that was peanuts compared to some of the financial pains I've faced.

When I resigned my four thousand-strong pastorate in Louisville at the age of 32 to embark on an evangelistic ministry, my assets—including library, furniture and insurance—came to less than $20,000. My total cash was $217. But I didn't mind. I had given practically everything I had to the church program, and had done it with joy.

God blessed me. In my new work I had 20 invitations come in for every one I could fulfill. By the time I was 45 the ministry was established and growing solidly. But then we decided to launch what is now known as the Haggai Institute for Advanced Leadership Training. This was a far bigger venture. In order to provide funds I used all my savings, and borrowed a large amount of money from Atlanta's First National Bank.

The bank refused to lend the money to the Institute as the Institute had only just been established, so I had to take the loan personally—a responsibility that weighed on me heavily. We had quite a few problems, and by the end of 1969 prospects were so bleak financially that a rogue thought came into my mind, an urge to cut my losses and move into a new career. The trouble was, I knew that wasn't God's will, just as I'd known it all those years before when I'd become a salesman. Then, just as I was in the middle of the "slough of despond" over my finances, I got a call from a good friend, Dr. Wendell Phillips.

I ought to tell you about Wendell. *Time* magazine described him as the world's largest oil concessionaire. He led the most prestigious archeological ventures, including the Cairo to Cape Town Venture on which the chief archeologist was Dr. William F. Allbright of Johns Hopkins University. Wendell had accompanied me when Sir Cyril Black arranged for me to speak to members of Parliament at Church House, Westminster, London, and introduced me when I spoke to the Southern Baptist Convention Pastors' Conference in New Orleans. In turn I had introduced him to government leaders, and many business and professional friends of mine. We had enjoyed many enriching experiences together.

Wendell called to make me an offer. He said he would give me a million dollars if I would give him one year of my life to help him develop contacts in Asia and Latin America. In addition he would give me a percentage of the royalties should any of these contacts turn out to be profitable. In short it was an offer that would have gone toward getting the Haggai Institute off the ground.

A few days later he called the house. I was out, and he spoke to Chris, my wife.

"Did John tell you that I called him, Chris?"

"No, tell me about it."

He told her the offer he'd made.

She asked, "What did John say?"

"He just laughed."

"That means he's not interested."

Wendell called me back a couple of days later and said, "What's the matter? Not enough money?"

I responded, "Your job's too small."

It was a tough decision to make, but I had to accept the pain of financial pressure in order to move towards that higher goal I knew God had called me to: the evangelization of the world through credentialed national leaders.

I've known plenty of other people who have chosen the same kind of sacrifice. In the 1960's I met a young banker whose genius had created a sensation in the financial community. No obstacle seemed to stand in his way. He could have moved to the very top of his profession, but he felt that he wanted to do more with his life than amass capital and build a reputation. Consequently, with his wife's agreement, he resigned his banking position and undertook some activities that enabled him to bring his Christian commitment and professional expertise to bear on the men and women in the marketplace who regard Christianity as a once-a-week affair that is irrelevant to the rest of their lives. The decision brought financial hardship but he and his wife accepted it because they believed they were called to a higher goal.

One of my own colleagues at the Haggai Institute, Michael Youssef, has been through some incredibly troubled times. At the age of 19 he fled from Nasser's Egypt to Beirut, enduring the most straitened circumstances, sometimes going without food (an unusual experience for a young man whose family were prominent in Assiut). He fled to Australia in order to follow what he believed to be God's calling. Today he has a world ministry. He earned his Ph.D. at Emory University and is now respected as one of the world's outstanding young Christian intellectuals.

The fact is, we are all prepared to suffer pain if we believe that pain will achieve some higher good. Think of your own experience for a moment. Often you do it in very mundane circumstances.

For instance, you probably don't enjoy sitting in a traffic jam for an hour every day. But you do it because you like your job and you want to provide for your family. You probably don't enjoy spending 12 hours a day poring over your textbooks. Nonetheless you do it because you want to pass your exams and improve your employment prospects. You work overtime. You give up social activities of your own for the sake of spending an afternoon with the kids. You do weight lifting and running to make a place on the football team. You look after an elderly parent. You save money you could spend on yourself to buy someone an expensive present. You spend arduous hours doing scales on the piano. You reduce your sugar intake on the advice of your doctor . . .

We all invest our time, our money, our attention, and our energy in things that, at the time we do them, are not very enjoyable. Some are only mildly disagreeable, others are frankly unpleasant and tough. They all limit us, and keep us from doing some other thing we'd rather do. In short they are pains. *But we take them on anyway because we know that in the long term they lead to some greater good.*

We are so used to this idea of working for reward that often we do not think of calling the work itself a "pain." More common terms are "duty" and "discipline." Yet some things we volunteer to do—like giving blood or having an operation—are physically painful, and some common *situation pains*—like a lousy job—remain distressing even when the pain is dulled by our "getting used" to it.

Yet we won't subject ourselves to pain indefinitely. There is an equation that links the level of pain we are willing to endure to the importance of the end to be achieved. Paul alludes to it in Romans when he writes: "Scarcely for a righteous man will one die: yet peradventure for a good man some would even dare to die" (Romans 5:7).

Giving up your life—the ultimate pain—is not a deed to be taken lightly. If a man is going to risk his life he will want to be satisfied he is doing it for a good cause. And such causes do exist. Most of us would risk death to save a loved one from danger. Many have risked death by volunteering to defend their country in time of war.

You might think that since these two relationships—with family and nation—provide the highest motives, they are therefore the most capable of inducing a person to endure pain. But this is not always so. Certainly as far as the nation is concerned there is an element of conscious calculation. The extent to which the individual is willing to sacrifice himself for the sake of the state depends on whether he perceives the state's interests as worthwhile. Vietnam showed us that patriotism alone could not stop someone from tipping the pain equation in favor of dodging the draft.

This is not true of religion. The young recruit at the front may suspect his death for the fatherland is not the sweet and fitting thing his general has led him to believe. But the novice at his prayers is far more likely to persevere. A general can be wrong. A country can be wrong. But not God. God is the rock around which all else is a surging sea, the one fixed point around which all other points revolve.

This unswerving conviction of "rightness" a believer has about his religion means that, if he takes it seriously, he will be quite ready to suffer for it. The security forces in Lebanon have had to confront the problem of Muslim extremists for whom martyrdom is a privilege. Buddhist priests in the Far East have been known to burn themselves to death with kerosene to demonstrate their indifference to the body.

From the outside this behavior can look totally irrational. Common sense tells us that a person driving a truckload of explosives into the side of a building is a waste of human life. But then what a person considers to be common sense is dictated ultimately by his outlook on life, and that depends on what he or she sees as the "rock" in the moving sea. If that rock is Allah, then what looks like an irrational suicide to the outsider is for the person involved a completely rational decision based on what his religion tells him to be the truth.

This is no different in principle from the behavior of the prophets of Baal on Mount Carmel:

> They cried aloud, and cut themselves after their manner with knives and lancets, till the blood gushed out upon them (1 Kings 18:28).

Of course religious observance doesn't come to extremes like this for most people in the world. The pains accepted in the service of belief are of a far milder kind. Fasting. Periods of prayer. Presenting gifts or sacrifices. Wearing certain types of clothing. It's different in every religion. But every religion down to the simplest animism and ancestor worship, has its own internal rationale, and each one demands the endurance of pain in some form for the sake of spiritual advancement.

Christianity has had its share of hair-shirted ascetics, it's true. John the Baptist, who lived off honey and locusts in the desert, has been followed by a whole string of determined souls who have sat on pillars, hung in cages, flogged themselves, lain naked in the sun, and walked barefoot in the snow, all in the name of Christ.

Also, from the earliest days there has been a tradition of martyrdom for the truth of Christ, and a willingness on the part of Christian missionaries to face the bitterest hardship in order to spread the gospel. Paul's tally of pains endured for the sake of his apostleship may have been the first, but it was by no means the last:

> Of the Jews five times received I forty stripes save one. Thrice was I beaten with rods, once was I stoned, thrice I suffered shipwreck, a night and a day I have been in the deep; in journeyings often, in perils of waters, in perils of robbers, in perils by mine own countrymen, in perils by the heathen, in perils in the city, in perils in the wilderness, in perils in the sea, in perils among false brethren; in weariness and painfulness, in watchings often, in hunger and thirst, in fastings often, in cold and nakedness.
>
> Beside those things that are without, that which cometh upon me daily, the care of all the churches (2 Corinthians 11:24-28).

These were pains of a very special kind. They came with the calling and are not the sort many Christians experience unless there is a period of persecution or unless God has called them into a very tough ministry. Most modern examples are to be found behind the Iron Curtain, or in the extreme Islamic states of the Middle East.

To take one example, Dr. John Sung, the son of a Chinese Methodist pastor, smuggled his way to America to get an education. On completion of his Ph.D. at Ohio State University, he was offered top positions at the University of Minnesota and with the Standard Oil Company. But in 1929 he returned to China, put aside his western clothes for the blue cotton robe of the Chinese peasant, and spent the next 15 years preaching, two or three times a day, 11 months of the year, until he died at the age of 44. His life was not wasted. One of Singapore's leading multinational executives said, "It was the influence of John Sung that created the climate in the Malayan Peninsula in which business was able to grow and thrive as it does today."

There are countless other stories like that of John Sung. But they are not all found in the less-developed areas of the world.

My own mother and father had a strong desire to serve as foreign missionaries. I remember as a preschooler hearing my father at family devotions ask the Lord to "send us some place to minister that is so difficult nobody is willing to go there." The door never opened to a foreign mission, but the prayer was answered nonetheless. In fact two prominent missionaries of the thirties and forties—Carl Tanis and Paul Metzler—volunteered that it was an area far more difficult than either of their mission fields.

Though there were three very wealthy people in the church, my father's salary was $14 a week. It never increased in five and a half years. And although the town was home to some of the dearest and godliest folks you could ever hope to meet, it also contained some outright ruffians. Dad's life was threatened more than once. One time, when they took exception to a sermon Dad had preached from the book of Hebrews, they set fire to a 50-foot cross and detonated three torpedoes in our backyard. My brother and I were terrified, and vowed that we would return one day to exact retribution on such men. Thank God, when we grew up our anger was changed into pity. But my parents' persecution and hardship for the sake of the gospel were real, and they were taken on voluntarily. Dad didn't have to stay there, yet he carried on for years.

Such is the spirit of Christian mission. However, there is one type of pain every Christian will suffer, whether he looks for it or not. Not because of persecution. Not because of rejection, bereavement, loss, change of circumstance, or any other factor we've looked at so far. It is a pain that comes, as it were, "with the territory." You can't be a Christian and not experience it, just as surely as you can't go into a sauna without feeling the heat.

We might call it the "pain of salvation."

11

God's Second Answer to Pain

The pain of salvation is a major theme in the New Testament. Paul writes about it in the sixth chapter of Romans:

> Know ye not, that so many of us as were baptized into Jesus Christ were baptized into his death? Therefore we are buried with him by baptism into death: that like as Christ was raised up from the dead by the glory of the Father, even so we also should walk in newness of life. . . .
> Likewise reckon ye also yourselves to be dead indeed unto sin, but alive unto God through Jesus Christ our Lord. Let not sin therefore reign in your mortal body, that ye should obey it in the lusts thereof. Neither yield ye your members as instruments of unrighteousness unto sin: but yield yourselves unto God, as those that are alive from the dead, and your members as instruments of righteousness unto God (Romans 6:3,4,11-13).

It's an experience we're all familiar with.

In a more ideal world than ours the convert, having seen the error of his ways, would spend the rest of his life in joyful submission to the will of God. Every opportunity to please God rather than himself would bring him unspeakable pleasure. Every chance to deny the self-will Adam chose in Eden would have him singing hymns of joy.

Unfortunately, we all know that isn't the way things are.

Conversion is followed by a life of difficult, hard-fought surrender to the will of God. The heart that has turned to God carries along with it a crowd of instincts that incline to disobedience and sin. We still want to watch TV instead of going out

131

to make that important visit. We still get mad at people and think unholy thoughts. We're still tempted to compromise our beliefs at work for the sake of a winning promotion. We often find prayer and effort and worship a bore.

It is almost as if there are now two versions of us—one good and one bad—struggling for control of the same body. And this is almost exactly the way Paul expresses it. By becoming a Christian I have shoved my old nature—the "old man"—out of his accustomed place. I want my new nature—Christ—to take charge. But the old man isn't going to give up without a fight, and so I am constantly assailed by temptations to do things the way I did before.

This causes me pain. It can't do otherwise because the old man and the new man are both "me," and whenever one has the upper hand the other is constricted, limited, pained.

The cry Paul utters in Romans 7:24—"O wretched man that I am! Who shall deliver me from the body of this death?"—is the cry of the new nature perpetually harassed and badgered by the old. The Christian is desperate to please God and frustrated at his failure to do so.

But you and I know that we feel just as much pain in having to surrender our will as we do in indulging it. C.S. Lewis said that for us as fallen men "to render back the will which we have so long claimed is in itself . . . a grievous pain." That pain begins the first time our parents scold us for doing wrong. It takes on a new meaning when we come to Christ. And then it goes through the process of sanctification till death and resurrection separate us forever from that troublesome old man and his fallen desires.

Of course the pain is more acute for some than for others.

I don't mean to suggest that the Christian life is one long testimony to moral failure. Far from it. And we have been given the assistance of the Comforter that we might not fall foul of temptation, but rather overcome it. Nonetheless it is a conflict we will all know. And Paul assumed as much when he advised his readers to actively "crucify" the old man.

In the 1970's Jerry Nims, founder and president of Infinioptic Inc., developed a new approach to multidimensional photography. It could be applied not only to still photography, but also to motion pictures and even to X-rays. The research and development for a product like that was expensive, and any sensible businessman would have gone for the backing of another large company.

But when Jerry received an offer worth millions he turned it down.

The reason was that much of the sum had been put up by the publisher of America's best-known pornographic magazine, with the agreement that Jerry would relinquish a small part of the rights to his new invention to that publisher. As a Christian, Jerry felt he could not do that. He did not want his product to be used in any way that did not honor the Lord. So he chose to go ahead without the investment, to grow slowly when he could have expanded in top gear. In short, he chose the pain of salvation.

He didn't have to do it. He was making the same kind of decision as Ruth did in the Old Testament, when after the death of her husband she opted to return to Bethlehem with her mother-in-law, Naomi. She didn't belong in Bethlehem— she was a Moabitess. Leaving her people must have been going against the grain, and it would have been quite reasonable for her to follow Naomi's other daughter-in-law, Orpah, who had also been widowed, back to their own native land. But she didn't:

> They lifted up their voice, and wept again: and Orpah kissed her mother-in-law; but Ruth clave unto her. And she said, Behold, thy sister-in-law is gone back unto her people, and unto her gods: return thou after thy sister-in-law. And Ruth said, Intreat me not to leave thee, or to return from following after thee: for whither thou goest, I will go; and where thou lodgest, I will lodge: thy people shall be my people, and thy God my God . . . (Ruth 1:14-16).

Going to Judah wasn't the easy option, but it was the right one. And so it is with us. Jerry refused that backing for the same reason we all accept the pain of our Christian commitment. Because as believers we know it's better to take the narrow way to God's Kingdom than the broad, easy way to destruction.

What Paul says about tribulation in Romans 5 applies just as aptly to every salvation pain:

> Not only so, but we glory in tribulations also: knowing that tribulation worketh patience; and patience, experience; and experience, hope: and hope maketh not ashamed; because the love of God is shed abroad in our hearts by the Holy Ghost which is given unto us (Romans 5:3-5).

And here we come to the vital point.

We really don't mind suffering pain for the sake of our faith. We are willing, as James says, to "count it all joy" when we "fall into divers temptations" (James 1:2). We don't mind depriving ourselves of worldly pleasures for the good of our souls. We don't even mind persecution if we are persecuted for the sake of Christ. And the reason we don't mind is that these pains are the direct result of our faith. We chose the pains when we chose the faith, and we accept the pains because we know the faith is right. In a way, we have volunteered to suffer.

At the same time we naturally make a distinction between these pains (pains with a purpose) and all other pains (*people pains* and *situation pains*) that come to us, sometimes disastrously, and seem to have no point whatever. The Soviet Christian languishing in a Siberian labor camp at least knows he is there for his witness to the gospel. The minister laid low with cancer can make no sense of his condition at all. His church is under pressure, his family is anxious. It cannot, he feels, be anything other than the clear will of God to raise him up, release him from his pain, and restore him to effective service.

Maybe it is a person like this who picks up the imaginary book on healing I talked about at the start of the last chapter.

Who musters all his faith for healing. Who isn't healed. Who cannot understand why God hasn't heard his prayer.

What such a person hasn't understood is one of the most important points I want to make.

The apparently obvious distinction between pains with a purpose and pains without a purpose is really a false one. For the Christian every part of life can contribute to sanctification, and that includes even the most random, senseless suffering. If we receive a pain, therefore, we receive something that has meaning and purpose, even if we do not understand it.

To put that another way, if we pray for release from pain and do not get it—if God does not give us His first answer to pain—then we are *not cut adrift to suffer a fate we can neither understand nor resist.* We have the chance to receive God's second answer to pain, which is something like this:

"The pain you have is something I allowed for a greater good you may never know in this life. All I ask is that you trust Me, and be ready to receive the special blessings that I can give you only through this experience."

That is why "purpose" is the second element in the formula: I WILL WIN OVER PAIN WITH PRAYER, PURPOSE, AND PERSISTENCE. To suffer meaningless pain is the cruelest fate imaginable. However, it is a fate the Christian will never have to endure. If you are a Christian in pain, you are standing in the center of God's plan. Your pain may be the random result of living in a fallen universe, but it's not there because God is punishing you or neglecting you. On the contrary, God is watching over you in love.

I'm not going to pretend that's an easy answer to take.

I doubt if any of us, given the choice of God's first or second answer, would choose the second. Nobody wants to live with a disagreeable experience. But the problem is not presented to us theoretically. It is presented tangibly, in the form of a pain that we feel, dislike, and need to deal with. A chronic illness, a bereavement, a put-down. And we have to come to terms with it somehow whether we want to or not. Which means, if God does not heal us or put things right, we have to listen to His second answer, and say yes or no to it.

Let me emphasize. There is nothing second-rate about being faced with this decision. You have not failed. If you can pray with a clear conscience, having done as much as you can to "clear the lines" between you and God, you stand every bit as much in the will of God as the healed, released, or pain-free person.

I am even tempted to say, more so, because pain offers an opportunity, an incentive, that the easy, pain-free life will seldom give us. That was why Harold John Ockenga said in Chattanooga, "I don't believe God has ever used anyone in a powerful way who has not first suffered." Many years of ministry worldwide have taught me the truth of that statement. Suffering somehow brings us into the presence of God with a depth and seriousness we'll never be motivated to have in an easy life. So much so that I doubt whether anyone has ever made a serious commitment to the Lord who has not first gone through a crisis.

I believe this to be the second great reason why God has allowed pain to remain in the world. As I said in chapter 3, pain shatters the illusion of comfort and permanence that so easily besets us in our modern, materialistic society. But that is not its only use. It can also be a positive help, a means of grace that enables us in spiritual terms to achieve far more than we would have otherwise.

The principle is firmly embedded in Scripture.

Nobody except Satan had any doubts about Job's piety—if Job were alive today he would probably rank higher than Billy Graham and Mother Teresa on the scale of Christian virtue. But for all that, he never got a straight answer, from his friends or from God, as to why he had suffered. God didn't say to him,"Well, it was just that Satan came along one day and we had this little wager . . ."

But that said, two things are undeniable. One, that through his experience of pain Job encountered God in a deeper way than he'd ever done in his prosperity. And two, that through his pain and his encounter with God he turned out a better person. As he says:

> I have heard of thee by the hearing of the ear: but now mine eye seeth thee. Wherefore I abhor myself, and repent in dust and ashes (Job 42:5,6).

We see the same process at work in the New Testament in the life of Paul. It is known that Paul was dogged by a pain that had nothing to do with his calling as a Christian or as an apostle. Paul himself never referred to it explicitly. He just called it his "thorn in the flesh."

Reading between the lines it seems to have been a problem with his eyes—a pretty severe handicap for a man like him. Considering Paul was responsible for taking the gospel to most of the Roman world, and also for codifying much of the church's doctrine, you might think God would have let him see properly. Not so. Yet Paul himself is aware, in retrospect at least, that his pain had its purpose.

His reaction to it is a clear example of a man seeking God for his first answer to pain, and gratefully accepting the second:

> Lest I should be exalted above measure through the abundance of the revelations, there was given to me a thorn in the flesh, the messenger of Satan to buffet me, lest I should be exalted above measure.
>
> For this thing I besought the Lord thrice, that it might depart from me. And he said unto me, My grace is sufficient for thee: for my strength is made perfect in weakness. Most gladly therefore will I rather glory in my infirmities, that the power of Christ may rest upon me (2 Corinthians 12:7-9).

Saying yes to grace

"My grace is sufficient for thee" is perhaps the essence of God's second answer to our pain.

It isn't a fancy, pious way of saying "Just grin and bear it." That would indicate a totally different approach, one based on stoicism, finding the grit and determination in yourself to ignore the pain and carry on as usual. That sort of stiff upper lip may build empires, but it won't make saints. The whole point of grace being sufficient is that grace is a real source of strength and comfort.

You don't need any special strength of your own to have grace. In fact the one qualification is that you have no strength at all. It is the weak person, the one who feels he is sure to be overwhelmed by his pain, who is most able to experience the perfection of God's strength.

Ironically, that means that whatever task God has for you to do, your pain is precisely the equipment you need to accomplish it. Maybe, as it did in Paul's case, your weakness will counteract some trait in you that would spoil things when left to itself. Or maybe the pain you have is important in God's plan.

This brings us to the heart of our faith. Jesus Himself knew that the pain He was about to endure in the crucifixion was an evil hidden like a black jewel in the crown of God's purpose. And it was precisely because He saw that pain in the context of its purpose that He was determined not to evade it:

> Then said Jesus unto him, Put up again thy sword into his place; for all they that take the sword shall perish with the sword. Thinkest thou that I cannot now pray to my Father, and he shall presently give me more than twelve legions of angels? But how then shall the scriptures be fulfilled, that thus it must be? (Matthew 26:52-54).

Remember—the formula of this book is: I WILL WIN OVER PAIN WITH PRAYER, PURPOSE, AND PERSISTENCE.

We need prayer because without God there is no answer at all to pain. We need purpose because if God does not give us his first answer to pain, purpose is the key to victory. But this purpose, undergirded by God's grace, has to be real for us every day. We can't just switch it on like a light and then sit under it. We have to seek it out, take it in like food, and digest it. What use is purpose if we only have it for a few days? No use at all. That's why we need the third element in the formula—*persistence*.

I can best illustrate this from my own experience.

Chris and I never questioned God's wisdom in permitting Johnny to be so badly injured. Some of our friends could hardly believe it. But the issue never came to our minds. We knew that God was too wise to make a mistake, too holy to do wrong, too loving to inflict a hurt. We may not have understood God's purpose at first, but we knew He had one.

Sure, we saw Johnny's pain as an evil.

Knowing that God's grace was sufficient for us as a family didn't absolve us from the responsibility of relieving Johnny's pain. Long after we had accepted his condition as God's calling we persisted in our efforts to give him better communication skills, wider experience, and more mobility. The ability to improve the situation even a little was part of God's grace. A new drug or new treatment was like God saying, "Thus far it is My will for the pain to be removed."

To the extent that Johnny remained in pain, which was a considerable extent, I can testify that God's grace was indeed sufficient. As for God's purpose, I admit I sometimes puzzled over it at the time. Not in the sense of suspecting God had made a mistake, but of wanting to make the best decisions in the situation. It really did seem, on the face of it, that more could be accomplished if only God would give us His first answer to pain. Looking back, though, I begin to understand a little of God's plan.

For one thing, Johnny's pain, which could have been so destructive, had a beautiful effect on those who were close to him. I can see, for instance, how Chris's character matured and deepened through knowing and caring for Johnny. I still marvel at her willingness and determination to keep me free for ministry. When Johnny had gone through a string of bad days and we literally feared for his life, Chris insisted that I carry on as usual. "You must carry on your work," she'd say. "I don't want you to hold back on your commitments." She had taken on an almost superhuman task in caring for Johnny at home; yet she never tied me down, and didn't complain that I wasn't pulling my weight.

In spite of his illness Johnny wasn't simply an extra problem to build other people's Christian character. He was an important, almost indispensable, part of my ministry. I mean that with all my heart. I'm not sentimentalizing a bad situation, or trying to make it seem better than it was. I really did depend on Johnny. I depended on his listening ear and his moral support. Most of all I depended on his prayer.

You might not think a child like that could even make a decision for Christ, let alone pray. But he did both.

Johnny came to some of my evangelistic crusades, and often showed a rather embarrassing spontaneity in support of the preacher! But it took Chris and me a long time to realize that his restlessness at the end of the sermon was more than physical discomfort or distress at the strange surroundings. When it dawned on Chris at a crusade in a football stadium in Mississippi that Johnny wanted to respond to the appeal, she was faced with a dilemma.

"Johnny," she whispered, "you want to go forward with the others?"

"Yeah," Johnny blurted.

Chris looked across the field. She knew the effect it would have if she took Johnny forward. Everyone knew about Johnny. For him to make an open profession of faith would lay us open to accusations of exploiting him and trying to manipulate the audience.

Chris hesitated.

"That's wonderful, Johnny," she said eventually, "but let's wait until we get home. I'm sure we can arrange for you to go forward in our church and give your heart to Jesus. Won't that be better?"

Johnny said nothing. But he broke out in a sweat as the appeal went on, and bitter disappointment registered on his face when he realized Chris wasn't going to take him.

When she got back to the motel Chris asked me what we were going to do. We both wanted Johnny to have this experience in the same way as any other person would, and both knew the dangers that went with it. We procrastinated.

The next night, the closing night of the crusade, I was aware of Johnny thrashing about in his chair while I spoke. I used the traditional form of invitation, asking people to bow their heads and to raise their hand if they wanted to accept the Lord. Involuntarily my eyes drifted towards Chris and Johnny. I could see he was trying to lift his hand. Chris tried to quiet him.

We had still made no decision about it. But as I spoke, emphasizing that this was the last night of the crusade, the last chance for people to offer their lives to the Lord, I heard the clicking of Johnny's leg brace against the side of his chair. The thought came to me that it might be this very night the Lord called him home. What if we had an accident on the way back and our son's life was snuffed out?

Chris must have been thinking something similar because she began slowly to push Johnny's chair forward. They came over the end zone and across the field. When I saw them I knew, in spite of my misgivings, that Chris was doing exactly the right thing. Not many people saw them at first, but as they did the truth of our son's motivation spread across the stadium like an electric charge. The impact of Johnny's courage, his unashamed witness, gave the meeting a whole new dimension.

At that moment Johnny was just the same as the rest of the people in that meeting. He was a penitent youth, sorry for his sins, eager to enter into a transforming encounter with the Lord Jesus. In that encounter all the restrictions imposed on him by the weakness of his body mattered not at all.

"Lord Jesus," Chris prayed quietly, leading Johnny, "I know I am a sinner."

"Yeah!" said Johnny.

"I know Jesus died on the cross to save me from my sins."

"Yeah!"

"And now, right here, I accept Jesus as my personal Savior."

"Yeah, yeah!"

It was a majestic and beautiful moment, and it had an incredible effect. What a family reunion we had back at our room!

"Not only was Johnny's life changed tonight," Chris said with tears in her eyes, "but I'll never be the same person again either."

There was a knock on the door. It was the chairman of the committee.

"You can't leave," he said quickly. Then his eye fell on Johnny. "God bless you, son. You touched us all tonight."

For a moment silence hovered in the room. Then the chairman turned to me. "Stay another week, Dr. Haggai," he said. "There's a tremendous moving of the Holy Spirit in this town. You must stay!"

As Johnny grew in the Lord he became a warrior in prayer. He would spend hours praying. I don't know anyone who became more enthusiastic about the ministry in the Third World. I kept Johnny fully informed about the work that became the Haggai Institute—the victories, the challenges. I'm only sorry I didn't share more of the problems with him. Talking to him was a therapy for me. I found myself emphasizing the positive, and knew that Johnny was praying and praising God in it all.

The older he became, the stronger his confidence grew in God. I could tell him I needed $10,000 by noon on Monday and I knew that my son was praying. I knew also that come noon Monday he'd be expecting a call to say the prayer was answered. We were in partnership, "laborers together with God" (1 Corinthians 3:9). And if I never fully understand in this life what God's purposes were in Johnny's very special, very hard existence, I am satisfied at least that he fulfilled an invaluable calling. Certainly I could not have asked for a better son.

Let's take a moment to recap.

We've said that God has two answers for the person who seeks Him from the place of pain.

The first answer is the answer of gradual or immediate release, performed by supernatural intervention or permitted through modern medicine. We should always, like Paul, seek this answer before we consider any other, knowing that God loves to see wholeness and freedom from pain, and is able to bring instant relief if He so wills.

Our prayer, though, must always be in the pattern laid down by Jesus in the Garden of Gethsemane: "Not my will, but thine be done." This is in recognition of the fact that Christian faith is a calling to pain as well as a calling from it. And if, after prayer for release, we find God is not telling us to escape, but rather to embrace the pain as part of our calling, we should thank God for the special way in which He is leading us.

Winning over pain, you see, isn't necessarily killing it at the outset. Few military conflicts are won as easily as that. Often it will be a lengthy campaign, with advances and setbacks. But I can promise you one thing. If that is your calling, God will back you up with all the armies of heaven so that you can achieve the purpose He has personally selected for you. Remember the formula:

I WILL WIN OVER PAIN WITH PRAYER,
PURPOSE, AND PERSISTENCE.

I realize the prospect of future pain is daunting. I went through 24 years not knowing whether the next day would bring the pain of continued suffering or the pain of bereavement. But, to use the military analogy again, the same is true of war. No one looks forward to it. Churchill knew the challenge he was taking by declaring war on Nazi Germany. But he got stuck in there and did what he felt was right.

Churchill could have said no to the challenge of the Second World War. He could have sat idly by while the Nazis grew in strength and overran the whole of continental Europe. But he was convinced that would have led to defeat. He reasoned that if he refused to act it would only be a matter of time before he too became a victim of German expansionism, and Britain fell to the Nazis.

The same is true for us. We can say no if we want to when God gives us His second answer to pain. But saying no will accomplish nothing for us. It won't send the pain away. It will only deprive us of the plan God has for us to win over it, and the special blessings that will come to us on the way.

It is far better to walk in Paul's footsteps, and to accept that what God takes away from us He takes so that our hands may be free to grasp some higher gift. "Most gladly, therefore, will I glory in my infirmities, that the power of Christ may rest upon me" (2 Corinthians 12:9).

I think my mother did that. She had not one, but nine major medical problems, including angina, emphysema, and pernicious anemia. The doctors predicted confidently that she would not live through 1936. But mother took on her pain with a holy defiance, trusting that her days were in God's hands. She finally died in 1979 at the age of 80, having remained mobile and able to accomplish her work until a few months before her death.

And that brings us to the hardest thing I want to say about pain.

The Valley of the Shadow

It would be a mistake to believe that any of us will get away without suffering pain. We won't. As we've said already, pain is part of the human condition, although it varies in its intensity. Sometimes it is very mild, hardly noticeable. At other times it is extremely severe, and we can have a lot of trouble coping with it.

But I am not certain that even severe pain is the bottom line.

David wrote the following familiar verse in Psalm 23:

Yea, though I walk through the valley of the shadow of death, I will fear no evil: for thou art with me; thy rod and thy staff they comfort me (Psalm 23:4).

I've heard a lot of preachers dismiss this a bit too lightly. "Oh," they say, "there is indeed such a thing as the valley of the shadow of death, but we must remember that it is only a *shadow*. For a Christian, even a suffering Christian, such an experience has no real substance."

I want to make it quite clear that it does. True, a shadow is a shadow. But if I see the shadow of a bear in the forest I shall not be saying to myself, "Never mind, it's only a shadow, it has no substance." I'll run like crazy, because I know that where there's a shadow of a bear, there's a real bear not far behind!

Don't misunderstand me. I don't mean to imply any lack of faith in God. His rod and staff are there to support me and comfort me. But the threat is real. And I gain no comfort by persuading myself that it is not. There is no such thing as a "pretend" pain—something that seems like a pain until we smarten up and stop letting ourselves be frightened by it. Pain is real. It arises from real life. It really hurts us, even when we have faith.

In addition, I believe there are times when pain is not only hard to cope with, but impossible to cope with.

I say this because I don't want anyone God is calling to win over pain the hard way to think he or she is letting the side down when it all gets to be too much. There can be moments crossing a river when the current sweeps you off your feet, when you are being carried by a force that is stronger than you are. That doesn't matter. The important thing is that finally you reach the other shore without drowning.

Similarly with pain. It is not essential that you are always able to keep your footing. Any Christian who has been in severe pain will tell you there were times when from his point of view the struggle was as good as lost. Times when "my feet were almost gone; my steps had well nigh slipped" (Psalm 73:2). At such a moment, when the tide of pain carries you off, the promise of Psalm 23 comes into its own. God's rod and staff are with you keeping you from going under when your own strength has failed.

It was for this Henry Lyte prayed in his famous hymn:

Abide with me: fast falls the eventide;
The darkness deepens; Lord, with me abide;
When other helpers fail, and comforts flee,
Help of the helpless, O abide with me . . .

Lyte, of course, was talking about the ultimate pain of death. But though this experience is often associated with death I believe it can come in other circumstances too, notably with bereavement.

To be deprived of someone we love is probably the severest pain any of us will have to suffer. Pain hits us in all sorts of areas. In our emotions, in the arrangement of our daily schedule, in our planning for the future. Suddenly we must make a mammoth readjustment to life without the person whose presence had for years been a centerpiece of our existence.

The resulting pattern of pains we call bereavement is deep and complex.

A bereaved person can feel all sorts of strange things. Shock. Numbness. Anger. Guilt. Painful memories. Hopelessness. None of these have much to recommend them morally. As Christians we feel a vague duty to win over them, control them, subdue them. But not only would this be ineffective, it would also be detrimental to us, because these feelings are part of coming to terms with loss, a process of readjustment that is essential for most people if they are to put bereavement behind them and return to a normal life.

Given time, the feelings pass naturally like a freight train rumbling past a rail crossing. They're not pleasant—all the more so because we feel we ought not to be experiencing them—but the key to winning over them isn't to try and derail the train, but to let the pain wash over and recede in its own time.

Of course, it's not hard for me to illustrate this immersion in pain from my own experience.

During the last two or three years of his life Johnny endured constant pain, day and night. Sometimes he would just look at us and mumble "Umn, umn, umn . . ."

"Pain?" his mother would ask.

"Yeah."

Often it was impossible to locate the pain. In his final years he developed a constriction of the intestines.

"It can be as painful as kidney stones, as painful as childbirth," his doctor told us.

"Is there no medication?"

"There is," the doctor replied. "But to administer it to Johnny would be fatal."

Johnny had to be hospitalized frequently. We took him with us on a trip to Singapore, but he was in great pain all the way. The only consolation was a ray of hope given to us by a hotel maid who suggested acupuncture. A few months later I was given the name of a specialist who had recently taken up a practice in New Jersey. We brought him to Atlanta at a cost of $1,000.

He gave Johnny a cursory examination.

"Can you help him?" I asked.

"Possibly. We might be able to improve his speech. Maybe get him to wheel his chair himself. But there are no guarantees."

That was almost unbelievable.

"How much would it cost to have you proceed with the treatment?" I asked.

Dr. Kim at least was frank.

"With your travel, hotel costs and all, it could be between seventy-five and a hundred thousand dollars a year."

We talked it over with Johnny. There was no way we could run to that expense. "It's just beyond our reach," we told him.

"Yeah," Johnny agreed in quiet resignation.

We took Johnny with us to Australia, where our national youth organization named him their permanent chairman. Johnny managed the trip better than at any other time.

Encouraged, Chris came with me on my next trip down under, leaving Johnny in the capable hands of Christina, a friend from Belfast, and Mother Barker. I don't know why—maybe he missed us—but we soon got an emergency message that Johnny had taken sick and been admitted to the hospital. Chris went back immediately.

I half expected to lose him, but Johnny held on. When I returned I made up my mind I was going to make the rest of his life as good as possible.

"We'll move to Hawaii," I told him.

Johnny's eyes widened.

"I mean it. We'll move to Honolulu as soon as you're fit to travel."

But that day never came. Johnny grew weaker. He showed some improvement in December of 1974 and on into the new year, but it was only a temporary reprieve. In spite of the occasional bright day, he grew increasingly listless. He was in constant pain.

Early in 1975 I had to make a trip to Chattanooga. When I called home that night the news was bad. I came back immediately.

"Johnny," I said as I stepped to his bedside, "you got a cold, Buddy?"

He could barely look up at me.

"Remember. As soon as you can snap out of it, we're going to Honolulu, just like we said."

But Johnny's lips puckered faintly in the way they did when he knew he was going to be disappointed. He knew we'd never get there as well as I did. I stepped away.

He weakened over the next few days. We maintained a round-the-clock vigil. Instead of keeping in touch with home from the office, I kept in touch with the office from home. Johnny hardly seemed to sleep. He was emaciated, unable to eat. He constantly tossed his head back and forth, moaning.

The doctor offered to have him put in the hospital.

"Should we?"

"Well, frankly, about all the hospital could do is delay things some."

I looked at Johnny, and turned away.

"Would it make it any easier on you, Mrs. Haggai?" the doctor asked.

Chris shook her head. "No, I gave him up a long time ago, doctor. Let him stay here. He's happier at home."

It was a long day. We tried to keep out of the room so that Johnny could have some peace. But he was going downhill fast.

At midnight the doctor returned.

"I don't know how he can remain conscious," he said. "With all that pain he should have been comatose before now."

The telltale rattle appeared in Johnny's throat. I leaned over and whispered, "Can you hear me, Buddy?"

He opened one eye just a little. But his breathing grew steadily shallower, his face more jaundiced. Finally at two o'clock in the morning he vomited blood, took one last breath, and was gone.

I heard Chris's voice beside me.

"Thank God," she said calmly. "He's free at last."

12

Free at Last

Alice in Wonderland finishes with a court scene where the Knave of Hearts is tried for stealing the proverbial tarts.

Various witnesses are called, including Alice, without advancing the case much further, and the Queen—a kind of walking pain—is anxious to bring the matters to a decisive conclusion:

> "Let the jury consider their verdict," the King said, for about the twentieth time that day.
>
> "No, No!" said the Queen. "Sentence first—verdict afterwards."
>
> "Stuff and nonsense!" said Alice loudly. "The idea of having the sentence first!"
>
> "Hold your tongue!" said the Queen, turning purple.
>
> "I won't!" said Alice.
>
> "Off with her head!" the Queen shouted at the top of her voice. Nobody moved.
>
> "Who cares for you?" said Alice (she had grown to her full size by this time). "You're nothing but a pack of cards!"
>
> At this the whole pack rose up in the air, and came flying down upon her: she gave a little scream, half of fright and half of anger, and tried to beat them off, and found herself lying on the bank, with her head in the lap of her sister, who was gently brushing away some dead leaves that had fluttered down from the trees upon her face.
>
> "Wake up, Alice dear!" said her sister. "Why, what a long sleep you've had!"

Lewis Carroll isn't talking about death. But it is analogous of death. The scene changes abruptly, and Alice has the

151

feeling that she is being overwhelmed as the cards rise up and fall on her. But this sense of overwhelming merges with another feeling—one of liberation, waking into a real world where the strange laws she was subject to in her dream no longer apply.

That is what Chris meant on the night of Johnny's death when she said, "He's free at last."

For so many years Johnny had been trapped in a kind of dream. His real self, the inner self, the essential Johnny, was hidden in a broken body. He had never been able to express himself properly. He'd never been able to move in a coordinated way. His whole experience of life from birth to death had been marred by pain. It was as though we never saw the real Johnny at all. At best we caught only brief glimpses of him, as though through the bars of a cell door.

But at the moment of his death that door was opened.

Just like Lazarus in Jesus's parable, who had squatted at the rich man's gate, having his sores licked by the dogs, Johnny was released from every pain he suffered. He no longer struggles with simple words. There is no need to endure long, painful nights. He is free to go, to be his full self in the presence of his Savior. He no longer sits in his chair, but walks and runs in the fields of heaven. I know that, like Lazarus, "now he is comforted" (Luke 16:25).

Johnny always liked us to talk to him about heaven. On the night of his death I recited to him the twenty-first chapter of Revelation. It's about release from pain, but not just in this life, and not just for individuals. You might call it God's third answer to pain—His final answer:

> I saw a new heaven and a new earth: for the first heaven and the first earth were passed away; and there was no more sea.
>
> And I John saw the holy city, new Jerusalem, coming down from God out of heaven, prepared as a bride adorned for her husband. And I heard a great voice out of heaven saying, Behold, the tabernacle of God is with men, and he will dwell with

them, and they shall be his people, and God himself shall be with them, and be their God.

And God shall wipe away all tears from their
eyes; and there shall be no more death, neither
sorrow, nor crying, neither shall there be any more
pain: for the former things are passed away.

And he that sat upon the throne said, Behold, I
make all things new (Revelation 21:1-5).

In that day—the day of resurrection, the day when God
wraps up forever the sorry business of human rebellion—
pain will vanish permanently.

But notice how *all* aspects of pain are dealt with.

First, there are to be no more *people pains*. All relationships
will be restored to harmony, beginning with the most important—our relationship with God. He will no longer be hidden
from us. We shall be His people, and He shall be our God.
And because we are at one in that most important of relationships, we will be at one with each other—together, as it were,
the holy city; together the bride adorned for her husband. We
cannot be rejected anymore. We cannot be separated by
death.

Second, we will suffer no more *situation pains*. On earth
we might be displaced, impoverished, injured, or aged. We
might be subject to all the miseries that confronted Adam
when he left the safety of the Garden. But at the end of time
there will no longer be armed cherubim guarding the way
back to Eden. We shall live next to the very tabernacle of God.
"God is with men, and he will dwell with them" (Revelation 21:3).

Pain will be removed because it has outlived its useful
function.

In heaven we will not need "disagreeable experience" to
turn our hearts back to God. There will be nothing for pain to
warn us of, no further limitations laid on us. More than that,
pain will not even affect us as a memory. The former things
will pass away like Alice's dream—swamped by a new, bright

vision of the future. Everything, ourselves included, will be made new.

This is the hope that enables us to bear pain as part of our Christian calling. We can trust that however God answers our prayer on pain, that answer is in His great purpose for the redemption of the world, and given to fit us for our moment of "waking" in the resurrection.

As Paul told the Roman Christians, this highest of prizes is worth all the pain we will endure:

> For I reckon that the sufferings of this present time are not worthy to be compared with the glory which shall be revealed in us. . . . For the creature was made subject to vanity, not willingly, but by reason of him who hath subjected the same in hope, because the creature itself also shall be delivered from the bondage of corruption into the glorious liberty of the children of God. For we know that the whole creation groaneth and travaileth in pain together until now. And not only they, but ourselves also which have the firstfruits of the Spirit, even we ourselves groan within ourselves, waiting for the adoption, to wit, the redemption of our body (Romans 8:18,20-23).

If you are a Christian, and suffering a pain you can do nothing to remove, be sure there will come a day when that pain is discarded, just as a plaster cast is discarded when the broken limb is healed.

That day may be coming very soon. But if God does not take your pain away immediately, don't blame Him.

Don't get angry.

Don't feel misused.

Don't give up hope.

Your pain has a purpose. I can't tell you what that purpose is—that is something you will discover in your own walk with God. It may be a marvelous discovery, a grace, like Paul's, which once received makes you glad you went down the road of suffering with God at your side.

That is true for me. I could look back over the last 30 or 40 years and bemoan the pains I've suffered. I could feel resentment at God for allowing Johnny's life to be spoiled by his injury, and Chris's life to be restricted by her care of her son. From a human perspective I would have every right to do that.

But I don't.

I give thanks. I give thanks to God for His special grace to Chris and Johnny and me. I give thanks for all the good times we had together in spite of the pain. I give thanks for the way God allowed our hard experiences to mold us into shapes that look a bit more like His Son, Jesus. And I give thanks, most of all, that God gave us the strength in our pain to see His purpose worked out. I know that in His wisdom He has led us down the right road.

So, to finish, let me summarize briefly the steps that will take you to the solution to your pain:

1. Remember the formula for winning over pain: I WILL WIN OVER PAIN WITH PRAYER, PURPOSE, AND PERSISTENCE.
2. Take courage that God is with you.
3. Examine your own heart and situation in the light of His Holy Spirit, to understand the nature and causes of your particular pain.
4. PRAY daily to receive His answer to your pain, whatever that may be.
5. If God does not take away your pain, then discover and fulfill His PURPOSE in that pain.
6. Keep on praying. Keep on seeking. Have PERSISTENCE.

That way you *will* win over pain.

You will be a victor, an overcomer.

And not only that. You will be among that crowd of disciples who have followed faithfully in the footsteps of the Master, and received the crown of glory:

> Wherefore seeing we also are compassed about
> with so great a cloud of witnesses, let us lay aside

every weight, and the sin which doth so easily beset us, and let us run with patience the race that is set before us, looking unto Jesus, the author and finisher of our faith; who for the joy that was set before him endured the cross, despising the shame, and is set down at the right hand of the throne of God (Hebrews 12:1,2).

Book II

WINNING OVER

OVER

Introduction

I'm Afraid—You're Afraid

Let's face it—we're all afraid.

No human being is immune to this most basic of emotions. In fact, it is an emotion we share with many members of the animal kingdom. But unlike animals—who seem to fear only definite and immediate threats—we can fear threats that have never been made, even threats that will never come into existence. It is possible for us to be afraid of something, like a newspaper, that by its very nature poses no threat at all!

The human being is capable of fearing almost anything. Naturally, some fears are more common than others. A recent study by Illinois Institute of Technology revealed that middle-class Americans tend to fear financial problems (losing their jobs, paying the bills, and so on), the deterioration of their health, and difficulties in social, business, and marriage relationships.

For such people—and that probably includes most of us—fear often does little more than nag the subconscious, giving them a vague feeling of disquiet about their home or their finances. Yet for many, fear has grown like a tree until it overshadows them from morning till night. Did you know that phobia, the severest form of fear, affects no less than 13 million Americans, qualifying it as the country's number two health problem? "Next to marital difficulties, alcohol and drug problems, phobias are the most common reason we see people," says Richard A. Chaifetz, president of Chicago's Comprehensive Psychological Centers (quoted in *Business Week*, April 21, 1986).

Of course, not all fear is bad. As we shall see, there is such a thing as legitimate fear, and this is not only permissible, but essential to self-preservation. The real subject of this book is illegitimate fear—fear that serves no useful purpose and wrecks the lives of those who suffer from it. Fear of this sort, whether it is mild or acute, is about as useful to you as a toothache. Putting up with it is like trying to run the 800 meters with lead weights on your back.

I tell you frankly: You will never succeed in achieving your goals while you are hampered with fear. I'll give you an example.

Fighting fear

At the age of 62, I made a promise to myself: I was going to learn how to ski.

I'd wanted to do it for years. I don't mean that sedate form of the sport called cross-country skiing, either. In a way, I would have preferred that—it's safer. But the little voice inside me said, "No. It's downhill skiing or none at all. You're going to go flying down the slope with the best of them."

I swallowed hard and gave in. I got in contact with John Bolten, a friend of mine who lives in Germany, and told him my plans.

"Are you serious?"

"Yes. Now what do I do?"

"Get a ski instructor."

"Where?"

"Austria. The best ski instructors are Austrian."

I told him I'd set aside some time to visit Austria, and he offered to arrange the details of the venture. I don't mind telling you I was scared stiff! But I was also excited, and after a few days I had told so many people that I couldn't back out without doing serious damage to my credibility.

They didn't encourage me. For every person who sounded pleased at my taking up the challenge, there were at least 20 others who tried to talk me out of it. The range of arguments they used was stunning. They began by appealing to my instinct of self-preservation. "Your muscle tone isn't what it used to be, John," said one. "If you get on that ski slope, you'll be going so slow some speedy downhill skier will hit you like you're a brick wall." Another added gravely, "You will doubtlessly break a leg."

When I resisted those ideas, they started in on my conscience. "John, if you fall over and you're laid up in a plaster cast, what's going to happen to your ministry? Don't you think it's ridiculous for a man of your age to try to act like a teenager?" And: "Do you really think this is consistent with your reputation as a mature leader who has written a major book on leadership? Won't this ridiculous project you're so determined to undertake destroy your credibility?"

Of course they were right, but my plans were already being noised abroad. Even if the compulsion left me, which it showed no signs of doing, it was too late to go back now. My only option was to control my fear by taking every precaution I could.

I called John Bolten.

"What can I do to minimize the risk of injury?"

"Get your legs in shape. It's important that your legs be in first-class shape."

So every day I got on my Air Dyne Schwinn bicycle and peddled for 30 minutes at a time. In a few months my legs were in better shape than they had been in for years.

But I was still feeling afraid.

I decided to employ self-affirmations.

"I have the genes," I told myself. "My father played tennis until he was 85. My grandfather competed in ice-skating contests on the Charles River in Boston when he was nearly 70. I can learn to downhill ski.

"Mastering the art of downhill skiing will not only give me a lift, but it will encourage many of my vegetating friends to undertake a more vigorous lifestyle.

"Learning to downhill ski will give me greater rapport with young people whom I am trying to influence for world evangelism.

"Since I won't be able to think about anything but the skiing when I'm on that slope, it will be a good activity to relax me after months of sustained and concentrated work."

There was no aid that I did not make use of. Every time I had the opportunity, I watched television programs on downhill skiing. I read articles in magazines, looking hard at the pictures and impressing them on my mind.

I bought a book on skiing, written by four news reporters from the British paper, *The Sunday Times.* People like William F. Buckley said it was one of the best books ever written on the subject. I read it carefully. I read about skis, ski boots, and ski clothing. I read every word from beginning to end. I read about the snowplow procedure for stopping. I read about the "stem christie" and the "grand wedel." I read about how to get up when you fall down and about ski etiquette.

In addition, I talked to everybody I could think of who skied. I asked them, "What's the single most important thing to remember about downhill skiing?"

They told me always to keep the weight on the downhill ski, to keep the point of the uphill ski just a little bit ahead of the point of the downhill ski, to face down the fall line, and to put your hips into the mountain. Did it make sense to me? Not exactly, but I listened hard.

I did everything I could think of to overwhelm the fear of the task to which I'd set myself. I even went to orthopedic specialists to get their input regarding the project I was about to undertake. Ironically, the specialists were the most encouraging!

Finally, 12 months after I had first phoned John Bolten, I arrived on the Austrian ski slopes. I was greatly encouraged by the applause of my wife and friends, who noted out loud even very slight improvements in my style, and expressed the conviction that I was learning fast and would ski well. At the age of 63, I became a downhill skier.

So when I say that fear stands in the way of achievement, I am speaking from my own experience. Any important undertaking, from writing a book to learning how to ski, comes with a price tag attached, and that price is measured in the currency of fear.

It is sometimes said that fear diminishes as you grow in experience. In a way that is true, because a very basic human fear is fear of the unknown, and so what has become familiar to us will also be less likely to make us afraid. But fear never vanishes entirely, and curiously enough that is really an advantage.

I remember talking in 1966 to the late Dr. William Culbertson, then president of the Moody Bible Institute. I said, "Dr. Culbertson, I'm 42 years old. I've preached around the world. I've pastored churches. Yet to this day, I don't know what it's like to get up before a group of five people—let alone five thousand—without getting the butterflies in my stomach."

"Thank God," Dr. Culbertson boomed. "When the time comes that you no longer have the butterflies, stop preaching. God will be through with you."

You see, fear has its uses. It is like a guard standing at the gate of opportunity. Every time we wish to take advantage of an opportunity, we have to overcome the guard. Maybe you think God is making life unnecessarily hard for us by barring our way like that. I don't think so. Fear may be dangerous, but it also teaches us to value what we aim for. "If it ain't worth fighting for, it ain't worth having." Fear puts us on the alert and forces us to give of our best. Like the seasoned opera star, we need it at the threshold of every performance.

Be warned, therefore. It is not my intention in writing this book to help you eliminate fear. I couldn't do that even if I wanted to, for God has so arranged things that fear will always be standing guard at the gate of opportunity, whether we like it or not. My aim is not to remove the guard once and for all, but to show you how to overcome him at each new conflict and so achieve your goals. Learning this method of "combat" by internalizing the principles taught in the Bible will give you the mastery every time.

Before you begin

Fear is probably the greatest cause of wasted potential. How many people down through the ages failed to achieve because they turned back from opportunity at first sight of the guard? If you have not read the book *Profiles in Courage* by former President John F. Kennedy, I suggest you read it. You will see what benefits accrued to the United States and to the world as a result of six men mastering fear.

My own favorite example of the victory over fear is Mother Teresa, the tiny nun from Yugoslavia whose heart is big enough to include people of every rank, intellect, culture, and creed. Her life is a parable of the mastery of fear. Fear of poverty, fear of disease, fear for personal safety, fear of being misunderstood.

In 1986, Mr. Ed Stanley, the outgoing president of the Young Presidents' Organization sent me a transcript of Mother Teresa's address to the YPO convocation. So powerful was the impact of this frail little lady on those men and women (who represent the world's business leadership under 50 years of age) that scores of them said they could never be the same. They said they planned to return to their homes and implement the challenge Mother Teresa had delivered to them by precept and example.

Ask yourself now what challenge God wants *you* to take up—a challenge that will enrich your life and honor God—which lies beyond your reach because of fear.

There is no shortage of challenges available. Businesses need to be established. Schools need to be founded. Churches need to be planted. Books need to be written. Laws need to be enacted. Vaccines need to be discovered. Pollution needs to be controlled. Who knows? You may be just the person to meet one of these needs, or one of a thousand others.

Whatever your challenge is, I pray that this book will encourage you to work toward the mastery of fear and the fulfillment of your unique potential.

"Are you sure it'll work?" you ask. The answer is yes, I am sure. Sure, that is, provided you satisfy one basic condition. A close family friend said to me, after reading *How to Win Over Worry*, "I read your book, but I still worry."

I chuckled and said, "How many times did you read it?"

"Once."

"Do you really believe that reading the book once, at the age of 53, is going to correct a habit pattern you've been developing over more than half a century?"

She said she got the point. I hope she did—and I hope you get it as well. Reading this book once will not wave a magic wand over your fears and liberate you from bondage to them. I suggest you read and reread it. I suggest you make notes in the margin or inside the back cover about passages that have a special relevance to you. I suggest you write out specific goals and time targets to help you apply its methods.

You would do well to take a hint from Paul J. Meyer of Waco, Texas, founder of Success Motivation Institute and the acknowledged authority on self-motivation. He says of his courses: "If you expose yourself daily to this material, you will gain the benefit of one of the most powerful learning techniques known—spaced repetition. An idea very seldom is absorbed the first time it is presented. To become a usable part of you, ideas must be presented over and over. Psychologists estimate that most ideas are presented at least six times before they are fully accepted and internalized."

Meyer produces his material in both audiocassettes and written manuals. He instructs his clients to listen to each cassette, one at a time every day for six days before going on to the next. That's in addition to reading the same material twice a week. If they can do both at the same time, so much the better.

There's no cassette on sale with this book. But that shouldn't keep you from picking out the passages most important to you and making your own cassettes. If you can get the information going in through your ears as well as your eyes you will learn from it more efficiently. I doubt if you will be able to read or hear "enough." A book that has made a revolutionary change in my life and work is one I have read through 13 times. I've read some chapters scores of times, and one chapter 100 times!

To start with, though, I advise you to read this book through fairly quickly, just enough to familiarize yourself with it and to get the gist of the argument. You will find further instructions at the end, but don't bother about those for the time being.

Please do not use this book as a replacement for the Bible. I heartily recommend that you devote the first moments of every day to reading the Bible, a book that is more important to your mastery of fear than any other. To help you, you may want to secure a Bible concordance, look up the word "fear" and make a study of the passages that deal with it. You will find I identify some of the main passages later on.

I wish you well. As I write this book, I pray that God will use it to help and bless you. Should you have questions about anything I've written, please write me at Box 13, Atlanta, Georgia 30370. I will answer your query. God bless you.

Part 1

LIVING DANGEROUSLY

1

Fear in Focus

A fundamental human fear is the fear of the unknown. What we cannot predict, explain, or understand is likely to make us afraid. That is why children are afraid of the dark and cautious of strangers—both present situations over which they have no control, and in which the love of those they trust does not protect them.

Adults also experience fear of the unknown. Consider the scare caused by AIDS, a viral infection scantily understood at the time of this writing, over which medicine has little control, and against the progress of which loved ones are powerless to intervene. Typhoid, cholera, and leprosy do not induce the same fear as AIDS because they are known diseases—medical science has examined them and found cures which, at least in the West, are available to sufferers. At the present time there is no cure for AIDS. In that sense it is unknown. Consequently it is an object of fear. People lose their jobs and are ostracized by former colleagues because they carry the AIDS virus.

There are many less dramatic examples than AIDS of our fear of the unknown. In a way, nearly every fear we have involves the fear of the unknown, as every fear is rooted in the future, and no one can predict with certainty what is going to happen in the next minute, let alone the next week or year. I expect you've had the experience of fearing some future event and then, when it came, finding it wasn't half as bad as you expected. The object of our fear is usually less intimidating when seen face-to-face than it is when projected in the imagination. A friend of mine, who dislikes injections and was horrified at the thought of having an inoculation for polio, was relieved to step into the doctor's office and be given a drop of serum on a lump of sugar!

Understanding what was previously unknown can go a long way to dispelling fear, as my friend found out. But understanding does something else too—it helps to solve the problem to which the fear has become attached. Understanding is 90 percent of the solution to any problem—ask anyone who's taken an exam in mathematics! It is true in all areas of life. The administrator who understands what is causing the cantankerous behavior of a staff member is 90 percent of the way to sorting it out. The golfer who understands what is causing him to slice is 90 percent of the way to correcting his swing.

It stands to reason that if a fear is linked to a specific problem, as it is with AIDS, fear will be countered by understanding. AIDS will only be an object of fear as long as science is baffled by it. Once a cure or a vaccine is found, it will no longer be feared. In fact, it may be regarded with insufficient caution, as other veneral diseases have often been since the introduction of penicillin.

What is true for individual fears is also true for fear in general.

Your particular fears may or may not involve the unknown. Either way, you can be sure that those fears are made worse, not by the unknownness of the thing you fear (you may be well acquainted with it!), but by the unknownness of fear as an entity. Say your fear is in the area of personal finance and you are afraid of losing your job or of not being able to make ends meet. The chances are you already know a lot about employment prospects at your place of work, and the options open to you through the services of a bank. But how much do you know about fear?

I would guess not much. We tend to experience fear rather than analyze it. Yet I've just said that understanding a problem is 90 percent of the solution. And isn't fear a problem? If it is, we would be well advised to study it before we go much further. And that is why the first two sections of this book are about the nature and effects of fear.

How fear fits in

The first recorded case of fear in the Bible comes in the early chapters of Genesis. Until their sin, Adam and Eve lived in harmony with God and with the rest of the created order. The economy of life for prefallen man was supremely simple: he was to have dominion over all living creatures, and all living creatures were to be given vegetation for food. Genesis pictures an idyllic pastoral scene in which man and woman carry out their twin responsibilities to worship God and look after His creation:

> God blessed them, and God said unto them, Be fruitful, and multiply, and replenish the earth, and subdue it: and have dominion over the fowl of the air, and over every living thing that moveth upon the earth.
> And God said, Behold I have given you every herb bearing seed, which is upon the face of all the earth, and every tree in which is the fruit of a tree yielding seed; to you it shall be for meat. And to every beast of the earth, and to every fowl of the air, and to every thing that creepeth upon the earth, wherein there is life, I have given every green herb for meat: and it was so (Genesis 1:28-30).

What follows is that Adam and Eve destroyed their communion with God through disobedience. In that, they stand as symbols for every human being who has ever lived.

But notice the changing role of fear in the story of the Fall. In their prefallen state, the only fear Adam and Eve knew was the mild and useful fear that all good men have in the face of justice. We might call it "respect." As long as they inclined their freedom to the love of God, the prohibition against eating from the tree of knowledge affected them no more than we are affected by the death penalty for murder. If we are responsible citizens, we don't refrain from murdering someone because murder is against the law. We refrain because it is in our nature to refrain—conscience makes the act abhorrent to us. In a society made up entirely of responsible citizens, the law against murder would be unnecessary because nobody would want to kill.

So it was in Eden. By nature Adam and Eve had no appetite for the forbidden fruit.

But appetite can be aroused. We haven't all been tempted to pick up a gun and shoot somebody, but none of us can deny having experienced the temptation to retaliate. And it is once we have been provoked that fear begins to operate. When somebody insults you, it isn't usually humility that keeps you quiet (most people would love to lay their detractors out cold!). You suffer in silence for fear of embarrassing others or making yourself look like a fool. It is exactly the same mechanism that makes the penal code a deterrent to crime. In a society with no punishment, crime will be committed with insolence; but where crime is punishable, the criminal will think twice before breaking the law.

It is significant that when he tempts Eve, the serpent starts by *assuming* her compliance: "Yea, hath God said, Ye shall not eat of every tree in the garden?" (Genesis 3:1). He hints strongly that this was an unreasonable demand for God to make, and Eve falls for the suggestion hook, line, and sinker. Instead of affirming her belief in God's commands and replying, "Yes, He has said that, and I agree with Him," she allows herself to take the serpent's standpoint. In effect she says, "I don't know why, but God doesn't want us eating from the tree of knowledge, and since He will punish me if I do, I'm not going to go near it."

She is wide open. She has declared that her obedience stands on fear, and not on her natural goodness. Mentally she has already fallen; all that separates her from the act of disobedience is her fear of retribution. This fear the serpent is swift to allay:

> The serpent said unto the woman, Ye shall not surely die (Genesis 3:4).

Having soothed her fear (and no doubt she was very willing to have it soothed), he proceeds to whet her appetite a little more, and with no fear left to deter her she soon falls, dragging her husband after her. But the result is ironic—their newfound knowledge, far from raising them to the promised equality with God, only returns them to a state of subjection. In their innocent fear of God they had enjoyed limitless freedom. Now that they have tried to take God's place, it is fear that calls the tune:

> The eyes of them both were opened, and they knew that they were naked; and they sewed fig leaves together, and made themselves aprons.
>
> And they heard the voice of the Lord God walking in the garden in the cool of the day: and Adam and his wife hid themselves from the presence of the Lord God amongst the trees of the garden. And the Lord God called unto Adam, and said until him, Where art thou?
>
> And he said, I heard thy voice in the garden, and I was afraid, because I was naked; and I hid myself.
>
> And he said, Who told thee that thou wast naked? Hast thou eaten of the tree, whereof I commanded thee that thou shouldest not eat?
>
> And the man said, The woman whom thou gavest to be with me, she gave me of the tree, and I did eat.
>
> And the Lord God said unto the woman, What is this that thou hast done? And the woman said, The serpent beguiled me and I did eat (Genesis 3:7-13).

Adam and Eve had never before known what it was to be afraid. But this shift in their experience of fear was a natural result of their disobedience. I use the word "natural" because just as in their prefallen state it was "natural" for them to know God as a benefactor, so after the Fall it was "natural" for them to know Him as a judge. One act of disobedience was enough to fix the abyss of sin between them and the Creator.

Now that the abyss was in place the threat of retribution was no longer remote; it was immediate, tangible, real. For the first time they had something to fear. Hence the fig leaves and the frantic passing of the buck.

We might note that all of the fear referred to in the Eden story was legitimate; that is, it all served a useful purpose. Even the fear that made Adam and Eve hide from God was legitimate—after all, the judgment of God is not to be taken lightly. However, Adam and Eve's reaction reveals something more basic about fear, something that characterizes fear in all its forms.

It is this: fear does not exist in isolation. It is a *response to danger.*

The dependence of fear on danger is made clear in its very definition. Merriam-Webster's dictionary describes fear as "an unpleasant emotion caused by the anticipation or awareness of danger." You can never be scared, as it were, in the abstract: you are always scared of *something* even if you cannot say precisely what that something is.

The first point to learn about fear, then, is that it is a God-given potential designed for our protection. Eve would not have felt the deterrent power of God's command in Eden if she had not already possessed the faculty of fear. True, as long as they remained in a state of innocence, Adam and Eve had no practical use for this faculty. But they did not remain in innocence. And at the moment that intuitive harmony with God and the natural environment disappeared, when the first couple was cast out of Paradise and the ground was cursed through their sin, fear became not only a possibility but a necessity.

Today, as Ashley Montagu aptly expressed it, "to be human is to be in danger." He might have said, "to be alive is to be in danger," because fear is not the exclusive property of human beings. Fear—the basic, physiological response that increases the heart rate in readiness for flight or defensive action—affects the wild beast fleeing from the leopard, just as it affects me when I see another driver about to run into my car. The response is instinctive and essential. And incidentally it gives rise to many of the euphemisms we use to describe fear, such as "gooseflesh" or "the shivers":

> The heart beats faster. Breathing is accelerated, and the glands are stimulated to greater activity. The muscles become taut, preparing for struggle or flight. A strain is placed on the whole physical system. . . . Fear is an elemental alarm system. It is an indispensable part of our means of self-preservation. A fearless man would have difficulty remaining alive for a single day in the tangled confusion of traffic in any large metropolitan city (G. Ernest Thomas, *Faith Can Master Fear*).

Fearless men, in fact, frequently do come to grief. A farmer living downwind from Mount Saint Helens had been warned of the possible eruption of the volcano and refused to move. He perished. So, too, did 300 residents of Cameron, Louisiana, who defied a flood warning.

So I am not going to tell you to get rid of your faculty of fear. You need it to tell you when you are in danger. In this uncertain world, fear is a gift to be thankful for. Fear may be unpleasant. But if it wasn't, you wouldn't take any notice of it!

So get it into your head right now that fear in *itself* is an asset. It is there to put you in a physical and mental state where you are most capable of tackling whatever danger is ahead of you. Think how useful fear is when there's a man behind you with a gun in his hand! And think also how useful fear is on a societal level. After all, it is fear that is largely responsible for adequate defense arrangements. Certainly fear lay behind the provision of hospitals and sanitariums for the treatment of tuberculosis in the early years of this century. It is probably doing the same now for research into the treatment of AIDS.

Be realistic

You will never be able to escape from danger. To attempt to do so is pointless and counterproductive. Danger will confront you in any enterprise you engage in, and wherever danger is, there will be fear. The person who avoids danger because he doesn't like fear will not be fulfilling his potential. As I pointed out earlier, sidestepping fear means sidestepping the challenge of life and passing up the opportunity of achievement. Of course, fear is a nasty experience. But the answer is not to avoid it, but to use, transcend, and overcome it. How else did Sir Edmund Hillary get to the top of Mount Everest, or Neil Armstrong to the moon? How else has anyone achieved anything that involved more risk than spilling ink on his pants?

But maybe you don't want to face up to your fear. In that case, two options are open to you.

One option is to cut and run. To cop out. To avoid places, people, and situations that stimulate fear. That was what Adam and Eve were doing hiding among the trees. They were trying to put off the dreadful moment when they would have to confront God. Of course, it didn't work. Fear will nearly always track you down in the end. But even if it doesn't, the chances are you will fall into a fear far worse than the one you are trying to escape from. Remember what happened to Jonah? God told him to go and preach to the Ninevites, and Jonah, calculating that the Ninevites would have him for breakfast if he turned up denouncing their wickedness, promptly set off in the opposite direction.

But God refused to let him off the hook:

> The Lord sent out a great wind into the sea, and there was a mighty tempest in the sea, so that the ship was like to be broken. . . . So they took up Jonah, and cast him forth (Jonah 1:4,15).

In the end, Jonah was persuaded to go to Nineveh, and the whole city repented in dust and ashes. Jonah was running not just from his fear, but from God, which explains why God put such a terrifying obstacle in his way. But the conclusion of the story gives hope to any fearful person. Whoever is following God's way can expect God's help. If you are serious in reading this book, therefore, and serious in desiring to apply its

Scriptural solution to fear, you may be assured of God's assistance. If God brought the Ninevites to repentance, He can subdue your fears.

The second option open to you is covering up—getting out the fig leaf and trying to hide your embarrassing fears from those around you. This not only fails to conceal fear, it actually makes fear worse.

I'll explain in the next chapter.

2

Three Disguises of Fear

The story of Adam and Eve tells us something we know from our own experience: fear has an insidious power over us.

When we are afraid, we are driven to perform actions alien to our usual pattern of behavior. Until fear entered their lives, it had never occurred to Adam and Eve to sew fig leaves together for clothing. Clothing had never been necessary. They turned tailor because knowledge made them ashamed. Suddenly they felt unpresentable to God, to each other, and to the outside world. As a result, they tried to disguise their nakedness with clothing.

Today, we go a step further than Adam. Adam, at least, was willing to admit his fear. When God asked him why he was hiding, he said simply, "I was afraid." Most people today try to hide not just their own perceived inadequacies, but the very fact of their fear. In a culture where the virtues of strength and courage are held in high regard, fear is a kind of inadequacy. Consequently the world is full of fearful people desperately pretending to be fearless. And let's be frank about it—it is a pretense. As long as you refuse to tackle fear at the root, it will continue to grow. And especially as you get on in years and you are faced with more legitimate objects of fear (serious illness or death, for example) the effort of pretense will become insupportable.

My mind goes back to a man about my own age whom I met in my 20's. At that time he was handsome, bright, flamboyant and, I must say, arrogant. He cut a wide swath in his peer group. He got things done. Whether you liked him or not, you could not ignore him. I met this man for the second time about ten years ago. He had changed. His wife had left him. He was hated by his children, two of whom had gotten into

He was hated by his children, two of whom had gotten into serious trouble with the law. He had been crippled with arthritis. What struck me was his quietness and sensitivity, the ease with which I could talk to him. But at the same time, I could not shake off the urge to pity him. As I said to a friend later, "I almost preferred him the way he was." Fear had worn him down.

I've seen it countless times. I've lived long enough to recognize a girl who masks her secret fears with excessive attention to her face and figure. She projects charm and vivacity. But even if she is genuinely beautiful (and girls of this sort often are), age knocks the props out from under her. The wrinkling of the skin and the changing contours of her figure gradually erode her confidence until the old fears show through.

Simon Peter wrestled with fear (read Mark 14). On the face of it, Peter was a bombastic character. He himself declared that though everyone else fall away, he would stick by Jesus to the end. When Jesus foretold Peter's betrayal Peter covered up his fears with loud assertions of loyalty: "If I should die with thee, I will not deny thee" (Mark 14:31). But when it came to the test, fear won out.

> A little after, they that stood by said again to Peter, Surely thou art one of them: for thou art a Galilean, and thy speech agreeth thereto. But he began to curse and to swear, saying, I know not this man of whom ye speak.
>
> And the second time the cock crew. And Peter called to mind the word that Jesus said unto him, Before the cock crow twice, thou shalt deny me thrice. And when he thought thereon, he wept (Mark 14:70-72).

Here is a fine example of the power of fear. Peter could brag in front of his friends, but under duress he could neither hide his fear nor stop it from controlling him. Later, in the safety of darkness, he reproached himself bitterly. Yet his betrayal was inevitable, not because he was helpless, but because he refused to be helped. In adopting a disguise for his fear he had probably fooled even himself. There is no hint of hypocrisy in his brave promise to Jesus. But by placing so much confidence in his own abilities he neglected in Gethsemane the one opportunity given to him to confront his fear instead of covering it up:

> He cometh, and findeth them sleeping, and said unto Peter, Simon, sleepest thou? Couldest not thou watch one hour? Watch ye and pray, lest ye enter into temptation. The spirit truly is ready, but the flesh is weak (Mark 14:37,38).

In the long run, disguises do nothing to remove fear, you can paint over the rust on your automobile, but paint isn't going to stop the bodywork from falling to bits. If you think it is, you are deluding yourself.

Disguises, besides being ineffective, are also harmful. They distort your personality and corrode your relationships. How could they not? When you adopt a disguise for fear, you are compensating for it by behaving in a way that is not natural to you. Would you spend the rest of your life playing the role of Othello or Lady Macbeth? Of course you wouldn't. If you did, you would soon find yourself under lock and key. Yet there are millions of people today walking around so heavily disguised that, ironically, the first thought that comes to a person who meets them is that they're trying to hide something. The disguise misfires. It is meant to manipulate the responses of others, but it only undermines the mutual love and trust that are essential for a balanced relationship.

Fear has three common disguises: strength, saintliness, and love.

The disguise of strength

This was Peter's disguise. Fear masquerading as strength seeks to impress others with feats of daring, and to create the illusion of competence by projecting a powerful personality.

There is nothing wrong with a powerful personality, and not all men and women who come across like that are trying to conceal fear. Strength of character is a mark of the Spirit, even in those who by nature are quiet and reserved. As Paul said of himself, "When I am weak, then am I strong" (2 Corinthians 12:10). This authentic power, though it organizes and motivates effectively, is never overbearing. The powerful personality adopted as a disguise, however, will come across to others as a desire for domination. It doesn't motivate, it suffocates.

Consequently it is self-defeating. The fearful person suspects a gulf between himself and his fellows, and because he doesn't have the assurance that issues from a spirit dominated by the Spirit, he tries to compensate for his own lack of self-confidence by dominating others. This sets up a tension between his real self (the self that wants to be loved and accepted) and his assumed self (the self that projects bravado for purposes of manipulation). It also fails to achieve its objective. You cannot force another person to give you love and acceptance, for the more strength you display, the more likely you are to drive him away from you. And so the fear intensifies. I am not joking—I have seen men of wealth and prominence attempting to overcome their fear by hiring public relations men to "puff" them. I've watched them act with unwarranted aggression toward their employees. They have taken these measures to disguise fear. They will go to ludicrous lengths to curry the favor of the public.

The man or woman disguising fear with strength is doomed to unhappiness. Compare Paul with Nero. The apostle Paul suffered appalling hardship for the gospel. For the greater part of his life he was on the run, in prison, or in danger of being killed. "Surely," you say, "he would have been more content had he experienced the blessings enjoyed by Nero— wealth, influence, and an almost limitless circle of admirers." Yet you would have to go a long way to find a happier man than Paul. And Nero, who craved Rome's acclamation, not only as its finest emperor, but also as its most talented musician and charioteer, died by his own hand at 32, a frustrated dissolute.

A fearful person using the disguise of strength suffers terrifying symptoms.

1. *He can never be himself.* Projecting strength leaves him in a state of perpetual competition. He must always go one better if he's going to retain the admiration of those around him. And if he's going to do that, he's also forced to conform to their standards—otherwise, there is no basis on which to judge the winner. So he is enslaved by the lifestyle of his peers. He sends his children to their school, drives their make of car, and wears their brand of clothing. He builds a summer home on the same lake, joins the same clubs, and goes on the same tours. He is not free to fulfill his own potential, and when he encounters people who are, he can only respond by trying to belittle them.

2. *He can never enjoy his success.* He is driven to move for the sake of moving, to strive for the sake of striving, and above all to keep ahead in competition with his peers. There is no chance for him to take a rest, to look back on all he has done and, without reference to anybody else, enjoy his achievement for its own sake. His habit of activity will drive him, even in the absence of defined goals. Having nothing to aim for, he doubles his activity, and often ends up dropping dead of a heart attack.

3. *He can never enjoy others.* He is too busy evaluating them, measuring them, and comparing them to himself. He would take no pleasure in others anyway. He wants them not for who they are, but for what they can give to him.

4. *He can never be satisfied.* If the person living on bravado survives long enough, he will eventually be forced to slow down. And when he has time on his hands to think, he will likely be devastated by a sense of failure. He has fortified his confidence by demeaning his underlings and gloating on the downfall of his superiors. He has not admitted that he was afraid. But what has he achieved that will be of any lasting

value, or even of fleeting satisfaction to him? And what has he done to himself? Paul wrote to Timothy that he must "not quarrel but be gentle to all, able to teach, patient, in humility correcting those who are in opposition . . ." (2 Timothy 2:24,25 NKJV). That is a strength of character bravado will never produce.

The disguise of saintliness

If strength comes across to the outsider as domination, saintliness comes across as sanctimoniousness.

Of course, there is a proper saintliness. The word translated "saint" in the New Testament actually means "set apart," so strictly speaking a saint is anyone, lay or ordained, male or female, liturgical or nonliturgical, who is set apart by the indwelling life of Christ for a life of service—in other words, any Christian. It is hoped that every Christian will also be saintly in the common sense of the term, that is, outstandingly virtuous.

However, there is the world of difference between being saintly in this sense (as evidence of the work of the Spirit) and appearing saintly (for the sake of impressing others). Appearing saintly is a popular way of disguising fear. It is also good for concealing a host of other unpleasant traits, as tricksters, charlatans, and dishonest salesmen down the ages have been delighted to discover.

> How doth the little crocodile
>   Improve his shining tail
> And pour the waters of the Nile
>   On every golden scale!
>
> How cheerfully he seems to grin,
>   How neatly spreads his claws,
> And welcomes little fishes in
>   With gently smiling jaws!
>   —Lewis Carroll
>   *Alice in Wonderland*

If you are in the business of looking saintly, you will find yourself in good company. Paul blows the whistle on a few aspiring "saints" in 2 Corinthians:

> Such are false apostles, deceitful workers, transforming themselves into the apostles of Christ. And no marvel; for Satan himself is transformed into an angel of light. Therefore it is no great thing if his ministers also be transformed as the ministers of righteousness; whose end shall be according to their works (2 Corinthians 11:13-15).

But wait a minute, you say. Surely Paul is talking here about the unregenerate? Of course he is. But if the devil can daub himself in greasepaint and pass himself off as an angel, think how much easier it is for a Christian, under the influence of fear, to mimic the appearance of virtue!

I'll let you in on a secret. You can nearly always spot this phony saintliness—all you have to do is see how it is expressed. False virtue gives itself away by telling you, not what it does, but what it *doesn't* do. When I was a boy, I learned to spot a phony saint a mile off. Many church people I knew considered themselves dedicated Christians on the strength of their abstinence. They didn't drink. They didn't smoke. They didn't dance, play cards, or go to movies. But you should have seen some of them in church! They could lie, cheat, covet, and even split congregations in two with their fractious spirits.

Their list of official sins was ridiculously selective. Apparently they had never studied the works of the flesh Paul enumerates in Galatians 5:19-21. If they had they would have seen that 11 of the 18 he names are sins of attitude. The very projection of saintliness is a form of deception, and therefore a sin. It was exactly that sin for which Ananias and Sapphira lost their lives in the early church (Acts 5:1-10). Nobody would have blamed them for holding back part of their estate. But to hold back part, when they pretended to have given it all, was gross dishonesty.

I am in no doubt that fear lies at the root of much assumed saintliness. How many times have I been in a church business meeting when some headstrong, stubborn-willed trouble-maker has stood up and said, "As I prayed, the Lord told me that this is the action we must take. . . ." A person like that is using his saintly reputation to manipulate others. He lines up his opinion in such a way that anyone opposing him seems to be opposing the will of God. He may deserve the good reputation he has. But no degree of spirituality or success can turn a man into an oracle. If he thinks it can, then he has unconsciously fallen victim to his own public relations, and now that he sits on the top of the pile, he cannot bear the thought of being voted down, criticized, or given bad press. In short, he is afraid.

Fear disguised as saintliness degrades the personality in several ways.

Through pride. Fear is proud often through dogged insistence of its own humility. I had a professor who had the unthinking vanity to repeat to his students in class, "Teacher is humble, teacher is humble."

Through condescension. Fear is critical, always putting others right. But the habit of using phony saintliness to criticize others ultimately brings about its own downfall. The fearful person hopes through criticizing others to secure his own position. But criticism is like a drug—the more you dole out, the more you need to dole out to achieve the same feeling of superiority. In the end, you will repulse even genuinely good and tolerant people.

Through inflexibility. When you are filled with fear and endeavoring to cover up with saintliness, flexibility is difficult, if not impossible. Any deviation from your tick list of "don'ts" so threatens your sense of adequacy that you must rise up in censure.

Through unreality. A person wearing saintliness as a disguise has left the real world and taken flight in fantasy. In doing this, he lays a guilt trip on others who think that his saintliness is real. They think, "I could never be as good as that," without realizing they are being made to chase a mirage. In moments of rational reflection, the person may feel himself stretched across the yawning chasm between the saintliness he has assumed and the inadequacy of his real life. At that point he develops another fear—that of being found out.

It might do him good! There is no progress without honesty. As a young man visiting a country church in the Piedmont section of South Carolina, I heard a story that would have amused me had it not been so painfully true. During a Wednesday night prayer meeting at the Baptist Church, the pastor asked for testimonies. "Just stand up and tell what the Lord has done for you." One after another stood up and thanked God for His saving grace, His sustaining power, and His answers to prayer. Finally one man got up and said, "I thank God I don't cuss. I don't drink. I don't run with wild women. I don't gamble. I don't steal."

The pastor said, "Bill, we're few in number here. We know each other well. We really have no secrets from one another. Let's be honest. Let's level. What's your besetting sin?"

Bill replied: "Lying, dadburn it. Lying!"

The disguise of love

This disguise works on a more personal level than strength or saintliness. But like them it has two faces. From the inside, love used as a disguise for fear seems like generosity and self-giving. From the outside it comes across as possessiveness.

Many people are simply afraid of losing somebody close to them—usually a child or a spouse. Consequently they go out of their way to help, advise, and protect the person. A mother who has a possessive relationship with her daughter will show excessive concern about any area in which the child must eventually exercise independent judgment. She will express strong and often censorious opinions about the daughter's choice of friends, vocation, place of residence, and partner in marriage. All this is done in the name of love. She wants "the best" for her child, and will stop at nothing to get it. In reality, however, it is likely that she wants the best only for herself, and that the fear of losing her daughter drives her to influence the girl's decisions with a view to allaying her own fears.

Predictably, like strength and saintliness, this sort of "love" has the effect of actualizing fears rather than dispelling them. Possessiveness smothers. The child, deprived of her independence as she enters teenage years, desires it all the more and sees her mother as the obstacle to obtaining it. Eventually there is an argument. The daughter leaves home. The mother, who is devastated, tells herself that her love has been repaid with ingratitude, and wallows in self-pity. Yet there would have been no separation had she dealt with her fear when it first appeared. As it was, she accepted the fear, tried to disguise it with what she called love, and reaped the consequences.

The genuine article

All three disguises of fear—strength, saintliness, and love— are destructive in their effects. They produce the negative personality traits of domination, sanctimoniousness, and possessiveness, which will destroy the very relationships they were intended to protect and build. They are counterfeits crafted by fear. But the counterfeits must not be allowed to detract from the genuine virtues on which the disguises are modeled.

For that reason, I want to finish this chapter by looking briefly at the lives of three men I have been privileged to know, in whom true strength of character, true godliness, and true generosity have shone out like the sun.

Probably nobody has had a stronger influence on my life in regard to Christian giving than Guy Rutland. For one thing, he gave as much thought and preparation to his giving as he did to his business. For another, he neither sought nor needed public exposure as an incentive to give. Since his death, his family has learned of the enormous help he gave to people they knew nothing about.

Certainly no one invested more hours, more effort, and more dollars than Guy Rutland did in Haggai Institute. He served for 13 years as its treasurer. In that position, he could have exerted a lot of pressure to achieve ends inconsistent with the stated aims of the organization. He never did. In fact, this business tycoon would say, "John, we are looking to you for leadership. We believe God has sovereignly given you the vision. You make clear to us what needs to be done, and we are going to follow you to the best of our ability under the leadership of the Holy Spirit."

Another such person was Cecil Day. He died at 44, but he accomplished more in that time than most of us could achieve in a life twice as long. Though he gave enormous gifts of money, time, and influence to the Institute, not once in all the years I knew him did he display any possessiveness over its work. He refused to stifle it for his own interest.

Once we ran into a financial crisis so severe that the Institute faced closure. We needed immediate answers, so I phoned six trustees and asked them to meet me at the Executive Park Hotel in Atlanta. Amazingly—considering their heavy schedules—all six came without hesitation. After prayer and discussion, they came up with a sound solution, one that did not entail any immediate additional outlay of money from them (they were already giving to the limit). As we were walking out of the building, I remember Cecil, then 39, turning to me and saying wistfully, "I wish I had a group of men I could call on the spur of the moment, who would come up with answers like that!"

I realized then, for the first time, what a uniquely capable and consecrated group of men and women undergirded my ministry.

A third man was Arnold Browning, a wealthy hotel and real estate businessman from the Bay Area in California. He hadn't heard of the Haggai Institute until he was 61 years old. But from that time until his death at 78 he, too, gave unstintingly of his money, influence, and time. He would drop everything to arrange a meeting in the Bay Area and invite outstanding business leaders to learn about the organization. At the time of life when most men are slowing down, he was traveling as far as Singapore for the work of the Institute.

Had any one of these men been gripped by fear, the story of my ministry at the Haggai Institute might have turned out very differently. None of them were. Each of them had a strong personality. Each had impeccable financial credentials. Each acted in genuine Christian love.

Their lives are demonstrations of the victory over fear—the same victory you can have through the power of God.

Part 2

How Scared Are You?

3

The First Degree—Rational Fear

In the introduction to this book, I said that your fears can be classed as legitimate or illegitimate.

Legitimate fear can be a problem, but it will be a much greater and more complex problem if it has become illegitimate. But how exactly are the two distinguished? At what point does a legitimate fear become illegitimate?

The key to understanding this is the all-important relationship between fear and danger, for as we said, fear doesn't exist in a vacuum—it is a response.

Rational fear

The intensity of fear (how scared we feel) depends on two factors.

The first factor is the *level of danger* encountered. If you are young and at the peak of fitness, you will probably not fear for your health. There is no danger, nothing to be scared of. If, on the other hand, you are middle-aged and have a persistent pain in your chest, there will be cause for concern, and you will experience a corresponding level of fear. If you then consult a doctor and he says you have developed an incurable heart condition of which you are going to die in two weeks, your fear will intensify.

The greater the danger, the fiercer the warning signals the body sends to the conscious mind.

You might think that the difference between legitimate and illegitimate fear is a matter of intensity. But this is not so. If it were, high levels of danger would always make your fear illegitimate, which is nonsense. Imagine yourself walking in a forest one day and hearing a rustling sound in the undergrowth. You creep forward, hoping to catch sight of a squirrel or a fox, and then, as you push aside a branch, you get the shock of your life. It's a grizzly bear. All at once your heart jumps into your mouth, the hairs stand up on the back of your neck, and you break out in a cold sweat from head to toe. Scared? You are almost crazy with fear. If you could climb, you would already be a hundred feet up in the nearest pine tree!

Nobody could say your fear in that situation is illegitimate. It is acute, because the level of danger is acute—you're in real danger of being torn limb from limb. All those abrupt changes in your metabolism are your body's way of giving you the best possible chance of escape. If you found yourself standing ten yards from a grizzly bear and your body did not respond in that way, your chances of survival would be significantly reduced.

But what is helpful when you are face-to-face with a grizzly bear can be a handicap when you are dealing with ordinary dangers. Say you are going for a job interview. There is no threat to your life here, but you badly want the job, and there is a danger that you won't get it. As a result, your pulse rate increases, beads of perspiration form on your brow, and your throat gets so tight you can hardly speak. By the time you go into the prospective employer's office and shake hands with him, you are showing all the physiological signs of panic. You blow your chances through excessive and unnecessary fear.

The lesson is this: in order for your God-given capacity for fear to function effectively, it is necessary that the *level of fear you experience* be in proportion to the *level of danger you confront*.

This proper correspondence between fear and danger is what makes a fear legitimate. Fear that arises out of (and is appropriate to) a certain level of danger is *rational fear*. It makes an accurate assessment of the level of danger faced, and creates the conditions in which evasive action may be taken.

The role of *rational fear* in response to the nearness of a grizzly bear is obvious. But *rational fear* operates just as efficiently when the danger is mild or, statistically, a matter of chance. If you met a smaller animal than a grizzly bear in the forest, *rational fear* would still make you cautious of going too near it. *Rational fear* prevents you from walking casually along the edge of cliffs. It urges you to take out life insurance so that your family will be provided for in the event of your death. It makes you look for traffic before you cross a highway, get the right vaccinations before you travel abroad, and make prudent plans for your children's education.

Remember, fear is not wrong in itself. It is part of your survival mechanism. Provided that your fear is rational, it will always be legitimate. To be afraid of walking on thin ice is to show a just regard for the natural laws God has written into the world. To be afraid of falling ill or having an accident (to the extent that fear moves you to get medical insurance) is neither paranoia nor a lack of faith in God's providence, but the simple wisdom of precaution.

Let me give you an example.

A friend of mine said to me recently, "Travel is treacherous. The terrorists are accelerating their efforts. Your life has already been threatened in Indonesia and in Australia. You've been under house arrest in Pakistan. In the '60's, you visited an area in Afghanistan where no Americans had been invited. Don't you think you're being reckless?"

I responded: "I'll tell you what I told my son Johnny when he got so upset about my visiting Vietnam back in the '60's. 'Johnny,' I said, 'Daddy is safer in Vietnam in the will of God than in Atlanta, Georgia, out of the will of God.' "

"That may be true," my friend said. "But I've often heard you quote the wise words of the psalmist: 'Keep back thy servant also from presumptuous sins' " (Psalm 19:13).

"Okay. But since I believe that my travel is essential to carrying out my God-ordained mandate, I must go."

"Then why don't you let me provide you with some bodyguards? I'll underwrite full salary and expenses for three bodyguards, so you will have protection every hour of the day."

I thanked him for his generosity, but I wasn't moved.

"What good is a bodyguard? Did bodyguards keep President Reagan from being shot? Did bodyguards protect John Kennedy or Robert Kennedy or Martin Luther King or Moro or Somoza or Sadat?

"You may think I'm foolhardy, but I will tell you that having three bodyguards only makes you more visible. I take sensible precautions. There are usually at least two, often five or six people with me wherever I go, in different rooms of the hotel or different seats of the plane. I announce my itinerary to the appropriate people. When I'm in a country that's under the cloud of oppression or terrorism, I let the hotel staff know where I'm going, how I'm traveling, and when I expect to be back. I tell them whom to contact if I don't return at the announced time."

That is my way of dealing with the threat of terrorist reprisals. The fear is perfectly rational, but it is in proportion to the danger. If it wasn't, I'd have two bodyguards standing behind my desk as I write.

I have some less spectacular dangers to combat, too.

As a typical American, I have learned that I have a weak stomach when it comes to foreign food. Once, when I was overseas in 1969, I got so sick I thought I would die—in fact, I didn't much care if I did! As a result, whenever I'm traveling in places where I suspect my stomach will not tolerate the food, I restrict my diet to guarantee hygiene. Rice and tea are always safe because they have been boiled. So are fruits like the banana, from which you can remove the skin. I also take some toast and, occasionally, marmalade. I remember once being served a glass of Coke, which a generous waiter had loaded with ice cubes. I knew Coke would be fine, but I feared that the ice cubes might have been made with contaminated water. To be safe, I sent it back.

More recently, I went for a sophisticated medical checkup in Germany. The doctors told me I should treat myself a bit more kindly. "Get more rest," they said. "Spend more time in interesting diversions, and take more time when you travel between areas of varying climate. Try not to spend more than four or five hours flying in one 24-hour period."

Following their instructions is requiring a complete overhaul of my lifestyle. But I'm doing it. Why? Because I have a *rational fear* that if I push myself too hard I'll die before my time. The doctors said that given my genetic structure and God's blessing, I could live to be 90, like my father. But if I am going to get those extra years, I need to take care of myself so I'm fit to enjoy them.

Paul talked frankly about his fears. When he wrote to the Corinthians, "I was with you in weakness, and in fear, and in much trembling" (1 Corinthians 2:3), he did not mean that he distrusted God or was losing grip on his faith. In the next verse he says, "My speech and my preaching was not with enticing words of man's wisdom, but in demonstration of the Spirit and of power." How could he demonstrate God's power and at the same time be afraid? Easily, because his fear was a natural, God-given faculty to respond to the very real danger he was in. The pressure was constant:

> When we were come into Macedonia, our flesh had no rest, but we were troubled on every side; without were fightings, within were fears.
> Nevertheless God, that comforteth those that are cast down, comforted us by the coming of Titus (2 Corinthians 7:5,6).

For Paul, fear came with the territory of his apostolic office. We never hear him praying to be delivered from this fear. But when he asked for prayer from the Ephesians that he might fulfill his duties as an evangelist, it appears, though he doesn't say so explicitly, that he was seeking to transcend and overcome the fear of persecution.

> Pray for me, that utterance may be given unto me, that I may open my mouth boldly, to make known the mystery of the gospel, for which I am an ambassador in bonds: that therein I may speak boldly, as I ought to speak (Ephesians 6:19,20).

So *rational fear* is something we all can and should experience for our own well-being. It is what we might call the "first degree of fear," that is, fear in its normal and proper proportions. In short, it is legitimate fear. Fear in the first degree is still unpleasant. In its way, it still needs to be won over. But it does what fear is meant to do; it focuses our attention not on itself, but on the danger giving rise to it. We are more powerfully aware of the grizzly bear than we are of our terror of the grizzly bear. We are more powerfully aware of the danger of quicksand than we are of our fear of falling into it.

This is not true of fear in the second and third degrees, as we shall see. But before turning to them, I want to look briefly at two distinctions you will find helpful in examining your own fear.

Fear-objects and fear-scenarios

Whenever a fear is focused—in other words, whenever we say we are scared of something rather than just scared—we are relating our fear to some tangible object, event, or circumstance. But when we do this we may be referring to one of two things: the fear-object, or the fear-scenario. The two are so closely connected that we easily confuse them.

Suppose you tell me you have a problem with fear, and I respond by asking you what you are afraid of.

"Flying," you say.

"Okay," I reply. "Do you mean that the fact of being carried several thousand feet above the ground in an airplane is, in itself, what terrifies you?" You think for a moment and then admit that it's not. "So what scares you?" I ask.

You answer, "The thought that while I'm strapped into my seat, the plane might crash, and I'll be burned to death or suffocated by the fumes."

Although you began by saying that flying is the experience you are afraid of, it is, in fact, not flying, but crashing that you fear. Crashing (and consequently dying an unpleasant death) is the real fear-object. Flying is frightening to you not for itself, but for what it might lead to. If airplanes were, and had always been, roomy, comfortable and absolutely safe—and if bicycles were proven to be lethal—you would probably say you were scared of cycling instead. Actually, in statistical terms, you are far safer in a plane than on a bike! Nonetheless you have come to associate your fear of crashing with flying. Flying is your fear-scenario.

The tendency to confuse the fear-object with the fear-scenario is characteristic of the way fear spreads. Fear-objects are always specific. One of the horrifying features of the society portrayed in George Orwell's *1984* is the way the authorities identify personal fear-objects and then use them to torture captives—in the case of Winston Smith, with rats.

Even what we recognize as a single fear-object may, in fact, be a collection of them. Crashing in an airplane, for example, involves several fears: the fear of death, the fear of pain, the fear of confinement, and so on. We are justified in calling the crash a fear-object because it is an event in which those particular fears will almost certainly be realized. But we cannot call flying a fear-object. It is only a situation in which crashing is a logical possibility. In fact, the plane almost always lands safely at the end of the flight.

So in the case of *rational fear*, where might fear-scenarios occur? The answer is in any situation where there is clear risk. The marine in active service will see the battle as a fear-scenario. For a woman in a deteriorating marriage relationship, the fear-scenario may be that her husband will get involved with another woman. In both cases, the fear-scenario is clearly distinguished from the fear-object. The precise object of the marine's fear is the possibility of death, injury, pain, or the loss of companions. For the woman, it is the total breakdown of her marriage.

Wild Wood fear and Big Bad Wolf fear

In both of the examples I've just given, the fear is rational. In both, there is an object and a context to the fear. But if you look more closely at what the two people are actually scared of (the fear-objects) you will see a difference.

The marine's fear is largely impersonal. He looks into the future and sees there a "thing," or series of "things," that may happen to him. If he is wounded in action, it will be another person who has pulled the trigger or thrown the grenade. But the two men will not know one another. Their relationship will be defined by their allegiance to their respective sides in the conflict.

Conversely, the woman's fear is largely personal. It is one person in particular to whom she is married. A soldier can be shot by anyone, but a wife can be betrayed only by her husband. What she fears, therefore, is not the experience of betrayal in the abstract, but the jarring of an important relationship by the action of the other party. Where the marine fears violation, the woman fears rejection.

I give these two types of fear-objects special names: *Wild Wood fear* and *Big Bad Wolf fear*.

In Kenneth Grahame's *Wind in the Willows*, the Wild Wood is the place nobody goes. Except the Mole, the bumbling hero of the book, on whom the warnings of the other animals are totally lost until, one day, he ventures in:

> The pattering increased till it sounded like sudden hail on the dry-leaf carpet spread around him. The whole wood seemed running now, running hard, hunting, chasing, closing in round something or—somebody? In panic, he began to run too, aimlessly, he knew not whither. He ran up against things, he fell over things and into things, he darted under things and dodged round things. At last he took refuge in the deep dark hollow of an old beech tree, which offered shelter, concealment— perhaps even safety, but who could tell? Anyhow, he was too tired to run any further, and could only snuggle down into the dry leaves which had drifted into the hollow and hope he was safe for the time. And as he lay there panting and trembling, and listened to the whistlings and the patterings outside, he knew it at last, in all its fullness, that dread thing which other little dwellers in field and hedgerow had encountered here, and known as their darkest moment—that thing which the Rat had

> vainly tried to shield him from—the Terror of the
> Wild Wood!

The quote gives a flavor of the terror of the Wild Wood. It's a terror familiar to us all, a sense of foreboding and threat, an awful feeling that something terrible is just about to happen to us. The Wild Wood is thus a good metaphor for all those fears that revolve around the anticipation of disaster. Anyone who expects that something unpleasant is going to befall him is suffering from a *Wild Wood fear*. At some point in the future, he feels, some specific event is going to change his life unalterably for the worse.

My fear of becoming a target for terrorists is a *Wild Wood fear*.

Another common example is the fear many elderly persons have of falling. The danger is real—elderly folk who are frail do sometimes fall and injure themselves, and sometimes even die because they cannot reach a phone to call an ambulance. Falling is thus a *rational Wild Wood fear*. So is the possibility of domestic violence for a woman whose husband is drunk and aggressive, and the threat of persecution for the Christian believer who is living under an oppressive regime.

Seeing some disaster in store for you is obviously a strong motive for trying to avoid it. And this gives *Wild Wood fear* an important application as a deterrent to crime—a useful way of exacting obedience from persons not inclined to give it. The fear-object is punishment: in theory, the fear of what will happen to him if he is caught deters the wrongdoer from committing a criminal act. Whether or not it does so in practice is a moot point, for children still disobey after threats of a spanking, just as drug smugglers will risk the death sentence to run heroin. They are winning over their fear, but wrongly, because fear used as a deterrent protects society from damage in much the same way as fear of injury protects the individual from damage. A country with no fear of the law would quickly destroy itself.

In a way, all fears have at their heart the "anticipation of future disaster." But there is one group in which the disaster is of a specially personal type, and I have called these *Big Bad Wolf fears*.

Big Bad Wolf fear always occurs within the victim's social circle. It may focus on his wife, parents, children, employer, employees, colleagues, or members of his church. The common feature is the breaking of existing relationships, such that he suffers a measure of rejection. Often it exists alongside other emotions, as when a child feels guilty over some misdemeanor and fears rejection by his parents if they find out. As the story of the Big Bad Wolf suggests, rejection can take an uncomfortably tangible form. The three pigs may have suffered a breakdown in relationship with the wolf, but he also threatened to huff and puff and blow their house down. Real-life examples aren't hard to find either. Domestic violence is rejection written in the language of physical pain. The loss of employment brings rejection, not in an abstract or emotional sense, but in the form of financial hardship.

Let's recap.

We have said that the first factor affecting the intensity of fear is the level of danger, and that as long as it is in proportion to the danger we face our fear is rational. We have seen how examples of *rational fear* demonstrate the difference between the fear-object (what we're really scared of) and the fear-scenario (the situation in which those fears may be realized). We have also seen how fear can be classed as *Big Bad Wolf fear* or *Wild Wood fear*, depending on whether the fear-object is personal or impersonal.

It is an enormous help to begin your victory over fear with a careful analysis of the enemy. I recommend that you take a while now to think about your fear. Can you distinguish the real fear-object? What are some of the fear-scenarios that haunt you? Most important, can you honestly say that your fear is *rational fear*, that it is proportional to the danger that inspires it? If you can, then your fear is legitimate. Though you dislike it, it is not an enemy—the fear is helping you by turning your attention to danger.

And if your fear isn't *rational fear*? Read on!

4

The Second Degree—
Exaggerated Fear

We have seen how the intensity of fear, "how scared we feel," depends on the level of danger. But that is not the only factor it depends on.

In the last chapter I talked about my fear of terrorism. I justified it as a *rational fear* because, first, the danger is real, and second, my response to the danger is proportional to its size. Consequently I am satisifed that my fear is legitimate. I am not overreacting to the danger by hiring a crowd of body-guards and a bulletproof automobile. Nor am I treating it too lightly by failing to take sensible precautions for my safety.

Now all of this relies on a mental faculty called *perception*.

Because I see the danger in its proper perspective, I am able to respond to it rationally without squandering my money on unneeded security measures or leaving myself unprotected. I rely on correct perception. In our daily experience we are always relying on correct perception. Take visual perception as an example. When you drive, shave, write, or throw a ball, you assume that what you see is a true representation of reality. If your visual perception were wrong, you wouldn't survive. Have you ever tried drawing pictures while looking in a mirror? It's a constant effort just to make a line go in the right direction. You rely on correct visual perception to coordinate your movements.

In the same way, you rely on correct mental perception to control your fear. Without that right perception, fear comes out of the servant's quarters and sits down at the head of the table.

The rationality gap

Imagine you could measure levels of danger on a scale, as you can measure people's heights and mark them on a graph.

203

At the bottom of the scale would come trivial dangers like having injections, and at the top, serious dangers like being kidnapped or being attacked by a grizzly bear.

Now, imagine that for each danger, you could mark with a cross the level of real danger and the level of *perceived* danger. What would happen if you tried out a few of the fears we've looked at so far—the *rational fears*?

In each case, the two crosses would fall in the same place. The person facing a grizzly bear has both his crosses near the top of the scale, because he quite rightly perceives the danger as acute. On the other hand, the person going for a smallpox vaccination has them near the bottom of the scale; there is no risk of serious injury, and after a brief moment of pain it will all be over.

Because their fears are *rational*, the actual danger and the perceived danger are on a par.

But what happens if the man going for his vaccination is frightened of needles? In fact, he dislikes them so much he even considers playing hooky and not going to the doctor. Is the danger any greater for him than for the other people having the vaccination? Of course not. The difference lies in his perception of the danger. For him, the cross showing the level of perceived danger is placed far higher on the scale than the cross showing the real danger.

We might call the distance between the two crosses the *rationality gap*.

It shows the amount of distortion present in a person's view of reality. The wider the *rationality gap*, the greater the distortion, and the greater the fear. That's why perception is the second factor affecting "how scared we are." It doesn't take a high level of danger to make a person afraid—all that's required is that he perceives a high level of danger. You probably realized that when you were eight years old and told your kid sister there was spider on her back!

The *rationality gap* is what moves first degree fear into the second degree. *Rational fear* gives way to *exaggerated fear*.

I use the term exaggerated because there is still a logical connection between the fear and the fear-object. The man who is scared of needles is justifiably scared, because having an injection is seldom a pleasant experience. The problem is that his fear response is out of proportion to the danger. Fear at the prospect of pain or discomfort is normal and is part of the body's defense mechanism. But he doesn't need to be as scared as he is. In his fear, he is exaggerating the danger.

"Okay," you respond. "I see that. But this man who fears needles has almost nothing to be scared of. I, on the other hand, fear something that is really dangerous."

I agree. I have used that example for the sake of clarity. In fact, most people with *exaggerated fears* can point to a fear-object much more dangerous than a vaccination. But that the danger is real and frightening is precisely what gives exaggerated fear its power. The fact that it is also unlikely to happen and perhaps easily avoided doesn't reckon in the calculations of the one who fears it. As is often the case, fear arises out of ignorance, misinformation, inadequate understanding, and the sheer impossibility of working out the odds.

On top of which other factors combine to make the situation worse. A major one is the high monetary value of scare stories as copy for newspapers and TV. Shootings, ghastly murders, rapes, massacres, accidents, and epidemics can always be relied on to increase the circulation and boost the ratings, but selecting materials of this sort inevitably gives a falsified account of the world, pumping it directly into the living room of the reader and viewer. If a morning news program reports a shooting in New York, feelings of fear associated with extreme violence are produced around thousands of breakfast tables in the rural Midwest. Are those people going to get shot themselves that day? The odds are less than one in a million. Yet they feel a twinge of fear. They feel another twinge when a report comes in about threats made to American travelers by terrorist organizations.

All of these matters are legitimate objects of fear. My point is simply that our culture tends to magnify them, making it easier to develop *exaggerated fear*.

The man whose perception is true will know that the threat posed to his personal safety is negligible. Nobody in his town has been shot for a hundred years. As for terrorism, he knows that in the particular countries he plans on visiting, he is unlikely to be a target.

Contrast that with the man who has exaggerated fear. Hearing about the shooting, he goes out and buys a handgun ("just in case") and for good measure keeps a loaded rifle under the stairs. And he certainly won't leave the country. Forget that long-promised trip to Europe he was going to take his wife on this year. They will go to Florida instead.

What I'm talking about here is one of the big problems of fear—that is, the power it has to control us. I'll return to this important effect of fear in chapter 7. For now, let's look in more detail at some of the common objects of *exaggerated fear*.

A short checklist of scares

1. *Illness—violation of the body*. Sickness and incapacitation are major fear-objects. Nobody likes to think that he might suffer a stroke, go blind, become chairbound or require a colostomy. Illness reduces the quality of life. Consequently a healthy person often harbors a fear of falling ill, and an ill person—especially if he has a progressive disease like cancer, multiple sclerosis, or AIDS—fears the worsening of his condition.

As a fear-object, illness comes in numerous forms. For the cancer patient, the object is narrowed to that one disease, and narrowed even further to the various pains, discomforts, and indignities to which he, as an individual, may be subjected by that particular cancer. At that stage his fear is likely to be rational. He knows more or less what is in store for him. The danger is real. And sometimes this very proximity to danger helps him to face up to it and win over fear.

Ironically, *exaggerated fear* of illness is more common among the healthy. The mother of a preacher friend of mine, a lovely and compassionate woman, suffered from the time of young motherhood the fear that she would die from cancer. When she did finally die (in her mid-70's) it was of a heart attack. She spent 40 years fearing the wrong ailment. But even if she had feared heart attacks for all that time, would it have done her any good? I doubt it!

Like all fear-objects, the fear of illness frequently comes packaged in a fear-scenario. The classic modern example is that of contact with an AIDS patient. But in general, the fear-scenario will be any situation where the fearing person thinks infection can be passed on or injury sustained (injury, in this case, can include medical treatment—especially if it is carried out by a dentist!). He may even fear certain places not for the perceived threat of illness, but simply because they remind him of it. Consequently he may be uncomfortable at having to visit a sick friend in the hospital.

A special category of illness (in the wider sense of violation of the body) is assault, an act of violence against the individual deliberately carried out by others. Rape belongs to this group; so, too, do mugging, torture, and crowd violence. The traumatic nature of all these experiences makes them objects of intense fear, the more so if a person has already been subjected to them once. Such a person will probably have vivid fear-scenarios. A woman who has been raped, for instance, may fear darkness, seclusion, or men. Clearly this fear has a rational basis. For a woman whose work takes her into situations of high risk, the fear of rape is a *rational fear*. But that very fact fosters an *exaggerated fear* of rape in women who are really not at risk.

It is possible to have the fear of assault vicariously—that is, not for yourself, but for someone you love. A young friend of mine who got married recently said to me, "The Lord will probably get even with me by giving me daughters. He knows how terrified I'll be when they get old enough to go out with young men. I know how I behaved in my teens, and it'll be torture thinking that these young men might be behaving in the same way!" His smile was too thin to hide the depth of meaning behind the remark. *Exaggerated fear* was already doing a number on him.

2. *Impoverishment—violation of finances.* By impoverishment I do not necessarily mean bankruptcy. The fear of impoverishment comes to the blue collar worker as an anxiety over

making ends meet, just as it comes to the New York financier when his stock crashes. As with illness, the fear-scenarios are many and varied. For some, the loss of employment or the calling in of a loan would be a fear-scenario. For others, it might be the unexpected addition of a family member, extra heating bills, or an event such as burglary. In personal finance, more than any other area, a person's thoughts are ruled by the question, "What would happen if . . . ?"

I am no psychologist, and I have not read any studies on the comparative response of men and women to financial stress. But after years of extensive contacts in the business world, I have come to the strange conclusion that while men are more prone to the vice of greed, it is in women that fear of poverty makes its greatest inroads into the mind.

Two years ago, I heard Dr. Gateri of Nairobi, an internationally respected psychiatrist, offer the opinion that the most pervasive fear in women is insecurity. My experience seems to bear this out. I have observed some women of great wealth suffering torments at the possibility that they would wind up in the poorhouse. Also, it is worthy of note that although the really big money in America is in the hands of women, it is men who do most of the big giving. I do not say this out of prejudice. Women are among the biggest donors to our organization. But as a group, they seem less willing to give large amounts than men, despite the fact that wealthy widows often have more money and more liquidity than their husbands had while they were alive. The reason? I am convinced it is *exaggerated fear*.

I am old enough to remember the Great Depression of the late '20's and '30's. During the intervening years I have watched men and women, who fear a repeat of those tragic times, take protective action that actually reduced their net worth. I know of some who to this very day keep their savings in cash. They refuse to trust banks or savings plans. Consequently in the last two decades high interest rates have stripped the value of their money by 60 percent.

3. *Bereavement—violation of relationships*. In a recent survey, *Psychology Today* (February, 1985) canvassed its readers to find

out what they were most afraid of. "More than 1,000 people responded," wrote Elizabeth Stark, "and chose death of a loved one overwhelmingly as their greatest fear. This was followed by serious illness. Financial worries and nuclear war tied for third."

Every normal person dreads the thought of losing a loving spouse, a devoted child, or a respected parent. But *exaggerated fear* lives in anticipation of bereavement. In my first church, I met a couple who had waited 14 years before God blessed them with a beautiful baby boy. But as soon as he was born they started to fear for his life. They stopped coming to church because they wanted to give every moment to the child. They were terrified by the thought that they might lose him. They would go to ridiculous measures to make sure he wouldn't catch cold, get his feet wet, or contract a disease. The regimen became oppressive. They smothered the child with doting concern.

Tragically, in spite of all their attentions, the lad died suddenly when he was only seven years old. A few months after the initial trauma of his death, the couple came back to church. They told me, "God, in His mercy, took the little boy to Himself—for the benefit of the child and to bring us back where God wanted us." They had been the victims of *exaggerated fear*.

As a footnote, I will add that bereavement doesn't only occur as a consequence of death. A woman whose husband travels in the Middle East may fear "bereavement" through kidnapping. Families living under totalitarian regimes are constantly afraid that a loved one may suddenly join the ranks of the "disappeared."

4. *Death—violation of life*. Death is the ultimate fear-object. It is a constituent of many other fear-objects (for instance, illness and old age), and a feature of many fear-scenarios (for instance, flying, war, and nuclear holocaust).

History records that those who were conscious at the time of death, and died outside the faith, have been tormented by it. The famous rationalist philosopher Thomas Hobbes died crying "Oh, it's a fearful leap into the dark!" Voltaire, seeing hallucinations of Christ at the foot of his deathbed, raised himself on one elbow and hissed, "Take that black man out of the room. Crush the wretch." Mariba could only beg for sedation.

It may seem that there is no cure for the fear of death. But I assure you there is. After living for 63 years, I tell you flatly that the Christian believer can win over the fear of death, from the moment he knows it is imminent.

One day a lady asked Dwight L. Moody if he was afraid to die. He told her he was. She remonstrated with him, saying she had heard him preach that God gave grace to die. He replied, "Madam, God does give grace to die. Right now He has given me grace to live. When the time comes for me to die, He will give me grace to die." Later Moody had a stroke and was rushed from Kansas City to his home in Massachusetts. Just before he died he said, "Earth is receding. Heaven is opening. This is my coronation day." God did give Moody grace to die as He had given him grace to live.

Even Dr. Daniel Drew, founder of Drew Theological Seminary, faced death triumphantly. His family had been called to his bedside. The doctors knew the end was near. Since he gave no sign of consciousness, one of his daughters asked, "Has he gone? Has he gone?" Her sister replied, "Feel his feet. Feel his feet. Nobody has ever died with warm feet."

At that Dr. Drew opened one eye and said, "Joan of Arc did." Then he died.

David said: "Whenever I am afraid, I will trust in You. . . . In God I have put my trust; I will not be afraid. What can man do to me?" (Psalm 56:3,11 NKJV). Trust in God overwhelms fear—even the fear of death. And if the fear of death can be beaten, you can win over any fear.

Bob Pierce, founder of World Vision, phoned me a few days before he died. He said, "John, I've told the doctors to remove the life support systems forever. So after I am taken off them, I will go into a coma and then pass over to be with the Lord. I want you to hook up your recorder because there are certain things I want to tell you before I go."

I still have in my possession the one and a half hours of recorded conversation with Bob Pierce I made on that day. Bob Pierce was in right standing with God, and anyone who has put his trust in God through faith in Jesus Christ's redemption on the cross of Calvary can face death unafraid. As a child of God on the threshold of death Bob Pierce knew, like Moody, that God gives grace to die.

You see, you can win over fear, even the fear of death.

5. *Rejection—breakdown of relationships*. The first four exaggerated fears on my checklist have been examples of *Wild Wood fear*, the fear of impersonal disaster. But it is equally possible to exaggerate the other sort of fear—*Big Bad Wolf fear*. Here the interest focuses not on the fear-object (rejection is the only fear-object in *Big Bad Wolf fear*) but on the ways in which it is expressed; in other words, on the fear-scenarios.

Rejection, in fact, lies at the root of a good many social fear-scenarios. Its most obvious guise is simple fear of criticism—having your opinions, ideals, actions or motives scorned by others. Fear of criticism can occur on its own, or be implicit in the fear of failure. Failure, in turn, plays a leading role in other common fears, such as fear of responsibility, fear of social interaction, and fear of taking examinations. All of these ''high risk'' situations the person with *exaggerated fear* will try hard to avoid. But others are more difficult. For example, old age, a complex fear-scenario, includes the threat of rejection through the weakening of your faculties and inability to form and maintain lifelong relationships. Finally, the fear of rejection is even present in guilt, the nightmare of what others would think of you if they ever found out about your past misdeeds.

I'll pick up on just one of those fear-scenarios, that of old age.

A very forthright Atlantan called Charlie Outlaw lived to the age of 86. He was a dynamic character. Almost single-handedly he brought Billy Sunday to Atlanta for a series of massive meetings. I doubt if there was a single major evangelical personality who came to Atlanta in the middle years of this century who did not know Charlie Outlaw. His apartment, shared with his wife Nell, an author, was guest quarters for people from all over the world.

But as Charlie Outlaw approached death he became a recluse. No pastor was allowed to visit him. Even his close friends were kept away. The reason was, he had developed an *exaggerated fear* that if people saw him in a weakened condition it would spoil the positive impressions that had built up about him over the years. He wished to die with dignity. But to do this, he had to grapple with the fear of old age—the fear of rejection.

5

The Third Degree—
Irrational Fear

I assert again: fear is fundamentally an asset. It recognizes danger and puts the body in a state of red alert until the danger is past, evaded, or overcome.

What I have called *exaggerated fear* is fear armed with binoculars. It sees big dangers a long way off, and small ones as though they were big. It overreacts, because the *rationality gap* separates the actual level of danger from the danger perceived by the fearing person. Naturally you can overreact a lot or a little. *Exaggerated fear* doesn't have to be intense. You need only one stamp to mail a letter. If you put on two, you are wasting stamps in the same way you would if you put on 15.

Exaggerated fear, however, does share one feature with *rational fear*. Both are able to distinguish a real danger and a false alarm. They are both logical.

But suppose a person is scared of worms—those pink, wriggly things you dig up in the garden. Believe it or not, the condition has a name. It's called *helminthophobia*. Now there is absolutely no way you can convince me that worms are dangerous. They won't sting you. They won't give you blisters. They don't carry infectious diseases. They won't poison you or suck your blood. They are totally harmless.

But try telling that to a helminthophobic! He won't listen. For him, that poor little helpless worm is a source of grave danger. As soon as he sees it he goes prickly all over and wants to get out of the way. He's so frightened he wouldn't dare tread on it. Why? I certainly have no idea. His perception isn't magnifying a danger, it's manufacturing one. He is seeing danger where there is really no danger at all. He is, in fact, suffering from fear in the third degree—*irrational fear*.

(In case you think I'm joking about the fear of worms, I'll tell you about a girl I know of who was terrified of them. She

213

lived in a basement flat in Vancouver, separated from the street by a long path. When it rained the path was covered with worms. She was so afraid of them that she would leave the house only if her boyfriend carried her!)

In practice, the distinction between *exaggerated fear* and *irrational fear* is a little hazy. There are some *exaggerated fears* where the danger, though real, is so small or so remote that the fear response is effectively irrational. These, together with the purely *irrational fears*, go to make up the class of anxieties the psychologists call "phobias."

Merriam-Webster's dictionary defines phobia as "an exaggerated, usually inexplicable and illogical fear of a particular object or class of objects." And phobia, according to *Business Week* (April 21, 1986), is on the increase. As a mental health problem it is second only to alcoholism. James O. Wilson, director of the Phobia Centers of the Southwest in Dallas, estimates that a single phobia, the fear of flying, is causing the airline industry to lose $1.5 billion a year.

What is the phobic afraid of? Sometimes nothing at all—or at least nothing he or anyone else can identify. But where the fear is focused, the list of fear-objects is virtually endless. At least three hundred phobias are common enough to have a specific name.

Mild phobias are widespread and, in most cases, fairly inoffensive. Serious phobias lead to all sorts of problems.

In 1972, the year of his reelection, Richard Nixon was being hailed by some as the brainiest president since James Madison. He had notched up some great achievements—détente with the Russians, a visit to Mao in China, the policy of floating the dollar. He was a "shoo-in" for a second term. George McGovern had about as much chance of winning that election as a snowflake has of surviving in the watery bosom of the Potomac. But Nixon developed an *irrational fear* of losing, and it drove him to one of the greatest political follies on record—Watergate. He didn't need to misuse the power of his office, but fear drove him to it. And today, though he is much admired as a speaker, writer, and political advisor, he is remembered as the first president to resign rather than face impeachment.

Phobia isn't only a scourge of politicians. My father's two brothers married sisters. In their late 80's they are still beautiful women. But when they were teenagers their mother had an *irrational fear* for their safety. So much so that every time a man came to read the gas or electricity meter, she would lock them in a back room. She did the same when the postman came. In fact, she did it when any man came. I believe it was only the fact that they married so young that saved them from emotional damage through their mother's fear.

I don't know what experiences lay behind that woman's behavior. But I know what lies behind the fear many Jewish people have of Germans. The Holocaust must go down as one of the foulest outrages in human history. And yet I'm not certain that the fear of Germans (Teutonophobia, to give its proper name) is a *rational fear* or even an *exaggerated fear*. There is no logical connection between the atrocities committed by the Third Reich and the individual German the Jew meets today, and only a tenuous one between Nazism and the modern nation of Germany. As with hospitals and illness, the fear is one of reminiscence.

That doesn't mean it's always easy to decide how dangerous a situation is. For instance, there was an orgy of killing in Indonesia following the failed Communist coup of September 30 - October 1, 1965. Estimates of the numbers slain range from 400,000 to more than two million. Among the dead were two family members of a friend of mine, innocents who had been killed in the panic. Their murder moved two local men to seek out the self-appointed executioners. When they found the murderers, they jumped them, beheaded them, and brought the severed heads to my friend in a burlap bag.

"We have avenged you," they said.

But my friend replied, "That is wrong. God says, 'Vengeance is mine. I will repay' " (Romans 12:19).

Why had the two men killed the executioners? Maybe it was a way of striking back at an impersonal evil. At any rate, the fear that they might be the next victims of those particular men was an *irrational fear.*

Irrational fear is the worst kind of fear. It has the widest *rationality gap*, and therefore gives the sufferer the most distorted view of reality. Of course, the fear-object may be trivial, or the fear mild. If you have a drastic phobia associated with lemon-scented geraniums or Scotland's blue-footed boobies, your lifestyle is unlikely to suffer! However, I think it is true that most phobias, and especially the common ones like agoraphobia (the fear of open spaces), are at best inconvenient, and at worst completely debilitating.

In God's power you can win over any irrational fear. There is absolutely no doubt about that. However, it is only fair to say here that you should not restrict your options. I trust you will find this book to be of vital assistance. But if your problem with fear arises from having a *rationality gap*—a faulty perception of the world—you may also benefit from consulting a reliable psychiatrist. I cannot, as a writer, necessarily pinpoint for you as an individual what we are turning to in the next chapter—the causes of fear.

6

What Does Your Fear Feed On?

Like pain, fear is a faculty we are born with. According to some psychologists there are some fears (noise, being alone, and falling) that babies have more or less from birth. But most fears are learned:

> Children pass through a sequence of fear stages. In the first year loud noises, strange or unexpected stimuli, and threats of bodily harm are mostly feared. Mother's departure becomes feared in the second year. The third year ushers in many fears, mostly auditory but also large objects, rain, wind, animals, and the dark (which often persists through to the sixth year). In the fourth year visual fears predominate, but in the fifth auditory fears again prevail. Five year olds show less fear, but the end of the sixth year may bring many fears—especially auditory stimuli and sleeping alone . . . (R.D. Kahoe)

Ideally all this ought to result in a balanced adult who experiences fear only in the first degree. In practice it does not. The God-given potential for entirely *rational fear* is corrupted to a greater or lesser degree in all of us. Our social environment exerts constant pressure on us, like a crosswind on an airplane, blowing us off course from first-degree fear into second-degree fear. The process begins in infancy and continues throughout life.

But what are the factors that contribute to it? It is important to our understanding of fear that we know not only what we are scared of, and in what way, but also what experiences give strength to that fear. So test out your fear in this chapter, and find out what it feeds on.

Childhood programming feeds fear.

Childhood programming is what ought to produce a mature and rational sense of fear. You may attribute the fact that it does not to one of several factors:

1. *The use of scare tactics.* One day when my son Johnny was three years old, a well-meaning relative who was trying to get him to eat said, "Now, Johnny, if you don't eat your food, a big bear will come and eat you."

Johnny's eyes opened wide. So did mine. I said to the relative, "Do you realize how you would respond if I could convince you that there was a real bear in the next room ready to come in here and eat you? Johnny believes what you tell him. I don't want you ever to make a statement like that to him again."

The relative had done it out of love and an innocent desire to help Johnny eat. It's an easy mistake to make. But I believe it is a mistake all the same.

A parent who blithely uses terror to get his way with children deprives them of the ability to look at danger rationally. He loads them up with pessimistic expectations and makes them targets for fear in later life.

2. *The role modeling of fear symptoms.* Children learn by imitation. If they see their parents exhibiting fear, they will exhibit fear. A woman wrote to an advice column asking why her three-year-old child had fits of trembling. She was, she added, an incredibly fearful person herself. That was the reason. Children of fearful parents are doubly exposed, for they lack the protection of the parents' confidence and suffer from the example of the parents' fear. So it is passed down from one generation to the next.

3. *The making of unrealistic demands.* Many parents are never satisfied. If a child gets a B at school, he is told he should have made an A. If he gets an A, then he should have made an A +. Consequently the message picked up by the child is not that achievement is rewarded, but that failure is criticized. Naturally he doesn't want to be criticized. The parents know that, and they are relying on it to motivate the child to higher

standards of attainment. But at the same time they are programming the child to fear.

No matter how innocent the motive, it is cruel to lay a guilt trip on children. My cousin asked his father one day, "Dad, why is it when you give your Christian testimony, you tell people what a bad boy you were before your conversion, but when you talk to us, you tell us what a good boy you were?"

Good question.

4. *The blows of disaster.* Some apparently random events can leave scars of fear on a child. I remember when I was nine hearing that the three-year-old daughter of some neighbors had moved too close to the warm heater one morning. When she turned around her little sweater caught the flame, and before the family could come on the scene to help her, she had been hopelessly burned. She died within 24 hours.

Her funeral was the first funeral I had attended. I shall never forget how the father wept. He wailed. He was convulsed with sobs. I had never heard a man cry audibly before, and it terrified me. Even now, 54 years later, I can feel the pain of that bereavement. Had it happened ten years later, it would not have been half so vivid. Because I was a child the impact was tremendous.

Media violence feeds fear

It seems curious to me that intelligent people who dismiss the effect of violence on the screen happily accept the logic of spending millions of dollars to advertise a product between programs. If a 30-second ad can persuade you to change your brand of wash powder, what is half an hour of violence going to do to you?

A few years ago, two beautiful young mothers were in a city park near my home. They worked at a bank and went to the park for lunch. One day two men jumped them, molested them, and tried to kill them. One of the women got away. The other, the daughter-in-law of a dear preacher friend of mine, was kicked so viciously that her heart literally exploded.

The attack was given wide coverage in the media. By chance, the reporting coincided with the showing of a TV film that portrayed a similar crime. The effect was staggering. I know people who, as a direct consequence of that event, installed burglar alarms, bought firearms, and put in wrought iron window bars, solid doors, and dead-bolt locks on their doors. Many of them also had their houses and grounds fitted with emergency lighting that could be flipped on at the turn of a single switch, illuminating the entire area.

An even better measure of the effect of media violence is the response of those who know America only through its television programs. Many of my friends in Asia are convinced that life in the United States is just as they see it on *Miami Vice*. They wouldn't dream of visiting me. When I tell them I have never seen a man shot, never seen a gun battle in my town, never even seen a person robbed, they stare at me in disbelief. They exemplify the point made to me by my colleague, Dr. Harold Keown, who has years of experience in psychology of communication studies, that aggressive and violent behavior shown on the media produces fear and anxiety in the viewer.

Pain feeds fear

"Beware of dogs" is one warning that always captures my attention. I got my first bite, courtesy of a neighbor's dog, when I was only four years old. I think the growl terrified me as much as the bite, though he certainly took some skin with him.

Some years later, cautious inquiries to another dog owner elicited reassurances. "Fido never bites anyone. He's just a good watch dog, but he won't attack." He did.

The last straw came several years ago when I returned from a trip overseas. My wife had phoned me while I was away to tell me she'd been given a beautiful little dog called Brownie. I'd forgotten all about Brownie until I arrived in Atlanta at two o'clock in the morning. Not wanting to cause a disturbance, I opened the door quietly and crept in. But before I could switch on the light there was an explosion of canine belligerence that sent my hair straight up. For the next ten minutes

I went at it with this beast, determined to end his miserable life as soon as I could get my hands on him. He was saved by my wife, who had been awakened by the noise and came in to break up the fight. One word from her and Brownie turned as nice as a bowl of peaches and cream.

To this day, I am terrified of strange dogs. I'm okay once I've been introduced to them—politely and officially. In fact, we've recently acquired another dog, indelicately named Pookie, who I am relieved to say shows every indication of liking me. But the fear remains. I tell my friends, "If you want me to visit you, chain up the livestock before I arrive!"

Far deeper and more pervasive than physical pain is emotional pain. For instance, I can think of one of America's most eligible Christian bachelors whose influence and effectiveness is limited because he will not trust any woman. His wife had so shattered his confidence by her wanton sexual behavior prior to finally leaving him, he felt he was the laughing stock of the city.

The physical pain of a dog bite cannot remotely approximate the soul and heart pain this man has endured. Unfortunately, he has not demonstrated the necessary maturity to face up to the fact that one errant woman does not represent all womanhood, one intolerable marriage does not represent all marriages, and one unconscionable rejection does not represent all female behavior.

He has allowed the continual replay of his pain to make him the hostage of an ever deepening fear.

Feelings of inadequacy feed fear

Moses is a perfect example of this. Read Exodus chapters 3 and 4, where God gives Moses his job interview for the leadership of Israel. A more diffident candidate you could not hope to meet. God tells him all the mighty victories in store for him, and all Moses does is look for excuses:

> Moses said unto the Lord, O my Lord, I am not eloquent, neither heretofore, nor since thou hast

spoken unto thy servant: but I am slow of speech,
and of a slow tongue (Exodus 4:10).

In other words, "Send somebody else!" Moses tried to
evade his calling because he felt inadequate. He dug in his
heels. In the end, God got angry with him and said, "Okay, if
you insist on working from behind the scenes, I'll get your
half brother Aaron to be your mouthpiece." I wonder if later
on Moses didn't regret letting his fears get the better of him.

It's no use measuring out your wheat by someone else's
bushel. You will come out depressed because their bushel
isn't the same size as yours. Don't compare yourself with
others all the time. Accept the fact that God will provide for
you the necessary adequacy to accomplish whatever He calls
you to do. This is His special provision to you to win over fear.

Ego defense feeds fear

It is also true the other way around—fear feeds ego defense. The two exist in symbiosis. Because a person is afraid of
losing his credibility he defends his ego by building up his
image with others. But the more he builds up his image, the
more insecure he gets.

I personally know some Christian celebrities who go to
unbelievable lengths to arrange testimonials on their own
behalf! Of course they launder the idea. The person who
actually fixes up the dinner with government, educational, or
business leaders probably ends up thinking the testimonial
was his own idea. But the sole purpose of the event is to build
up the ego of the man at the top of the organization—an
ordinary man who is trying to camouflage his ordinariness
by orchestrating the praise of others.

It reminds me of the man who felt so inadequate that he
asked to be paged at a convention so he would come to the
attention of the people he wished to impress.

A distorted concept of God feeds fear

Often I have been asked why God permits terrorism, futile
wars, torture of innocents, and so on. There is a phony logic at

work behind this question. The Bible says God is all-powerful and all-loving. For suffering to exist in the world He has made, therefore, implies either that He loves us but is helpless to prevent our suffering, or that He could prevent it if He wanted to but prefers to watch us suffer.

The logic is phony because it leaves out the doctrine of human sin. We don't have to fear that God's hands are tied. They are not. He is omnipotent. Nor do we have to fear that He laughs at our suffering. His love, like His power, is absolute. The weak link in the chain is the ability of the sinful world to receive that love. It is when we refuse to trust God, in the totality of His power and love, that we become subject to fear.

The only way God could impose peace on the world would be to robotize our wills and rob every human being of the power of choice. He has not chosen to do that. He has given every person a free will. If someone prostitutes that power of choice to unworthy ends, don't blame God. If someone comes into my home, lights up a cigar, and flips the ashes on the floor so that the curtains catch fire and the house burns down, I would be foolish to blame God for the destruction of my home; it was that careless fellow who flipped his cigar ashes on my floor.

It never ceases to amaze me how people who fight among themselves in their own homes somehow seem to think that there can be peace and serenity in a world made up of people just like them. As long as we enjoy the divine gift of free choice, we are also saddled with the responsibility of the results those choices bring about.

7

Fear Feeds on You!

In the end you are the prize entrée on the menu of fear.

Having a fear is like having a cancer. It is always there, hidden inside you, always sapping your strength and breaking your concentration. Even *rational fear* can be destructive in its effects. What is popularly called "shell shock," for instance, is really nothing of the kind. It is a form of mental breakdown resulting from the prolonged endurance of *rational fear*—a conflict, if you will, between a soldier's natural fear on the battlefield, and the sense of duty (or perhaps the fear of punishment for not performing it) that makes him stay there.

You cannot hide fear. Its destruction begins by feeding on you, and then moving into your social and physical environment. Let me illustrate.

There are many avowed evangelicals who profess a strong faith in the Bible. But scratch the surface a little, and you will uncover a strange paradox. While they believe in the Bible, they also harbor a perpetual fear that research in theology or the spade in archeology will one day uncover something to disprove the very Scriptures they profess to believe. The result? There is a setting in motion of precedents and policies that stifle legitimate scholarship.

Again, for nearly 20 years I tried, in every way I knew how, to get an appointment with a man whose behavior signaled the message that I had offended him. He would not answer my letters. So I went through intermediaries, some of his closest friends, in the hope of seeing him. All to no avail. Now the Bible says that if there is a problem between me and my brother, I must go and talk to him about it. But how can I do that if I cannot reach him? He is one of that growing number of Christian celebrity untouchables. Their phones are unlisted. They live in a compound behind a high wall or

225

in a remote area where normal access is impossible. When they move they are surrounded by a huge entourage and insulated from the real world by a coterie of assistants and bodyguards. To me that behavior spells one word—fear.

I was once asked on a television interview, "Dr. Haggai, after your extensive world travels, what is the most amazing observation you have made?"

"You mean in the United States or overseas?"

"In the United States."

"The most amazing observation is the prevailing insecurity of the average American."

"Did this surprise you?"

"It shocked me. I couldn't believe it."

I still cannot, and yet the years have only confirmed and reconfirmed the observation.

A child wants to go to a certain event. The mother has to call every other mother in the neighborhood before she can make up her mind. A family decides to go on a vacation, but they have to find the "in" place before they finalize their plans. If that colorful evangelist Cyclone Mac (Baxter F. McClendon) were still alive today, he would say, "They're all like baloney sausages, stuffed with the same thing and wrapped in the same cover. Bite one in California, and it tastes exactly like one bitten in New Jersey."

I was flying one night across the country. During the flight, while nearly everyone was asleep, I turned on my individual light to read my Bible. A young man across the aisle said, looking at the Bible, "Oh, reading from Jeremiah, are you?"

"Yes, are you a Christian?"

"I'm a Jew."

"Where is your native home?"

"Jerusalem. I was born, reared, and educated there."

"Where do you live now?"

"Dallas, Texas, where I serve as a professor at the University of Texas. Before that I taught at McMaster's University in Canada."

"Well, I guess that the adjustment to this hemisphere was made when you moved from Jerusalem to Canada, and the move from Canada to Dallas was probably an easy move, with virtually no change except the weather change."

"That's not true. The minute I crossed the Canadian border, the stress factor zoomed up at least a thousand percent."

"I can't believe that. Explain it to me."

"In the United States you brag on your individualism, but you demonstrate a herd instinct. I'll give you an illustration. In Canada, I drove a 1968 Chevrolet. Nobody seemed to be upset with that. I lived in a particular house in a particular section of town. In Dallas, while they'll not come out and say it, they communicate nonverbally that driving a 1968 Chevrolet when you are a man in my position is not acceptable, and they let you know in a hurry what type of home and what part of the city you need to live in and where your children ought to go to school. These people seem to be filled with fear that they are not going to be accepted."

I told him that I thought his judgment was somewhat harsh, but I've never forgotten that midnight conversation with the young Jewish professor from Dallas.

The lesson is transparently clear: *fear has the most insidious power over its victims.*

The ruins of fear

Illegitimate fear in general—*exaggerated* and *irrational*, *Wild Wood* and *Big Bad Wolf*—has a stunning list of destructive effects.

1. *Fear means lack of influence.* Imagine you're at a lecture, and the speaker gets up and says: "I don't know why they called me to speak on this subject. I'm really not qualified. There are scores of people who are more qualified than I am— in fact, many of them are in this room. I really don't want to waste your time, so if there's somebody else here who'd like to speak instead . . ."

Doesn't exactly inspire confidence, does it? Fear undermines personal dynamism. Instead of being a person who knows where he is going and emits an enthusiasm that motivates others, you perpetually apologize and thus decrease your influence in the group.

My brother Tom is one of the world's premier speakers to business and professional groups. He passed on to me an astute observation a couple of years ago. "When a speaker like Mr. So-and-So, who gets $5,000 for every speech he makes, comes to a group and tells them what a hectic schedule he has kept and how many miles he has traveled and how little sleep he has had, he really does himself a disservice. The people sponsoring him did not scrape up the money for the honorarium in order to hear about his fatigue. They came to hear his oration and receive benefit from his insights. Why would he, one of the most accomplished speakers in the world, resort to currying sympathy from the audience?"

Tom didn't need to elaborate. The man was afraid. He wanted to neutralize his audience so they would be favorably disposed to him.

2. *Fear means truant thoughts.* Fear divides the mind much like worry and keeps the fearing person from focused thinking. Consequently he has little control over his thoughts. They range freely across the possibilities of disaster and tend to create a sense of panic and crisis that reinforces fear.

A friend of mine who works with the elderly in Scotland knows a couple with an *irrational fear* of mice. They think that if a mouse gets under their floorboards, it will ceratinly get into the roof, and once it's in the roof, it will certainly chew through the power cables and cause a short circuit and begin a fire. Truant thoughts have inflated the fear of mice into a fear of death.

The apostle Paul did not allow fear to confuse his thinking. He was absolutely committed to the spreading of the gospel, and while he was a man of mortal mean and mold, he could say of the hindrances he faced, "None of these things moves me." He directed his thoughts to good and edifying subjects. And he advised the Philippians to do the same:

> Finally, brethen, whatever things are true, whatever things are noble, whatever things are just,

whatever things are pure, whatever things are of good report, if there is any virtue and if there is anything praiseworthy—meditate on these things. (Philippians 4:8 NKJV).

Truant thoughts do not deal with love, truth, justice, or anything else that is positive. They entertain fantasies of harm—premature death, the child's flunking out of school, the betrayal of friends, or the leaving or death of a spouse.

What is the answer to truant thoughts? There is only one: Christocentricity—putting Christ where He ought to be, at the center of your life. Christ requires thoughts, as well as actions, that honor Him. So every thought should be brought into captivity to the obedience of Christ (see 2 Corinthians 10:5).

I remember accompanying the venerable Dr. Robert G. Lee, my favorite role model as a pastor, back to his study after a meeting. During the business session of that meeting he had burst out, "If you people who are always criticizing me knew how little your criticism meant, you would save your breath."

Because Dr. Lee loved me, he allowed me certain liberties, so I said to him rather wistfully, "Dr. Lee, I wish I could come to the place where criticism of other people did not affect me adversely."

He looked at me and said, "Oh, John, when I think of the hours I've wasted in the course of my life fretting about the criticisms of others—hours I could have utilized writing or visiting or memorizing—it would depress me if I gave much time to it."

That he didn't give much time to brooding over criticism was a measure of his power over fear.

3. *Fear means boredom.* Boredom is the side effect of implementing a no-risk policy in your lifestyle.

The fearful person often refuses to mix socially because he fears his looks are not adequate, his conversation is dull, his opinons are shallow. The fears may be groundless at first. But just like a car engine deteriorates through lack of use, so does a person's ability to socialize, and he will often get to the stage where experience corroborates his suspicions. He withdraws, not wanting to be hurt. But on the other hand, he doesn't want to live alone. He has more potential than his fear will allow him to express. As a result he suffers boredom.

4. *Fear means struggle.* Men who are short of stature know how painful it can be to lack those few vital inches. As a child, it's humiliating to be on the end of the group in every class picture, to be shorter even than the girls. It can affect your health! I am informed by our director of administration, Lieutenant Colonel (retired) Norman Vaughn, that studies done at West Point show short men to have more heart attacks, more health problems, and more often more difficulty in getting along with their peers. In fact, there is an Arabic proverb that runs, "Be careful of the man who is too close to the ground."

Many short men have overcome the fears associated with their height. Alexander the Great, Napoleon, and John Wesley were all only five feet tall. More often, though, the fear produces a constant struggle to compensate. For example, a short boy at school will often try to excel at sports, not through love for a particular sport, but in an effort to win the approval of his fellows and overcome the fear of his short stature.

A less rational form of the same mechanism is what the psychologists call obsessional neurosis. Here a fearing person adopts an obsessive habit that he feels will keep danger at bay. There is no logical basis for his choice. If I try to touch wood everytime I express a hope, or try not to walk on the cracks between paving stones, the action will do nothing to avert danger. More likely, it will only result in my fear being intensified when I forget to do it.

5. *Fear means financial errors.* It was fear that led to the 1929 Wall Street crash. People were buying stocks on a 90 percent margin. If the stock was $100, they would put up $10 and borrow $90. When the stock dropped to $50, they were required to put up another $40, which they didn't have. They were making financially disastrous decisions. Why? For fear of losing out on potential wealth.

Contrast that with the conduct of a businessman who came to America from Europe in the year of the crash. I know the story well because I know his son. This man brought all of his savings to the United States to set up business here. America was his chief market, and President Hoover had put 100 percent duty on the merchandise the business man was making. He was practically forced to move from his native Germany to America if his business were to remain viable.

When he got here, this German businessman found that nearly everyone he met told him the same thing: "Put your money in the market. You can make millions." But he resisted. He did not give in to the fear of losing out on a quick kill, the fear of being unable to compete with others who would certainly outstrip his economic growth if the market continued to rise. Of course, it didn't. The market crashed. In a matter of months, the men who had urged him to play the market had lost everything. Some were reduced to peddling apples and pencils on the street. Others committed suicide. He was sitting on a pile of cash.

Shortly after the crash, this German businessman was able to buy a 100,000-square-foot factory in Massachusetts for $25,000 cash. It was the start of one of the most incredible success stories in the annals of American industry. Today the company he founded is one of the most prestigious on the "Big Board"—the New York Stock Exchange.

6. *Fear means time dissipation.* I read yesterday that journalists don't have mental blocks because they are always working toward a deadline.

A deadline is a lifeline. Perfectionism can be unrealistic—after all, nobody really achieves full efficiency at work. It's better to do all your work at 96 percent of your potential than it is to do only half of it at 98 percent. In writing, certainly, the art lies in plunging in and not standing on the side waiting for the pool to be perfectly still so you can see the bottom. The British novelist John Braine, who wrote *Room at the Top*, advocated that you get at least 60,000 words down on paper before you begin to exercise your critical faculties.

Why is it so hard to push ahead and get things done? Probably because action means forging into the unknown, abandoning the familiar territory of what you have done before and trying your hand at something new. Fear procrastinates. And once it is in control, fear will supply you with a thousand good reasons for procrastinating.

Take the case of that strange creature, the professional student. He never moves more than five miles from the campus. He gets his degrees, goes on to postdoctoral studies, locks himself firmly in the ivory tower of academia. He never comes in contact with the real world. He is secure in an intellectual environment where no demands are made of him beyond the exercise of his own narrow expertise. He seems to be productively employed, but he's not. He is dissipating time in the illusion of productivity because he is afraid to take a risk and leave the academic nest. Fear chews away at his life.

7. *Fear means conformity.* One day a man approached my evangelist friend, Eddie Lieberman, who was holding a meeting in a southern town. The man had a large Bible under his arm and a broad grin on his face. He pumped Eddie's hand.

"I want you to know, hallelujah, bless God, amen, that we sure love the Lord, and hallelujah, amen, and blessed be God, we are walking in the light and in the power of the Spirit!"

Eddie smiled, said "God bless you," and walked on.

Next day another man, with a similar Bible and similar grin, approached him and gave him the same line. This time Eddie interrupted. "I know where you're from."

"Yes? Where?"

Eddie mentioned the group, whereupon the man said, "Oh, I guess you could tell us because we are all so different."

"No, the truth is, you're all exactly the same."

I've come across the same phenomenon myself. Some years ago, I met some friends who expressed their Christian faith in a totally unique vocabulary of super-saint trigger words. I wanted to be gracious, but I knew that if the average person heard them, he would think they were on an outing from the insane asylum. I determined not to play ball, and next time I met one of them on the street I asked him how he was.

"Isn't Jesus precious?" he replied.

I nodded. "I know how Jesus is. How are you?"

That floored him.

I know it says in Scripture that we are not to be of this world. But it also says we have to be in it. People will recognize the language of Zion without us festooning it in catchphrases. As ambassadors of God, it is our duty to pay due regard not only to the laws and customs of the kingdom of heaven but also to the culture of the people to whom we have been sent. The use of religious jargon is a sign of fear—a way of reinforcing the point that we are members of a certain in-group. This doesn't mean that we ought to adopt the jargon of the world through fear of being seen as oddballs. Fear should not make us conformists to any mere cultural trait, Christian or otherwise.

8. *Fear means godlessness.* Fear leads to godlessness because it opposes faith. I'll look at this further in a later chapter. But note how in the story of the storm, found in Mark 4:35-41, the disciples were forced into godlessness through their fear.

Terrified by the sudden storm, they woke Jesus, who had gone to sleep in the bottom of the boat. "Master, save us!" they cried. "We perish!" Jesus arose and rebuked the wind, and the sea became as calm as a millpond. "Why were you so fearful?" he asked them.

They could have replied, "Are you kidding? In all our years at sea we've never seen a storm like that, and you call us fearful?" They didn't, probably because they realized that being in the presence of Jesus turned their old assumptions upside down. Jesus had said when they left the shore, "Let's go to the other side," not, "Let's go out in the middle of the lake and drown." Why had they not believed that when the storm came up? Simply through fear.

9. *Fear means health problems.* Fear is closely related to worry, and tends to produce the same physical effects. Prolonged

illegitimate fear puts the body under a strain that is only meant to be endured in short bursts, for engagement with immediate danger. Among other things, fear causes tension in the muscles, restriction of the cardiovascular system, pressure in the head, and intestinal problems like duodenal ulcers.

10. *Fear means premature death.* The accumulation of stress cannot help but wear down the body and shorten life. Consequently I class the toleration of fear, when the fearing person knows he can do something about it, as a socially acceptable form of suicide, slower but just as effective as blowing your brains out with a gun or taking an overdose.

Fear kills in other ways. It kills in the culture of the Australian aborigines through "pointing the bone," a ritual in which psychosomatic death, induced by fear, follows in a person who has been condemned by the witch doctor. It kills in the West through a person's unwillingness to seek medical treatment. My Uncle Bill died at 49 from a strangulated hernia because he feared having surgery. Another man, whose nephew is a dear friend, died of a heart attack because he was so surprised to find, having convinced himself and everyone else that surgery was going to kill him, that he had come through alive!

Fleeing from the Big Bad Wolf

In addition to the complications of fear I've listed above, there is a wide range of specifically social difficulties that arise from *Big Bad Wolf fears*. To live in constant fear of rejection by others is to cripple yourself socially. It affects your work, your marriage, your leisure time and casual contacts. You live, like pigs in the story, in dread of the Big Bad Wolf.

If you have a fear founded on rejection, I suspect you will have trouble with the following.

1. *Forming relationships.* Making friends with someone involves risk. Starting a romantic relationship involves even greater risk. The fearful person will need a lot of persuading to begin a venture like that. And once he has begun, fear will

tend to make him too sensitive. Fear comes home from a party and replays every word and every nuance, interrogating them for signs of indiscretion. It is afraid of giving offense and upset at receiving it. It is also prone to wild flights of imagination.

I have seen long-standing friendships wrecked because one party, like Shakespeare's Othello, became possessed of jealous fears. I know of a man whose neighbor moved across the country after living for years in the same town. When the neighbor didn't write, his friend felt rejected and wrote a nasty letter, thus beginning an exchange of abusive correspondence which ruptured the friendship. In fact, the reason for the neighbor's silence was his involvement in an automobile accident. He had been on the critical list for months.

2. *Accepting responsibility*. The fearful person never wants to be in the place where the buck stops. If he is going to make a mistake, he would rather do it in private. So to avoid criticism he cancels meetings, misses deadlines, sidesteps personnel problems, and delays, delays, delays.

Some women avoid responsibility in the home, too. They spend their days munching on potato chips and watching soap operas. They don't plan in advance. Their shopping is haphazard. They don't keep their checkbooks reconciled or retain receipts for income tax purposes. They oversleep, leaving their children to shift for themselves in getting ready for school. The house usually looks like the last visitor was a tornado.

3. *Taking criticism*. The fearful person is rarely willing to learn from criticism. I know some writers who are capable of reaching the best-seller list, but who will not take criticism from editors. As a result they lose out and thousands are deprived of their valuable insights.

One of the most gifted men I've ever known lost his health and his company through repeated outbursts of fear-inspired temper. He saw behind every critical comment the danger of his losing control. Ironically, it was this very fear that wrested control of his multinational organization from him. His trumpcard in policy arguments was the threat to resign. He played it whenever he wanted to get his own way, and it never failed. Never, that is, until he played it once too often. After one of his raging scenes, culminating in a threat of resignation, a board member quietly moved to accept his resignation "with regrets."

The vote was unanimous.

4. *Facing confrontation*. No great goal was ever achieved without bringing the protagonist into confrontation with his opponents.

It's easy to write letters, easy to make others do the dirty work, easy to spiel off from behind a podium. But fear will not willingly confront another person and argue out differences. Paul wrote to the Galatians about how he had had to shame Peter into confronting the Judaizers. Peter, who had been the first Christian to take the gospel to the Gentiles, later lost the courage to do it. He tried to fudge the issue by appeasing them. Fear had gained the upper hand.

5. *Braving failure*. I was one of four boys in my family. One died in infancy. The youngest of the survivors, Tom, was ordained a minister, as I was. This put a lot of pressure on Ted. People would make remarks to him. "You say your father is a minister, and your two brothers are ministers?"

Ted's story

"Yes, they are."

"Isn't it interesting that you should not have gone into the ministry?"

Loaded question! How would you have answered it without coming across as defensive? I recoiled at hearing him baited like that and sometimes cut in to defend him. "God knows that while there are some men outside the ministry who should be in it, there are many more in it who should never have gotten there!"

Ted was 16 months my junior. I made good grades at school; Ted horsed around. He graduated only by the grace of the principal. Yet he went on to become a celebrated electrical engineer and led the project that put the SYNCOM satellite into space. I didn't know until his funeral that much of the

AWAC surveillance system was the product of Ted's scientific genius. How easily all that could have been lost had Ted given in to his fears of failure. I know he had them. But he had the strength not just to overcome his failures at school, but to risk further failure by defying the opinions of others and being his own man, doing what he knew was right for him.

For me, Ted stands out as a shining example of a man who won over fear. If you want to follow him, turn to the next section.

Part 3

How To Win Over Fear

8

Fear—And Fear Not

I want to make one point clear before I go any further.

Many of the so-called solutions to fear are psychological—they are ways of training your mind not to go overboard on the fear response, or of learning to tolerate an irrational fear stimulus (like worms) without breaking out in a cold sweat. These methods have their place; I do not disparage them. In fact, I recommend some of them in this book. But you must understand that they are not a complete answer. There is only one place where total freedom from fear can be found, because it is in that one place alone that the deepest causes of fear are healed. The place is the person of God.

The old fear of God

Winning over fear—and I mean really *winning*, not just learning to live with it—begins, paradoxically, with fearing in the right way.

Look at this passage from the Gospel of Matthew:

> Fear not them which kill the body, but are not able to kill the soul: but rather fear him which is able to destroy both soul and body in hell.
>
> Are not two sparrows sold for a farthing? And one of them shall not fall on the ground without your Father. But the very hairs of your head are all numbered. Fear ye not therefore, ye are of more value than many sparrows (Matthew 10:28-31).

Jesus has been talking to the disciples about persecution. Don't be under any illusions, He says. Follow Me, and you will be like sheep in a wolf pack. You will be tried and

241

scourged. You will be turned into refugees. You will be hated so much that even members of your own family will betray you.

For the full story, read through Matthew 10:16-27. It's not comfortable reading, is it? Jesus lists experiences, the prospect of which would scare any normal person to death. And then, suddenly, He puts the warning in context: "fear not them which kill the body . . . but rather fear him which is able to destroy both soul and body in hell. . . ." In other words, put your fears in the right order of priority. The torturer, the accuser, and the Judas are all legitimate fear-objects, but they are not to be feared as God is.

The Bible is adamant in its teaching that fallen man's first and most appropriate response to God is fear. It was with good reason that Adam hid in the bushes and said "I was afraid." He had disobeyed God's explicit command, and so has everyone else since. Adam enjoyed a unique privilege, however, inasmuch as his judgment was immediate. He had just enough time to sew a few fig leaves together before he heard God come out for His evening stroll in the garden. Consequently, Adam had the opportunity neither to reconcile himself to his guilt, nor to anesthetize his conscience and forget what had happened.

The same cannot be said of Adam's descendants. What makes much human sin so reprehensible is the shamelessness with which it is committed. Every sinner, perhaps, thinks twice when he reaches the gates of death, but in the meantime, on the far-roaming highways of life, he strides on in the happy delusion that his journey will never end and that he will not be held to account for his actions on the way:

> As it is written, there is none righteous, no, not one: There is none that understandeth, there is none that seeketh after God. . . .the way of peace they have not known: there is no fear of God before their eyes (Romans 3:10,11,17,18).

Brazen ignorance of the fear of God can be traced in a direct line from Cain's murder of his brother in Genesis 4 to the atrocities you saw reported on the news last night. The man with no fear of God makes himself an enemy of God, and the place of enmity with God is fertile ground for every other sort of fear: the fear of loss that results in fratricide, and the fear of embarrassment at the ballot box that results in rigged elections and military oppression.

But if the refusal to fear God is the gateway to folly, the converse is also true: that, as the writer of Proverbs puts it, "The fear of the Lord is the beginning of knowledge" (Proverbs 1:7). It is the beginning of many other blessings, too: longevity (10:27), confidence (14:26), life (14:27), and satisfaction (23:17). The Wisdom writers of the Old Testament urge on us again and again the magnitude of God's blessing to those who fear Him:

> He will bless them that fear the Lord, both small
> and great (Psalm 115:13).

> The Lord taketh pleasure in them that fear him,
> in those that hope in his mercy (Psalm 147:11).

Mary picks up the same theme in the New Testament, when she says in the presence of Elizabeth, mother of John the Baptist:

> He that is mighty hath done to me great things;
> and holy is his name. And his mercy is on them that
> fear him from generation to generation (Luke
> 1:49,50).

What does it mean, then, to fear God?

Practically the only New Testament Greek term for "fear" is used here by Mary, and also by Jesus in Matthew 10. It is a strong word, meaning literally "to be terrified of," which at first makes the contexts of its use a little strange. Mary links fear with mercy; and Jesus, advocating the fear—the terror—of God, goes on to emphasize His fatherly care.

An impossible combination?

Not quite. You see, man's relationship with God must begin with profound fear because, like Adam, we have disobeyed him. You, I, and everybody else have at some time been, as it were, hiding in the undergrowth, desperately trying to cover ourselves with fig leaves. We are guilty, and we know it. For some people, this guilt, this sense of utter unworthiness, lingers on to undermine every area of life. But it ought not. Guilt is the right place to start, but the wrong place to stay.

There is a famous passage written by John in one of his epistles:

> My little children, these things I write to you that you may not sin. And if anyone sins, we have an Advocate with the Father, Jesus Christ the righteous. And He Himself is the propitiation for our sins, not for ours only but also for the whole world (1 John 2:1,2 NKJV).

John is not writing to just anybody. He is addressing a readership of Christians, and it is Christians—those who have let guilt lead them to repentance and faith in Jesus Christ—for whom the propitiation, the sacrifice, is effective. I remember Dr. Chandu Ray expressing it perfectly when he lifted his voice and said of Jesus, "He is the annulment of our guilt."

To have your guilt "annulled" is to enjoy a totally new status before God. That status is unaffected by fresh guilt. It goes without saying that one of the first things any of us do after we are converted is sin. Becoming Christians doesn't make us immune to that. But sin cannot turn us back into nonbelievers. When we confess our sins, we do so not in order to secure our status, but because that status has already been secured. It is like the child apologizing to the parent, not in order to become a child, but because he is already a child and does not want to grieve the parent.

True Christianity could thus be defined as "the religion of the clean conscience." This is made possible through the fear—the terror—of God. Fear produces repentance, and repentance produces the blessings of a new status before God—a new status which I hope by now you have received.

But there is something else, too.

The new fear of God

When the new status is bestowed, the old sin-inspired terror of God should be transformed into a new sort of fear—fear in the sense meant by the Wisdom writers of the Old Testament. It has two elements.

1. *Fearing God means holding Him in awe and respect*. The most common word for "fear" used by God's people in the Old Testament would not describe the experience you have while watching a horror movie. Rather, it is the fear you might feel the first time you see the Grand Canyon, or are ushered into the Oval Office to speak to the president of the United States. You might call it "reverence."

Reverence shares with what I've called the "old fear of God," and with other fears in general, a sense of being overwhelmed. What scares us about a fear-object, be it a righteous God or a grizzly bear, is the gut-feeling that we are vulnerable in the presence of someone or something greater and more powerful than we are. Reverence balances that feeling with the assurance of safety. The man at the Grand Canyon is awed by its immensity, but at the same time he feels as though he belongs, as though he has a right to be there. The man about to shake hands with the president knows that he is accorded the rights and privileges of a citizen, though his heart is in his mouth.

Still, reverence gives neither man permission to take liberties. Only a churl would turn his nose up at natural beauty; and if the man visiting the White House took advantage of the occasion to give offense, he would receive short shrift from the security staff.

This fine balance of safety and respect, privilege and responsibility, lies at the heart of the "new fear of God." It causes Paul to write to Ephesians about "submitting yourselves one to another in the fear of God" (Ephesians 5:21); and to the Philippians to "work out your own salvation with fear and trembling" (Philippians 2:12). In both passages the sense of the word fear is "reverence." Peter sums it up neatly in his first epistle:

> As he which hath called you is holy, so be ye holy in all manner of conversation; because it is written, Be ye holy; for I am holy. And if ye call on the Father, who without respect of persons judgeth according to every man's work, pass the time of your sojourning here in fear (I Peter 1:15-17).

2. *Fearing God means trusting His providence.* The safety inherent in reverence springs from a state of dependence. The Grand Canyon is representative of the environment, just as the president is representative of the state. We depend on both for everything we have.

We depend far more fundamentally on God, in Whom "all things consist." In the Sermon of the Mount, Jesus is in no doubt as to Whom we should be thanking for our daily bread:

> Therefore take no thought, saying, What shall we eat? or, What shall we drink? or, Wherewithal shall we be clothed? (For after all these things do the Gentiles seek:) for your heavenly Father knoweth that ye have need of all these things. But seek ye first the kingdom of God, and his righteousness; and all these things shall be added unto you (Matthew 6:31-33).

The parallel passage in Luke goes on: "Fear not, little flock, for it is your Father's good pleasure to give you the kingdom" (Luke 12:32), and then proceeds to suggest a few practical ways of demonstrating fearlessness: "Sell that ye have, and give alms. . . ."

That "fear not" tolls like a signal bell through the pages of Scripture. The message is hammered home on over 300 separate occasions, in the Old Testament and the New. To fear God is to trust in His provision for your need. If you are a believer, God will meet your needs just as He met the needs of the Israelites when they journeyed in the wilderness. His promise is like a blank check given into your hands—a check which the fear of God will help you cash.

Time to decide

The whole problem of winning over fear boils down to one issue: whether or not you are willing to fear God. In the fear of God is contained, in embryo, the solution to all others. To fear God is to "fear not."

I emphasize the phrase "in embryo" because the spreading of this new kind of fear to the extremities of your being will take time, and will not become reality at all without your willing cooperation. You must give yourself to the task with the same commitment you would use in raising a child, or studying for a college degree. Without that patience and perseverance and determination you will probably give up. But I promise you this—in learning to fear God, you will receive not just victory over your fears, but many other blessings besides.

At this point, I want you to ask yourself two questions:

The first is: *Am I really honest enough to admit I have a fear?*

If you have read this far, I hope you are. I hope you have thought very carefully about fear and its disguises, and done your best to unmask it. But check all the same to make sure that it's not hiding away behind a screen of semantics. It is the easiest thing in the world to call your fear "prudence," or "caution," or some other fancy name. Lay it bare. Expose the fear for what it is.

The second question is: *Do I really want to win over my fear?*

Think carefully about that. Fear has some payoffs. It can give you a sense of worth, a false comaraderie at a coffee klatch, or material for conversation at a dinner meeting, in a Sunday School class, or over the backyard fence. You can talk about "great challenges" or "profound obstacles" or "serious threats." You can get a kick out of swapping fear stories with friends. If the stories are wild enough—about kids getting on drugs or having abortions, or about local racketeers threatening the community—you may obtain a certain notoriety in your little circle of friends.

There is a sense in which holding on to fear can give its own crazy, distorted, convoluted security. It is that security you will have to give up if you want to be rid of your fears. Winning over fear will mean leaving it behind forever. Are you sure you want to do that?

If you are, go on to the next page so we can get down to business.

9

The Timothy Formula

The key to winning over fear is to be found in the most fearful man in the New Testament.

His name is Timothy. He accompanied Paul on some of his journeys, and the apostle, who was not his real father, nonetheless seems to have developed a fatherly affection for him. Timothy took part in some important and dangerous missions across what is now Turkey and Greece. But he was a man with a problem, and his problem was fear.

Timothy's life exemplifies one of the most debilitating effects of fear—ineffectiveness. He seems to have been very gifted. God had set him apart for crucial work in the church, and for this work Paul and the elders had laid hands on him. Yet he fought constantly against the desire to hold back, to shy away. The word used of him, in fact, bears that particular meaning—timidity.

He was so sensitive that when Paul sent him to the troublesome church of Corinth, Paul also relayed special instructions to the church so that Timothy wouldn't be unduly disturbed by his reception:

> Now if Timotheus come, see that he may be with you without fear; for he worketh the work of the Lord, as I also do. Let no man therefore despise him: but conduct him forth in peace, that he may come unto me: for I look for him with the brethren (1 Corinthians 16:10,11).

There's no doubt Paul believed in Timothy's potential. The two letters he wrote to Timothy, which are preserved in the New Testament, are letters of encouragement and advice. But Paul knew of Timothy's weakness. The second epistle, written, it seems, to allay the young man's anxiety over Paul's imprisonment, overflows with assurance and concern:

> . . . I have remembrance of thee in my prayers
> night and day; greatly desiring to see thee, being
> mindful of thy tears, that I may be filled with joy;
> when I call to remembrance the unfeigned faith
> that is in thee, which dwelt first in thy grandmother
> Lois, and thy mother Eunice; and I am persuaded
> that in thee also. Wherefore I put thee in remem-
> brance that thou stir up the gift of God, which is in
> thee by the putting on of my hands (2 Timothy
> 1:3-6).

Apparently Timothy's fear had risen to such a pitch that he
doubted his calling. He even doubted his faith. Fear was
undermining his ministry, paralyzing him, preventing him
from living and working effectively.

What is Paul's answer?

Well, he brings Timothy back to the fact of his faith—his
fear of God. Through faith, he says, Timothy has been given
all that he needs for a successful and victorious life. What
about this timidity, this fear Timothy feels—is that a gift of
God? Emphatically not, for "God hath not given us the spirit
of fear; but of power, and of love, and of a sound mind" (2
Timothy 1:7).

Power, love, a sound mind (literally, self-control). That is
the summary of Paul's solution to fear. Three gifts that are
yours for free in the grace of God, if only you will take them.
In the next three chapters I am going to look at them in more
detail. Right now, I just want you to remember them. For
convenience, I've expressed them in what I call the "Timothy
Formula":

① DYNAMISM + ② DEVOTION + ③ DISCIPLINE =
DELIVERANCE FROM FEAR

Learn it and remember it, because it is the key to your victory
over fear!

10

Deliverance Through Dynamism

Everyone wants (power) over fear. The sort of power dyna-
mite has to blast rock out of a mine. The sort of power the
dynamo has to generate electricity. The power of dynamism.

Is this power to be found inside you? There are many
people around who will try to persuade you it is. A central
technique employed by psychologists in the treatment of fear
is called "behavior modification." The theory is quite simple—you put the fearing person into the very situation that
makes him afraid, and then teach him to respond to it differently. Up to a point it works. A man told to tackle his fear of
big bridges by traveling repeatedly over small ones can now
manage a four-mile span. Some people terrified by airplanes
can now journey by air.

But it only works up to a point. A report in *Business Week*
(April 21, 1986) says of this form of therapy, used to treat
phobias at a clinic in Rockville, that "for many phobics 'cure'
is a relative term. Psychologist Ross reminds patients that
phobias can reappear months or even years after seemingly
successful therapy. The aim of therapy, she says, is to give
sufferers 'the ability to lead a normal life without avoidance.' "

In other words, the power offered is of a very limited sort.
The strategy aims not so much to eradicate fear as to contain
it. And for this open-ended solution to your problem you can,
according to *Business Week*, pay up to $1,300 for a 16-week
course.

Now in case you haven't clued in already, I'll say again that
winning over fear God's way will involve you in much more
than four months of therapy sessions. What God asks of you
is a complete turnaround in your values, priorities, and lifestyle. Some people will make the mistake of seeing this as a
"price" for treatment, as though God expected them to repay

Him by going to church on Sunday or turning religious. It is not. What God gives, He gives entirely free. The transformation of your whole person is not the cost of the treatment, but the means by which it is effected. You win over fear by becoming a new person under God. If you refuse that transformation, you may still find some help with your fear, but you will never really win over it.

The reason is clear when you think about the resources at your disposal. On your own you have simply yourself, your own determination and strength of character. That isn't enough. If it were, you wouldn't have a problem with fear, and you wouldn't be reading this now. All right, then—let's assume you pay your $1,300 and go to consult a leading authority on fears and phobias. He recommends therapy. What have you got now? The same as you always had, with a teaspoon of psychological method and maybe a pinch of extra confidence. In short, nothing has really changed.

By way of contrast, I'll give you a snatch preview of the "dynamism" in the Timothy Formula.

Paul talks about it in the first chapter of Ephesians. His prayer for the Ephesian church is what I pray for you:

> That the God of our Lord Jesus Christ, the Father of glory, may give unto you the spirit of wisdom and revelation in the knowledge of him: The eyes of your understanding being enlightened; that ye may know what is the hope of his calling, and what is the riches of the glory of his inheritance in the saints, and what is the exceeding greatness of his power to us-ward who believe, according to the working of his mighty power, Which he wrought in Christ, when he raised him from the dead, and set him at his own right hand in the heavenly places, far above all principality, and power, and might, and dominion, and every name that is named, not only in this world, but also in that which is to come: And hath put all things under his feet (Ephesians 1:17-22).

You can tell how enthusiastic Paul is about God's dynamism—he doesn't stop long enough to end a sentence!

Read it over again, slowly. Let it soak into you. This power Paul is writing about is the power God is ready to release into your war against fear. Paul could hardly have found a stronger term to describe it than "exceeding greatness." It is the same power that brought the world into being, and governs the motion of the universe. It is the same power that sliced open the Red Sea, and moved in a pillar of cloud before the tribes of Israel. It is the same power that raised Jesus Christ from the dead, and set Him in the place of highest authority, putting everything under His dominion. We are not in the playpen here. Thermonuclear warheads, the sun, or the accumulated energy of the entire cosmos cannot begin to compare with the power of God.

No wonder Paul later describes God as "him that is able to do exceeding abundantly above all that we ask or think, according to the power that worketh in us . . ." (Ephesians 3:20). Such power, active in the lives of ordinary men and women like us, cannot fail to exceed our expectations. And since fear comes under the heading of "all things," there is no doubt that victory is ours through faith in God.

Power at work

I said earlier that Paul was subject to a great many rational fears. I am convinced that no one could have endured the stress he did who was not filled with this dynamism, this power of God. But how did the power work in practice?

Paul gives us a tantalizing insight in his letters to the Corinthian Church. Take this excerpt from his description of the work of an apostle:

> We are hard pressed on every side, yet not crushed; we are perplexed, but not in despair; persecuted, but not forsaken; struck down, but not destroyed—always carrying about in the body the dying of the Lord Jesus, that the life of Jesus also

may be manifested in our body.

For we who live are always delivered to death for Jesus' sake, that the life of Jesus also may be manifested in our mortal flesh. So then death is working in us, but life in you.

But since we have the same spirit of faith, according to what is written, "I believed and therefore I spoke," we also believe and therefore speak, knowing that He who raised up the Lord Jesus will also raise us up with Jesus, and will present us with you.

For all things are for your sakes, that grace, having spread through the many, may cause thanksgiving to abound to the glory of God.

Therefore we do not lose heart. But though our outward man is perishing, yet the inward man is being renewed day by day.

For our light affliction, which is but for a moment, is working for us a far more exceeding and eternal weight of glory, while we do not look at the things which are seen, but at the things which are not seen. For the things which are seen are temporary, but the things which are not seen are eternal (2 Corinthians 4:8-18 NKJV).

Notice how Paul's entire outlook is transformed. He doesn't overcome his fear by using a psychological technique—the overcoming is implicit in the transformation. Consequently, though he feels fear as a natural God-given faculty for recognizing danger, he doesn't suffer illegitimate fear. That death is "at work" in him, through constant risk and stress, is relatively unimportant. Provided he is serving the church, and God is being glorified, his present hardships are a mere "light affliction." Like clouds, they are here today and will be gone tomorrow.

Not many of us would describe what he went through as a "light affliction." But for Paul such dangers were a seeding bed where the power of God could grow. "I can do all things through Christ which strengthens me," he wrote to the Philippians, ". . . and my God shall supply all your need according to his riches in glory by Christ Jesus" (Philippians 4:13,19). Was he comfortably ensconced in a posh penthouse apartment when he said that, or sitting in some magnificent Roman high-rise in a recliner, watching color TV? Was he munching on chocolates, writing his letter with a $150 gold pen, under a six-way lamp, on nonglare paper? Hardly! When Paul said, "I can do all things," he was cooped up in one of Nero's cells awaiting execution.

The Western mind rebels at that concept. To us it seems only good sense for a man in Paul's position to go about his business using the most comfortable divine gifts of wealth and influence. We cannot understand how "I can do all things" goes hand in hand with total powerlessness. We cannot understand how the attainment of goals is furthered by perpetual exposure to danger and pain. Yet for Paul the two are as inseparable as magnets. He was happy to forgo even the blessing of health for the sake of the kingdom. Why? Because the greater his weakness, the greater his capacity to receive the power of God:

> Therefore I take pleasure in infirmities, in reproaches, in necessities, in persecutions, in distresses for Christ's sake: for when I am weak, then am I strong (2 Corinthians 12:10).

This topsy-turvy logic has some pretty shattering implications, though I am not concerned with those now. I emphasize the point only to make it clear that God's dynamism is not available to us because we are strong, but rather because we are weak. And the weaker we are, the more available it is.

It follows that we must be honest about our weakness. It is a universal human failing to put on a brave face and pretend everything is okay when it plainly isn't. Assuming that sort of "power" for the sake of keeping up appearances only compounds the problem by preventing us from receiving the real power. We are doing ourselves no service if we talk down our fear instead of facing up to it as a weakness. Paul was so determined not to lead the Corinthians into this particular error that he deliberately exposed himself to fears in order to show that it was God, and not he, who had the power over them:

*Very
Imp.*

> I was with you in weakness, and in fear, and in much trembling . . . that your faith should not stand in the wisdom of men, but in the power of God (1 Corinthians 2:3,5).

Paul knew Who was the Source of that power and how important it was to stay "plugged in" by faith in Christ. Take the plug out, and the lamp will fail. Keep it in, and a light is shed that drives back every shadow of fear. Think of every bad experience that could ever happen to you—contemplate all of your worst fears—and you will still be able to say with Paul, ". . . in all these things we are more than conquerors through him that loved us" (Romans 8:30).

When I was a boy, I read the story of the martyrdom of John and Betty Stamm. It made an indelible impression on me. They were beheaded, but by all accounts they remained calm and serene right up to the moment of their execution. That was the spirit of dynamism.

The Christian superperson

Finally, let me add a word of caution.

I have used Paul as an example of dynamism because his circumstances and his faith are painted in the Scripture with bold colors. The two together make a striking combination. But I am aware that by doing this I run the risk of reinforcing a minor heresy of the evangelical churches, namely that Paul is a champion of faith who should be imitated in every possible respect.

Clearly there are many ways in which we should imitate him. He invited believers to do that. But God's dynamism in Paul, like God's dynamism in everyone else, is to some extent a unique phenomenon. We are not all meant to be miniature Pauls or Paulines. The Bible doesn't commend uniformity of character and gifts, and in practical terms, for everyone to strive for the sort of personal dynamism that Paul had is as ridiculous as using all the power in your house for toasters and nothing else. So I'd like to explode the myth of the forthright, extroverted, omnicompetent Christian superperson. You can be dynamic and ungodly, just as you can be reserved and deeply spiritual! I doubt whether Paul himself would have matched our mental stereotype if we'd met him. So why lay so much stress on appearances?

God's dynamism does not necessarily result in a "dynamic" personality. It may do so, but it is important to recognize that the quiet person can be filled with God's power just as easily as the loud and boisterous one, only in a more low-key and unpretentious way. To go back to the analogy of electricity, some people are toasters, others are lights, still others are burglar alarms. Someone may be an electric toothbrush. It doesn't really matter—the important point is that you are to be filled with God's power to perform your own special task.

Of course, right now your purpose in plugging into God's power is to tackle your fear. We have seen that weakness is no obstacle to that. In fact, if we take Paul's example seriously, it appears that weakness provides the opportunity to use God's power.

But if Paul had written to Timothy, "Fear is overcome by power," none of us would be much further along. We need something to get a grip on dynamism, a handle on the drill to help us use it.

That handle is love.

11

Deliverance Through Devotion

I am calling love "devotion" for a special purpose.

Love, in common parlance, is fast losing the rich flavor of meaning it possesses in the Bible. A character on a TV drama is likely to tell a women he loves her, and ten minutes later be suing for divorce. I don't deny that the scriptwriter had in mind a strong emotion when he used the word "love." The problem is he never went beyond it. The same happened in the '60's and early '70's when love was taken up as a political slogan. Everyone agreed with the Beatles that "all we need is love," but because love was understood as an emotion, it had about as much effect on world affairs as throwing feathers at a tank.

Love is more than emotion. It involves commitment. You know that well enough if you have children. People without children are apt to sentimentalize family life, as though it were all beach parties and barbecues. Now I'm a great believer in the family, but I also know that parents are put to the test. There are times when children are desperately annoying, when they get under your feet, break windows in the greenhouse, or ask you to do something at the moment you're stepping out the door. If love were all emotion it would be conspicuously absent at a time like that! But, in fact, it isn't absent. We love our children even when they drive us crazy. We are committed to them.

It is this committed love I am calling devotion. But how does this committed love, this devotion, help us as a "handle" for power? Well, the answer starts not with our devotion, but with God's.

Know you are loved

The same distinction I have made between emotional love and committed love also applies to God.

I don't know how many times I've heard people say "God is love," or something similar, as though the existence of a benign Old Man snoring gently on a cloud of cotton wool was supposed to be a comfort to the sick and suffering. Is God's love so remote He pays no attention to evil, injustice, and cruelty? Or is He blithely sleeping through it all? Let's assume for a moment that this God is not asleep, but that He cares enough about His human family to intervene when evil gets the upper hand. What might He do, if His love were ruled directly by His emotions?

The answer is difficult to think about. After all, God's family hasn't paid much attention to Him over the years. If we are annoyed by the occasional disobedience of our children, just imagine the weight of provocation that bears on our heavenly Father. Why on earth should he still love us? Look what happened in the days of Noah: "God saw that the wickedness of man was great in the earth. . . . And the Lord said, I will destroy man whom I have created" (Genesis 6:5,7).

God, after that single act of judgment, tempered justice with forbearance because of the commitment of His love. In Hebrew, there is a special word for it, translated in the King James Version as "kindness," "loving kindness," and "mercy." It means love with commitment, love that does not walk out when the other party gives offense. It is used frequently, for there are plenty of times in the Old Testament when God's people push His patience to the limit:

> Nevertheless my loving kindness will I not
> utterly take from him, nor suffer my faithfulness to
> fail. My covenant will I not break, nor alter the thing
> that is gone out of my lips (Psalm 89:33,34).

God's devotion, in fact, is what turned the Old Testament into the New, what makes Christian faith possible. As Paul says in Romans, "God commendeth his love towards us, in that, while we were yet sinners, Christ died for us" (Romans 5:8). Mere emotional love is incapable of commitment like that. It turns aside and says of the disobedient, "They've

very
&mp <

made their bed—now they can lie in it!" If God's love had <
been a matter of feelings, there would have been no incarnation, no cross, no redemption.

But Christ died. God acted in expression of His love for us
though we had done nothing to deserve it. And this action
had two effects.

First, it provided concrete evidence that God cares for us.
I'm not talking about the sleepy benignity of the Old Man on
his cotton wool cloud. "Care" here is the kind of practical love
and support a father extends to his children, watching out for
them, protecting them, ensuring the best for them, even—
and I don't say it lightly—disciplining them if they go astray.
Trust in the Father's devotion to us is what Jesus encouraged
when He said, "Come unto me, all ye that labor and are heavy
laden, and I will give you rest" (Matthew 11:28). Peter advo-
cates it in his first epistle: "Humble yourselves, therefore,
under the mighty hand of God . . . Casting all your care
upon him; for he careth for you" (1 Peter 5:6,7). And, of
course, Paul refers to it in that famous passage from Romans 8:

> We know that all things work together for good
> to them that love God, to them who are the called
> according to his purpose. For whom he did fore-
> know, he also did predestinate to be conformed to
> the image of his Son, that he might be the firstborn
> among many brethren (Romans 8:28,29).

So be assured that whatever fears you face, you face them in
company with your heavenly Father. In the crucifixion, Jesus
faced reduction of human fear. He knows what it's like, and
He overcame it. Nothing that will happen to you in the
future, none of those fear-scenarios you toy with in your
mind, will come to pass unless the experience is for your
ultimate good. Take comfort from that.

Make love your aim

The second effect of God's love expressed in Jesus is to
provide us with an example to follow. And it is in the following of this example that we have our handle on the power of
God.

Example is really too mild a word. To love was the only one of Jesus' instructions He called a commandment. Listen to Him talking to His disciples on the night of the Last Supper:

> "This is my commandment, that ye love one another, as I have loved you. Greater love hath no man than this, that a man lay down his life for his friends . . . . These things I command you, that ye love one another (John 15:12,13,17).

Once again, this love is more than emotion. Jesus isn't asking us to generate mushy feelings for each other. It isn't even good enough to talk about love, as though saying it were the same as doing it. "Greater love hath no man than this, that a man *lay down his life for his friends*." The love God wants us to have is a practical love, the self-giving love Jesus showed us on the cross. Without that practical expression, the love in us will be as meaningless as the electrical signals in a telephone wire are without an earpiece to turn them into words. Unexpressed, love is unintelligible.

This love, which I am calling devotion, is distinguished by its own Greek word in the New Testament—*agape*. My own personal definition of *agape* is "the outgoing of the totality of your being to another in beneficence and help." Almost invariably the writers of the epistles unpack it like a suitcase, to show you what is really inside.

> Put on therefore, as the elect of God, holy and beloved, bowels of mercies, kindness, humbleness of mind, meekness, longsuffering; forbearing one another, and forgiving one another, if any man have a quarrel against any: even as Christ forgave you, so also do ye.
> And above all these things put on charity, which is the bond of perfectness (Colossians 3:12-14).

So love is something we do, not something we feel. But how does that help us use the power of God to overcome fear?

It helps in three ways.

1. *Love repels fear*. In his first epistle John says, "There is no fear in love, but perfect love casteth out fear" (1 John 4:18). In other words, there is a quality about love itself that dissolves fear as the sun melts the winter snow. As Albert Barnes says in his commentary:

> Nothing will do more to inspire courage, to make a man fearless of danger, or ready to endure privation and persecution, than love. The love of country, and wife, and children, and home, makes the most timid bold when they are assailed, and the love of Christ and of a dying world nerves the soul to great enterprises, and sustains it in the deepest sorrows (*Notes on the New Testament*, 1949).

2. *Love directs the attention outward*. Fear is fundamentally selfish and introspective. When I am afraid, I fear something that is going to happen to me. Even when I am afraid for someone I love, my fear contemplates my own suffering, my own bereavement. Fear turns me in on myself.

By contrast, devotion is outer-directed. In loving, you find your attention taken up with the happiness and welfare of others. This has the salutary effect of putting your own worries in perspective, for it is the easiest thing in the world, when you are looking inward, to think your fears are unique. Being outer-directed also means, very often, that your mind is buzzing so loud with other people's interests that you simply don't have time to be afraid.

And what if you have a *Big Bad Wolf fear*, where the other person is actually the object of the fear? Well, love helps there, too, because when you love someone you begin to see the difference between the person and the twisted circumstances that have placed him in a position of animosity towards you. "Father, forgive them," said Jesus as the soldiers nailed him to the cross, "for they know not what they do" (Luke 23:34).

The evangelist David Wilkerson found that love helped him in this way when he came face-to-face with the gang leader Nicki Cruz. That gang leader became a friend and colleague. So remember, you may find that loving an enemy makes him into a friend. You might just find he wasn't an enemy in the first place!

3. *Love brings its own reward*. In modern psychiatric jargon I'd reexpress this as "love produces positive feedback." Isn't that a bit selfish? Not really. *Big Bad Wolf fear*, particularly, is encouraged by lack of communication. Haven't you ever heard somebody say, "I don't like so-and-so, she doesn't smile much." I wonder what so-and-so would think if she knew what an effect her gloomy face was having on her colleagues! Devotion expressed in something as simple as a smile can open up bridges of communication and end the negative interaction that fosters suspicion and fear on both sides.

The trigger

Devotion that releases dynamism is part of the transformation the Holy Spirit works in the life of the believer. It undermines the foundations on which fear is built and sets up a new structure in the personality of assurance and trust, against which fear is powerless.

But this structure does not build itself. The Spirit may be the architect, but you are the foreman, and this means that you must have a conscious determination to keep at the job. Maybe you find that a bit daunting. "The problem," you say, "is that it's so hard. Like Nehemiah rebuilding the walls of Jerusalem under the eye of his enemies, I find I'm constantly distracted by my fears."

Well, I am going to show you how you can turn that very fact to your advantage.

Many kinds of fear—and especially *Big Bad Wolf fear*, where the fear-object is rejection by others—come to us, as it were, "on cue." Fear, after all, is a warning signal. It is meant to alert us to danger. So imagine your fear is associated with your boss at the office. Your fear-object is rejection (a snub, a lost promotion), and your fear-scenario is any sort of confrontation with your supervisor. Looked at rationally, the boss is about as much fun as a sore toe. But he is not an ogre. You would be able to handle him if only you hadn't developed an *exaggerated fear* of meeting him.

In that kind of situation you can use devotion directly—not just as a new lifestyle that makes you strong against fear, but as a way of addressing yourself to particular fear-objects. All you need do is determine that whenever you feel the fear, you will put love into action. When the boss comes into the room, instead of ignoring him, say, "Hi! How are you?" Do that, and you will have won a decisive victory over your fear. Why? Because you've given it a new role. You've turned fear into a reminder to love.

I used the image of the handle on the power drill to describe the relationship of dynamism and devotion. When you use fear as a reminder to love, it becomes the trigger. You win over fear by making it work for you. Before, when fear came, you used to say to yourself, "Oh dear, I'd forgotten about that until you reminded me." Now you can say, "Thanks! If you hadn't shown up I'd have missed a chance to show love!"

Redeployed in this way, fear turns up some unexpected benefits. The criticism of others suddenly appears as a free education in improving our performance. The betrayal of friends becomes a chance to show thought for others. And, not surprisingly, many anticipated rejections are averted because our own behavior is no longer reinforcing the pattern of rejection.

Let me illustrate.

When I was 12 years old, my father took me to Camp Barakel, where he was chaplain and main counselor. One day we had to drive to Battle Creek, Michigan, about 50 miles away, but hadn't gone 14 miles before the car stopped. We had run out of gas. This was extraordinary because we'd just filled up. Dad got out to take a look. He soon found the problem. Somebody had driven a spike into the gas tank.

This was a blow. In 1936 Dad's weekly income, which had to feed a family of five, was slightly more than half of what today's American government reckons as the minimum wage. He and my mother certainly lived on faith! The car was an old jalopy, a 1930 Chevrolet. I sometimes say to people that we worked on that car from Monday through Saturday so we could drive it on Sunday. Yet we couldn't have done without it.

As soon as I saw the damage I knew who was responsible. He was a miserable little rascal, a double-distilled bully, and a cocky, incorrigible troublemaker. I wasn't alone in my loathing for him. But when I exploded to Dad, he scolded me and told me not to jump to conclusions.

Fortunately, Dad was able to get help on the highway. We returned to the camp for dinner, but I didn't eat. As the oldest child in the family, I was always concerned about the family finances, and I couldn't imagine how Dad was going to get money to replace the gas tank and fill up for the journey home. My fear turned into hostility when I saw Dad perched on the edge of the dock with his arm around the shoulders of the same little monster who had spiked his tank.

I could not understand Dad's attitude. Yet it is my view now, more than half a century later, that Dad's response made a positive and lasting impression on the boy. He was revealing the spirit of the Lord Jesus. He had every reason not to— he was a young man with three growing boys and a wife whose sickness put a constant drain on funds. He could have let fear of impoverishment drive him into a rage. But he subdued his fear, and turned it into an opportunity for love.

In 1972, I was conducting meetings in the public buildings in Portugal. During that time, the chairman of the crusade, Mr. Matthys Van den Heuvel, hosted a black-tie banquet for the leaders of business, government, education, religion, the media, the professions and the arts. It was as elegant and impeccably executed an affair as I've ever attended. The purpose of Mr. Van den Heuvel and his wife was to present the gospel of Christ Jesus.

I was delighted and surprised at the eager interest of the audience in the teachings of the Bible. After the program was over, the Swiss representative (in Portugal) of one of the large Swiss pharmeceutical companies walked up to Mrs. Van den Heuvel, a raven-haired Swiss lady of high standing who, along with her husband, subjugated everything they were and had to the communication of the gospel.

"This has been a fascinating experience for me," he said. "You have given me the opportunity to meet people I have long wanted to meet. I must tell you, though, I am an atheist."

Mrs. Van den Heuvel looked him in the eye, smiled graciously and said, "Oh, I am sorry."

"Why are you sorry?"

"Because God is so big, and you are so little, and you will need Him. And you don't even know where to go for help. I feel so sorry for you. I will pray for you."

His eyes widened. I learned a lesson from that. Mrs. Van den Heuvel didn't try to rebut him. She didn't argue. She didn't give him a polemic on the resurrection of Christ. She just showed genuine Christian compassion and love in a way that man could not ignore.

She might easily have succumbed to fear. She might have thought, "Here's this man, one of the most important foreign businessmen in Portugal. He is well connected. Since we are both Swiss, he may belittle me when he sees our mutual friends in Switzerland. He may think I'm a fanatic."

None of that. She simply turned the temptation to fear into an opportunity for love—and who knows what effect that had on the man's eternal destiny?

Using fear as a trigger works even on very extreme fears.

A while ago, a woman was attacked and raped in Atlanta by a group of young felons. It was the kind of attack that could leave enduring scars and cause petrifying fear every time an unknown man said good morning to her, be it in a country club or a church, an office or a school. Those scars never appeared, because she turned the temptation to fear into an opportunity to love. She forgave the men and made known to them her concern for their conversion. It had a powerful impact on them, and it released her from the traumas of fear.

I had a friend in Grand Rapids, Michigan, whose wife, eight-year-old son and and baby daughter were murdered by the man who was rooming with them. The 1929 depression wasn't long past. The boarder was an educator; he had needed accommodation, and my friend had needed the money.

It would have seemed natural, after the triple murder, for my friend to fear for the safety of loved ones every time he left home. But no. Instead, he started writing to the murderer and even paid him an occasional visit at the Michigan State penitentiary. He did it for 50 years. And far from being scarred by fear, my friend was one of the most radiant men I have ever known. He had won over fear through love.

I am absolutely convinced that the answer to fear in all shattered relationships is love. Joseph, who rose from slavery in Egypt to second in command to Pharaoh, was reconciled to the brothers who had abducted him as a child. He might still have feared them years later when they appeared before him as victims of famine, asking for grain. He might have been prompted by fear to turn them away empty-handed. But he was not. He used the temptation to fear as an opportunity to love.

In all broken relationships, fear can be won over by love. Children who suffered abuse from their parents can win over fear. So can the victims of abuse in marriage—and I mean men as well as women. John Wesley suffered abuse from his wife. She threw hot coffee in his face, pulled him up by his hair, and humiliated him before those he was preaching to. Yet the very fact that history has forgotten Mrs. Wesley is testimony to the power Wesley had over his fear. Like Joseph, he turned the temptation to fear into an opportunity to love.

But, of course, that doesn't come about by magic. Fear may be the trigger on the power drill of dynamism, but it's up to you to press it. If fear comes along, and you don't turn it into opportunity, you are back where you started. So how do you take yourself in hand?

12

Deliverance Through Discipline

Dynamism, devotion and discipline aren't three separate techniques from which you make a selection or rejection according to a whim of the moment. They form a single coordinated approach to the problem of fear. Apart from the other components, each one is about as much use as a single player on a football field.

You could summarize their relationship like this: "To apply dynamism through devotion requires discipline."

Discipline is the quarterback of the outfit. Without it, nothing works. Of course, inspired by pity or conscience, you can practice devotion on the spur of the moment. If a member of your church congregation is dying in the hospital, for instance, you might make a mental resolution to visit him once a week. Assuming he lasts only a month, you will have no trouble keeping the promise. But what if he has a remission? Will that original impulse of love or pity keep you driving to the hospital every Sunday afternoon for two years? I doubt it! In order to maintain your commitment you will need a motivating force that does not fade—a quarterback who keeps the team organized right to the end of the game.

But there lies the problem with discipline. "If I cannot rely on love to motivate me," you say, "how can I be sure of exercising the required discipline? Might I not wake up one morning and think, 'Today I really can't be bothered with this?' Where is my discipline then?"

My answer is that you are thinking of discipline in the wrong way. Naturally, you cannot be certain how you will feel on any given day in the future. More likely than not, on some days you will prefer to neglect your commitments and do something to please yourself. But discipline isn't a *feeling* that you ought to do your duty. Such feelings, if you get them, originate in your conscience. They will prompt you, but they can never force you to do something you are "not in the mood for" or "can't be bothered with."

Discipline is a momentum of good habits. It is easier to push a moving car than to move a stalled one. Discipline is like that. It is harder to overcome the initial inertia, but it gets easier as the new habits sink deeper and deeper into your personality. Eventually the momentum is so great that stopping is harder than continuing. Consequently when I talk about developing discipline, I am not trying to infuse you with a new state of mind, a new feeling, or a new way of looking at commitments. I am recommending a set of positive actions which, with about the same amount of effort you would put into jump-starting a car with the cable connections to a power source, you can use to get your spiritual life moving under its own power.

I know that God is the source of all true power. That doesn't release you from personal effort and responsibility. God gives you breath, but *you* must do the breathing. He doesn't do it for you.

These positive actions all work toward the same objective—opening your life and consciousness to the Holy Spirit. There are two reasons for this.

One, the love through which dynamism is released cannot be generated by your own willpower. Let's face it. Most of us do a poor job of loving even our friends and family, let alone those who make us afraid. Are you really capable of loving an intimidating boss, your critical colleagues, or the men who wrecked your home in a burglary with an open, self-giving love? Not in your own human strength. We need the vital, renewing touch of the Holy Spirit on our lives if God's amazing transformation is going to set us free from our fears.

Two, discipline in spiritual matters is the foundation for all other disciplines. You cannot hope to have the self-control necessary to win over fear if you are not willing to learn the discipline of fellowship with God, whose love is the antidote to all fear. Be disciplined in your relationship with God, and self-control in other areas will follow naturally.

Five divisions of discipline

1. *Quiet time*. The most powerful countermeasure against
fear is the awareness of walking in fellowship with God.
That's why beginning each day with a quiet time is so essential.

Let me put before you this question. If Jesus were with you
in His human form and promised to live in your home, go
with you wherever you went, advise you on every decision,
and personally encourage you during every depression—
would you then suffer fear? I don't think you would. Now
consider what Paul meant when he wrote to the Colossians
about "Christ in you, the hope of glory" (Colossians 1:27). He
is not with us; He is *in* us. God has sent His Holy Spirit to
guide us into all truth, to undergird us with power, to illumi-
nate us with His light.

"But that's not the same as seeing Him," you say.

I agree—it's better! All you need do is draw the benefits of
God's presence within you. The best way to start is by the
disciplined use of your quiet time.

I once traveled for three weeks with Dr. and Mrs. Han
Kyung Chik of Korea. Every morning they were up at five
o'clock for the dawn prayer meeting. This man—pastor, educator, humanitarian, statesman, author—not only begins his
day with at least one hour of quiet time, but he bows his head
inconspicuously in prayer before every activity, event, and
conversation. I have watched him visit businessmen in their
offices. He would sit down, and for perhaps 15 seconds he
would quietly bow his head and close his eyes. I knew he was
committing that particular conversation to the Lord.

What a deterrent to fear! What a guarantee for God's victory! I have no doubt that Dr. Han's serenity, after a life of
harassment by the Communists (who on several occasions
dispossessed him and chased him out of home and town) can
be attributed to his quiet time with God. His face is a mosaic
of cheerful calm.

What does a quiet time consist of? Chiefly, two elements:
prayer and Bible study. It is a time of communing with God,

being in His presence in an undisturbed and conscious way. If you are married, or have a good friend, you will know what it is like simply to be with somebody you are close to. Contact doesn't depend on words alone. Yet words are important. There are matters we want to make known to God, wrongs we want to confess, blessings for which we want to give thanks. And there are promptings from the Holy Spirit that we hear either in meditation or through reading God's Word, the Bible.

Bible study, of course, doesn't have to be tied into a personal quiet time any more than prayer does. I applaud a group of high-powered young businessmen in Atlanta who meet for a Bible study every Friday morning. They find it inspiring and mind-broadening to cross denominational barriers to fellowship with their peers in the study of God's Word. I have talked to some of these men, and have every reason to conclude that God uses this Friday morning Bible study to still their hearts and to dissipate the fears arising from their professional concerns.

I could go into a lot more detail on both aspects of the quiet time. I won't, because I've covered the topic extensively elsewhere. If you want further guidance I suggest you look up the fourth section in *How to Win Over Worry*, where I devote four chapters specifically to prayer. Remember, quiet time is a key to victory over fear.

2. *Fellowship*. One of the blessings of the Friday morning study group I referred to is that it combines fellowship with God and fellowship with others.

That second sort of fellowship is important. Contemporary society—especially in America, with her frenetic lifestyle and TV churches—too easily squeezes out fellowship with others. But the Bible clearly teaches that no Christian is an island. It isn't an unwarranted distortion of the text to render 1 John 4:20 as follows: "How can you say you love God whom you have not seen, when you have no fellowship with your brothers whom you have seen?"

At the time of this writing my father is 90 years old. He attends Sunday school faithfully. He hasn't missed a week since 1923. Even when he was in the hospital for surgery, one *Father* of the classes he taught met in his hospital room so he would be able to keep up his record and minister to the business and professional men who make up his class. Dad attends every Sunday morning worship service, every Sunday evening service, every Wednesday night prayer meeting. He attends every church function including revival meetings and Bible study weeks.

In his knowledge of the Bible, and of Greek and Hebrew, Dad is probably the equal, if not superior, to any of the ministers to whom he listens or for whom he prays. His pastor, Dr. J. Hoffman Harris, who built the church from a handful of people to a membership of over five thousand while founding 27 thriving daughter churches, would be the first to agree to that. And yet Dad is unstinting in his praise for the younger man. "I don't believe there is anywhere in the world a man more compassionate and more gifted in the area of pastoral leadership than Dr. Harris," he exults.

Dad lives alone. He drives his own car and takes care of his own meals. He speaks an average of three times a week. He prays for long periods at the break of each day. He has read the Bible through 102 times. But he does not allow that to anesthetize him with the needle of smugness, or seduce him with the idea that his background or advancing years exempt him from the need for fellowship.

Though he is 25 years past normal retiring age he displays no evidence of fear. I attribute this remarkable lifestyle to discipline that touches every area of his life—quiet time, physical exercise, dietary control, reading, memorizing, and so on. But it is his fellowship with others that I believe keeps him youthful in spirit and attractive to other people. When a group of youngsters went on retreat recently, they insisted on taking him along. He was the center of attention. They marveled that he could play the piano, and marveled even more that he could play the cornet at the same time!

We all need fellowship, and we all benefit from it. On one occasion when my wife and I were relaxing for a couple of days in Florida, we attended the Wednesday night prayer service of the First Baptist Church. Dr. Avery, for years the senior pastor, squinted his eyes as he looked in my direction. Finally he said, "Is that John Haggai I see back there?"

I assured him it was.

He then went off into an effusive expression of appreciation that we had come to the meeting, and bemoaned the fact that so few people on vacation followed our example. I was downright embarrassed! We had come because we felt we needed to come, because we wanted fellowship. Dr. Avery was loading us up with laurels we didn't deserve.

The point is that fellowship enriches not only the lives of others, but your own life as well. And that is a powerful ally against fear.

3. Testimony. I can't explain it, nor can I back up my argument with chapter and verse, but I have been convinced for some time that those who exercise the discipline of telling what God has done for them receive, whether or not they realize it, a freedom from fear.

Testimony reinforces faith, and fear cannot cohabit with faith.

I think of the late R. G. Le Tourneau, inventor and manufacturer of earth-moving equipment. He would come to my crusades in the '50's and '60's and give his testimony on a Saturday night. No matter where this man was, he would talk about the Lord. I think of Bob Glaze, the Dallas businessman and civic leader; Paul Meyer, the president of the Success Motivation Institute; John Bolten, a multinational businessman living in Germany; and Otto Bohl, the European investment banker—men who discuss their faith as easily as they discuss their families. Observing these men convinces me they are free from fears that hold so many men hostage.

Businessmen Stanley Tam has testified by writing a book about his Christian odyssey. You read between the lines of his book robust faith, not wretched fear. I've never met Stanley Tam, but I was in Toronto recently to address a group of business and professional people, and at my table two men (one of Canada's leading developers, and the Canadian head of Apple Computer) mentioned his name. They told of the powerful impact Stanley Tam had made on them. They were fascinated by his life and witness, and wanted to know more about him.

When I talk about giving testimony, incidentally, I'm not referring to those earnest believers who testify only in religious circles, at church services and convocations. I mean those who do their testifying "in their stride," who are able to integrate testimony into their everyday conversation as naturally as they would the weather, the World Series, or Soviet-American relations. In many ways, testifying on home ground is too easy. When you talk about your faith to those outside the cozy confines of the church, you are taking a far greater personal risk. And even though I am sure that those who testify in this way do not publicize their spiritual experience in order to overcome fear, years of observation have shown me that it has this effect.

I heartily recommend, therefore, that you make it part of your spiritual discipline to witness naturally and easily about what the Lord has done in your life.

(4.) *Obedience*. Not everyone is brilliant. Not everyone has a high IQ. Not everyone is handsome or beautiful. Not everyone is well-connected socially or from a famous family. Not everyone is wealthy, charming, or sensitive. But anybody, anybody at all, can be obedient.

Obedience dissipates fear, just as disobedience fosters it. Think of Saul in the Old Testament. God had told him not to bring back any livestock from the enemy camp. He disobeyed. He could not resist taking a few of the prize cattle and the best sheep. When the prophet Samuel demanded an explanation, Saul began a long and sanctimonious diatribe on how God had blessed him and given him victory in battle. Samuel cut in with a truth that, to his dying day, Saul never really grasped: "To obey is better than sacrifice, and to hearken than the fat of rams" (1 Samuel 15:22).

Study the life of Saul and I think you will agree he was a man dominated by fear. There was no observable reason for him to be afraid. Physically, he stood head and shoulders above his companions. Vocationally, God had picked him out for leadership. Spiritually, in his life and leadership role, he enjoyed the mentoring of the prophet Samuel. Financially, he was rich. He had everything going for him. Why was it he fell into the clutches of fear? There is only one explanation—disobedience.

On the other hand look at the experience of Dr. Harry Ironside. Almost 60 years ago Moody Memorial Church asked Dr. Ironside to become its pastor. Since Dr. Ironside worshiped with the Plymouth Brethren, this put him on the spot. The Brethren do not believe in an ordained clergy. They believe in the priesthood of all believers, which to them means that any member of the church, and not just the pastor, can bring a message to the meeting.

Dr. Ironside had a real battle with his conscience. He told his friends, "I received this call from Moody, and in prayer I said, 'Lord, what about the Brethren?' Yet a second time the call came, and once again I asked the Lord, 'Lord, what about the Brethren?' A third time the call came from Moody for me to become the pastor, and I asked, 'Lord, what about the Brethren?' It was then that the Lord said to me, 'Harry, you go to Moody, and I'll take care of the Brethren.' "

The Brethren always respected Dr. Ironside, and he always loved them. But he had to obey, and in obedience he had victory over his fears. I had the pleasure of knowing Dr. Ironside. My wife was one of his favorite soloists. He requested her to do solo work at his anniversary services when she was in Chicago. I am still impressed, favorably impressed, with his easy demeanor and his continuing victory over fear—a victory which, being privy to some of his devastating personal heartaches, I know wasn't cheap.

God asks hard decisions of all of us from time to time. Believe me, the right way is always the way of obedience. It may not seem like it at the time, but the road God takes you on will always bring you safely through your fears.

5. *Service*. My mother never knew good health. She suffered from pernicious anemia, emphysema and angina, among many other ailments.

Forty-five years before her death the doctors said she would not live. She lived to be 80 years old. And throughout the course of her life, with great discipline, she served others. My father said that she could write legibly in such small handwriting that she cheated the post office back in the days of the one-cent postcard! She could get more on a postcard than most people can in a letter. Into her later years she kept up her correspondence with friends all over the world, a constant stream of messages that gave hope, encouragement, and spiritual counsel.

From the human standpoint mother had every reason to be terror-stricken. The hours she spent in doctors' offices, the regimen of medication and shots—all this would have been too much for most people to handle. But in serving others she forgot herself, and demonstrated that fear cannot coexist with love.

13

Getting Off the Ground

I could have called this chapter "Discipline Two." Remember that formula?

$$\text{DELIVERANCE FROM FEAR} = \text{DYNAMISM} + \text{DEVOTION} + \text{DISCIPLINE.}$$

Discipline has two uses. The first one—the vital need to be disciplined in your spiritual life—I have discussed already. But you also will need to be disciplined in maintaining and executing your overall strategy against fear.

The reason is simple. Think about the individual soldiers in an army. Each is only a man, with a limited amount of strength. Each is probably strangely fearful on the eve of a battle. What gives the army its strength? I submit that the crucial factor is discipline, a dedication to duty that turns a group of individuals into a fighting unit. Did the armies of Rome sweep across the ancient world because they were better equipped or more courageous than their enemies? No. They founded and established the great empire of Rome on the bedrock of an iron discipline. And what about the famous King Harold at the Battle of Hastings—was he defeated by William the Conqueror in 1066 because he lacked swords or armor? No. He lost because his men, in panic, broke their lines at a crucial moment in the conflict. They were undisciplined.

Your discipline can be the deciding factor in the battle against fear. Develop it, and your life will be enhanced. Neglect it, and the fight for a productive and fulfilling life is all but lost.

What I purpose to do in this chapter is suggest a step-by-step program for you to follow.

279

I emphasize that it isn't a new piece of advice given in addition to the formula. The advice Paul gave to Timothy is wholly adequate to overcome fear; in that sense I have nothing to add to it. But as I said in the last chapter, the three elements of the formula cannot be put into effect one at a time, anymore than you can walk using only one leg. Success in your battle with fear comes by using the three elements in combination. This program is designed to do exactly that, to help you "get off the ground" by applying the Timothy Formula to your own personal situation, and start living that new quality of transformed life that will sound the death knell for your fears.

You are waiting in the departure lounge. You have your boarding card in your hand, waiting for the boarding call. In a few moments you will strap yourself into your airplane seat in anticipation of the takeoff. Before takeoff, I want to ask the question posed at the beginning of this section, a question to which I hope you've already given a firm positive answer: Are you 100 percent committed to making this life-changing journey against fear?

I cannot affirm long or loudly enough that to handle fear you must face reality.

In "Trouble Ahead Needn't Bother you," Jackie Robinson, Brooklyn Dodgers baseball star, recounts an important lesson learned August 19, 1945, the day Branch Rickey, former President of the Brooklyn Dodgers asked him to become the first Negro to play in major league baseball:

> "Mr. Rickey," I said, "it sounds like a dream come true—not only for me but for my race. . . .There will be trouble ahead—for you, for me, for my people, and for baseball."
>
> "Trouble ahead," Rickey rolled the phrase over his lips as though he liked the sound. "You know, Jackie, I was a small boy when I took my first train ride. On the same train was an old couple, also riding for the first time. We were going through the

Rocky Mountains. The old man sitting by the window looked forward and said to his wife, 'Trouble ahead, Ma! We're high up over a precipice and we're gonna run right off.'

"To my boyish ears the noise of wheels repeated "Trouble-ahead-trouble-ahead. . . .' I never hear train wheels to this day but what I think of this. But our train course bent into a tunnel right after the old man spoke, and we came out on the other side of the mountain. That's the way it is with most trouble ahead in this world, Jackie—if we use the common sense and courage God gave us. But you've got to study the hazards and build wisely. . . .

"God is with us in this, Jackie," Mr. Rickey said quietly. "You know your Bible. It's good, simple Christianity for us to face realities and to recognize what we're up against. . . .We've got to fight out our problems together with tact and common sense."*

I love my brothers and sisters in Christ, and I don't say this as a put-down, but frankly, unreality has paralyzed a large segment of the Christian church in its viselike grip. How often I've heard church members stand up and say, "Jesus saves; He keeps; He satisfies!" while their faces are long enough to suck marbles out of a gopher hole. Others, wearing tense expressions, shout their praises so loudly they remind me of cheerleaders desperately trying to rally supporters whose team is losing the game.

Pretending that everything is okay is not the solution to your fear, even if the pretended behavior is what your friends expect of you. A man who has fallen overboard doesn't think to himself, "I'd better not shout for help; somebody might think I'm in trouble." He yells like crazy until he catches the attention of someone who throws him a life belt. His need

*Norman Vincent Peale, ed., *Faith Made Them Champions* (New York: Prentice-Hall, Inc., 1954), p.238-39.

dictates his actions. And if you have a problem with fear, that's the way it should be for you. Acknowledge it. Bring it out into the open. You don't have to go around your church or office telling your friends about it, but at least don't hide it from yourself.

Step One—Analyze your fear

Once you've got the fear in your sights, take a long hard look at it.

You may find it helpful to set aside an hour or two in quiet solitude, with a notepad, to make sure you have recorded every facet of your fear. Use the categories I suggest in Part 1 of this book. Divide the fear-object(s) from the fear-scenario(s), pinpointing as accurately as you can what persons or events you fear. Decide whether it is a *Wild Wood fear* or a *Big Bad Wolf fear*, or a combination of the two. Become thoroughly acquainted with your fear, just as a skilled hunter becomes thoroughly acquainted with the habits of his prey.

Now turn your attention to the danger on which the fear is based. Is there a difference—a *rationality gap*—between the danger as it really is, and the danger as you perceive it? You may find that a hard question to answer, because levels of danger can be difficult to assess. But try to find out everything you can about the danger. Is that disaster you are so afraid of really likely to occur? How often does it occur to people like you? And what about the results? Is the event you fear going to leave you physically or mentally incapacitated, financially ruined, socially devastated, or just a bit out-of-pocket and a little shamefaced? Believe me, there are many Americans who nourish tremendous fear over trivialities.

It may help to gain a perspective on your own fear by comparing it with the fear of trusted friends. Say you have a teenage daughter about to leave home for the university, and you are terrified something may happen to her. She may get hooked on drugs, compromise her morals, or lose her faith. You will probably know a couple with a daughter in college.

What has been their experience? Is there anything about life at the university that is really dangerous? How do your friends cope with any dangers they imagine their daughter has to face? Are they able to cope with it?

This analysis of your fears and possible dangers may lead you to one of the following conclusions.

First, you may feel your fear reaction is entirely justified. If you are about to undergo major surgery, for instance, you will probably feel fear in anticipation of pain or possible death. You may also fear that you will be unable to provide for your family and loved ones. You have legitimate cause for fear.

Second, you may feel that the danger before you is making you more afraid than it should—in other words, you are suffering from *exaggerated fear*. A lot of women facing major surgery fear rejection through the deterioration of their youthful beauty. It is true that younger women are more likely to attract a certain sort of attention from the opposite sex. But there is vastly more to a person than a shapely figure and a flawless complexion. Fear of aging in that situation is usually *exaggerated fear*.

Third, you may feel incapable of distinguishing the real danger from the perceived danger.

This confusion may arise in two ways. Let's assume that you are about to take a trip to a country in the midst of civil war. Just before you go, you hear there has been a flare-up near the city you plan to visit. How much danger will you encounter? You don't know. You may be in no danger at all. On the other hand, you may be risking your neck! You are frightened because of a lack of information about the danger. And rightly so. As long as you cannot quantify the danger ahead, your God-given faculty of fear will urge you to be cautious.

But imagine now that a reliable authority tells you your destination is completely safe. Fear can no longer be justified from lack of information. Yet you continue to feel scared. You are convinced, in the teeth of evidence to the contrary, that you are going to be blown up or shot down the moment you step off the plane. When someone tries to reassure you by showing you newspaper reports that verify the safety of the area, you refuse to believe the reports. You are incapable of distinguishing the real danger from your perception of supposed danger.

Clearly your problem in the last instance is far more serious. With the best will in the world, you cannot close the *rationality gap* and consequently your view of reality is distorted. You are like a blindfolded man trying to cross a busy highway. If this is your situation, I advise you to enlist the expertise of a good friend, or perhaps a pastor or reliable professional counselor, to provide you with a touchstone—an outside view of your fear that is not blinkered by your faulty perception. If you are crossing that highway, you want to go with someone who can see the traffic!

Step Two—Confront your dangers

The object of the first step is to see your danger as it really is. Until you can do that you will never be able to act effectively against it. Your faulty perception may immobilize you as it immobilized the Israelites when the 12 spies whom Moses had sent to reconnoiter the land of Canaan returned.

> They told him and said, We came unto the land whither thou sentest us, and surely it floweth with milk and honey; and this is the fruit of it. Nevertheless the people be strong that dwell in the land, and the cities are walled, and very great: and moreover we saw the children of Anak there. . . .We be not able to go up against the people; for they are stronger than we (Numbers 13:27,28,31).

You can detect in this passage how faulty perception led these men to overestimate the danger and saddled them with *exaggerated fears.* Only Joshua and Caleb saw the danger in the true context of God's call to them to occupy the Promised Land. But seeing the danger correctly wasn't the same as overcoming it. The danger was still great enough to tempt the Israelites back to the security of bondage and brick making in Egypt. Another move was called for, a move that I am calling the second step of the strategy for winning over fear. Moses wasn't content to see the danger for what it was; when he saw it, he led his people to confront it.

If you haven't already read the biography of Paul J. Meyer, founder of the Success Motivation Institute, I suggest you do it. It's an object lesson in confronting danger.

Paul Meyer started from zero; some people might say he started from below zero. He had no money, no connections, no college degree. Yet by the age of 25 he had built the largest insurance business in history. Two years later he was flat broke, the victim of crooked dealing in the parent company's leadership. At this point his preacher friend and mentor, Dr. William M. (Bill) Hinson, introduced Paul to Jarrell Mc-Cracken, Hinson's old college friend. As a result of that meeting, Paul Meyer joined forces with McCracken, the founder of WORD, then a neophyte and struggling publishing company in Waco, Texas.

When Jarrell McCracken visited Paul Meyer's magnificent Miami home, he chuckled and said, "We can't afford to pay you." Paul offered to come to WORD on a straight commission basis. In no time at all he had put WORD on the map. But his commissions compared favorably with the net profit of the entire company! This was not acceptable to the company, and a parting of the ways resulted. Once again Paul Meyer was left with a family, no position, and no income.

He went to see Bill Hinson, who gave him this advice: "You're at your happiest when you're helping other people move toward their potential. Why don't you start a business designed to help thousands of people in the same way you're already helping a few, face-to-face?"

At first the idea seemed ludicrous. There were any number of ways a project like that could run aground. But Paul Meyer looked coolly at the dangers, and after making meticulous plans, he launched Success Motivation Institute. He now does business in 75 countries of the world, and is the leader of a firmly established, financially sound organization.

Like Moses, Paul Meyer could have let himself be paralyzed by the thought of what might go wrong. After all, things had gone sour for him on previous occasions. He refused to allow previous setbacks to distort his perception with *exaggerated fear*. He confronted danger and planned to knock it out.

Of course, there are as many ways of confronting danger as there are dangers to confront. But these various ways of confronting danger do have a common feature—what we might call "active engagement with the problem." You would be surprised at how often a little effort on the part of the fearing person puts an end to danger. Never let fear fool you into thinking there is nothing to be done. As King Solomon said in Proverbs, "The soul of the sluggard desireth, and hath nothing: but the soul of the diligent shall be made fat" (Proverbs 13:4).

I'll show you how this type of confrontation can work in two areas.

First with *Wild Wood fear*. You and I both know that life is uncertain, that there are no ultimate guarantees. Almost anything *might* occur in your life. So what does "active engagement" mean in this situation?

The most obvious answer is: precaution. Precaution is the first objection of *rational fear*. It is because you fear your children may catch polio that you take the precaution of having them inoculated. It is the fear of leaving your family destitute that impels you to take out an insurance policy. It is the fear of injury that stops you from driving a car without brakes.

One of the inconveniences of yielding to an *exaggerated fear* is that it drives you to take precautions for which there is no real demand. Fear of injury in an automobile accident is useful if it stops you from driving off in a faulty jalopy, but obstructive if it renders you unable to do any driving at all. That sort of behavior hardly merits the name "precaution." It does not address the danger, only your fear and your distorted perception. You are really running away from the fear-scenario, the experience which, in your heart, you know will stimulate your fear.

Active engagement means taking the bull by the horn, or rather, taking the car by the steering wheel and the controls, and forcing yourself to do what your perception tells you is dangerous but in fact is not. How else will the dynamism that God promises to release in your life strengthen you against fear? Confrontation is vital, just as it was vital for the Israelites to cross the Jordan and enter the Promised Land. Occupation of the land God had promised to them remained only a theory, an idea, until they took positive action to possess it.

But remember, too, that when Joshua led the people over to the Promised Land, he didn't send a telex to all the Canaanite kings inviting them to join in a collaborative effort to fight him! He invaded the land of strong peoples and walled cities one at a time. In the same way, it would be sheer folly for you to attempt the conquest of your fear of road accidents by jumping behind the wheel and heading for the most crowded freeway. The first time it may be enough for you just to get into the driver's seat. The second time you might start the engine. The third time you could put the car in gear and drive a few yards down your driveway. Start with what you can do, and go on to conquer your fear stage by stage.

I strongly recommend that you use this suggested program as a guide in writing out your personal program for winning over your specific fears. Break up your program into a series of small steps that will take you from sitting in the driver's seat to motoring around town.

A program is a form of discipline. It will help you work on your fears consistently. It will give you the means to monitor and measure your success. Stick to it, and it will carry you forward to ultimate victory. It may be awhile before your "Promised Land" is subdued and you can drive happily in the rush hour. That is not important. The point is to progress a little bit every day. That way you build your confidence until you can face what was once an unassailable fear-scenario.

I can think of no finer example of victory over *Wild Wood fear* than the habit pattern of the former treasurer of Haggai

Institute, the late Guy W. Rutland, Jr. I'm sure many businessmen questioned the soundness of his unique generosity. Fear restricted the giving of many of these businessmen who observed Guy with awe. Guy Rutland understood the line attributed to Jim Elliot, the missionary martyred by the Auca Indians in Ecuador: "He is no fool who gives what he cannot keep to gain what he cannot lose." Guy lived as modestly as I do. The difference was he didn't have to. His gift check for Haggai Institute arrived on the first of every month, and even though there were lean times in the trucking business, as in every other business, you could never tell when those times had settled on him by the size or timing of his gifts. He had conquered *Wild Wood fear* in an area of life that terrifies most people.

2. The second area where "active engagement" can overcome the danger is in *Big Bad Wolf fear*.

What I said about the fear of automobile accidents also applies here. And consider also that the real damage you sustain through rejection (domestic violence and work layoffs excepted) is often limited. "Sticks and stones may break my bones," the old proverb says, "but words will never hurt me." Tackling your fear of rejection by avoidance, therefore, is overkill of an even worse sort than refusing to drive for fear of an auto crash. It stands to reason that the hermit will not be rejected. But who wants to be a hermit?

To illustrate, I am going to take an example from one particular kind of *Big Bad Wolf fear*—the fear of having past misdeeds exposed, a fear that often finds expression in guilt.

I have been involved in literally hundreds of protracted church meetings, but I can only point to two city-shaking revivals. A revival is a movement of God that results in His people getting right with Him, confessing their sins, making restitution, and setting a new course laid down by the Holy Spirit. One such revival was released by the Spirit of God on the little city of Lancaster, South Carolina, in 1949. For the first 12 nights of the meetings, the evangelist did not give an invitation to the audience to make a public decision. Yet people were getting right with God in the quiet of their own homes. It was incredible by normal standards. Some went back to the principal of the high school with their diplomas in their hands and confessed, "We cheated our way through school. We don't deserve this. We want to make arrangements to earn a legitimate diploma."

One man—a deacon, if you please!—phoned the Gulf Oil distributor at two in the morning and said, "Bill, I've owed you $55 since 1929." (That was a princely sum in 1929, believe me.)

Not surprisingly, the distributor barked back to the deacon, "You're drunk. Go back to bed."

"No, I must get this debt settled. I'm coming over to see you."

And he did. Before daybreak the Gulf Oil distributor found the record of the 20-year-old $55 debt owed by this deacon, a debt the distributor had written off as an irretrievable loss years before.

During these same meetings a young woman, later to become my secretary, was working as secretary to Mr. Marshall of the Marshall chain of furniture stores in South Carolina. She said to her boss, "Mr. Marshall, have you heard about the meeting over at Second Baptist?"

"Meeting!" he cried. "H——, that's no meeting—that's a revival! I've had more people come in to pay off bad debts in this last week than I've had come to me in all the years I've been in business. And every time they've said it was because they'd gotten right with God over at Second Baptist."

He wasn't the only one whose attention the revival had arrested. People from out of town would visit and exclaim, "It seems that this whole town is upbeat and smiling." People by the hundreds who had been enslaved by fears of the exposure of past misdeeds were set free. Wherever they could do it without hurting innocent people, they confessed not only to God but to the persons injured. One man was so smitten by grief over a major theft he had committed that he determined to return the money. When he found that the victim of his larceny had long since died, the repentant thief calculated the total amount stolen plus the appropriate interest for the intervening years in addition to a 20 percent add-on, and gave the entire amount to the Lord's work. He couldn't make the full payment all at once, but he added a percentage of the restitution amount to his regular weekly tithe (ten percent of his income) until full restitution had been made.

Of course, you need to bear in mind factors about confession as a form of active engagement against fear. For one thing, your confession must not cause unnecessary suffering to innocent people. You must always avoid this. The principle is, "Confess to whom confession is due." It is neither fair nor honorable to relieve your own fear by loading pain on somebody else. Another factor is this: in neutralizing one danger you may lay yourself open to another. At a highly publicized campus revival in the '60's, a beautiful young coed, convulsed by guilt, confessed to promiscuous relationships with many of the boys. When the revival ended she was hassled by so many of the young men on campus that she left the school with tears and a broken heart to seek peace and anonymity in a distant university.

Step Three—Censor your input

In 1951 a church in Chattanooga, Tennessee, extended a call to me to become pastor. I was 27 and had just finished an extraordinarily happy ministry in Lancaster, South Carolina. One of the few clouds to have crossed my horizon in Lancaster was an incident involving a mean and disturbed man who, for reasons of churlishness and cantankerousness, had been removed by the deacons from a position of church leadership with the unanimous backing of the congregation. I think he would have fought the decision, but since he could not take on the entire congregation, he stopped attending the church and took every opportunity to scandalize its leadership.

I had almost forgotten about the affair until, two days after I had preached my valedictory sermon in Lancaster, the sheriff phoned to tell me he had a warrant out for my arrest. The sheriff was a good friend who was understandably embarrassed. He attended my church regularly on Sunday nights though, regrettably, I never had the joy of seeing him profess faith in Christ. He said, "Preacher, I don't want to come out and serve you this summons, but I'd be grateful if you'd come into my office." This I did as soon as I hung up the phone.

When I arrived at his office he was sitting pensively behind his desk. His crimsoned face and set jaw signaled his embarrassment and his anger at my accuser. The accuser was none other than the disgruntled church member who had taken unbelievable steps to have me arrested and forced out of the ministry. He charged me with defaming his character.

Arrangements, legally circumspect to the last detail, were made for me to enjoy my freedom pending the decision of the grand jury which was to meet several weeks hence. The possible punitive action was not nearly as distressing to me as the thought that this matter inevitably would go before me to Chattanooga, and my new ministry would die aborning. I was certain that no amount of explanation on my part would undo the damage. Worse, I saw the possibility of a termination to my ministry, period.

I had enough other burdens to carry without adding this to my load. And, still worse, Christine, my wife, was on the threshold of exhaustion from the care of our four-month-old, cerebral-palsied son.

I think you'll agree that my situation provided grounds for *rational fear*. At only 27 years of age I was in danger of having my character assassinated and my ministry shot down like a clay pigeon. Yet, my wife can testify, I didn't lose an hour's sleep over it.

How did I handle the situation?

Obviously, I analyzed the danger. And I confronted it head-on with all the means at my disposal. First and foremost, I committed the entire matter to God in prayer. Then I sought the advice of the finest legal minds—churchmen who understood both the law and the Bible. I thus secured my freedom of movement so that the case should not delay my departure to Chattanooga. To ground me, after all, was what my opponent most wanted. As I heard from several people later, he planned "to delay that preacher's move so long he won't have bread on his table."

But I did something else, too. You see, it would have been easy for me to start feeling, thinking, and behaving defensively at best, or guilty at worst. Once a charge has been leveled at you, you can find plenty of people, most of them good and innocent people, who are prepared to entertain the notion that the charge just might be true. It was, therefore, vital for me to protect my mind from negative input. I made a point of not listening to any doubtful criticism. I forced myself to think and act as though the grand jury's throwing out the case as fraudulent was a foregone conclusion.

That's exactly what the grand jury did. In fact, I was advised to sue the man. I didn't. In a short time, I learned he had quit the church altogether and, I'm sorry to say, died prematurely, an embittered and unforgiving old man who seemed to hate the world. But I think I can say honestly that during the whole unpleasant business I never suffered from *exaggerated fear*. And certainly one important influence on that episode was the grip I, by the grace of God, maintained on my own mind—the way I censored input.

What input you need to censor naturally depends on the object of your fear. A nervous investor would be well advised not to dwell on the opinions of the bearish commentators. A woman with breast cancer will more easily win over fear if she refuses to feed her mind on the horror stories that wickedly sensational journalists write about mastectomy. Anyone anywhere will lead a happier life when the environment is surcharged by positive and affirmative feedback from others. The principle is delightfully simple. Every day you are feeding your mind, just as you are feeding your body. If you feed your mind on a junk food diet of depressing, negative, and pessimistic ideas you will end up ravaged by fear.

Perhaps you never thought about that before. Think about it now. A healthy mind is vital for victory over fear. Make it a discipline to put every new idea you receive through the grid of "sound-mindedness." Don't just swallow somebody else's opinion. Exercise a bit of critical judgment. Ask yourself, "What authority does this person have for saying that?" or "Why should all his gloomy predictions apply to me?" You will probably find that most of these unsolicited ideas have very little power over your life. If that's true, why waste time on them? You can't possibly derive any benefit from exposing yourself to them.

So, when you suspect that a book, an article, a film, or a meeting is just going to trouble you with fear, avoid it like you would the plague. Nobody is compelling you. Would you eat a slice of moldy bread? Of course not. Then why should you have to feed your mind on stuff that tastes lousy and makes you ill?

Step Four—Cultivate your love

Your aim in winning over fear is to be able to live as though your fear never existed.

When the ordinary person talks about his "aim" it is understood that he has not yet achieved it. It is hooked up like the last car of a freight train bound for a long period of hard slog through hundreds of miles of mountain terrain before reaching the destination. If he aims to be a millionaire he will expect to spend the first few years in relative poverty. If he aims to conquer Mount Everest he will know there is a price to pay in arduous fund raising, training, and climbing. Looked at in these terms, aiming to win over fear would mean putting off, perhaps for years, the rewards of winning.

Fortunately, for two reasons we are not required to assign this meaning to the word "aim" when we use it to describe our fight against fear.

First, because, as we've already seen, fear is overcome a piece at a time. That is nonsense with regard to wealth or mountain climbing. Either you have become a millionaire, or you have not; either you have reached the summit, or you have not. Of course, I'm not denying there is an element of struggle involved in the fight against fear. But the man who tackles his fear of accidents on the road by driving a little farther each day is *already achieving his aim*. He is conquering fear progressively, as the Israelites did in occupying Canaan.

Second, there is the important matter of attitude. Look at the Israelites. They didn't cross the Jordan merely hoping to find a home on the other side. They didn't say, "Boy, I surely hope those sons of Anak will let us stay here." They crossed over in the assurance that victory was already theirs. Part of the secret of their success was in their assuming the role of victors from the outset. They reinforced the success of the enterprise with a positive mind-set.

You can observe this principle at work in the lives of the New Testament Christians. Read Acts 16 and see what potential fears confronted Paul and Silas on their visit to Philippi. They had hardly begun their work before the rulers of the city had them thrown into prison on trumped-up charges:

> When they had laid many stripes upon them, they cast them into prison, charging the jailor to keep them safely: who having received such a charge, thrust them into the inner prison, and made their feet fast in the stocks (Acts 16:23,24).

What did Paul and Silas do? Did they accept the idea that they were done for? Did they surrender to fear? Just the opposite. "And at midnight Paul and Silas prayed, and sang praises unto God: and the prisoners heard them. And suddenly there was a great earthquake . . . " (Acts 16:25,26). Even in the stocks of a maximum security prison, Paul and Silas knew they were "more than conquerors" through the love of God. Victory was theirs not next month, not even next morning, but right during the very time they were in the stocks.

That means you must stand your aim on its head. Winning over fear isn't something you are going to achieve some day in the far distant future. You already have the victory—if you claim it and act upon it. You already have power over the fear that stops you from driving, socializing, taking responsibility, or whatever. You have it because you are a redeemed child of God*, living by the life-transforming principle of devotion. Why then do you feel as if power over your fear is some dim and distant objective? Well, probably habit! You have thought that way for so long it's hard to break the thought mold. You haven't yet used God's gift of discipline to release devotion and dynamism.

This step—using discipline to cultivate love—is the fourth and final step in your fight against fear.

I've already said that one way of taking this step is to let fear act as a reminder to love. Employ this procedure at every opportunity. But remember, there are other ways of cultivating love, too.

First, consciously push yourself into a new mold. Ask yourself, "How would I think, speak, and act if I had never suffered from this fear?" Write out a few ideas that you can follow up. If you have been afraid of meeting new people, for example, get into the habit of looking at them with smiling eyes while extending a firm handshake. If you so fear financial trouble that your giving has dwindled, resolutely take action to give in the amount and with the regularity God commands.

Second, perseveringly give thanks in faith for your victory over fear. By all means use your quiet time to ask God for strength, but don't fail to thank Him for the extra step you managed yesterday, and for the inevitable victory of your next step today.

Third, see yourself winning over fear. When you think of fear-scenarios, deliberately picture yourself confronting the danger, and in the power of God, subduing the fear and coming through safely. Until now your visualization has all been negative. That's what fear-scenarios are all about! Turn that around, so that fear-scenarios become success-scenarios.

*If you are not a redeemed child of God, turn to Chapter 21 in my book *How to Win Over Worry* to understand what it means to be a redeemed child of God, or write to me at Box 13, Atlanta, Georgia 30370, and I will be happy to tell you how you may be a redeemed child of God and know it.

Fourth, make your self-affirmations work for you in the conquest of fear. Write the affirmations on cards, mount them on frames, attach them to the sun visor of your windshield, place them on the wall, learn them, and repeat them to yourself whenever you have a free moment.

In his book *The Practice of Godliness*, Jerry Bridges of Navigators rephrased the virtues of love in 1 Corinthians 13 in terms of motivational statements:

- I am patient with you because I love you and want to forgive you.
- I am kind to you because I love you and want to help you.
- I do not envy your possessions or your gifts because I love you and want you to have the best.
- I do not boast about my attainments because I love you and want to hear about yours.
- I am not proud because I love you and want to esteem you before myself.
- I am not rude because I love you and care about your feelings.
- I am not self-seeking because I love you and want to meet your needs.
- I am not easily angered by you because I love you and want to overlook your offenses.
- I do not keep a record of your wrongs because I love you, and "love covers a multitude of sins." (Jerry Bridges, *The Practice of Godliness*, NavPress).

If you will make these motivational statements your own affirmations, you will go a long way toward cultivating love and winning over fear.

You repeat self-affirmations every day anyway. Simply change them from fear affirmations to faith affirmations.

Any positive and relevant statement will do—for instance, "Claiming God's power over my thought life, today I shall love and not fear." I recommend that you choose Scripture verses that you can legitimately apply to your special situation. Philippians 4:13 is appropriate: "I can do all things through Christ which strengtheneth me;" or John 14:27: "Peace I leave with you, my peace I give unto you . . . Let not your heart be troubled, neither let it be afraid." To find verses suited to your particular situation, I suggest you dip into the Psalms. Some Psalms, Psalm 91 for example, are a solid source of strength in danger. You will find undergirding help in reading such portions of Scripture out loud when you are tempted to feel afraid. Read them repeatedly until you know them and they have become a part of you.

Finally . . .

Finally, a brief note for you if you suffer a special sort of fear.

I have written this book to help those whose problems arise from a wrong reaction to danger. Obviously, winning over fear will involve the confrontation of danger, but most readers, I think, will discover the danger of which they were so afraid to be much less threatening than they originally perceived it to be.

But what if your danger is acute—acute enough to give you valid reason to believe that while you have been stung badly once, you are almost certain to be stung again?

I think, then, your problem is of a different sort. Of course, you will experience fear—that is only natural. But it is the danger, not the fear, that you need to overcome. Your fear is *rational fear*, fear that's doing its job. And so, hard as it may be for you to believe, it is on your side. Your total experience is not so much one of fear as one of pain. I could here enter some remarks under that heading, but I simply cannot do it justice in the space available in this volume. I have treated the problem fully in the companion volume to this one entitled, *How to Win Over Pain*. If you feel you are suffering this special sort of fear, I urge you to read the companion volume.

Part 4

FLYING BY FAITH

14

Sufficient unto the Day

Have you started to put those four steps into practice? If you have, you are airborne.

Maybe now you would like to take a glance out the window and consider what holds you up. What is the spiritual aerodynamic that supports the structure of dynamism, devotion, and discipline? I haven't majored on it so far; nonetheless it is a principle implicit in practically every chapter of this book. It's called faith.

Faith is the essence of fearing God. Without faith, the Bible says, it is impossible to please Him. God will not accept us on any terms other than those of our total powerlessness and His absolute provision. He has, in Christ, accomplished all that is necessary for our spiritual and material well-being. The most we can contribute to the process is our receptiveness—our "yes"—to the gifts of God, from the day we repent to the hour we are received into glory.

That "yes" must not be spoiled by greed. Greed is the great downfall of the spurious "name it and claim it" theology, and the fund-raising endemic in modern America that treats faith as a form of financial investment. On the other hand, our "yes" must not be delivered so tentatively that it borders on mistrust. We are urged by Jesus to live in straightforward, practical dependence on our heavenly Father:

> Therefore we take no thought, saying, What shall we eat? or, What shall we drink? or, Wherewithal shall we be clothed? (For after all these things do the Gentiles seek:) for your heavenly Father knoweth that ye have need of all these things. But seek ye first the kingdom of God, and his righteousness; and all these things shall be added unto

you. Take therefore no thought for the morrow: for
the morrow shall take thought for the things of
itself. Sufficient unto the day is the evil thereof
(Matthew 6:31-34).

This advice follows the point made by Jesus that a man
cannot serve two masters (Matthew 6:24). He must decide
whether he is throwing his lot in with God, or with mammon—with the life of faith, or with the covetous pursuit of
wealth for wealth's sake.

But as ordinary men and women, this presents us with a
problem. We all need at least some material wealth—food,
drink, and clothing—and we are not convinced we can rely
on God to provide it for us. Reason goads us with the apparently *rational fear* that faith will let us down. At the same time
it warmly commends the alternative pioneered by the Gentiles—that if you want a job done you had best do it yourself.

In the end, then, the options open to us in life are two:
faith, or fear. We seek first the kingdom, believing that the
rest will follow, or we take so much thought for the morrow
that today is exhausted in a futile attempt to make the future
secure.

I say the attempt is futile because there is no way to predict,
let alone counter, the evils that may befall us. The most we
can hope for, if we put our trust in material goods, is to
accumulate so many of them that our ultimate insecurity is
forgotten. But then, isn't faith just as futile? God may be good
at reassuring us over ultimate issues—death, salvation, and
so on—but when it comes to paying the grocery bill at the end
of the week, aren't we better off with mammon?

I answer that with an emphatic "no."

If we don't have everything by faith, we have nothing at all.
Faith isn't a means by which we earn extra commissions on
our sanctification, nor is it a religious window dressing on
prudence. It is the air we breathe. And it is to the shame of
Christianity that our churches today are filled with men and
women who loftily sing "Holy, holy, holy" on a Sunday

morning, but live the rest of the week on the principle of fear. They are too afraid to trust God to guide them with their money, to guide them in their businesses, and to direct them in their relationships, their careers, and their social calendars. They are Christians only in theory. In practice they are atheists.

Jesus challenges us to faith in even the most everyday matters:

> If God so clothe the grass of the field, which today is, and tomorrow is cast into the oven, shall he not much more clothe you, O ye of little faith? (Matthew 6:30).

If I were not convinced that God honored faith for our every need, I would not be writing a book about winning over fear. There is only one principle by which your fear can be eradicated, and that principle is faith. Faith alone is the basis for utilizing the Timothy Formula of dynamism, devotion and discipline. Faith alone opens us to the limitless resources of God's power.

You may be thinking, "If that's true, I wish I had a bit more of it!" Well, it's not a matter of having "more" or "less" faith. You can't measure it in gallons like gasoline. We can only talk metaphorically about "having" it, for faith is essentially something you do, a way of living on the premise that God may be taken at His word. It exists always in the present moment; and as it exists, it overwhelms fear just as a roller covers old paint in a brand new gloss. Faith improves health; it improves relationships; it improves personal productivity; it improves devotional life; it improves self-image and personal influence. It makes all things new.

This book, then, is about learning to live in faith, because faith is the direct opposite of fear.

The now of faith

There is one more point about faith that you should know. I began this book by talking about a fundamental human fear, our fear of the unknown. It is this—our sheer ignorance of what lies in store for us—that makes mammon so appealing. In mammon's ample bosom we find some comfort against the future, not a freedom from fear exactly, but the illusion of being prepared for danger when it comes. We walk into the Wild Wood clutching a pistol.

Outside the realm of faith, that is about as much victory over fear as a person can hope for. There is no way of achieving the ideal, of knowing for certain that the Wild Wood contains only mice and buttercups. Such certainty is withheld even from the Christian. But the Christian has one big advantage over the man without faith: he is required to live only one day at a time. The man carrying his pistol into the Wild Wood is anxious about situations, narrow passes, deep recesses, and dark corners that he has not yet come to. But the Christian is told to "take therefore no thought for the morrow: for the morrow shall take thought for the things of itself. Sufficient unto the day is the evil thereof" (Matthew 6:34).

You might look on that as shortsightedness, "ostrichism." It's not. We are talking about the ancient doctrine of faith in the providence of God.

In the life of faith we live without guarantees, just as the Israelites did in their wilderness journey. We walk in a desert, hardly knowing what lies before us, certain that the environment is incapable of sustaining us. Our insecurity, our fear of the unknown, makes us wish we were traveling not in the wilderness, but across a fertile land where milk and honey were available on demand every day of the year. Yet here we are. We have no food—only a God who leads us on and says, "Trust Me."

What God provides for us in the battle against fear is utterly and completely adequate. But like the manna He gave to the Israelites, it is delivered only in daily rations:

> When the dew that lay was gone up, behold, upon the face of the wilderness there lay a small round thing, as small as the hoar frost on the

ground. And when the children of Israel saw it, they said one to another, It is manna: for they wist not what it was. And Moses said unto them, This is the bread which the Lord hath given you to eat. . . .

And they gathered it every morning, every man according to his eating: and when the sun waxed hot, it melted (Exodus 16:14,15,21).

To win over fear, you must get used to living in the "now" of faith.

God's provision for you in your fight against fear is made today, here, now. The future is in God's hands. He controls it. And He will give you strength for tomorrow when tomorrow comes. Until then you must focus on your present situation. Why do anything else? Precaution is your only way of influencing the future, so when you have taken all sensible precautions, you may as well leave it be. Train your energy on the day, the hour, the moment in which you are living. And as you have need, so God will supply.

By faith, you will win over fear.

15

Lambs to Lions

Reading this book won't deliver you from fear.

Agreeing with this book won't deliver you from fear.

Asking God for deliverance won't deliver you from fear.

You must act. Deliverance starts, proceeds, and finishes with you. Not because God hasn't done everything necessary for your deliverance, but because He will not step in and do what you can do for yourself. He has given you the Timothy Formula—but it's up to you to apply it.

You have read this book through once, enough at least to get the gist of it. Now go back to the beginning and read it through again. But this time do it more slowly, concentrating on those parts which you feel apply especially to you. As you read, jot down on a notepad an analysis of your fear in the terms I have suggested in the opening chapters. In other words, put *Step One* into effect. Then draw up a personalized campaign plan. Make sure that you are attacking your fear on the three fronts indicated in *Step Two*, *Step Three*, and *Step Four*. Find a way of confronting your danger. Adopt a specific policy to guard your input. And organize your lifestyle to cultivate the love of God. State your intentions in the form of a to-do list, and incorporate a comprehensive review of your progress into your daily devotions. If you want to, share your new regimen with someone else who can encourage you and keep you on your toes!

Remember, God has not given you a spirit of fear. He has given you a spirit of power, of love, and of self-control. Organize yourself to receive that gift and your fear will be finished. The perfect love of God flooding into your life casts out fear. It turns you from a lamb into a lion.

Are you ready to begin? If you are—congratulations! Victory is yours!

Book III

WINNING
OVER
Worry

Introduction

Every time I write an article for a magazine or a manuscript for a book, I grapple with the problem of worry—the divided mind. Will some of the statements come back to haunt me 20 years from now? Will the views expressed subject me to the ridicule of my peers? Will statements made be misunderstood by sincere people with the result that they will suffer hurt, though my aim was to help? Will some of the readers conclude the material was superficial and frivolous? Will I, after the publication of the book, conclude that the hours and energy and, yes, emotional pain, invested in producing the manuscript didn't pay off; rather that it turned out to be a travesty of productive enterprise? Will the publisher give the book fair exposure?

The initial edition of *How to Win Over Worry* (1959) got very little attention from the publisher. In less than two years, the publisher's sales representative announced to bookstore owner Bob Hawkins the publisher's intention not to reprint the book after the present edition was exhausted. Bob Hawkins owned two bookstores in Oregon at the time. He said, "That book cannot go out of print." In vigorous terms he gave reasons why it must be reprinted. To prove his point of the book's importance, he ordered 500 hardback copies. Some people would think that an order of 500 hardback copies for two modest-sized bookstores in a modest-sized city would be foolhardy. Bob sold them all within two months.

What Bob Hawkins did for that book got it off the ground. Had I known of the publisher's plan at the time to not reprint my book, I'm sure I never would have written another book. Since Bob's purchase of those 500 copies of the book, it has now been translated into 18 languages and gone through more than 50 printings.

Just last night my brother Tom called to tell me that a lady under psychiatric care had been given a copy of this book. When she went to the psychiatrist he told her she was doing much better and asked how she accounted for it. She told him she didn't know. He then asked if she had done anything differently. She simply mentioned that she had read the book *How to Win Over Worry.* He asked to see it. He has now ordered a supply because he wants to give the book to some of his patients.

One of the South's prominent business tycoons saw me at the airport in San Antonio, Texas, early one morning. He asked if I was John Haggai. I said yes. He then told me how God had used that book to avert his suicide at the very moment he had the .38 revolver to his temple ready to blow out his brains. His daughter had picked up a copy of the book in London. It helped her so much she wanted her father to read it too, so she left it on his bedside table.

God used the book to avert the planned suicide of one of London's highy publicized and world-famous impresarios. A friend of his asked me to autograph a copy for this impresario. On the day when he was ready to pull the trigger of the suicide gun, he heard a thud. He went to the upstairs railing across from his bedroom to see what caused the noise. He looked down to see the postman had pushed a parcel through the slot. He opened the package, saw my book, read it, found meaning for his life, then placed a transatlantic phone call to thank me.

The internationally renowned Dr. Paul Yonggi Cho, founder and pastor of the world's largest church (membership over 600,000), came to my hotel in 1970 and told me that ten years earlier God had used the book *How to Win Over Worry* to meet his deep needs during the time of sickness and depression. When I saw him ten years later, he told me he had preached from the book on several occasions.

The late Mr. Stanley Kresge told me that he and his wife had read one chapter of *How to Win Over Worry* each morning, along with their other devotional materials, during their quiet time until they finished the 25 chapters of the book.

I read it periodically myself, since I need it. I did not create the ideas. I simply put down the truths that I found.

It encourages me greatly to know that this volume has sold over half a million copies in the United States and, in abridged form, three times that number overseas. The writings have crossed the threshold of hundreds of thousands of homes I shall never visit, and the influence of this book will touch the lives of millions of people I'll never meet. Despite all that encouragement, I still must keep my guard up against the monster of worry.

Reading this book through once and agreeing with its principles will not eliminate worry. I suggest that you read it and reread it. Make notes in the margins or inside the back cover of passages that have special relevance to your need. Write out specific goals with time targets to cope with your problems relating to worry. Devote the first moments of every day to reading the Bible. This is more important to your mastery of worry than reading any other book.

The formula for winning over worry is **Praise** plus **Poise** plus **Prayer** equals **Perfect Peace**. You must win over worry before you can master any worthwhile undertaking in life.

I pray this book will encourage you to work toward the mastery of worry and thus to move toward your potential.

Should you have questions about anything I've written, please write me at Box 13, Atlanta, Georgia 30370. I will answer your query. God bless you.

Part 1

Surveying the Problem

1

Meet Public Enemy Number One

You can die of worry.

It's not a cancer. It's not caused by a virus. If you're afflicted by it no doctor in his right mind would say you are physically ill. Nonetheless worry is a potentially fatal condition.

And it's spreading. Let me introduce you to an astounding and terrifying fact: According to Mike Gorman, the Executive Director of the National Mental Health Committee, half of all hospital beds in the United States are occupied by people suffering mental disturbance. Half! And in his book *Every Other Bed* he predicts that in the near future the proportion will rise to two thirds. That means two out of every three hospital places are taken up by the victims of mental illness, at a cost of billions of dollars a year.

Listen to the *Supplement to the American Journal of Psychiatry*, July 1985, in a report titled "Research on Mental Illness and Addictive Disorders: Progress and Prospects":

> In the United States, 15 percent to 22.5 percent of the population has some form of mental illness . . .
>
> One percent of the population will develop Schizophrenia. Over 9 million currently have affective disorders. Five percent of the population suffers from generalized anxiety. Ten million adults and three million children abuse alcohol, and millions of individuals abuse drugs.
>
> Major mental disorders, alcoholism and drug addiction disrupt the lives of 32 to 45 million people in the United States each year.

Take the lowest estimate in that report—15 percent suffering some form of mental illness. Reckoning on the basis of the

317

1980 census figure of 226,545,805, that means 33,981,870 people. In other words the number of mentally disturbed in America today exceeds the entire population of Canada. The root cause? Worry!

Look at the statistics on suicide in the United States. In 1972 24,280 people committed suicide. By 1982 the figure had risen to 28,200. Now the 1987 *Information Please Almanac* states that "suicide claims the lives of at least thirty thousand Americans annually." At a conservative estimate that's over 6,000 more suicides per year today than 15 years ago. Statistically speaking you're more likely to kill yourself than you are to be killed by someone else.

And of course killing yourself doesn't just mean jumping off a bridge. The evidence has piled up over recent years that worry causes death through a wide range of physical disorders. In 1982 6,700 people died as a result of ulcers in the stomach and duodenum. And that's just ulcers. We were shocked in World War II to hear that a third of a million of America's finest young people had been killed in combat. But did you know that, over exactly the same period, one million—three times as many people—died of heart disease right where they were in the USA?

Read the excellent book by Dr. Edward Podolsky, *Stop Worrying and Get Well*. It deals with the correlation between worry and heart trouble, worry and blood pressure, worry and rheumatism, ulcers, colds, thyroid malfunction, arthritis, migraine headaches, blindness, and a host of stomach disorders. The fact is that worry causes any number of physical malfunctions, and those malfunctions can kill. Dr. Alexis Carroll spelled it out to one group of worriers: "Businessmen who don't know how to fight worry die young," he said.

Is worry a problem that only afflicts top-level executives? Not on your life! People from every echelon of society worry. A leading physician has stated that 70 percent of all medical patients could cure themselves if only they got rid of their fears and worries—he knew, because he'd suffered a stomach ulcer for exactly that reason. Or take the testimony of two outstanding doctors who set up the Medical Arts Clinic in Corsicana, Texas. They told me that the first complaint of more than 70 percent of their patients is: "Doctor, I can't sleep." Why? Worry!

Let me give you an example of the effect of worry.

Several years ago a pastor friend of mine, Eddie Lieberman, was asked to try and help a young lady apparently suffering severe depression. He went to see her. She told him she was sick, that she didn't love her husband anymore (he was overseas in the Armed Forces at the time), and that she wanted a divorce. Her physical state was deteriorating badly, and in fact she soon became a total paralytic.

Besides being a pastor, Eddie Lieberman is trained as a psychologist. He declined an invitation to become the first case psychologist in one of our leading Baptist hospitals only because he wanted to pursue his first calling—to the gospel ministry. And his instincts as a psychologist told him something was drastically wrong with this girl, so he requested permission to admit her to Duke University Hospital.

There she confessed to her psychiatrist that she'd received a letter from her husband telling her he'd fallen in love with another girl. It was he, not she, who wanted to initiate divorce proceedings. She had never told anyone about this, but bottling it up had caused severe anxiety, and anxiety had led to paralysis. Eddie Lieberman tried to help her, but it is almost impossible to help someone who fundamentally has no desire to be helped. She refused to face the facts. Today, when she should be a lively, vivacious woman in her mid-thirties, she is a morose paralytic bound for a premature grave. The culprit: Worry.

Worry is not a disease. But it causes disease. And like a disease, it is contagious—in fact several outstanding psychiatrists believe it is more contagious than scarlet fever or diptheria. So much so that in the West today, and particularly in the United States, people worry about worry. Pick up a popular magazine and you are likely to find an article about stress or anxiety. "How to Face Your Fears, Tensions and

Worries" was a headline I read in the *Pageant* not so long ago. *Reader's Digest* for the same week devoted eight and a half pages to the subject of "The Inner Secret of Health." It seems we have an almost obsessive desire to get rid of our worry. Worry is public enemy number one.

How does worry work?

The New Testament word for worry is translated "take thought" and "be careful". J. B. Phillips correctly translates it "worry."

The word "worry" comes from the Greek word *merimnao* which is a combination of two words: *merizo* meaning "to divide" and *nous* meaning "mind" (including the faculties of perceiving, understanding, feeling, judging, and determining).

Worry, then, means "to divide the mind." Worry divides the mind between worthwhile interests and damaging thoughts.

The apostle James states the unhappy condition of the person with the divided mind:

> A double minded man is unstable in all his ways (James 1:8).

You will notice that James says that the man with the divided mind is unstable in *all his ways*. He is unstable in his emotions. He is unstable in his thought processes. He is unstable in his decisions. He is unstable in his judgments.

Peace of mind requires singleness of mind. The worrier robs himself of peace of mind by dividing his mind.

Worry divides the feelings, therefore the emotions lack stability.

Worry divides the understanding, therefore convictions are shallow and changeable.

Worry divides the faculty of perception, therefore observations are faulty and even false.

Worry divides the faculty of judging, therefore attitudes and decisions are often unjust. These decisions lead to damage and grief.

Worry divides the determinative faculty, therefore plans and purposes, if not "scrapped" altogether, are not fulfilled with persistence.

Worry in the extreme leads to *abulia*—loss of the power to will. Why? The mind is so divided it cannot act in one channel. It is like the mule who stood between two haystacks and starved to death trying to decide from which stack to eat.

Abulia is often termed a "nervous breakdown." In such a breakdown, pressures have so built up as a result of divided-mindedness that the victim ceases struggling with his problems and responds in a depressed and passive manner.

Worry is the cause of heartbreak, failure, misunderstanding, suspicion, and most unhappiness.

Is there any home which has gone "on the rocks" that cannot point to "the divided mind" as the cause? It may be that the husband's mind was divided between the wife and another woman. It may be that the wife divided her mind between the husband and "Mama." Her mind may have been divided between an inexcusably possessive preoccupation with her children and her God-ordained responsibilities to her husband. It may be that the mind was divided between home responsibilities and selfish, personal desires. It may be that the husband divided his mind between an inordinate ambition to succeed and his responsibilities as husband and father. With just a little thought you can come readily to many other possibilities or certainties which have divided the mind and wrecked the home.

Who can determine the percentage of school failures effectuated by "the divided mind"? Preachers' sons, believe it or not, confront difficulties in their youth. That goes for preachers' daughters as well. If they are "model children," the parents of other children hold them up as a pattern of behavior with the result that their friends detest them. If, on the other hand, they are normally mischievous, the other children appreciate them and their parents detest them. I have a brother who was so sensitive to the fact that he was a preacher's son that he deliberately made poor grades so the kids wouldn't think of him as a "goody-goody." Worry ruined his grades. He has an excellent mind. This fact has since been proven by his collegiate scholastic records. He graduated with honors in a difficult field from one of the nation's leading universities.

Do not some children fail in school because of discord in the home—discord that divides their minds between their scholastic responsibilities and the possible outcome of the domestic "cold war"? Do not some children bungle their school opportunities simply because they are neglected at home? They feel unwanted and therefore they create havoc at school in order to get the attention that they do not get at home.

Only the Lord knows how many businesses have been torpedoed by worry—the divided mind. There was a man who opened a hot-dog stand. His business grew. He expanded. Soon he had a chain of stands. He was making fabulous money. He sent his son to college. The son graduated with a major in Business Administration. This was in 1933. The father took him into the business. The son said, "You know, Dad, there's a depression on. Business is bad everywhere. Many businesses have gone into bankruptcy. We must be careful. Let's cut down our inventory, reduce our advertising budget, lay off some of the help, and tighten our belts." The father listened to his "learned" son and followed the advice reluctantly. Yes, you've guessed it. The son succeeded in dividing his father's mind between the principles of success and the potential threats of the depression. Soon their business folded. Worse yet, depressed by the financial reverses, the father lost his sparkle, his "drive," his optimistic outlook and began to deteriorate physically.

One of the best-known tycoons of our nation during this century made and then lost three huge fortunes. Why? Because he over and over again divided his mind between his business interests and "gold-digging" paramours.

One of the most bitter and cynical men I have ever known was a man loaded with talent. He had more ability than six typical men. He could have been a leading cartoonist, or a top-notch photographer, or a highly paid after-dinner speaker, or a humorist, or a prosperous realtor, or a topflight hotel executive, or a celebrated writer. He never amounted to anything. He saw men who obviously did not possess one fraction of his ability soar to the heights of success while he groveled in the mud. Those who knew him well knew the reason. It was a divided mind. He never came to the point at which he determined what he was going to do. He could not say with Paul the apostle, "This one thing I do." He would never throw all of his energies in a single project. He aimed at nothing, hit a bull's-eye, and then brooded over the result. He became critical of others who did achieve. With unparalleled cynicism he would rationalize his failure and deal out misery to all of his associates. His health broke completely. A distraught mind inevitably leads to a deteriorated body.

Worry is ravaging societies worldwide. It is slaying tens of thousands of people. It is infiltrating businesses and bringing them crashing down. It's passing through homes like a tornado, leaving in its wake bitter and frustrated parents, and insecure, terrified children. It is driving some to spend fortunes on psychotherapy, and heading others into psychiatric care. In America at least, it has virtually become part of the national culture. You could write on countless American gravestones the epitaph: *Hurried, Worried, Buried*.

So you're worried. It's your problem too. Worry is your personal enemy as well as a public enemy. But what are you going to do about it?

Well, there are many solutions to worry. Of those solutions, I assure you confidently, there is *only one that works*—the one presented by God in the Bible. I will be giving the formula for that solution in chapter 3. But in case you don't believe me when I say it's the only effective solution, take a look first of all at the other ways worriers try to cope with their problem.

2

Throw Away Your Popgun

A popgun is a fine toy for children. It gives them action and noise. It arrests their attention—for a time, at least. When a boy arrives at the age of adolescence, he no longer finds much interest in a popgun. And could there be anything more ludicrous and incongruous than a full-grown man whiling away his time shooting a little dime store popgun?

You cannot kill a bear or a lion or any vicious enemy of human life with a popgun. Men do not go hunting with popguns. Nor are soldiers equipped with popguns when called upon to fight an enemy.

Shooting a popgun probably takes as much effort as shooting a .22-caliber rifle or many other types of guns. Some popguns make as much noise as real guns. Apart from occupying the attention for a little while, making some noise, and requiring the exertion of some effort, popguns accomplish nothing.

The majority of worriers try to kill this vicious enemy, worry, with popguns. Figuratively speaking, that is. Let us mention a few of the more prominent popguns that are used.

There is the popgun of *flattery*. Flattery is a device used by many seeking to compensate for worry. By flattery the worrier endeavors to secure loyal friends in large numbers. He thereby seeks to immunize himself from danger by building around himself this wall of friends. It is his thought that there is safety in numbers. He reasons that if the dreadful probabilities he fears become calamitous certainties, he will be shielded by this wall of friends.

Obviously flattery accomplishes nothing except to give a temporary and a false security to the flatterer. The very dishonesty of this attempt ultimately adds to the worries of the worrier.

Flattery is mentioned and denounced over 30 times in the Word of God. Job says:

> He that speaketh flattery to his friends, even the eyes of his children shall fail (Job 17:5).

Again in Job:

> Let me not, I pray you, accept any man's person, neither let me give flattering titles unto man.
> For I know not to give flattering titles; in so doing my maker would soon take me away (Job 32:21,22).

The psalmist records the sinfulness and foolishness of flattery in Psalm 5:9:

> For there is no faithfulness in their mouth . . .
> they flatter with their tongue.

You remember the statement made in the previous chapter that worry is essentially divided-mindedness. Notice now how that fits in with the following words of the psalmist:

> They speak vanity every one with his neighbor; with flattering lips and with a *double heart* do they speak (Psalm 12:2).

The wisest man of history, Solomon, admonishes us:

> He that goeth about as a talebearer revealeth secrets: therefore meddle not with him that flattereth with his lips (Proverbs 20:19).

> A lying tongue hateth those that are afflicted by it; and a flattering mouth worketh ruin (Proverbs 26:28).

Another popgun utilized by many worriers is that of *criticism*. Psychologists tell us there are three reasons for this.

First, we criticize to elevate ourselves. Second, we criticize to project our miserableness. Third, we criticize the very thing of which we are guilty, or the thing which tempts us and troubles us the most.

No matter what may be your motive for criticism, the old saying is true, "It doesn't take much size to criticize."

Remember that popguns are used only by children and the popgun of criticism, like the other figurative popguns mentioned in this chapter, is used by the most immature personalities.

Worriers often resort to criticism to project their own miserableness. They are miserable and they want everyone else to be miserable. This obviously is not the answer to worry. In thus projecting their own misery, people succeed temporarily in getting their minds off their own problems. The tragic result, however, is that the relief is only temporary. In criticizing they are focusing their minds upon negative thoughts, and the mischief that inevitably follows negative thinking but adds to their worries. Consequently the depression becomes more intense.

It is true that "what Peter says about Paul tells more about Peter than it does about Paul." Or, in the words of the little couplet:

> Things that thou dost in others see, are the most
> prevalent in thee.

The Bible tells us that to the impure, all things are impure (Titus 1:15). To the dishonest, all are dishonest. To the untrue, all are untrue. When the worrier criticizes others, he certainly solves none of his own worries. He focuses his attention upon the miserable traits he sees in others which mirror his own condition. His mind is riveted to this destructively negative thinking in such a way that more fear-producing thoughts are bred to add to his already overstocked supply of fears.

Paul the apostle denounces the sin of criticism when in Romans 2:1 he says:

> Therefore thou art inexcusable, O man, whatsoever thou art that judgest: for wherein thou judgest another, thou condemnest thyself; for thou that judgest doest the same things.

What the worrier fails to realize is that in criticizing others he is revealing to the world what he himself is.

Another popgun that many worriers use in their endeavor to kill this vicious enemy of worry is that of *excessive activity*. This is only a temporary escape. Through this means they try in vain to conquer their worries, but they only postpone their misery with a temporary emotional intoxication. They think they are busy when they are only "nervous." (Later on you will understand why I put the word "nervous" in quotes.) They are like a worm on a hot rock. As one TV personality said, "They are as nervous as a long-tailed cat in a room full of rocking chairs." Spinning their wheels, they are going nowhere. They seem to have become infatuated with the twentieth-century beatitude, "Blessed are they that go around in circles, for they shall be called big wheels."

This feverish activity, motivated by the desire to escape rather than the urge to produce, solves no problems. It simply takes the mind for a brief spell off the fear-producing thoughts that cause the anxiety. This type of activity, instead of solving problems, actually produces more problems and thereby intensifies the problem over which victory is sought.

It is amazing how few people can stand their own company for 30 minutes without any action or device such as TV, radio, books, or any other prop. They do not know the meaning of the words of our Lord,

> Come ye yourselves apart into a desert place, and rest a while (Mark 6:31).

They take phenobarbital to go to sleep, Dexedrine to get started in the morning, and they stay tanked up on coffee to make it through the day. That which they call fervor is actually no more than emotional fever.

Another popgun used by many worriers in their vain effort to kill this vicious enemy of worry is the popgun of a *self-righteous resignation*. There is nothing righteous about this kind of resignation. You notice I said it is a self-righteous resignation. They will assert, "My cross is heavy, but I am determined to take it valiantly." This is almost blasphemous. Wherever the biblical injunction "take up thy cross" appears, it is referring to death to sin and death to self. This is the exact antithesis of the attitude just referred to. The Bible never refers to any problem, grief, or dilemma as a cross that some people are called to bear. The man who really bears his cross is the man who knows no worry. He has died to sin and to self. Thus he is invulnerable to destructive fears. He has peace because his mind is ever staid upon Christ and because he trusts in Christ.

Jesus never complained about the weight of His cross. However, He bore a cross. A real cross—a cross for you and for me.

Our Lord's disciples rejoiced that "they were counted worthy to suffer shame for His name" (Acts 5:41).

These people who respond to worry, fear, and anxiety with a self-righteous resignation say one thing, but they live another. They delude no one but themselves. Although they claim to want to bring glory to God, their faces would "draw a wart" on a tombstone. They repeat the sin of Jonah who said in Jonah 4:3:

> Therefore now, O Lord, take, I beseech thee, my
> life from me; for it is better for me to die than to live.

And the sin of Elijah:

> . . . It is enough; now, O Lord, take away my life;
> for I am not better than my fathers (1 Kings 19:4c).

This is not spiritual courage. This is disgusting cowardice. It is the most revolting type of self-pity.

Some worriers resort to the popgun of *alcohol* and/or *narcotics* in a vain effort to kill the vicious enemy of worry.

This gives them temporary exhilaration during which their minds may not be focused upon the fear-producing thoughts that cause them so much grief. However, this type of behavior only postpones the problem. It ultimately increases the agony.

Perspective is distorted under the influence of stimulants. This often leads to regrettable circumstances which result in an increase of the problems of the worrier. Who can calculate the damage done by the many plays (whether in book form, staged on Broadway, projected on the television or movie screen) which portray the unrequited lover desperately going down to the corner saloon to drink away his sorrows. The attitude that a drunken spree is the way to escape an agonizing situation produces pernicious results. The Japanese say: "A man takes a drink, then the drink takes a drink, and the next drink takes the man."

Solomon, the sage of the ages, speaks wisely when he says:

> Who hath woe? who hath sorrow? who hath contentions? who hath babbling? who hath wounds without cause? who hath redness of eyes?
> They that tarry long at the wine; they that go to seek mixed wine (Proverbs 23:29,30).

It is still true that:

> Wine is a mocker, strong drink is raging: and whosoever is deceived thereby is not wise (Proverbs 20:1).

Some worriers resort to yet another popgun. They seek to conquer worry by *positive thinking*. Now positive thinking is good. Certainly a person cannot have positive thoughts and fear-producing, worrisome thoughts at the same time. Nevertheless, the worrier needs help from outside—or to be more specific, from above. It is one thing to know what we ought to do. It is another thing to have the ability to do it. The Ten Commandments showed man what he must be and what he must do, but no man—our own Lord, the God-man excepted—has ever kept the Ten Commandments. It is one thing to know what we must be and what we must do, and another to meet the demands.

With all of my heart I believe in the power of positive thinking. Let it be understood, however, that God alone is the source of positive thoughts. Paul says in 2 Timothy 1:7:

> For God hath not given us the spirit of fear; but of power, and of love, and of a sound mind.

Positive thoughts do not constitute a useless "popgun" in this instance. Rather they produce the erroneous concept that man in his own strength can bring about the kind of mental attitude that will banish fear and worry. Man might just as well try to shoot an African lion with a popgun as to conquer his worry with his own self-inspired and self-produced positive attitude.

Later on in the book you will notice that much emphasis is given to positive thinking. Equal emphasis is also made on the basis of human experience and on the basis of God's Word that there is no such thing as peace except to those who have properly related themselves to the Lord Jesus Christ, the Prince of Peace. Apart from divine help, a proper mental attitude—one that gives peace—is totally impossible. A man's belief that he can be the source of a proper mental attitude is a Pollyanna notion that leads ultimately to frustration.

There are many other popguns used to slay the deadly beast, the enemy worry. Those who resort to the use of these various popguns reveal their immaturity and their helplessness. I do not say this disparagingly. God grant that this book will lead them to a proper relationship with God through Christ who is our Peace (cf. Ephesians 2:14). The first requisite for help must be that you *throw away your popgun*.

Thousands of people every year resort to the popgun of *suicide*. It goes without saying this accomplishes nothing. It is like a man cutting off his head to cure the headache.

One of the most heartrending articles I've ever read appeared on the front page of the May 21, 1931 edition of *The New York Times*. This article dealt with the suicide of Ralph Barton. Mr. Barton was an outstanding cartoonist, one of the nation's leading caricaturists. He was highly gifted, a great writer. His life ended tragically by his own hand.

In his suicide note he told about the melancholia he had been suffering. Apparently his fears nearly drove him mad. Read verbatim part of what he said in his suicide note:

> It (melancholia) has prevented my getting anything like the full value out of my talent, and the past three years has made work a torture to do at all. It has made it impossible for me to enjoy the simple pleasures of life.

Now I am taking the liberty of italicizing that part of his note which I want impressed upon you.

> *I have run from wife to wife, from house to house, and from country to country in a ridiculous effort to escape from myself.*In doing so I am very much afraid that I have brought a great deal of unhappiness to those who have loved me . . .
> *No one thing is responsible for this and no one person— except myself . . .*
> *I did it because I am fed up with inventing devices for getting through the twenty-four hours a day and with bridging over a few months periodically with some beautiful interest. . . .*

Poor fellow. Brilliant of mind! How tragic that a life such as his, filled with great possibilities for blessing his generation in the will of God, had to end in such tragedy!

He tried to kill the stalking lion of worry and melancholia with a series of useless popguns.

Throw away your popgun. This is your first step if you would conquer worry.

3

Worry Is a Sin

Worry is a SIN—a blighting sin that has become the subject matter of nonsensical satire.

Worry cannot be excused as an uncontrollable condition. It's amazing how easy it is to blame our problems on our heredity—our parents, grandparents, and forebears.

I chuckle inside every time somebody says to me, "Worry is not a sin for me; you see, my mother was a worrier and my father was a worrier and, therefore, I am a worrier."

I chuckle because it reminds me of the Vermont Republican zealot:

> A Democrat from the South asked this man living in Republican Vermont, "Why are you a Republican?"
>
> The Vermonter answered, "My father was a Republican, and my grandfather was a Republican, and, therefore, I am a Republican."
>
> The Southerner said, "Suppose your father had been a fool, and your grandfather had been a fool, then what would you be?"
>
> "Oh, in that case, I'd be a Democrat."

You cannot blame your worries on a congenital condition communicated through your blood, a condition inherited from your parents.

Worry is a sin. It is always a sin, and it is a sin for two reasons: Worry is distrust in the truthfulness of God and worry is detrimental to the temple of God.

1. *Worry is distrust in the truthfulness of God.*

When you worry you accuse God of falsehood.

God's Word says, "And we know that all things work together for good to them that love God, to them who are the

333

called according to his purpose" (Romans 8:28). Worry says, "Thou liest, O God!"

God's Word says, "He hath done all things well" (Mark 7:37). Worry says, "Thou liest, O God!"

God's Word says, "I can do all things through Christ which strengtheneth me" (Philippians 4:13). Worry says, "Thou liest, O God!"

God's Word says, "But my God shall supply all your needs according to his riches in glory by Christ Jesus" (Philippians 4:19). Worry says, "Thou liest, O God!"

God's Word says, "I will never leave thee, nor forsake thee" (Hebrews 13:5). Worry says, "Thou liest, O God!"

God's Word says, "He careth for you" (1 Peter 5:7). Worry says, "Thou liest, O God!"

God's Word says, "Take no thought for your life, what ye shall eat, or what ye shall drink; nor yet for your body, what ye shall put on . . . for your heavenly Father knoweth that ye have need of all these things" (Matthew 6:25a, 32b). Worry says, "Thou liest, O God!"

Worry is hypocrisy, for it professes faith in God and at the same time assails the reality of His truthfulness.

If it is highly insulting to call a man a liar (although the fact is that David probably spoke the truth when he said, "All men are liars"), how infinitely more inexcusable it is to accuse the sovereign God of falsehood. He is the God "who cannot lie."

> In hope of eternal life, which God, that cannot lie, promised before the world began (Titus 1:2).

> He that believeth not God hath made him a liar . . . (1 John 5:10).

2. *Worry is a sin because it is detrimental to the temple of God.*
If a group of vandals should crash into your church some dark night and succeed in shattering the stained-glass windows, ripping up the carpeting, smashing the furniture, wrecking the musical instruments, disfiguring the walls, and ravaging the Sunday school rooms, you would react with

justifiable anger and prosecute them to the full extent of the law. The laws of the land provide stringent penalties for disturbance of public worship and for destruction of church property. You would make the most of these laws, as well you should.

Yet worry is a far more inexcusable and grievous sin than this vandalism of church property. In all probability, these vandals were not professing Christians, while many who worry are. Furthermore, there is no inherent value in a church building. True, it symbolizes worship. It symbolizes the work and the Word of God. However, its only inherent value is symbolic. God does not dwell in the church building as such. He dwells there only as He dwells in the hearts of those who worship there.

God *does* dwell in the heart of every believer.

> Know ye not that ye are the temple of God, and that the Spirit of God dwelleth in you? (1 Corinthians 3:16).

> What? know ye not that your body is the temple of the Holy Ghost which is in you, which ye have of God, and ye are not your own? (1 Corinthians 6:19).

> Ye also, as lively stones, are built up a spiritual house, an holy priesthood, to offer up spiritual sacrifices, acceptable to God by Jesus Christ. (1 Peter 2:5).

> And because ye are sons, God hath sent forth the Spirit of his Son into your hearts . . . (Galatians 4:6).

Worry debilitates and even destroys the temple of God which is *your own body*, Christian! In chapter 1 we mentioned some of the detrimental effects worry has on the body—God's temple. Let's review for a moment. Some of the ailments caused by worry (according to Dr. Edward Podolsky to whom I referred in chapter 1) are heart trouble, high blood pressure, some forms of asthma, rheumatism, ulcers, colds, thyroid malfunction, arthritis, migraine headaches, blindness, and a host of stomach disorders apart from ulcers. It also causes palpitations, pains in the back of the neck, indigestion, nausea, constipation, diarrhea, dizziness, unexplainable fatigue, insomnia, allergies, and temporary paralysis.

Many other reasons could be given to substantiate the fact that worry is a sin.

Worry is a sin because it is symptomatic of prayerlessness.

> Moreover as for me, God forbid that I should sin against the Lord in ceasing to pray for you . . . (1 Samuel 12:23).

No one can pray and worry at the same time.

> Thou wilt keep him in perfect peace, whose mind is stayed on thee: because he trusteth in thee (Isaiah 26:3).

When you pray your mind is staid on Christ and you have His assurance of perfect peace. Worry is therefore banished.

Worry is a sin because of what it does to family life.

> Wives, submit yourselves unto your own husbands, as unto the Lord.
> Husbands, love your wives, even as Christ also loved the church, and gave himself for it.
> Nevertheless let every one of you in particular so love his wife even as himself; and the wife see that she reverence her husband (Ephesians 5:22,25,33).

These injunctions in the book of Ephesians are violated and disobeyed when worry is in the saddle.

Worry is a sin because it undermines our Christian witness. In Matthew 5:16 Jesus says:

> Let your light so shine before men, that they may see your good works, and glorify your Father which is in heaven.

Someone may say, "Oh, yes, Mr. Haggai, you can talk like that in an overly confident, pedantic manner. You are young and enjoy good health, but you don't know what I have to put up with."

Let me say, friend, that I too hold the distinction of having suffered a "nervous breakdown." The reason I put the words "nervous breakdown" in quotes is that most so-called nervous breakdowns do not originate with any organic problem in the nervous system. Actually, most of what goes under the label "nervousness" ought to be called mental maladjustment.

When I was 24 years old and pastor of my first church, I suffered one of those so-called "nervous breakdowns" which was but the culmination of stress, anxiety, and worry. I was full-time pastor of a church, taking 19 college hours, and conducting evangelistic campaigns. My wife felt sorry for me. My church felt sorry for me. My doctor felt sorry for me. But no one felt as sorry for me as I felt for myself. Finally the doctor ordered me to get away for several weeks of rest and diversion. My church graciously made this possible.

During those weeks of convalescence God spoke to my heart and showed me that my condition was not the result of any organic difficulty, but the result of the *sin* of worry. With gratitude to God I can say that since the fall of 1948 I have not lost five minutes of sleep over any problem, difficulty, tension, worry, or any adverse circumstance of life whatsoever. Today my physical condition is as perfect as can be. In fact, an insurance company returned to me the culmination of seven years of penalties I had been paying on premiums because of a condition in my 20's which they feared. I attribute the improved physical condition to the conquest of worry.

Worry is a sin. The Bible is the only book that deals adequately with the problem of sin. Quite logically, then, we go to the Word of God to find the solution to this problem.

> Rejoice in the Lord alway: and again I say, Rejoice.
> Let your moderation be known unto all men. The Lord is at hand.

Be careful for nothing; but in every thing by prayer
and supplication with thanksgiving let your requests be
made known unto God.

And the peace of God, which passeth all understanding, shall keep your hearts and minds through Christ
Jesus.

Finally, brethren, whatsoever things are true, whatsoever things are honest, whatsoever things are just,
whatsoever things are pure, whatsoever things are
lovely, whatsoever things are of good report; if there be
any virtue, and if there be any praise, think on these
things (Philippians 4:4-8).

Delight yourselves in the Lord, yes, find your joy in
him at all times. Have a reputation for gentleness, and
never forget the nearness of your Lord.

Don't worry over anything whatever; tell God every
detail of your needs in earnest and thankful prayer, and
the peace of God, which transcends human understanding, will keep constant guard over your hearts and
minds as they rest in Christ Jesus.

My brothers I need only add this. If you believe in
goodness and if you value the approval of God, fix your
minds on whatever is true and honourable and just and
pure and lovely and admirable (Philippians 4:4-8—
Phillips).

Now give thought to the words of our Lord in Matthew
6:25-34:

Therefore I tell you, stop being perpetually uneasy
(anxious and worried) about your life, what you shall eat
or what you shall drink, and about your body, what you
shall put on. Is not life greater (in quality) than food, and
the body (far above and more excellent) than clothing?
Look at the birds of the air; they neither sow nor reap nor
gather into barns, and yet your heavenly Father keeps
feeding them. Are you not worth more than they? And

which of you by worrying and being anxious can add one unit of measure (cubit) to his stature or to the span of his life? (Psalm 39:5-7). And why should you be anxious about clothes? Consider the lilies of the field and learn thoroughly how they grow; they neither toil nor spin; Yet I tell you, even Solomon in all his magnificence (excellence, dignity and grace) was not arrayed like one of these (1 Kings 10:4-7). But if God so clothes the grass of the field, which today is alive and green and tomorrow is tossed into the furnace, will He not much more surely clothe you, O you men with little faith?

Therefore do not worry and be anxious, saying, What are we going to have to eat? or, What are we going to have to drink? or, What are we going to have to wear? For the Gentiles (heathen) wish for and crave and diligently seek after all these things; and your heavenly Father well knows that you need them all. But seek for (aim at and strive after) first of all His kingdom, and His righteousness (His way of doing and being right), and then all these things taken together will be given you besides.

So do not worry or be anxious about tomorrow, for tomorrow will have worries and anxieties of its own. Sufficient for each day is its own trouble (Matthew 6:25-34—*Amplified New Testament*).

The passage in Philippians 4:4-8 constitutes the biblical basis for this book. Out of these verses the thesis of this book is lifted. As we progress, other Scriptures will be used to give added emphasis, insights, illustrations.

Now here is the formula for victory over worry:

Praise plus **Poise** plus **Prayer** equals **Peace**.

Subsequent chapters will amplify and develop this formula found in Philippians 4. The factors involved in praise and in poise and in prayer will be discussed. Suggestions—specific suggestions—will be made for the purpose of assisting you in putting this formula into practice.

Observance of this formula would sweeten the atmosphere of many homes, convert many a faltering business into a thriving success, significantly improve the scholastic level of many a student, give meaning and purpose to many an aimless life, and deliver many a person from a premature grave by curing what is now psychosomatic illness (that is, a physical disorder orginating in or aggravated by emotional turbulence) but which would, if left alone, deteriorate into organic illness.

Remember the formula: **Praise** plus **Poise** plus **Prayer** equals **Peace**. Write this formula in large letters. Place one on the mirror of your medicine cabinet where you shave or on the mirror of your dresser. It will be well for the husband to place one in a conspicuous place in the office where he works and for the housewife to have one placed over the sink or in some prominent place where it will catch her eye during the daytime. It will also be well if you will attach one to the sun visor in your automobile. You will find great profit if you will place this formula in several conspicuous places where it will command your attention several times during the day.

Let me further suggest that you memorize the verses found in Philippians 4:4-8. It will be helpful for you to repeat them aloud every morning and every night until they become a part of you.

Now you are ready to begin the discussion of the cure of this vicious sin, worry.

Part 2

PRAISE

4

The Requirement to Rejoice

Rejoice evermore (1 Thessalonians 5:16).

Rejoice in the Lord alway: and again I say, Rejoice (Philippians 4:4).

Delight yourselves in the Lord, yes, find your joy in him at all times (Philippians 4:4—Phillips).

You say, "But I don't feel like rejoicing. I don't feel like being happy." By that you mean that the circumstances engulfing you are not such as contribute to your happiness.

The majority of people who are chronic worriers make the ridiculous mistake of waiting until the circumstances engulfing them change. You must change the circumstances whenever possible, but happiness is not a state of becoming, it is a state of being. You don't acquire happiness. You assume happiness.

Notice that the verse (Philippians 4:4) is in the imperative mood. It is mandatory. Paul doesn't say, "If you are so disposed let me suggest that you rejoice." No. He says, "Rejoice in the Lord alway: and again I say, Rejoice." Literally it could be translated, "Keep on rejoicing in the Lord always: and again I say, keep on rejoicing." Make the joy of the Lord the habit pattern of your life. When you fail to do this, you sin.

You rejoice when you praise. You cannot praise God without rejoicing in God and rejoicing in the circumstances, no matter how unpleasant, which God permits.

The word *praise* in its various forms, and the word *rejoice* in its various forms, are mentioned more than 550 times in the Word of God. The very fact that this subject receives such repetitious attention in the Book of God indicates its importance.

In Psalm 34:1 David said:

> I will bless the Lord at all times: his praise shall
> continually be in my mouth.

Praise was the habit pattern of David's life even though, like you, David had many troubles and difficulties. He often passed through deep waters. One son, Adonijah, broke his heart. Absalom, another son, betrayed his father and tried to usurp his authority. Another son, Amnon, brought grief to David's heart when he committed adultery with his half sister, Tamar. You also remember how viciously Shimei cursed David on one occasion. Every Sunday school pupil remembers the story of Saul's persecution of David. Saul repeatedly sought David's life and with barbaric treachery hounded him. Yet in all of this David blessed the Lord and fulfilled the requirement to rejoice. God's praise was continually in David's mouth.

In Psalm 33:1 David admonishes us to:

> Rejoice in the Lord, O ye righteous: for praise is
> comely for the upright.

This is the injunction of the man who was "a man after God's own heart."

After Peter and the apostles had been beaten mercilessly for speaking "in the name of Jesus," they departed, "rejoicing that they were counted worthy to suffer shame for His name" (Acts 5:41).

You are entitled to no particular commendation simply because you rejoice when everything goes well. When, however, you have made praise and rejoicing the habit pattern of your life, you have arrived at that place where you not only bring glory to God, but you set up an immunity against worry.

Rejoice even on blue Mondays and black Fridays.

Though it seems that friends have betrayed you, neighbors are vicious and mean to you, relatives don't appreciate you, and tragedy overtakes you, you will conquer worry with the attitude expressed in Isaiah 12:2,4:

> Behold, God is my salvation; I will trust, and not be afraid: for the Lord JEHOVAH is my strength and my song; he also is become my salvation.
> And in that day shall ye say, Praise the Lord, call upon his name, declare his doings among the people, make mention that his name is exalted.

The late Mr. Owen Cooper of Yazoo City, Mississippi, is one of the nation's outstanding Christian laymen and one of Mississippi's top-ranking citizens. Sometime ago his beautiful home, representing the dreams and hard work of many years, went up in smoke. Some of the members of the family barely escaped with their lives. The fire completely gutted the home and destroyed nearly everything of value.

Shortly after the terrible fire, Mr. Cooper's pastor, Dr. Harold Shirley, told me that the entire family was in prayer meeting the following night. In that service Mr. Cooper arose during the testimony time and with a radiance that only God can give expressed his gratitude to the Lord for sparing their lives. He had learned years before the truth of Romans 8:28:

> And we know that all things work together for good to them that love God, to them who are the called according to his purpose.

Despite this calamity, the habit pattern of the Cooper family could not be affected adversely.

Remember what has been said previously. There is no condition or circumstance that can justify worry. Worry is a sin. Praise is an antidote to worry.

One of the most radiant Christian men I have ever met passed through a heart-crushing trial several years ago. To help augment the family income during the depression, he and his wife provided room and board for a "highly respected citizen." The man whom they took in turned out to be a Judas, a betrayer. He seduced my friend's wife with diabolical cunning. When she tried to break off the relationship he went berserk. He strangled her and then put her baby in the oven and turned on the gas, murdering the little one by asphyxiation. He then took the couple's eight-year-old son out into the garage and strangled him with a piece of wire. Then the depraved man returned to the kitchen, lay down on some chairs in front of the stove, with all the gas jets on.

The rescue squad was able to revive the viperous murderer. But my friend lost his wife and children in that one terrible series of tragedies.

This crushing blow would have upset the mental balance of a lesser man than my radiant Christian friend. In the strength of the Lord he actually went to the penitentiary to witness to the murderer of his entire family. The way my friend conducted himself through that ordeal and during the subsequent years has had an impact for good and for God that words cannot express. Of course he was grief-stricken. But through it all the joy of the Lord remained his abiding and unwavering possession.

You say you have troubles? Surely you do. We all have. When rejoicing has become the habit pattern of your life you are not a thermometer personality registering the temperature of your environment. You are rather a thermostat personality setting the temperature. You have learned, in the words of Paul to "Rejoice evermore" (1 Thessalonians 5:16).

Paul was no "ivory tower theorist." He urged the Christians at Philippi to "Rejoice in the Lord alway: and again I say, Rejoice" (Philippians 4:4). He was a prisoner in Rome. He did not say, "Cry with me," or "Mourn with me," but "Rejoice with me." What a hysterical time he could have had, waiting to be martyred. If he could rejoice in an hour like that, what excuse can we find for our anxieties?

To help you obey this commandment—obedience to which will revolutionize your life—let me suggest some helps.

5

How to Control Your Feelings

Think and act joyfully and you will feel joyful. You can control your feelings by controlling your thoughts and your actions.

It is a basic law of human nature that you will feel as you act or think. In other words, if you don't feel the way you want to feel, think and act the way you ought to feel, and soon you will feel the way you are thinking and acting—ideally this will be the way God wants you to feel. I will give you an illustration. Go to a quiet room, stand with your feet about a foot apart at the heels and at 45-degree angles. Clasp your hands behind your back, letting them hang loosely. Bow your back and neck and head slightly, maintaining complete relaxation of the body. Now start thinking resentful thoughts.

Did you observe what happened? Immediately you straightened up because of the contraction of your muscles. You became taut. Your thoughts, actions, and feelings are interrelated.

When a man comes into my study and sits down in a relaxed manner, placing the ankle of his right leg loosely over the knee of his left leg and leans back, I know he has absolute confidence in me. He has no fear of me, for a position of defense would be hard to assume from this posture.

Carry this over into your everyday life. When you are depressed and forlorn and feel that you have nothing but trouble, *smile. Throw your shoulders back. Take a good deep breath. Sing.* Better still, *force yourself to laugh.* Keep forcing it until you are laughing heartily. At first it will seem mockery, but I guarantee you, it will chase away your gloom.

You cannot think *fear* and act *courageously.* Conversely, you cannot think *courage* and act *fearfully.* You cannot think *hatred* and act *kindly.* Conversely, you cannot think *kindly* and act *hatefully.* Your feelings inevitably correspond to your dominant thoughts and actions.

Is this scriptural? Absolutely! God's Word says, "For as he thinketh in his heart so is he" (Proverbs 23:7).

Now once again read verse eight of our text and see how important it is.

> Finally, brethren, whatsoever things are true, whatsoever things are honest, whatsoever things are just, whatsoever things are pure, whatsoever things are lovely, whatsoever things are of good report; if there be any virtue, and if there be any praise, think on these things (Philippians 4:8).

Obedience to the command of verse eight will result in obedience to the command of verse four. As you think, so will you feel. Our feelings are revealed by our actions. For instance, when I see a man with his feet set at ten minutes to two and his lips at 20 past eight, who pushes his weight instead of carrying it, I say to myself, "Watch out. This man is a potential tyrant." When I see a woman nervously moving her wedding band back and forth on her ring finger, I often assume she is suffering from the itch—or more probably she and her husband are not getting along too well.

No, you may not be able to directly control your feelings, but you can control your thoughts and actions voluntarily. Therefore, in the strength of Christ, master your thoughts and actions and thus dominate your feelings.

It is impossible for you to "rejoice in the Lord always" and to worry at the same time. Furthermore, you cannot remove worry thoughts and fear thoughts by simply saying, "I don't want to be afraid. I don't want to worry."

If you would win over worry, discipline yourself to think upon the "these things" of verse eight. Chapter 10 will give added insight on this subject. Let your actions accommodate themselves to your thoughts. Discipline yourself to smile, to maintain good posture, to talk with a musical voice in a dynamic manner—in short, to act in a manner compatible with these positive thoughts.

Don't start tomorrow; start *today*. Start *now*. Your worries will flee. God will be glorified.

Mr. Robert E. (Bob) Glaze of Dallas, Texas, has distinguished himself as a Bible teacher, a patron of the arts, a civic leader, a family man, and a businessman.

He is a member of the President's Council of the Dallas Symphony Association. He has taught a Bible class every Sunday morning for 40 years or more, and he has been written up in such prestigious business publications as *Fortune* as an outstanding businessman.

Bob is a certified public accountant by profession. Things went very well for him from the time he was discharged from the Navy where he served as an officer during World War II. After several years as a comptroller for a large organization, he and three friends decided to go into business for themselves. The business collapsed within a year. Bob did not panic, did not go into the trough of depression, but he took control of his situation and, like a superb sea captain, skillfully maneuvered the ship of his life through dangerous and uncharted waters.

He would not compromise with just any position that came along. He determined what he would like to do and with whom he would like to be associated. His number-one choice was America's leading developer, Mr. Trammel Crow of Dallas.

Bob had heard that Trammel Crow was a fitness buff. So Bob got into first-class shape himself. He was 43 years old at the time. He made an appointment with Trammel Crow. During the interview, Trammel suggested they visit the fourteenth floor of one of his buildings. Bob had heard that Trammel did not take elevators but, rather, ran up the steps. When Trammel arrived at the fourteenth floor, Bob was right behind him. Later Bob chuckled as he recounted the experience and said, "I don't know if Trammel hired me because he thought I was a good man for the job or because he was impressed that I could stay with him up the 14 flights of stairs!"

The point I'm making is that Bob kept his focus so tightly on his objective that he did not permit a divided mind. He gave no room to worry at all. He controlled his feelings by controlling his thoughts and his actions.

And he secured the position he wanted to the delight of both Mr. Crow and himself.

In November 1986, Bob was rushed to the hospital with a severe case of pancreatitis. His sickness and the complications from it lasted for more than seven months. As I understand it, rogue enzymes were attacking vital organs and endangering his life. The cause of the problem was a bad gall bladder situation. However, Bob was so weak they could not take the chance of operating. For weeks on end, he was fed intravenously. Three times, according to the doctors, they nearly lost him. After his gall bladder surgery, Bob announced to the doctors the day he would go home. They were skeptical, but Bob acted on the conviction that the surgery was a success and that he would be home earlier than the doctors had originally suggested . . . and he was.

This is no appeal to foolhardiness. Bob would not be imprudent. He would be positive.

Today, in his late 60's, he is back at his usual pace, which would make the tongue of a vigorous young man hang out.

Bob is quick to acknowledge that God supernaturally intervened in restoring him to health. He and his wife Ruth believe that God heard the prayers of literally thousands of Christian friends around the world. And he is quick to give God the glory, as are all of us who had a share in helping to love him and pray him through this ordeal. However, I must quickly point out that Bob, during this time, never permitted himself to focus his attention on anything except the expectation that he would survive, get well, and live a vigorous and fruitful life.

I submit to you that God honored his faith and the faith of his friends—and God also honored the focus of his mind, which gave foundation to the kind of emotions that are helpful in healing.

If you have not read *Anatomy of an Illness* by Norman Cousins, I suggest you do it. Norman Cousins, the famous writer and editor, was not expected to live. He concluded that if bad emotions can induce illness, why should not good emotions contribute to health?

I'm not making an appeal for an empty-headed assault on reality. I am making an appeal for reality.

Did not the sage say, "A merry heart doeth good like a medicine"?

Norman Cousins controlled his emotions by controlling his thoughts. That's exactly what Bob Glaze did. Norman Cousins has lived a productive life for more than a decade after the doctor said he could not survive. And Bob Glaze came through his ordeal very recently, at the time of this writing there is every evidence to believe that God has great things yet for him to achieve—and by God's grace, he'll do it. He controls his feelings by controlling his thoughts and his actions.

Much damage is done to the cause of Christ by professing Christians who shout out their defeatism and negativism by the limp manner with which they shake hands, the listless way in which they walk, the sourpuss countenance they maintain, and the plaintive and whining way in which they speak. I believe that these people do more damage to the cause of Christ than all of the bootleggers, extortionists, whoremongers, drunkards, and the riffraff of society's gutter put together.

Several years ago as pastor of a large church in a Southern city, I faced problems that would have challenged my sanity had it not been for the grace of God. Though it was kept from the congregation, several of the leaders and I learned that one of the senior deacons was enmeshed in sin. To make matters worse, he showed no signs of remorse and evidenced no desire to repent. Evidence was also uncovered indicating that another prominent member was stealing over $100 a week from the Sunday school offerings. The pressure was on. The question was, "What shall we do? Shall it be made public? If it is made public, will not the testimony of Christ suffer irreparably? Will not the witness for God be hampered irremediably for years to come?"

In addition to these problems, my wife and I had a sorrow in our home. Our precious little son was totally paralyzed. He suffered from cerebral palsy as a result of birth injuries caused by an intoxicated doctor who has since committed suicide. The little fellow was hovering between life and death. Where was the answer to my despondency?

My mind was drawn to Psalm 1. As never before I learned to appreciate the wisdom of that blessed man who delights in the law of the Lord *day and night*. I did not want to feel as I was feeling. It was not a good testimony. Therefore, by God's grace I fastened my thoughts upon the "these things" of Philippians 4:8 and endeavored to act in a compatible manner. On several occasions I would get into my car, drive outside the city, and literally force myself to laugh and to sing. I'm sure some passersby thought I was crazy. But this procedure was what kept me from going crazy!

Think and act the way God would have you to think and act. Result? You will feel as you think and act. This will glorify God. It will help you give worry the brush-off.

6

Count Your Many Blessings

If you would utilize this tonic of praise as an antidote to worry, you must *count your many blessings.*

Here again you must "gird up the loins of your mind" and with sheer determined effort force yourself, if necessary, to focus your attention upon all of the blessings God has so lavishly bestowed upon you. Read the Psalms for help in this.

Your blessings may not be material blessings, but they are real blessings, nevertheless. Actually, no man has ever found joy simply because he acquired material gain. Joy does not consist in the abundance of our material possessions.

> . . . for a man's life consisteth not in the abundance of the things which he possesseth (Luke 12:15b).

For how much money would you sell the health that God has given to you? How much does your wife's love mean to you? Have you ever thoroughly evaluated the value of your child's devotion? For what amount would you sell your reputation if it could be put on the open market? What premium do you put upon the eyesight God has given you—and the capacity to hear, and to speak, and to feel, and to taste? Have you ever thought how impoverished you would be if suddenly you were to be deprived of all your friends?

We tend to take the manifold blessings of God for granted, don't we? Start counting your blessings; your heart will overflow with gratitude and your lips with praise.

You may have heard the following story:

> There was a king who was so unhappy that he dispatched one of his men to go on a trip and find a

happy man. The king ordered, "When you find the happy man, purchase his shirt and bring it back to me that I might wear it and also be happy." For years the king's man traveled and searched. He could not find a happy man. Finally, one day when he was walking in one of the poorer sections of one of the most impoverished countries he heard a man singing at the top of his voice. He followed the sound and found a man who was plowing a field. He asked the plowman, "Are you happy?"

The plowman replied, "I have never known a day of unhappiness."

The king's representative then told the plowman the purpose of his mission.

The plowman laughed uproariously as he replied, "Why, man, I don't have a shirt!"

Also speaking of gratitude are the following lines:
"I had the blues because I had no shoes
Until upon the street I met a man who had no feet."

Count your blessings. If it will help you, periodically take a piece of paper and write out your blessings. Praise God for the love of your wife, the affection of your children, your good health, the encouragement of your friends. As you exert some effort along this line, blessings by the score will come crowding into your consciousness and you will jump to your feet, your heart singing, "Praise God from whom all blessings flow!" And you will be honoring the Lord in obeying the exhortation of Philippians 4:4.

How precious also are thy thoughts unto me, O God! how great is the sum of them!
If I should count them, they are more in number than the sand: when I awake, I am still with thee (Psalm 139:17,18).

> Many, O Lord my God, are thy wonderful works
> which thou hast done, and thy thoughts which are
> to us-ward: they cannot be reckoned up in order
> unto thee: if I would declare and speak of them,
> they are more than can be numbered (Psalm 40:5).

Spurgeon, the great Baptist preacher of the last century, wrote of a young man who had suffered an accident in which he had broken his hip. The hip did not heal properly and it left the man crippled. Earnestly the people prayed that God would restore this young man to health and strength. Shortly after the people began their intense and concerted intercession on behalf of this young man, apparent tragedy struck—the young man fell and broke his hip again. Was his a tragedy? It would have been completely natural for him and for the intercessors to begin to complain, for it seemed as though the condition was much worse. Fortunately many of the intercessors—wise and mature Christians—saw God's hand in the entire affair. They began praising Him and thanking Him for the blessing. Now the hip was set properly. It wasn't long until convalescence under God's leadership had done its perfect work. The young man walked with no limp whatsoever. The tragedy was a blessing.

Count your blessings! Even when things seem to go wrong, thank God and take courage. Say with the apostle Paul:

> Most gladly, therefore, will I rather glory in my
> infirmities that the power of Christ may rest upon
> me (2 Corinthians 12:9b).

In 1950 the Lord blessed us with a precious baby boy. Due to a tragedy described in detail a little later in this book, the little fellow nearly died. God was pleased to spare him, but he was now totally paralyzed. He had a keen mind and normal inclinations and desires, but his body would not respond to the demands of his will. Oh, yes, it hurt—hurt him and hurt us. However, God gave him a marvelously sweet disposition.

Was his paralysis and condition as a cerebral palsy victim a blessing? Yes. *Definitely so.* Between the year of his birth and the year I resigned the pastorate to go into full-time evangelism I undoubtedly buried more little babies and small children and ministered to more sick children than any man in any pastorate. God had conditioned me in a special way for a peculiar and yet a blessed ministry that He was about to entrust to me. The life of my son was a distinct blessing. There are many ways in which I could demonstrate this, but they involve experiences locked up in the cherished and secret places of my heart and open only to God and our immediate family.

Johnny died in 1975, 16 years after the first edition of *How To Win Over Worry*. People came from as far as 5000 miles away to his funeral. One man who drove from a distant city said, "I never knew exactly how to express to Johnny what an inspiration he was to me. I wanted to come here, because I'm sure he's conscious of this service, and I just want him to know how much he meant to me."

Letters from every continent on earth poured in after his death—people telling what a blessing his life had been to them.

Christine, my wife, always looked upon Johnny's life as a special blessing from the Lord. That attitude takes the sting out of hurt and the power out of worry.

In one of the prominent nations in the news, an Asian nation, a young minister of the gospel preaches to between 1200 and 1500 people every Sunday. In that nation people have been slaughtered by the thousands. When I met with this remarkable leader in a neutral capital of the world, I said, "How do you handle the pressure of trying to maintain a ministry in a city and nation vocally committed to the destruction of Christianity?"

He smiled at me and said, "How good is God. What blessings He bestows!" I thought to myself, "This poor fellow didn't hear what I said." But then the minister went on to explain.

"God has put us in the eye of the storm. On one side are the Communists. On the other side are the Muslims. They are in such hostile combat with each other that by being in the center we are wonderfully protected. Better still, hundreds are coming to know Christ as Savior."

This man was not bemoaning his lot; he was counting his blessings. I don't think that worry finds him a suitable host.

During my visits to Vietnam in the late '60's and early '70's, I met with many Vietnamese people. One man stands out. He told me how he regretted the war, how sorry he was that it was necessary for American boys to come and suffer separation from home, injury, and even death. Then he said, "The greatest victory of this conflict is that the Americans and the Koreans brought the gospel to our village, and we who were in darkness came to know Jesus Christ." This man had lost members of his family. He had lost his business. His home had been burned to the ground. He knew how to count his blessings!

During the Korean conflict, 1950-53, Presbyterian missionary Dr. Harold Voekel had a penetrating and pervasive ministry among the troops—on both sides. He personally won to faith in Christ more than 150 North Korean soldiers, 20 of whom are now in the full-time gospel ministry.

It was Voekel who introduced my mother and father, so I have more than a casual appreciation for that gentleman. The characteristic that captured my attention every time I was with Dr. Voekel was his bouyant and resilient Christian optimism in any situation. He knew how to count his blessings, and worry never seemed to quite catch up with him.

"Count your blessings. Name them one by one, and it will surprise you what the Lord has done." And one of the greatest surprises will be the fact that you are no longer saddled by that monster, worry, who has been riding herd on you.

Let me urge again that when you become depressed and worried, take a piece of paper and literally force yourself to write out in detail every blessing that comes to mind. Concentrate. Think hard. Surely it will take time, but not as much time as worrying will. It won't take as much time as an interview at the psychiatrist's office and it will be considerably cheaper. Furthermore, in the strength of God you will be actively doing something about your own condition. This is much more effective than passively responding to psychotherapy.*

In chapter 7 consideration is given to a most important factor in the matter of praise.

*Please do not misconstrue what has been written as an expression of disregard for the effectiveness of all professional counseling and for its importance in certain situations. Nevertheless, there are many people who today are frequenting the offices of psychiatrists who could be enjoying mental and emotional health had they only taken certain precautions and observed the biblical formula—**Praise** plus **Poise** plus **Prayer** equals **Peace**—earlier in their life.

7

Anticipate Apathy

Don't expect to be appreciated. When you are appreciated it will be like the cherry on top of the whipped cream of your strawberry sundae—something a little special.

Let not your rejoicing be dependent upon appreciation shown to you.

Our Lord healed ten lepers. Do you remember how many came back to thank Him? That's right. One!

The late General Harry C. Trexler, a wealthy philanthropist and outstanding citizen of Allentown, Pennsylvania, was providing the financial needs for 40 college students in 1933, the year in which he died. Four months before his death he called his secretary in and inquired how many young men and women he was sending through college. She told him. With mixed bewilderment and grief he replied, "And last Christmas I got only one or two Christmas cards from this group."

Many times, when discussing this prevalent ingratitude, I have stated in a jocular vein, "Would you believe it? Why there are some people who don't even appreciate me!"

Expect ingratitude. Give for the joy of giving and soon you will be so thrillingly occupied with this privilege of giving that you will not have time to reflect upon the ingratitude of others.

Sometime ago I read about a man in New York who, over a period of more than four decades, helped more than 5000 young people secure positions in New York City. When discussing it sometime later he observed that only six had expressed gratitude.

Years ago there was a shipwreck in Lake Michigan. A powerful swimmer who was then a student at Northwestern University rescued 23 persons before he finally collapsed.

Some years after that, in Los Angeles, Dr. R. A. Torrey was telling the story about this young man's concern and his heroic deeds. To his astonishment he found out that the man, now old, was in the audience. In talking with the rescuer, he asked him what was the most significant thing about the rescue—the thing that stood out most in his memory after all the intervening years. The rescuer dropped his eyes and in a low voice said, "Not a one said 'thanks.' "

Have you ever read about Aristotle's ideal man? Here is the philosopher's definition of the ideal man. "The ideal man takes joy in doing favors for others; but he feels ashamed to have others do favors for him. For it is a mark of superiority to confer a kindness; but it is a mark of inferiority to receive it."

Paul reminded the Christians to whom he was speaking that "It is more blessed to give than to receive" (Acts 20:35). Therefore, let your joy arise out of the blessedness of giving, of helping, of doing. Not expecting gratitude, find your joy in the very act of service.

Years ago Samuel Johnson said, "Gratitude is a fruit of great cultivation. You do not find it among gross people."

I am sure you have noticed how many times when friends move away from us or we change residence to a distant city, how eloquent and emotional we are in affirming that we will stay in touch—we'll write letters, we'll phone, we'll visit. Think back and ask yourself how often such resolutions have been carried out, whether it was with your gang at the college dormitory, your buddies in the military service, your neighbors down the street, the friends you met on a 60-day cruise overseas, your coworkers at the office or factory, or whatever.

It's not that we intend to ignore our friends. It's the apathy within us that does the work. Unless you, yourself, take measures to counteract the apathy natural to all of us, you'll lose the benefit of continuing relationships and uplifting experiences. But when you have examined your own heart, you'll not find it so difficult to grasp why others are also apathetic.

Take the matter of class reunions. Usually there are one or two spark plugs in the class. Were it not for them, there would be no reunions. They are the ones that take action, aggressively contact all the other members, and take steps to bring about a completely delightful experience of getting together after years of absence from each other.

It was the sage who said, "He who would have friends must show himself friendly." And maintaining friendships takes discipline, time, and energy.

To the degree that you understand the natural inclination toward apathy in your own life and grasp the insight regarding those whom you feel should not be apathetic to you—to that degree you will increase your capacity for the component of praise, the deterrent to worry and its divided mind.

It is quite evident as you read the Pauline epistles that some of the very people whom Paul won to faith in Jesus Christ turned upon him and reviled him maliciously.

Do you know what is the basic sin? Someone answers, "Unbelief." No, if you will read Romans 1:21 you will conclude that ingratitude is at the root of all sin whether that ingratitude be active or whether it be passive:

> Because that, when they knew God, they glorified him not as God, neither were thankful; but became vain in their imaginations, and their foolish heart was darkened (Romans 1:21).

Was not ingratitude the root of the sin committed by Adam and Eve?

Consider it. The Lord Jesus Christ died for us "while we were yet sinners" (Romans 5:8). He suffered. He bled. He died—for *us*. Yet there are millions who, knowing this, refuse to accept Him as Savior and Lord. Why? Ingratitude!

Ingratitude is a universal sin. Expect it. Give for the joy of giving. Do for the joy of doing. Help only for the joy of helping. And you won't have time even to notice the prevalence of the sin of ingratitude.

Praise should be the habit pattern of your life regardless of the cold and even cruel treatment received from some whom you have helped.

8

Master the Art of Altruism

If you would conquer worry with this weapon of *praise* you must master the art of altruism.

Become genuinely interested in other people. Love your neighbor as yourself. Honor God by losing your life in serving others. By "others" I am referring not only to your employer or your family, but also to all those whom God gives you the privilege of serving.

An upset young college man sought counseling from Dr. George W. Truett who was pastor of First Baptist Church of Dallas, Texas at that time. The student had passed through troubled waters. He said he was ready to give up his faith and that he had lost all confidence in God and people. Wisely and patiently Dr. Truett listened to this young man. When the student finished his tale of woe, the wise and patient pastor asked the young man for a favor. The young man agreed. Dr. Truett then gave the young man the name of the hospital and the room number of a patient who was in need of a visit. Said the great-hearted minister, "I just don't have time to make the visit. You make it for me." The young man assented.

He came away from that hospital bed a new man. As a favor to the mighty pastor in Dallas, the young man determined to do his best. He did so well that he became genuinely interested in the patient. In so doing, his own difficulties and despair were dispelled.

Uncle Joe Hawk was one of the most radiant personalities I ever met. For more than half a century he was a member of the First Baptist Church of Cleveland, Tennessee. When I met him, he was 87 years old but younger than many 25-year-old-people. He attended every service I conducted in that good church in 1953.

Let me tell you a little about him and you will catch an insight into his sparkling vitality at 87. Years before, during the depression, the First Baptist Church of Cleveland, Tennessee was in straitened circumstances. Uncle Joe Hawk was a drayman. He had been blessed with a good business, but of course he was suffering as were the other businessmen during those oppressive years. Nevertheless, he forgot himself. This dear man lost himself in his concern for that church and its people, many of whom had not yet accepted Christ.

At the risk of putting a calamitous crimp in his business, Uncle Joe sold his two finest dray horses. He gave the money to the church. Because of his gift the First Baptist Church of Cleveland, Tennessee, stands as a mighty citadel for Christ today. Few people knew what he did. He did it without fanfare. In fact, many of the church members today are unaware of this tremendous sacrifice. Uncle Joe never got the money back from the church. He didn't expect to. He didn't want it. He gave it for the sheer joy of giving. He gave it to the eternal glory of God and for the spiritual profit of man. No man who is that interested in others has time to worry about his own problems.

When was the last time you sacrificed and sent anonymously a gift of $50 over and above your tithe to a college or seminary student who was having a hard time? When was the last time you gave something to someone anonymously— a gesture that could in no way profit you from a material standpoint?

Perhaps the mother next door is sick and in great need of help. Why not offer to take care of the children for a couple of days? True, they may be little monsters. That is all the more reason your help would be a great benefit to their mother. When your neighbor goes on vacation, why not offer to take care of the mail and send it on? Why not drop a line of appreciation to that teacher who has taken such an interest in your child and has made such a distinct contribution to his highest good? Drop a line of gratitude to your pastor for the message that was such a blessing to you. Encourage him. It will take only a few moments of time and a stamp.

Does not the Word of God tell us we are to esteem others better than ourselves?

> Let nothing be done through strife or vainglory;
> but in lowliness of mind let each esteem other better
> than themselves (Philippians 2:3).

Let me earnestly suggest that you determine to do something specific for someone every day—something for which no remuneration of any kind will be sought or expected. You may exclaim, "Shades of the Boy Scouts!" but this is what good religion is all about and besides, it will relieve you of that time you normally give to worrying. Your cup will run over with the joy of the Lord.

Go ahead, do it *now*. If it doesn't come to you easily and if you don't know how to begin, simply sit down and ask the Lord to guide you. With pencil and paper write down some things that come to your mind.

Perhaps the Lord will lead you to do the washing for the lady next door who has been hampered by her day-and-night care of sick children. Perhaps you will contact the head of some fine Christian college or one of our seminaries to secure the name of a student who is in great need. You will help him. You may be led to invite a serviceman to have dinner with you on Sunday (we are not as thoughtful along that line as we were during the war years). There is no point in my going on; you take it from here.

I am persuaded that my mother, who suffered major illnesses for the last 45 years of her life—she died at 80—lived such a long and fruitful life because of the way she immersed herself in serving others. When a family moved into the neighborhood, she would be there with some warm food while they were getting settled. When someone was sick, she would take a card to them, as well as some thoughtful little present. She maintained correspondence with hundreds of people around the world.

I think that serving others created in her a greater capacity to praise. She was a mild-mannered lady, quiet of demeanor, but a person of strong will and great capacity to care for others.

To this day, nearly a decade after her final illness and death, people all over the world will talk to me about her. They will tell me some little act of kindness that she had shown toward them. They will produce a postcard, a letter, or a greeting card that she had mailed to them.

One of her close friends died in 1939 in Massachusetts. Mother maintained contact with the four daughters, their spouses, and the grandchildren from 1945, when she left Massachusetts, until late 1978 when she became bedridden.

It is giving, not getting, that induces praise. It is serving, not being served, that develops the highest type of rejoicing. And, of course, no one can rejoice and worry at the same time. The two are mutually exclusive.

If you want to find real joy in living and a genuine escape from worrying, get involved in helping others. It will leave you no time to worry.

A friend of mine, Elmer G. Leterman, visited Honolulu in 1935. In those days, the main mode of travel from the West Coast of mainland United States to Hawaii was by ship. When Leterman descended the gangplank and was greeted effusively by friends who put leis around his neck and his wife's neck, he noticed there were hundreds of people disembarking whom nobody met. They were not given leis. He had hardly unpacked his suitcase at the hotel until he determined that as long as he was in Hawaii, he would meet every boat with a sufficient number of leis to welcome every person who did not have someone meeting him, and put a lei around his neck with the robust "aloha" for which Hawaiian hospitality is internationally known.

As it turned out, people whom he contacted in this way gave him multiplied millions of dollars of business over the next 40 years, even though he didn't show personal interest in people for that purpose. Elmer was a happy man, always upbeat. He had mastered the art of altruism. And it left no room for a divided mind.

Mr. Ee Peng Liang of Singapore is a man past retirement age who has earned the respect not only of the Singapore people, but of people around the world who have watched his humanitarian efforts over the years. He is a chartered accountant by profession and heads up a substantial business in Singapore. The man never ceases to amaze me in his capacity for remembering detail. I met him once. Periodically I will get a note from him with a warm greeting. There is absolutely nothing that I could do for him in a business or personal way except give him the assurance of the continuity of my friendship and respect. But Mr. Ee does not do what he does in order to get. He has mastered the art of altruism, and he impresses me as being one of the most worry-free men I have met in the course of my travels. He has a focused, integrated mind—not a divided mind.

I first heard of Mr. Ee through Mr. Fred Lang, who was for years the head of Dallas Community Chest. Whenever I've visited civic leaders in the Orient, I've been impressed by the numbers who know Mr. Ee and marvel at the contribution he has made to their understanding of the opportunities to help meet the real needs of people.

By all means, use common sense in your efforts to assist other people. Don't be like a certain young Cub Scout who had his own ideas on the subject. One night during a pack meeting the scoutmaster asked all those who had done their good deed for the day to lift their hands. All hands were lifted except the hand of one scout.

The scoutmaster barked out, "Johnny, go out and do your good deed for the day and don't come back until you have done it."

Johnny left. He was gone about 20 minutes. He came back. His clothes were in shreds. His hair was disheveled. His face was cut and bleeding.

The scoutmaster said, "Johnny, what have you been doing?"

Johnny replied, "I did my good deed for the day, sir."

"What was that?" asked the scoutmaster.

"I helped an old lady across the street, sir."

"Well," said the scoutmaster, "how did you get in that condition?"

"She didn't want to go," replied Johnny.

Use common sense in your effort to help others. During the darkest part of the depression a needy family was given an expensive pedigreed French poodle. Doubtless there is much good to be said about a French poodle. But the friend who gave the dog would have been much wiser and more helpful if she had taken the same money and purchased needed clothing and food for the family.

Assist the other person at the point of his greatest need. While doing so, remember "It is more blessed to give than to receive" (Acts 20:35).

Your genuine interest in other people will assassinate the monster of worry. Your positive thoughts of concern for others will crowd out the negative fear-producing thoughts of worry.

Reflect once again upon the concern our Lord showed for others. Even while dying, He cried out, "Father, forgive them for they know not what they do." While in the agonizing process of dying upon the cross He showed concern for His mother and made the finest possible preparation for her after His departure.

Man is as selfish as he dares to be. We are selfish by nature. The middle letter of sin is "I." The middle letter of pride is "I." It takes the cross experience to adequately cancel out the "I." Real Christian discipline in the strength of God is required to master the art of altruism, but the rewards are immeasurable—especially as they relate to the altruist.

Without exception the people who are always rejoicing are people who have mastered this art of altruism—people who are genuinely interested in others. This rejoicing chases away gloom and kills worry.

You will "rejoice in the Lord always" as you faithfully fulfill the injunction in Galatians 6:2-4:

> Bear ye one another's burdens, and so fulfil the
> law of Christ. For if a man think himself to be

something, when he is nothing, he deceiveth himself. But let every man prove his own work, and then shall he have *rejoicing* in himself alone, and not in another.

I share with you these same verses in the *Amplified New Testament:*

Bear (endure, carry) one another's burdens and troublesome moral thoughts, and in this way fulfill and observe perfectly the law of Christ, the Messiah, and complete what is lacking (in your obedience to it). For if any person thinks himself to be somebody (too important to condescend to shoulder another's load), when he is nobody (of superiority except in his own estimation), he deceives and deludes and cheats himself. But let every person carefully scrutinize and examine and test his own conduct and his own work. He can then have the personal satisfaction and joy of doing something commendable (in itself alone) without (resorting to) boastful comparison with his neighbor (Galatians 6:2-4).

Part 3

POISE

9

Our Impelling Motive

Let your moderation be known unto all men. The Lord is at hand (Philippians 4:5).

Have a reputation for gentleness, and never forget the nearness of your Lord (Philippians 4:5— Phillips).

Now listen to the fuller translation of the *Amplified New Testament:*

Let all men know and perceive and recognize your unselfishness—your considerateness, your forbearing spirit. The Lord is near—He is coming soon.

The word translated in the King James "moderation" can also be translated "suitable," "fair," "reasonable," "gentle," "mild," "patient," and "lenient." The word further carries the idea of "congeniality of spirit." After making a thorough study of the word you will inevitably conclude that I have spelled it correctly—poise—for according to Webster the word *poise* means "balance," "stability," "ease," "dignity of manner," etc.

What is the supreme inducement to poise? What is our impelling motive? What is the driving force that pushes us toward this goal? Here it is in a brief and meaningful message: "The Lord is near"! This is a literal translation of the words in the King James, "the Lord is at hand." In fact, the actual translation would be "the Lord near." Three words! No verb was used. It was not needed. It is abrupt to the point of the dramatic. It is a bolt of light.

The awareness of His nearness gives great calm in the storm and stress of life.

As a child, I was small and sickly. I was the prey of every bully on the school playground. One day during holiday time in the summer of 1934, I was in Grand Rapids, Michigan, with my cousin Alex Haddad. I had accompanied him down to Seymour Square to pick up some groceries for his mother. We had nearly returned to their little house on Burton Street when three big fellows in a pickup truck came by and shouted, "Haddad, get yourself and that blankety-blank Hebrew, Wop, Dago cousin of yours out of here before we mop up the gutter with you."

Immediately I cringed. I thought to myself, "Uh-oh, here comes another beating." Then I looked over at Alex, and my fears subsided; a peaceful calm replaced them. In fact, I started to smile.

That year, Alex was the AAU wrestling champion in the 175-pound division. At 15, he was much a man. His biceps were like cannonballs and his pectoral muscles were like marble slabs.

Strangely, Alex did not answer back. I said, "Alex, you're not going to let them get by with that, are you?"

"Well, John, you know what the Bible says: If they hit you on one cheek, turn the other."

I had never remembered Alex being that spiritual before, but I was in no position to contest his decision! So I kept walking with him toward the house. We went inside the little picket fence, and just as we got to the front door, he handed the other bag of groceries to me and said, "John, take these in to Mom. Tell her I forget something; I'll be right back."

I knew exactly what he had forgotten. I shoved the groceries inside the front door and then trailed him back down to Seymour Square. I knew exactly what he had in mind. He surmised that the insulting roughnecks were on their way to Miller's ice cream parlor. I got to the location just in time to watch Alex knock one of the three fellows out cold, addle a second fellow with another powerful punch, while the third ran away in stark terror.

I pushed back the shoulders of my four-foot-10-inch frame, brushed the palms of my hands together, and said to myself, "Anyone else?"

What had converted me from a terrified little boy to a calm and serene fellow of positive optimism? A simple answer: Alex was near.

Now, moving from the ridiculous to the sublime, I want you to know that the Lord is near. And living in the awareness of that fact brings about a behavioral change that cannot be explained in human terms. It's often the only major difference between a defeated Christian and a victorious Christian.

Fortune may have eluded you. Culture which you have sought so laboriously becomes ever more painfully remote. Professed love has betrayed you. All these may be true. But "the Lord is near"! There is no mockery in that statement. Those few words assure us, and they impel us to observe the mandates set down in Philippians 4:4-8.

This truth gives urgency and charm to the admonition set down by Paul in this fourth chapter of Philippians.

This statement can refer to Christ's nearness to us right now or to His Second Coming. The best interpreters so agree.

John Calvin, Bishop Moule, and Dean Vaughan all prefer the thought of Christ's present nearness. On the other hand, equally great teachers and commentators such as Dean Alford, F. B. Meyer, and Bishop Lightfoot, prefer the interpretation which is eschatological. They believe the emphasis is on the Second Coming of Christ.

Let us take advantage of the insights of both groups of commentators.

The Lord is near *locally*. "Thou art near, O Lord," sang the psalmist (Psalm 119:151a). And the apostle Paul echoes and glorifies the ancient song.

The Lord is near in that He indwells, by the Holy Spirit, the individual Christian. It is "Christ in you" (Colossians 1:27).

Then the Lord is near from the standpoint of His *availability*. The psalmist cried, "The Lord is nigh unto all them that call upon him" (Psalm 145:18). Here again the New Testament echoes the Old Testament. As children of God we have His ear because we have His heart. A distant Lord would depress us and distress us. An unapproachable Savior could not help us. Thank God, Christ is approachable.

> For we have not an high priest which cannot be touched with the feeling of our infirmities; but was in all points tempted like as we are, yet without sin.
> Let us therefore come boldly unto the throne of grace, that we may obtain mercy, and find grace to help in time of need (Hebrews 4:15,16).

In the exigencies and vicissitudes of life the Lord is near. The psalmist anticipated this truth again. He sang, "The Lord is nigh unto all them that are of a broken heart" (Psalm 34:18). Who has not known the distressful mystery of a broken heart! "God is . . . a very present help in trouble" (Psalm 46:1). The consciousness of Christ's availability induces poise.

Then the Lord is at hand *eschatologically.* He is coming again in clouds of heaven with great glory. I believe His coming is sooner than we think. Very real to the early Christians was the return of our Lord. He Himself declared it in no ambiguous terms.

Jesus may come today. In the silence and darkness of midnight His trumpet may sound and His awful glory blaze upon us!

Our love of His appearing is the greatest inducement to obedience of this admonition to poise in Philippians 4:5. Every injunction mentioned in this book—injunctions all rooted in His divine mandate to us—is more easily fulfilled when we are motivated by the continuous consciousness of the possibility that Jesus may come today. "Be ye also ready" (Matthew 24:44).

The return of our Lord viewed as possibly near should make us rich in Christian character. Contemplation of this truth will make us like Him who is our great Exemplar.

Remember the King James translation of Philippians 4:5: "Let your moderation be known unto all men. The Lord is at hand." The preferable translation of the last sentence is, "The Lord is near." The greatest inducement to poise is the consciousness of the nearness of your Lord. This is the greatest impelling motive to that poise that combats worry.

As you live in the consciousness of the nearness of the Lord, you will find strength that will enable you to observe the biblical formula for peace. You will find strength and inclination to observe the factors involved in the matter of praise.

You will find the factors relating to poise much easier to fulfill as you live in the consciousness of the nearness of your Lord. For instance, you will find that your thoughts are thoughts that please Him and therefore positive thoughts that will put worry on the run. As you live in the consciousness of His nearness you will realize a strength, not your own, enabling you to exercise the self-control that leads to poise and banishes worry.

You will also have victory in the matter of relaxation as you live in the consciousness of the nearness of your Lord.

In the matter of scheduling, the consciousness of the Lord's nearness is a great boon. We avail ourselves of His help. We know that "The steps of a good man are ordered by the Lord" (Psalm 37:23).

Living in the consciousness of the nearness of our Lord will dispel the clouds of pessimism and lead us into the sunshine of enthusiasm and optimism. You cannot live in the consciousness of His nearness and go around looking as if you were born in crab-apple time, put up in vinegar, and weaned on a dill pickle. People who act as though they were born in the kickative mood and the objective case are those who live oblivious to the nearness of the Lord.

With respect to every factor mentioned in Part 3 of this book, fulfillment is largely contingent upon your awareness of the nearness of the Lord.

It goes without saying that Part 4—"Prayer"—of this book is meaningless apart from the consciousness of the nearness of the Lord.

To sum up: The Lord is near *locally*. That should remind us that He is watching everything we do. The Lord is at hand with respect to His *availability*. That assures us of the needed resources to fulfill our every responsibility to Him and for Him. The Lord is at hand *eschatologically*. That reminds us He may come at any time. This induces us always to live in a way that would not shame us if He were to burst unexpectedly upon the scene.

In these three words, then—*the Lord near*—lies dynamic truth. These words are the steam of motive power generating attitudes and activities in fulfillment of the divine demands.

10

Poise Through Thought Control

Finally, brethren, whatsoever things are true, whatsoever things are honest, whatsoever things are just, whatsoever things are pure, whatsoever things are lovely, whatsoever things are of good report; if there be any virtue, and if there be any praise, think on these things (Philippians 4:8).

For as he thinketh in his heart, so is he: Eat and drink, saith he to thee; but his heart is not with thee (Proverbs 23:7).

In chapter 5 the truth was set forth that while we cannot control our feelings directly, we can control them indirectly by controlling our thoughts.

You can control your thoughts directly if you so desire. To be sure, it will take some discipline. Arnold Bennett, in his splendid book, *How to Live on Twenty-Four Hours a Day*, challenges the reader to think on any given subject every day for at least 15 minutes without permitting his mind to wander. I challenge you to try it.

Many people can brood for 15 minutes. They can worry for 15 minutes. But very few people can focus their attention on any given, and I might add worthwhile, subject for 15 minutes without permitting their minds to wander.

To repeat a statement previously made in this book, you cannot think fear and act courage. If you want victory over anxiety, you must develop the control of your thoughts which leads to that poise that conquers worry.

The wisest man of history assures us that we are what we think. That is true. In the words of Marcus Aurelius, "A man's life is what his thoughts make of it." Ralph Waldo Emerson states the truth in another way when he says, "A man is what

379

he thinks about all day long." Our dominant thoughts tend to externalize themselves.

It's an old trick, but school children still love to play it. One will go to Billy and say, "Say, you look terrible. Are you feeling well today?" A little later another one will approach him with a similar suggestion. And then a third. And a fourth. Soon the thought of his not being well becomes Billy's dominant thought—and he goes home sick!

In my first pastorate there was a young lady 29 years of age who maintained an expression on her face that looked like the advance agent of a coming cyclone. She *enjoyed* poor health! Her house was a mess and her general appearance looked like an accident going somewhere to happen. She would come out the front door after the church service and I would shake her hand. It was so limp I felt like handing it back to her. I would say, "How are you?" She would then proceed to tell her tale of woe. I was only 22 years old, but I learned one lesson in a hurry. I stopped asking her how she was. When I shook her hand, I *shook* it, believe me! I gave her my finest smile and said, calling her by name, "You look so much better. You must be feeling better." Believe it or not, within a few months she was looking better and apparently feeling better. With the help of some friends I dropped a seed thought into her mind which became a dominant thought and as she thought, so she became.

Paul says to think on the things that are true. Don't think on falsehood. Think on falsehood and pretty soon you will become false. Your heart will condemn you and your worries will increase.

Think on things that are honest, not dishonest. Your thoughts will tend to externalize themselves. If you think honestly, you live honestly. The word here could be translated, "honorable." Think on things that are honorable. Even if it is true, refuse to think about it if it's dishonorable.

Think on things that are pure. The word used here refers to all sorts of purity. As Peter would say, "Gird up the loins of your mind" (1 Peter 1:13a). An impure thought always precedes an impure deed. Keep your thoughts pure and your deeds will be pure. Pure thoughts are incompatible with worry thoughts.

Think on things that are lovely. This word means "winsome and pleasing." As you embrace thoughts that are winsome and pleasing you will bar from entrance thoughts that produce worry and anxiety.

The apostle Paul says, "Think on things of good report." The words *good report* come from two words meaning "fair-speaking." It could also be translated "attractive." Attractive thoughts will also deliver you from worry. Attractive thoughts will deliver you from being a sourpuss.

Paul then said, "If there be any virtue, and if there be any praise, think on these things." The word *virtue* comes from a word *aresko* which means "to please." Here again learn to control your thoughts so they will relate to that which pleases; they will be pleasing thoughts.

Under God, control your thoughts. Some people are miserable because they are indiscriminate with respect to the guests they invite into their minds. They think worry thoughts, fear thoughts, anxiety thoughts. They don't see the glass half full, they always see it half empty. They are not optimistic, they are pessimistic. They pride themselves by sanctimoniously saying, "I expect the worst so that I will never be disappointed." Expect the worst and you will get the worst. Thoughts of the worst dominating your life tend to externalize themselves into your outward actions so that you become the creator of the worst. You therefore create a self-destroying monster.

Do your own thinking. You must guard yourself even against the well-meaning but oftentimes negative influences and damaging advice of relatives and friends. They mean well, but they often do much damage. Don't leave your mind open to the negative influence of other people. Read the biography of any dynamic personality—any achiever—and almost without exception you will discover that discouraging remarks, poor advice, negative influences, and downright opposition were thrown across his path by the people who were the closest to him.

Misery loves company and worriers will do their best to drag you down to their level, as the following story illustrates.

> There were two farmers. One was a pessimist, the other was an optimist.
>
> The optimist would say, "Wonderful sunshine."
>
> The pessimist would respond, "Yeah, I'm afraid it's going to scorch the crops."
>
> The optimist would say, "Fine rain."
>
> The pessimist would respond, "Yeah, I'm afraid we are going to have a flood."
>
> One day the optimist said to the pessimist, "Have you seen my new bird dog? He's the finest money can buy."
>
> The pessimist said, "You mean that mutt I saw penned up behind your house? He don't look like much to me."
>
> The optimist said, "How about going hunting with me tomorrow?" The pessimist agreed. They went. They shot some ducks. The ducks landed on the pond. The optimist ordered his dog to get the ducks. The dog obediently responded. Instead of swimming in the water after the ducks, the dog walked on top of the water, retrieved the ducks, and walked back on top of the water.
>
> The optimist turned to the pessimist and said, "Now, what do you think of that?"
>
> Whereupon the pessimist replied, "Hmmm, he can't swim, can he?"

In the strength of God, control your thoughts. Let them be regulated according to the will of God. Such thoughts will lead to inner poise that is a shield against worry.

11

Poise Through Self-Control

Study the records of those whom the world calls great and you will observe that every one of them possesses this quality of self-control.

Many homes are wrecked through lack of self-control. Only God knows the number of churches whose testimonies have been irreparably neutralized simply because of this prevalent lack of self-control among the leadership. Businessmen by the thousands who are capable and qualified in every other respect receive only a fraction of their income potential due to this lack of self-control.

Never retaliate against your enemies. In so doing you may force them to pay the price of grief, but the resultant price of your own grief will be greater. The Bible tells us that we must love our enemies (Matthew 5:44).

While you are hating your enemies you are giving them the sovereignty of your own life. You are literally forcing them to dominate you. For instance, here is a man who has wronged you. You loathe him. Your loathing becomes a festering personality-sore. You so detest him you would not welcome him into your home. You would not permit him to fraternize with your relatives. You would not invite him to eat at your table or spend the night in your guest room. Yet, all the time, while you are hating him you are "entertaining" him in your blood-stream, in your brain cells, in your nerve fibers, in your muscles, and in the marrow of your bones. You are giving him power over your sleep, power over your blood pressure, power over your health, power over your happiness. You are *insisting* that he destroy your body and disintegrate your effectiveness. *Tragic!*

Some years ago *Life* carried an article on high blood pressure. In that article the statement was made that the chief personality trait of people with high blood pressure is resentment. What a price to pay for lack of self-control! They are paying financially in doctors' bills and medical assistance. They are paying emotionally with shattered nerves. They are paying in reduced efficiency resulting in decreased income. They are paying domestically in strife in the home resulting from the projection of their bitterness and misery. *What a price!*

Learn a lesson from our Lord in whose steps we are commanded to follow:

> Who, when he was reviled, reviled not again; when he suffered, he threatened not; but committed himself to him that judgeth righteously (1 Peter 2:23).

Well did the wise Solomon say:

> Better . . . is he that ruleth his spirit than he that taketh a city (Proverbs 16:32b).

Reflect for a moment upon the poise of the immortal Abraham Lincoln. In the anguish of his most grief-producing hours, he exercised poise. Had it not been for this quality it is doubtful that the war between the states would have ended in victory for the Union Army. It is highly doubtful his name would have been immortalized had it not been for this magnificent quality. Men in his own cabinet were disloyal to him, trying on several occasions to discredit him. To his back they made light of him, scoffed at his limited education, and sneered at his rustic ways. Realizing that their disloyalty was to him personally, and realizing further that they possessed qualities making them essential to our nation, the ex-railsplitter exercised self-control, disregarding the objectional characteristics of these colleagues.

In attaining the mastery of self-control you must learn how to *conquer criticism.* I do not mean that you can avoid criticism. Nor do I mean that you can subdue criticism. You can conquer it, however, with respect to its relationship *to you* personally.

Once again follow the example of our Lord who answered His critics so often with silence. Our Lord defended other people. He defended the Word of God. He defended the work of His Heavenly Father. He defended little children. *He never defended Himself!*
Usually you will find it wise not to answer your critics.

> Answer not a fool according to his folly, lest thou also be like unto him (Proverbs 26:4).

Your friends don't need an answer and your enemies won't believe the answer.

Unjust criticism is often a disguised compliment. It often indicates that you have excited the jealousy and envy of the critic. As the old adage goes, "No one ever kicks a dead dog."

It is wise to listen to criticism of yourself, but do it objectively. While listening, don't allow yourself to become emotionally involved. Sometimes you can profit greatly. If the criticism is just, do something about it. If the criticism is unjust, put it where you put your other garbage.

Clergyman are often criticized! If the minister wears a black suit, the critics say, "Who does he think he is—Digger O'Dell?" If he wears a sport coat, the critics question, "What is he trying to do, imitate a movie star?" If he has five children they respond, "He can't afford such a family. Why doesn't he use better sense?" If he has only one child they quip, "Doesn't he know the Bible says that we are to be 'fruitful and multiply'?" If he visits the poor they say he is showing off. If he visits the rich they say he is playing politics. If he drives a Buick they say he ought to drive a car priced within his means. If he drives a Volkswagen, they say, "What's he trying to do, embarrass us by letting people think we don't pay him enough?" If he preaches 30 minutes, they say he is long-winded. If he preaches 20 minutes they say, "What's the matter, didn't he study last week?" If he goes away to conduct meetings in another church they complain, "He ought to stay home and take care of the flock." If he stays home and never goes away, they howl, "What's the matter, doesn't anyone else want him either?" My father gave me some good advice when I entered the ministry. He said, "John, listen to what people say when they are mad. That's what they really mean."

A man flies off the handle. He says some nasty things. After he cools down he comes back and says, "I really didn't mean that." Of course he meant it! If he had not thought it, he would not have said it, for God's Word makes it clear that "Out of the abundance of the heart the mouth speaketh" (Matthew 12:34b). He didn't draw those words and thoughts out of thin air. They were in his heart.

While I am no disciple of Freud, I do believe in the so-called Freudian slips. When a person writes me a letter in longhand and he crosses out one word and writes down another, I may spend 15 or 20 minutes holding that letter up to the light trying to decipher the word crossed out. In all probability that was what he really meant.

When you respond to criticism volcanically, you lose possession of many of your faculties so that your thoughts become inaccurate, your decisions unwise, and your words regrettable.

Let me tell you a little habit I have formed which has served me well. By nature I am very explosive. After all, I am half Syrian and people from that part of the world are not usually phlegmatic. When God called me into the ministry, He impressed upon me the fact that by His grace my spirit must be completely dominated by Him if I were to be an effective ambassador of the Court of Heaven. I memorized and meditated upon 2 Timothy 2:24,25.

> And the servant of the Lord must not strive; but be gentle unto all men, apt to teach, patient. In meekness instructing those that oppose themselves; if God peradventure will give them repentance to the acknowledging of the truth.

Now here is the procedure I have followed when the provocation of unjust criticism has sorely tempted me to lose my head. Through sheer conscious effort I listen objectively. I look at the person who is venting his anger, but I do not see him, for in my mind's eye I am watching a moving picture. A huge elephant is walking down the street. I picture myself as that elephant. Over by the curb (and I am inclined sometimes to think, in the gutter) there's a little ant who is spitting at the elephant. Rather ludicrous, you say. Precisely. It helps my sense of humor. Now then, does the elephant stop and threaten the ant? Of course not. The elephant is unaware of the puny efforts of this pompous ant.

All I can say is that this certainly works for me and I have no copyright on it. It keeps me in complete possession of my faculties so that I can think clearly and quickly, talk judiciously, and act wisely.

An American statesman was once quoted as saying, "Never lose your temper except when you do it on purpose." That's a good statement and one that will bear much thought.

Let's go back to Abraham Lincoln for just a moment. While he was an occupant of the White House, some loquacious "smut-sprayers" and "character assassinators" spread the rumor that he was living with a black woman. What did the President do? Nothing. This man of poise had learned that in a fight with a skunk you might win the fight, but you will smell awful!

If as you've been reading these last few paragraphs you have caught yourself chuckling a time or two, good. Don't take yourself too seriously.

A vital relationship with God through Christ will result in self-control and you will refuse to respond to criticism with smug complacence, worldly courtesy, patronizing condescension, or vindictive retaliation. You will respond with *love* which is not compatible with fear, the basis of worry.

> There is no fear in love; but perfect love casteth out fear: because fear hath torment. He that feareth is not made perfect in love (1 John 4:18).

12

Poise Through Enthusiasm

Once again let me remind you that by poise we are referring to gentleness, fairness, and congeniality of spirit.

Enthusiasm is an indispensable ingredient. Some pseudo-
intellectuals may take exception to this. I reply simply that
most of what we do is done on the basis of emotional impulse
rather than intellectual impulse. I do not love my next-door
neighbor because of an intellectual theory regarding him.
Rather I love him because of an emotional impulse. You did
not buy that insurance policy because you intend to die
tomorrow and because through intellectual activity you
arrived at that sobering possibility. The main inducement was
strictly emotional. You saw your family destitute and in want
because of inadequate material resources. It was the emotional reaction of this that led you to buy the insurance policy.
You go to a football game. There you can tell no difference in
behavior between the spectator with a third-grade education
and the one with several doctoral degrees. They both respond
emotionally, with enthusiasm.

One of my hobbies is reading books on salesmanship. I
have a collection of over 40. Without exception each book on
salesmanship underscores enthusiasm as an essential quality
for success.

The leaders of this world always have been and are men of
enthusiasm. Adolph Hitler knew the power of enthusiasm.
His formula for speaking was "Say it simply. Say it often.
Make it burn." And the Austrian "paper hanger" became a
world figure who could not be ignored. Paul the apostle was a
man of enthusiasm as his own autobiographical remarks in
Galatians 1:14 and Acts 22:3 attest. He was so enthusiastic
about the gospel he preached that some of the people in
Corinth accused him of madness (2 Corinthians 5:13).

The man who never wonders at anything never does anything wonderful. That partially explains why the work of the Lord suffers so across the land. Thousands of people who profess a relationship with God through Jesus Christ have apparently failed to grasp what Christ has done for us and what our privileges are in Him. Therefore they come to church on Sunday morning with a face long enough to eat ice cream out of a pipe. You could ruin the greatest football team in the nation if you would fill the grandstands for four consecutive games with the average Sunday morning congregation.

No wonder communism spreads while the religion of Jesus Christ fails to keep pace with the population increase of the world. One thing you must say for the Communists—they are enthusiastic about their cause. Next Sunday when you go to church, watch the average person as he comes in. He shuffles along dragging his lower lip behind him. Then he slides into the pew and hangs his lower lip over the pew in front of him. He looks as happy as the skull and crossbones on an iodine bottle. No wonder he has no peace of mind. Remember chapter 5. You cannot act one way and feel another way. When you act sour, you are sour.

Some people who profess "religion" have talked about it for so long in negative terms and in pessimistic platitudes that a distorted concept has made its way into the thinking of the people whom they influence.

I heard of a man who walked into a hotel lobby and stood beside another man at the room clerk's counter. The fellow eyed his neighbor for a moment and then could not restrain himself from asking, "Are you a preacher?"

"No," said the neighbor, "I've just been sick!"

And I can well understand the little girl who came home from Sunday school and going up to Betsy, the mule, lovingly stroked her long head and said, "Bless you, Betsy, you must be a wonderful Christian. You look just like Grandma."

Not only is a lack of enthusiasm ruinous to the work of the Lord, it is also ruinous to happiness in the home, success in business, the making and keeping of friends, and achievement in any field.

There is no such thing as a well-adjusted personality apart from enthusiasm. There is no such thing as a satisfactory social relationship apart from enthusiasm. You reap what you sow. You sow the wind and you get the whirlwind. You sow a deadpan expression and that is exactly what you reap from the people with whom you associate. For what you give you receive in kind, but in greater degree. That is a fact that cannot be denied.

It was my privilege to have an interview with Ray Jenkins, the brilliant lawyer from Knoxville, Tennessee, who presided over the Army-McCarthy hearings. In the course of conversation I asked him his formula for success in speaking. He mentioned several things, but one thing remains paramount in my mind. "Don't ever speak on a subject about which you are not totally enthused." This statement came from the lips of a man who is considered by the people of Tennessee, and of the United States for that matter, to be one of America's outstanding trial lawyers.

> Whatsoever thy hand findeth to do, do it with thy might; for there is no work, nor device, nor knowledge, nor wisdom, in the grave, whither thou goest (Ecclesiastes 9:10).

Enthusiasm is essential to *industry* which is discussed in chapter 18. Enthusiasm is like steam. It impels action. Many people never become enthusiastic over anything, therefore they never *do* anything. Their lives become idle and negative and worrisome.

Enthusiasm tones up the whole life. You know men, and so do I, who constantly complain that they don't get enough sleep. They lament that they wake up every morning feeling as tired as when they went to bed. But what happens when they plan a fishing trip? They are awake before the alarm sounds at four o'clock in the morning—and feeling great! The explanation? Enthusiasm! All things being equal, the person who is enthusiastic turns out three and four times as much work as the person who is listless.

No great work has ever been done without enthusiasm. I give to God all the glory for the ministry of Billy Sunday. But let me state it flatly. Had it not been for his enthusiasm it is highly doubtful he would have so influenced this nation and even the world through a ministry that could not be ignored. Brother, he was enthusiastic!

To be sure, some people seem to be born with a greater capacity for enthusiasm than others. However, this is a quality that can be developed. It is developed by focusing the mind upon a worthwhile goal until the attainment of that goal becomes your "Magnificent Obsession."

The salesmen who succeed are enthusiastic salesmen. Musicians who succeed are enthusiastic musicians. Watch Leonard Bernstein on television! Have you not heard of some musicians who became so engrossed in their practice that they forgot even to take their meals? I submit to you that their achievements would be impossible without enthusiasm.

Enthusiasm leads to achievement. A sense of achievement—an awareness of accomplishment—is indispensable to poise and to peace.

If you go about your daily responsibilities in a listless and lackadaisical spirit devoid of enthusiasm, you are doomed to failure. Your failure will create anxiety and worry. Anxiety and worry will create failure. Thus you become the duped victim of a vicious cycle.

Remember that you cannot focus your attention upon two thoughts at the same time. When you are enthused, you are focusing your attention upon thoughts that crowd out the thoughts producing fears and worry.

See what Paul suffered:

> Of the Jews five times received I forty stripes save one.
>
> Thrice was I beaten with rods, once was I stoned, thrice I suffered shipwreck, a night and a day I have been in the deep;
>
> In journeyings often, in perils of waters, in perils of robbers, in perils by mine own countrymen, in

perils by the heathen, in perils in the city, in perils in the wilderness, in perils in the sea, in perils among false brethren;

In weariness and painfulness, in watchings often, in hunger and thirst, in fastings often, in cold and nakedness.

Beside those things that are without, that which cometh upon me daily, the care of all the churches (2 Corinthians 11:24-28).

Did he worry? Did he fret? No! A godly enthusiasm delivered him from self-pity and worry. Ponder his poise—poise through enthusiasm.

We are troubled on every side, yet not distressed; we are perplexed, but not in despair;

Persecuted, but not forsaken; cast down, but not destroyed;

For which cause we faint not; but though our outward man perish, yet the inward man is renewed day by day.

For our light affliction, which is but for a moment, worketh for us a far more exceeding and eternal weight of glory (2 Corinthians 4:8,9,16,17).

13

Poise Through Relaxation

Poise and relaxation go together like bread and butter and ham and eggs. You cannot maintain poise while you are tense. It is also true that you cannot relax and worry at the same time. Read the books *Progressive Relaxation* and *You Must Relax* by Dr. Edmund Jacobson.

Learn how to work under pressure without working under tension. This is possible if you have periodic breaks in your activities. That is, periodic rest periods. The rest may be a *change* in activity. It is only by this procedure that your heart continues to work for 70 years or so. And believe me, it *works*. It pumps enough blood through your body every 24 hours to fill a railway tanker. Every day it exerts as much effort as it would take to shovel 20 tons of gravel onto a platform as high as your waist.

If you think to excuse your tension on the alleged (and fanciful) basis of your responsibilities, forget it! No one has had the responsibilities that fell upon our blessed Lord. If anyone had cause for tension, He had. Yet He always remained relaxed. Even when they sought to kill Him, He moved quietly and unhurriedly out of their midst. Can you possibly picture our Lord in a frenzied hurry? To be sure, however, there was a definiteness to His walk and to His talk and to the totality of His activities. He said,

> I must work the works of him that sent me, while it is day: The night cometh, when no man can work (John 9:4).

Yet despite that fact, on more than one occasion when pressured by others, He said in substance, "My opportunity is not yet come. The time is not fulfilled." He is our Exemplar

395

in poise through relaxation. Hear Him as He says, "Come ye yourselves apart into a desert place, and rest a while . . ." (Mark 6:31).

Well did Vance Havner say, "The Lord told His disciples, 'Come ye apart and rest awhile,' What He meant was, 'Come ye apart and rest awhile or come ye apart.' " Well spoken words, Dr. Havner! It says that many were coming and going so they didn't have enough leisure to eat decently. You know some people think that they are busy when they are only nervous—rather, when they are only mentally maladjusted.

Now let us repeat J. B. Phillips' translation of verse 6:

> Don't worry over anything whatever; tell God every detail of your needs in earnest and thankful prayer, and the peace of God, which transcends human understanding, will keep constant guard over your hearts and minds as they rest in Christ Jesus (Philippians 4:6).

There is a rhythm, a cadence in all of nature. Plants reproduce themselves in their seasons and men in their generation. There is a rhythm, a cadence in all the action of nature— in our breathing, in the ebbing and flowing of the tide, in the rising and setting of the sun. One of the earmarks of the amateur musician is that he does not give proper observance to the rests.

Thomas Edison got by on four hours' sleep a day, we are told. However, he had the ability to "snooze" at almost any hour of the day or night. He was relaxed at all times. One of the most prominent of our contemporary psychologists has suggested that we need rest for the body and sleep for the mind. He goes on further to say that the man who stays free of psychic tensions gets by on less sleep than the man who gets tied up in knots.

The last year that Dr. Robert G. Lee was President of the Southern Baptist Convention he was in his 60's. During that year he traveled over 150,000 miles, built an auditorium that cost over one and a half million dollars, and received over

1200 new members into the 9000-member Bellevue Baptist Church in Memphis, Tennessee, of which he was pastor.

One of his members, a prominent Memphis surgeon, Dr. J. Murray Davis, told me that the secret of Dr. Lee's output was his capacity to relax. Dr. Davis said, "It is incredible how this man maintains such a pace despite his years." Then the surgeon recounted this incident in the life of Dr. Lee:

> One Sunday morning I went to make my hospital visits at six o'clock. Dr. Lee was also at the hospital visiting. He then taught our Sunday school class that morning and followed that by the delivery of one of his matchless sermons at the 11 o'clock hour. Immediately after the morning service he flew by chartered plane to Longview, Texas, where he delivered a baccalaureate address Sunday afternoon. He flew back to Memphis in time to speak at a special assembly of the Baptist Training Union in our church. Following that he delivered the evening message at the 7:30 evangelistic hour. After the benediction of the evening service he rushed to the airport where he boarded a plane for California. He flew all night and spoke Monday night to a large convocation in California.

What a pace! Remember: This was when Dr. Lee was in his 60's.

For over a quarter of a century Dr. Lee averaged more than ten visits a day. He preached in his own church a minimum of three times a week and he taught a Sunday school class 44 Sundays out of every year. After he was 40 years of age he built a church from a membership of 1300 to a membership of more than 9000 while all the time traveling and preaching outside his own city nearly as often as an evangelist. The secret? He knew how to relax! He knew how to pace himself! He worked under pressure without working under tension. Now in his 80's he probably preaches as often (if not more often) as any of our contemporary preachers.

Learn the rhythm of successful living. When you work, work. When you rest, rest.

When my father was 62 years of age he pastored a vigorous church in New York State. He slept only a few hours a night. He walked two miles a day. He was one of the best paddleball players in Binghamton, New York, and all his opponents were under 35. On his sixtieth birthday he played two sets of tennis. How did he do it? He knew how to relax.

On several occasions, when visiting him, I had some amusing experiences. He sat in his high-back rocking chair, and I sat across from him. Right in the middle of our conversation he said, "You must excuse me, son. I am going to take a few minutes' snooze." He laid his head back and slept (I have timed him, and he has slept for seven minutes!). Opening his eyes and returning to his alert form, he said, "All right, now. Where were we?"

Most great achievers maintain the practice of having a nap sometime during the day. It has been proved that a person will fare better with six hours of sleep at night and an hour of sleep every afternoon than with eight hours of sleep at night with no break in the day.

As a young man I realized that if I were to be productive, I would have to master the ability to relax and to sleep. I worked at it assiduously. In the late 1960's, I boarded Northwest flight 7 from Seattle to Tokyo. The now retired head of World Vision, Dr. Ted Engstrom, was on the same flight. He said, "John, people tell me that you can sleep like a baby on these flights, and you don't even take a sleeping pill. I don't believe it."

I grinned and said, "Well, Ted, I'm grateful to God. It's true."

Our flight lifted off. We had a meal, after which I read a paper and thumbed through a magazine. About an hour and a half out of Seattle, I stretched across the three seats and laid my head on three pillows just under the window. I slept like a baby until 30 minutes out of Tokyo. Ted couldn't believe it. I had not taken any sleeping pill.

In the late 1970's, my young colleague, Dr. Michael Youssef, and I were waiting for the delayed takeoff of a Pan American flight from Miami to Rio de Janeiro. Our destination was Sao Paulo, where I was to lead a seminar the following day. Finally, at 11 o'clock at night, the plane started rumbling down the runway. I turned to Michael and said, "I'm going to turn on this penlight and do some reading." In what seemed to be just a matter of moments, I was aware that the plane was still rumbling down the runway. I turned to Michael and said, "When in the world are we going to take off?" It was only the grace of God that kept him from reverting to his preconversion vocabulary. He was frustrated! He said, "This is Caracas, Venezuela. You have been sleeping so hard since we left Miami that we couldn't even shake you awake for the meal."

We stayed on the ground in Caracas for an hour. I then slept the four hours from Caracas to Rio de Janeiro. We made a quick transfer flight to Sao Paulo. I cleaned up, shaved, combed my hair. When we disembarked in Sao Paulo, I was ready for a full day's work.

Michael said, "Chief, I am willing to go anywhere with you, but the next time, I'm going to leave two days early."

I said to him what I've said to people all over the world, "One of the best investments of discipline and effort you can make is in learning how to relax so that you can get proper rest, whether it be in a full eight hours end to end, or whether it be six hours with snoozes throughout the day, or whatever is the best for you."

There's no way that I could have maintained my schedule over the past 24 years had I not learned the secret of relaxation. In 24 years I have made 66 trips around the world; written eight books and hundreds of inches of copy for brochures, appeal letters, and magazine articles; averaged a speech situation nearly once a day; administrated an organization that has offices in all parts of the world; and maintained my own personal study habits and responsibilities. Were it not for my ability to relax, I would be a physical and emotional basket case by this time. At an age that some consider appropriate for retirement, I thank God I'm still able to function with a great deal of energy and zest, but relaxation is one of the keys.

Relaxation is a component of poise.

The soil of tension and frenzy is productive of the plant of worry. Therefore, ask God to help you to develop poise through relaxation.

14

Poise Through Scheduling

By scheduling your activities you will make great strides toward victory in the matter of relaxation.

Scheduling leads to relaxation because it defeats frenzy and hurry. Scheduling and regularity go together. These infer order and system which are the best antidotes to hurry. Hurry is symptomatic of a weak mind, or at least a weakly organized mind. Without scheduling and organization there is foolish haste which leads to glaring mistakes which in turn lead to discouragement and tension.

Let me suggest that you once again read the autobiography of Benjamin Franklin in which he tells of his effort to master the 13 virtues. He was past 80 years of age when he wrote the autobiography and after passing the four-score year mark he confided that order was the one virtue he had never been able to conquer. It is probably one of the most difficult habits to perfect.

Yet order is so important. Through disorganization we do not know where we are and there is always fear of the unknown. Worry, like a buzzard, preys upon the carrion of the disorganized mind.

I was told of a state hospital in Illinois. One day one of the inmates ran out of the gate and down the road as fast as he could run. The orderly chased him, caught him, and brought him back. The next day another inmate did exactly the same thing with the same result. That happened ten successive days with ten different inmates. Now, if the ten inmates had fled at the same time, and if each had run in a different direction, nine of them would have escaped. However, they were not *organized*. That's why they were in the institution!

Plan your work and work your plan. Ask God for the wisdom to help you plan your work and then ask God for the

grace to enable you to work your plan. "The Lord is near."
Call upon Him for the needed wisdom and grace.

Just as He led Nehemiah to plan for and to organize the
work of the building of the wall around Jerusalem and just as
He enabled Nehemiah and the brethren to work the plan—
despite unspeakable opposition—so the Lord will enable
you, if you will but call upon Him, to so plan your work and
work your plan that you will fulfill the divine injunction to be
"always abounding in the work of the Lord."

Fatigue is caused mostly by boredom. When you have no
order—when you have failed to schedule your activities—you
lack the awareness of accomplishment. Conversely, when
you have wisely scheduled your activities under the leadership of the Holy Spirit, and when in His strength you are
performing your responsibilities on schedule, you get the lift
that comes from the awareness of accomplishment. There is
nothing more invigorating than the knowledge of tasks efficiently completed, and there is nothing more dispiriting than
the knowledge of unfulfilled responsibilities.

Paul enjoins us to be "redeeming the time, for the days are
evil." By His grace and in His strength we will fulfill our
responsibility to redeem the time and at the same time we will
conquer worry through poise by scheduling.

Korean Presbyterians invited me to be the evangelist in
1970 for the Seventh Decade Spiritual Revolution Crusade.
The chairman was Dr. Kyung Chik Han, pastor of the world's
largest Presbyterian Church . . . the Young Nak (meaning
"eternal joy") Church in Seoul. The crusade was of three
weeks' duration, with one week in each of three cities—
Pusan, Taegu, and Seoul.

For 21 days I was honored to be in the company of this
world leader.

Twice dispossessed of all—literally *all*—his earthly goods,
he had known the scourge of Japan's cruel occupation in the
40's and North Korea's atheistic terrorism in the 50's.

In 1956, with 27 North Korean refugees, Dr. Han founded
the Young Nak Church. Just after the outer structure of the

new sanctuary was completed, the North Koreans stormed across the 38th parallel and into Seoul, driving freedomloving Koreans southward . . . and ultimately nearly into the sea. The new sanctuary was used by the North Koreans as an ammunition depot.

Dr. Han and his people established three other Young Nak churches during their southern exile.

Back in Seoul in 1953, the work continued, and the statistics are impressive. The membership climbed to more than 16,000 by 1972. More than 100 daughter churches were established. Schools, orphanages, senior citizens' quarters, summer camp and spiritual retreat grounds and facilities, special ministries among the military groups, are but a few of the projects launched under Dr. Han's leadership.

Yet, the dear man never appears harried or hurried. I watched for three weeks—in vain, I might add—for any sign of pique or impatience.

Dr. Han met with his people every morning for the five o'clock to six o'clock dawn prayer meeting. What a way to start every day!

His life was and is a model of quiet achievement . . . for Christ. He is the master teacher of "The Stewardship of Time." I have heard him. Better, I have watched him!

He so schedules himself, so plans his work and works his plan, that without frenzy he discharges herculean responsibilities.

He knows God has given him adequate time to achieve all that lies within the divine will. In complete dependence upon the Holy Spirit of God, he moves peacefully and productively.

Relaxed and gracious, he infuses a "God is in His heaven, so fear not" mood into the room.

Dr. Han's life is a symphony of poise. The atmosphere of his home is the vestibule to heaven. Fellowship with this man of God bestows its own special benediction.

The Lord gives us the ability and the time to do *everything* He expects us to do. We have an obligation and privilege to utilize these God-given resources to the end that His will for us be fulfilled. Fulfillment of His will for us honors God and tends to dispel worry.

God help us to be able to say as our Lord while yet on earth could say:

> I have finished the work which thou gavest me to do (John 17:4b).

15

Poise Through Sidelines

Probably a preferable word to sidelines would be diversions. Beauty consists of contrasts, shades, varieties, and changes. "Variety is the spice of life."

The apostle Paul was not only a preacher; he was also a logician. Apparently he was interested in athletics, because he alluded to athletics many times in his epistles. Furthermore, his reference to Greek poets in Acts 17 seems to indicate he was conversant with poetry. Certainly no one could deny that he was also a master at understanding human nature.

David the king was a sportsman, a poet, a musician, a militarist, and a philosopher. And who could adequately evaluate the multiplicity of interests maintained by his son Solomon?

> And he spake three thousand proverbs: and his songs were a thousand and five.
> And he spake of trees, from the cedar tree that is in Lebanon even unto the hyssop that springeth out of the wall: he spake also of beasts, and of fowl, and of creeping things, and of fishes (1 Kings 4:32,33).

You will see here that Solomon was a sage—"he spake three thousand proverbs." He was a musician and poet—"and his songs were a thousand and five." He was a horticulturist—"and he spake of trees from the cedar tree that is in Lebanon even unto the hyssop that springeth out of the wall." He was an expert in animal husbandry—"he spake also of beasts." He was an ornithologist—"he spake of fowl." He was an entomologist—he spake "of creeping things." He was a piscatologist—he spake "of fishes."

405

Take the example of our own Lord. Study His parables and you will conclude that He was interested in and conversant with all phenomena and activities. Jesus was the Master Psychologist. He understood the laws of agriculture and horticulture. Our Lord displayed great interest in the sea and in fishing. He certainly understood the laws of anatomy and body function. He was an ornithologist and He knew animal husbandry.

Because of the broad interests of our Lord, men of every strata of society and rank of individuality and echelon of culture listened to Him with absorption. He could appeal to the religious and cultured and educated Nicodemus equally as well as He could appeal to the woman of ill repute from Samaria.

Diversion of interests, a hobby, or an avocation effectuate the balance that leads to poise. They bring the other dimensions into life that give life real perspective.

When Paul the apostle was forced out of Berea because of persecution and a threat to his life, he did not go to Athens and brood. He kept busy. In Athens he went down to the marketplace and listened to the dialogues of the philosophers. He studied the habit patterns of the Athenians. There he discovered their basic interests and their mental behavior. This turned out to be fruitful in the extreme. It wasn't long until they insisted that he go to Areopagus—to the top of Mars Hill—where only the great orators and the celebrities were permitted to speak. There he delivered the most masterful sermon ever preached by any man (our Lord excepted, of course). Through diversion he refused to give himself time to brood over his lot as a persecuted and a hounded preacher of the Word.

No man can honor God in a maximum way whose only interests are within the boundaries of a narrow and specialized field. Without a variety of interests you will not maintain any interest for long.

You see, this works hand in glove with the already mentioned importance of becoming genuinely interested in other people.

The brilliant pulpit orator from Louisiana, Dr. James W. Middleton, has been through enough to drive to despair and shatter the nerves of five rugged men. Recently he was out of his pulpit for nearly a year because of throat difficulties that subjected him to the surgeon's scalpel on two different occasions. His entire ministry seemed to be in jeopardy. Yet, as you listen to that matchless preacher, you are at once impressed with his poise—his sense of inner peace. As you hear that magnificiently controlled bass voice rising and falling, whispering and roaring, declaiming and appealing, like a mighty four-manual pipe organ under the domination of a master, you detect complete mastery. I am convinced that one of the explanations of his self-control and poise lies in his hobbies, one of which is horticulture. He has performed some amazing grafts of plants in tree stumps. He, too, is a sportsman—a fisherman and a hunter of no mean ability.

Dr. Roy O. McClain, former pastor of the First Baptist Church of Atlanta, Georgia, and selected some years ago by *Time* as one of the ten outstanding American clergymen, had several hobbies, among which were the raising of Shetland ponies, painting, the playing of the organ, and woodworking. These hobbies served as a balance wheel enabling him to honor the Lord in a maximum way through unruffled poise even though he was saddled with the titantic task of pastoring the largest congregation in the state of Georgia.

I seriously doubt Australian Dr. Ernest Watson the dean of Haggai Institute could maintain his Spirit-set pace were it not for the diversion he finds in swimming, music, and other outside interests.

President Eisenhower found diversion in painting and in golf.

The late Dr. Harry A. Ironside, who was deprived of an education past the eighth grade (I should say he was deprived of "schooling" past the eighth grade. His education was equivalent to that required to earn several doctor's degrees) found his diversion in poetry and in learning Greek and Chinese.

Dr. J. C. Massee, now deceased, formerly one of the nation's outstanding ministers, evangelists, and seminary professors, maintained a youthfulness and a virility usually associated with a man half his years. He found diversion in the study of words and in gardening, to mention but two of his many interests. When I last talked with him, I was uplifted and challenged by his spirit. When many men at his age (the mid-80's) would be complaining and dawdling, he was productively active. In discussing the blessings of the Lord upon his life, he said to me in a triumphant note, "My lines have fallen in pleasant places" (cf. Psalm 16:6).

You will notice that I have mentioned a number of clergymen. The reason for this is that ministers, more than any other group of men, have reason to get bogged down in the mire of routine responsibilities. They are on call 24 hours a day, seven days a week. They never have the satisfaction of knowing that everything is done. There is always another person to visit, another letter to write, another message to prepare. No wonder Dr. Wesley Schrader wrote the article appearing in *Life* some years ago on "Why Ministers Are Cracking Up."

For years I had looked with envy on people who did downhill skiing. I felt I could not afford the cost, and I knew, without a shadow of a doubt, I could not afford the time. However, I set my goal to take up skiing at 63. On my sixty-third birthday I drove to Hopfgarten, Austria, and for the next two-and-a-half weeks, I enjoyed the professional excellence of Austria's proverbial ski geniuses. In seven days, I was coming down the steepest slope of Hopfgarten Mountain. In nine days, I was feeling much more comfortable. Before I left, my Austrian friends gave me a videotape made by Austria's Department of Ski Instruction so that during the summer months I could rehearse the various moves by watching the video.

This is the first time I have had an athletic sideline to which I have devoted energy, enthusiasm, and resources. I tell you frankly that this sideline, skiing, has done as much to undergird inner poise and serenity as anything I have ever done.

For one thing, you cannot come down a steep ski slope and think about anything else except skiing. It's a marvelous way to force yourself to brush aside the multitude of energy-sapping little problems that are a part of daily living.

I'm not suggesting that you take up the sideline of skiing. I am suggesting that you find some sideline to which you can give wholehearted enthusiasm—a sideline that helps you to relax and that reinforces inner poise. Some women find diversion in mastering the art of cooking, in interior decorating, in gardening, in music, in writing, in all types of sports, and in a host of other interests.

Let me suggest that for added stimulus along this line you read Marie Beynon Ray's book *How Never to Get Tired.*

In Mark 6:31 when Jesus said to the apostles, "Come ye apart and rest awhile," the context shows that they did not go apart for a time of inactivity. Rather they went out to eat and then they engaged in a different form of activity. More times than not, rest is effectuated not by cessation of activity, but by change in the activity.

Jesus was always busy about His Father's business even though the pattern of His activity changed often.

Some men, it is true, find within the framework of their calling enough variation so that they maintain the poise that comes through diversion within the confines of their calling. This was true of Dr. George W. Truett.

The world-famed industrialist, the late R. G. LeTourneau, had an important appointment in his plant at Toccoa, Georgia. While in flight to Georgia the landing gear of his plane stuck. The pilot radioed ahead to the Anderson, South Carolina, airport and told them of his plight. Ambulances and a rescue squad rushed to the airport. The newsmen and the cameramen were on the spot ready to cover the landing. They made a good crash landing. When Mr. LeTourneau got out of the plane his first words, in substance, were, "Where's the car? Where's the car? I am already late for my appointment in Toccoa. Can you get me a car immediately?"

There is poise. I asked him one time when he took his

vacation. He said, "I never take a vacation. My work is my play and you never need a vacation from play." There was a man who through Christ and wise self-discipline learned the poise that conquers worry.

16

Poise Through Seizing the Day

In other words, live for today!

The songwriter D. W. Whittle understood this truth when he wrote,

Moment by moment I'm kept in His love,
Moment by moment I've help from above.
Looking to Jesus, till glory doth shine;
Moment by moment, Oh, Lord, I am thine.

The trouble with many people is that instead of "looking to Jesus" they are looking to tomorrow.

Yesterday is a cashed check and cannot be negotiated. Tomorrow is a promissory note and cannot be utilized today. Today is cash in hand. Spend it wisely.

This is the day which the Lord hath made; we will rejoice and be glad in it (Psalm 118:24).

Lowell Thomas had these words framed and hung on the walls of his broadcasting studio at his farm so that he could see them often.

If this verse is the convicton of your heart, it is impossible for you to worry.

Don't live in the past. On the other hand, don't live in the future. Paul was in the habit of "forgetting those things which are behind" (Philippians 3:13). While it is true that he was striving for future mastery, Philippians 3:12-14 makes it clear that his emphasis was on his opportunities and responsibilities during the present.

Give every moment your all. Give your entire attention to the work at hand, the person with whom you are talking or dealing. The Lord grants us time only in the quantity that we can use it—one moment at a time.

There is an illustration of our responsibility to live one day at a time in the story of the manna in Exodus 16. Now read this passage with special attention to the words that I have italicized.

> This is the thing which the Lord hath commanded, Gather of it every man *according to his eating, an omer for every man, according to the number of your persons* . . .
>
> And the children of Israel did so, and gathered, some more, some less.
>
> And when they did mete it with an omer, he that gathered much had nothing over, and he that gathered little had no lack; they gathered every man according to his eating.
>
> And Moses said, Let no man leave of it till the morning.
>
> Notwithstanding they hearkened not unto Moses; *but some of them left of it until the morning, and it bred worms, and stank* . . . (Exodus 16:16-20).

The Israelites were in need of food. The Lord provided for them a *daily* supply. He did not make available to them a week's supply. If they gathered more than a day's supply, all in excess of their daily requirements rotted. The truth is simply this: In the resources of God made available to you, *live for today.*

Here again our Lord is *the* example. He came to die. Through His death He would set up a kingdom—a kingdom not of this world, but a spiritual kingdom. Said Jesus, "To this end was I born, and for this cause came I into the world" (John 18:37).

The shadow of persecution and death constantly lay across His path. Nevertheless, He lived one day at a time and did not permit the grief, torture, and pain that faced Him to rob Him of perfect composure for today. Little children reveled in His company. Men who conversed with Him were aware of His total absorption with their own problems at that given time. Over and over again we can hear our Lord saying, "My hour is not yet come." In other words, He lived "moment by moment," one day at a time. Observe His matchless poise!

Don't be forever living in the future. As a Christian, look unceasingly for the Blessed Hope and Glorious Appearing of Jesus Christ, but while so doing, don't neglect your present work. Live in such a way that you would never be ashamed to meet Jesus no matter when He would appear.

In Acts 1:6 the followers of our Lord asked:

> Lord, wilt thou at this time restore again the kingdom to Israel?

Consider the answer of our Lord,

> . . . It is not for you to know the times or the seasons, which the Father hath put in his own power. But ye shall receive power, after that the Holy Ghost is come upon you . . . (Acts 1:7,8).

Our Lord replied by showing them that the finest possible preparation they could make for the future was a Spirit-led execution of the present. The proof that the child of God is looking forward to the Second Coming of Christ is made clear by his faithfulness in living *today* for the glory of God.

Montaigne said, "My life has been full of terrible misfortunes, most of which never happened." Many of us might say the same thing. How foolish of us to scuttle our opportunities and waste the privileges of this day which is slipping away with fantastic speed.

John Ruskin had on his desk a simple piece of stone on which was sculptured one word: *today.*

Osler gives good advice when he says, "Banish the future; live only for the hour and its allotted work. . . . Set earnestly at the little task at your elbow . . . our plain duty is "not to see what lies dimly at a distance, but to do what lies clearly at hand.' "

Yes, seize *today!* Richard Baxter left to us sage advice when he said, "Spend your time in nothing which you know must be repented of; in nothing on which you might not claim the blessings of God; in nothing which you could not review with a quiet conscience on your dying bed; in nothing which you might not be safely and properly doing if guests surprise you in the act."

Most of your misery is left over from yesterday or borrowed from tomorrow. In the dynamic of the Holy Spirit determine to live today to the glory of God. This is the day that the Lord has made. Paul would remind you to redeem the time for the days are evil (Ephesians 5:16). God has given you today. He has taken back all your yesterdays. All your tomorrows are still in His keeping.

The Lord graciously blessed us with a precious son. He was paralyzed and able to sit in his wheelchair only with the assistance of full-length body braces. One of the nation's most respected gynecologists and obstetricians brought him into the world. Tragically, this man—overcome by grief—sought to find the answer in a bourbon bottle rather than in the blessed Bible. Due to the doctor's intoxication at the time of delivery, he inexcusably bungled his responsibility. Several of the baby's bones were broken. His leg was pulled out at the growing center. Needless abuse—resulting in hemorrhaging of the brain—was inflicted upon the little fellow. (Let me pause long enough to say that this is no indictment upon doctors. I thank God for doctors. This man was a tragic exception. He was banned from practice in some hospitals, and, as mentioned previously, he committed suicide.)

During the first year of the little lad's life, eight doctors said he could not possibly survive. For the first two years of his life my wife had to feed him every three hours with a Brecht feeder. It took a half hour to prepare for the feeding and it took another half hour to clean up and put him back to bed. Not once during that time did she get out of the house for any diversion whatsoever. Never did she get more than two hours sleep at one time.

My wife, formerly Christine Barker of Bristol, Virginia, had once been acclaimed by some of the nation's leading musicians as one of the outstanding contemporary female vocalists in America. From the time she was 13 she had been popular as a singer—and constantly in the public eye. Hers was the experience of receiving and rejecting some fancy offers with even fancier incomes to marry an aspiring Baptist pastor with no church to pastor!

Then, after five years of marriage, tragedy struck! The whole episode was so unnecessary. From a life of public service she was now marooned within the walls of our home. Her beautiful voice no longer enraptured public audiences with the story of Jesus, but was now silenced, or at best, muted to the subdued humming of lullabies.

Had it not been for her spiritual maturity whereby she laid hold of the resources of God and lived one day at a time, this heart-rending experience would long since have caused an emotional breakdown.

John Edmund, Jr., our little son, lived 24 years and died in 1975. We rejoice that he committed his heart and life to Jesus Christ and gave evidence of a genuine concern for the things of the Lord. I attribute his commitment to Jesus Christ and his wonderful disposition to the sparkling radiance of an emotionally mature, Christ-centered mother who has mastered the discipline of living one day at a time. Never have I—nor has anyone else—heard a word of complaint from her. The people who know her concur that at 35 years of age and after having been subjected to more grief than many people twice her age, she possessed sparkle that would be the envy of any high school senior and the radiance and charm for which any debutante would gladly give a fortune.

Seize today. Live for today. Wring it dry of every opportunity. You have troubles? So do others. So did Paul who said, "Most gladly therefore will I rather glory in my infirmities that the power of Christ may rest upon me" (2 Corinthians 12:9b).

You seize the day. Don't let others seize it for you. Peer pressure in the United States robs too many of their individuality. There's no reason for you to engage in socializing just because that's the excessive pastime of your neighbors. If you want to socialize, if it contributes to your social desires without imposing upon you pressures that are counterproductive, go to it. However, I am appalled at the excessive and superficial socializing in which otherwise free people allow nonproductive activities to enslave them. They permit their minds to be divided between the idea "Is this what I ought to do?" and "What will they think of me if I don't go?" Take control of your own life. Go or don't go.

Because so many allow themselves to become enslaved to this superficial socializing, they never read a book, never memorize a poem, and never take that course at the university night school they had promised themselves they were going to take. In short, they rob themselves of the really important contributions to their lives and influence.

Unfortunately, our society has developed two extreme types of parents: those who abuse their children for whatever reason; and those who become hostage to their children for whatever reason.

In either case, I can assure you that the major reason is the divided mind. And in either case, the children suffer.

Let's take the case of the parents who become hostage to their children. They don't want their children to walk from the front door to the pantry. They must drive them there! Jogging for fitness is in. But for children, walking is out. These parents are determined that whatever the cost, they are to be a spectator at every activity in which the child has a part.

Consequently, we have had a 50-percent increase in obesity among children in the past ten years in the United States. The medical profession says that it's because of too much television and too little exercise.

How many children do you know today who are required to do chores? Even to make up their own beds, help wash the dishes or the car, take care of the lawn, or assist with the housecleaning? I submit to you that in many cases, the parents have split their minds between what they know they ought to do and what their peers are doing down the street.

I was in a vigorous and enjoyable debate with a man from Yorkshire, England. He said, "When I visit your country, I am appalled that so many can't make up their minds."

"What are you talking about?" I protested.

"I'll give you a perfect illustration: Junior asks his mother if he can go to a certain function. His mother then gets on the phone and calls the mothers of all of Junior's neighbors to find out what they are going to do. After having taken a poll of the neighbors, his parents then give Junior the verdict. What a terrible way to rear a lad. They are creating an atmosphere of indecision which is bound to have a deleterious effect on the boy."

I protested vigorously, but in my mind, I knew that more often than I cared to admit, what he said was true. And why do people act in this manner? The divided mind. It's divided between their responsibility as parents and their fear of acting in a way that is not consonant with the responses of the other parents down the street.

In short, they don't seize the day. They let the day—and their peers—seize them. And that does not make for mental health and emotional stability and a serene home life.

You develop greater poise when you determine to take time by the forelock and, under the leadership of God, shake it into obedience and make it your servant instead of your master.

People who worry about their health become hostage to the day instead of seizing the day. A friend told me of his mother who worried for 40 years that she would die of cancer. She died at 73—*from pneumonia!* Tragic! She wasted 40 years worrying about *the wrong thing.* Forty years she brought depression instead of delight to the hearts of her closest friends and members of her family. Forty years she divided her mind and her time between useful pursuits and worrying about cancer. Forty years her testimony for Christ was dimmed and her witness for Christ was diminished in power simply because she refused to live one day at a time—and to live that day to the fullest and to the glory of God.

Read it again:

> This is the day which the Lord hath made; we will rejoice and be glad in it (Psalm 118:24).

17

Poise Through Skill

If you would develop the poise that conquers worry, do everything you do the best you can and learn to master some skill.

The late Dr. M. E. Dodd well said, "Many are twisting a tune out of a hand organ when they ought to be playing a four-manual pipe organ. Many are satisfied to play with mud pies when they ought to be making angel food cakes. Many are crawling when they ought to be running. Many are building shacks when they ought to be building palaces."

First Corinthians 10:31 says:

> Whether therefore ye eat, or drink, or whatsoever ye do, do all to the glory of God.

Therefore if we are going to glorify God, we must do our best. There is no room for mediocrity in the life of the child of God. God deserves and demands our best.

> Hear ye the Master's call, "Give Me thy best!"
> For, be it great or small, That is His test.
> Do then the best you can, Not for reward,
> Not for the praise of men, But for the Lord.
>
> Wait not for men to laud, Heed not their slight;
> Winning the smile of God Brings its delight!
> Aiding the good and true Ne'er goes unblest,
> All that we think or do, Be it the best.
>
> Night soon comes on a pace, Day hastens by:
> Workman and work must face Testing on high.
> Oh, may we in that day Find rest, sweet rest,
> Which God has promised those Who do their best.

Every work for Jesus will be blest,
But He asks from everyone His best,
Our talents may be few, These may be small,
But unto Him is due Our best, our all.

Skill is essential to poise. The speaker who has subjected himself to rigorous discipline until he has perfected the craft of speaking is poised when he speaks. The speaker who has not paid the price of discipline and who comes to the pulpit or to the lectern half-prepared lacks poise. If he has any discernment he is tortured at the conclusion of his message as he reflects upon the mess he made of it. The anxiety produced thereby is totally unnecessary and could have been eliminated if he had simply paid the price in developing the needed skill. The same is true of the doctor, the lawyer, the salesman, the artisan, the athlete, the artist, the cook.

For a professing Christian to do less than his best is inexcusable. The Christian has the motive and has the resources for mastery available.

Tragic it is that there are few great musicians today. Few great orators. Few great financiers. Few great inventors. Thank God, however, there are still some who are willing to soar to the heights of the eagle though they know they will fly alone. For the glory of God and for their own peace of mind they are willing to climb the ladder of achievement even though they know that thorns on the rungs will pierce their feet.

Some time ago I had an interview with one of the greatest speech professors in America. He showed me seven pages of elementary voice exercises which to my amazement, he said he has practiced daily for 40 years. This man cannot tolerate mediocrity.

Paderewski practiced simple finger exercises for hours every day over a period of years. No wonder the musical world was hypnotized into the realm of ecstasy by the charm of his musical mastery.

Edison experimented multiplied hundreds of times before he successfully developed the electric light filament. While he was working on it a scientist in England said that anyone was a fraud who would say the electric light filament was a possibility. But Thomas Edison, who loathed mediocrity, kept on giving his best until success crowned his efforts.

Matthew Henry worked hours every day for 40 years in producing his *Commentaries*. They probably appear on the bookshelves of more clergymen than any other commentary. Why? Because, under God, Matthew Henry gave his best.

Jesus told the parable of the man who started the house but never lived in it. Our Master scorned a task half-done.

William Jennings Bryan for years unrelentingly, tediously, laboriously practiced the art of oratory. He never won a speech contest. Nevertheless he kept on. As a comparative unknown he attended the Democratic National Convention held at the Coliseum in Chicago in 1896. Here the years of self-denial and self-discipline paid off. It was past midnight. The people were weary. Many of them were leaving. He stepped up to the stand and delivered his famous *Cross of Gold* oration. This oration so masterfully delivered by the man who never won a speech contest catapulted him into the position of standard-bearer for the Democratic party. In less than 24 hours he had become a national figure. This mighty man of God had mastered the mechanics of the work for which God had called him and the record of his life is a glittering trophy and an imposing monument to the glory of God.

Peace of mind is dependent upon the awareness of divine approval. When we fail to give God our best, we fail to bring maximum honor and glory to His name. The consciousness of this failure produces anxiety and inner conflict.

There is no poise like the poise that accompanies the knowledge of mastery to the glory of God—mastery effectuated in the power of God.

Whatever may be your personal appraisal of television, I think you must confess with me that it presents one of the most stinging rebukes to the apathy of church leadership. Performers will work day and night to attain mastery in the field of show business. Some time ago, when Kate Smith was on TV, I read that for every hour that she was on TV she spent 18 hours in preparation. At that time she was on five hours a week. For five hours of TV entertainment she willingly worked 90 hours to bring to her viewers the finest programs of which she was capable. She did not have to do this for monentary reasons, for she is reputedly a millionaire several times over.

On the other hand, consider how shoddily we treat the Lord, and by "we" I am referring to professing Christians. Take an example. A soloist gets up to sing. Possibly he has rehearsed that particular number, but more probably he hasn't. He sticks his nose in the crease of the book and has to read every word. Imagine an opera star bound down to script and music! What conclusion do you come to? Yes, that's right. The opera star apparently is more devoted to the mastery of his profession than the average gospel soloist is to the glory of God.

In Philippians 4:13 Paul assures us:

> I can do all things through Christ which strength-
> eneth me.

You have the resources necessary to do what God requires of you. And in the fulfillment of His requirement you will have poise that conquers anxiety.

We like to do what we know how to do well. You are less likely to worry while you are doing what you like to do. Worry results from a divided mind. When you are doing what you like to do, your mind is occupied with one thing. "This one thing I do," said Paul. Dwight L. Moody said most people would have to alter that and confess, "These 50 things I dabble in."

The high school boy enjoys that sport most which he plays best. The housewife is contentedly happy when in the process of making a cake for which she is famous in the community. Watch Leonard Bernstein on television. For one solid hour he holds a capacity studio audience of hundreds of children spell-bound and charms millions of television viewers. He is totally absorbed. Obviously he enjoys it. Why? Because he is probably the world's greatest music teacher when it comes to explaining music to the masses. He apparently likes to do this because he has mastered the skill of doing it well. At the conclusion of the hour, even the television viewers detect that he is nearly exhausted, but supremely happy. Yes, I might add, he is poised.

Our high school principal, who also taught us American history, admonished us over and over again to "learn to do at least one thing better than anyone else can do it."

Have you not had this experience many times? Perhaps it was at a party, or maybe a picnic. You saw someone who seemed absolutely bored—thoroughly disgusted. That individual moped around on the sidelines, refusing to participate in the activities. Then, a game or a sport was proposed, the mention of which brought light into his eyes. He threw himself into that game, into that sport, with everything he had. He was skillful in that activity. Now his body was vibrant. His countenance scintillated. His conversation was spirited. Why? Simply because he was now poised. He was skilled in the particular activity and became congenially involved in the group. His mind was no longer divided. His interests were no longer diffused. Obviously he was supremely happy. The explanation simply lies in the fact that we enjoy doing what we know how to do well.

When Bedan Mbugua of Kenya came to Singapore for the course in advanced leadership, he was a pharmaceutical salesman. During the time in Singapore, he became enamored with the possibility of publishing a magazine that would communicate the gospel of Jesus Christ to people who might never come to church or be interested in religious things.

When he returned to Kenya, he pursued his goal. In less than three years, the magazine he was producing outsold *Time* and *Newsweek* in five of Africa's nations, including Nigeria. He later transferred the ownership and production of the magazine to another party, and he started yet another publication.

His story has been one of ever-increasing successes. He loves the work. He loves it, for one reason, because he's good at it, and he's good at it because he loves it!

I repeat, we like to do what we know how to do well. Bedan Mbugua understands magazine publishing. He understands not only the writing needs, the editorial needs, the demographics of the areas where he intends to sell the magazine, but he also understands the business aspects, marketing techniques, and all of the various elements essential to the production of an influential magazine.

If you would conquer worry, discipline yourself to the point of mastery in the field to which God has called you. It is also well for you to become competent in some other fields. This will redound to God's glory, your happiness, and other people's profit.

Jeremiah says:

> Cursed be he that doeth the work of the Lord deceitfully, (the margin renders it "negligently") and cursed be he that keepeth back his sword from blood (Jeremiah 48:10).

For your own peace of mind, excel in at least one thing. Concentrate all your forces upon some work. Gather in your resources, rally all your faculties, marshal all your energies, focus all your capacities upon mastery in at least one field of endeavor. This is a surefire antidote to the divided mind. Stop scattering your fire. Cease any half-hearted attempts to be superb in everything. Ascertain the will of God for your life. Enlist His help and strength through whom you can do all things. Strive for mastery, and experience worry-killing poise through skill.

18

Poise Through Industry

When you are idle you are subject to destructive thoughts, dangerous impulses, and perilous pressures from without. All these things contribute to anxiety.

Jesus Himself said, "I must work" (John 9:4). Jesus also said, "My Father worketh hitherto and I work" (John 5:17).

Work is divine in its inception. The old adage, "Idleness is the devil's workshop," is true.

Reflect upon the grief that idleness brought David the king. When he should have been in battle, he was home taking it easy. While idling about his palace he saw a sight which stirred his sexual passions. Still idle, he reflected and meditated upon that experience until it festered into the open sin of covetousness and then adultery. Those sins in turn led to the murder of Uriah, the husband of Bathsheba. Before long the entire affair was public knowledge. Talk about anxiety! I have no doubt that David at one point would gladly have died rather than lived through the grief and anxiety produced by the harvest of his idleness.

Paul the apostle had been pursued by hostility at Berea, and it was necessary for him to flee to Athens—alone! In Athens he could have holed up in some private room and felt sorry for himself. He could have brooded over the mistreatment he had suffered for the work of the Lord. He could have said, "I have been laboring night and day in Thessalonica and preaching faithfully in Berea. Now I will take it easy." Not Paul. Immediately he began an investigation of conditions in Athens. After acquainting himself with the conditions in this intellectual metropolis, he began to preach in the synagogue with the Jews and with devout persons in the marketplace daily. Soon his ministry attracted the interest of the philosophers, of the Epicureans, and of the Stoics. They requested a speech from him in which he would set forth his philosophy. He could have responded, "Oh, no. I was stoned and left for dead at Lystra. I was beaten and jailed in Philippi. I have just now been abused in Berea for this very thing—preaching the gospel of the Son of God, whom I serve." Paul was not of this stripe, however. Far from feeling sorry for himself, he shared with them this blessed gospel. At their behest he walked up the stone steps to the top of Areopagus, the ancient judgment seat of Athens where in the crescent of stone seats had sat the judges who 300 years previously had condemned Socrates to die. Here this ambassador of the Judge of the earth delivered probably the greatest sermon ever to come from the lips of mortal man.

Thorough preparation was an essential characteristic of Paul's ministry. As soon as God had saved him in Damascus, he immediately started preparation in Arabia and then in Jerusalem, developing skill (consider this against the back-drop of the preceding chapter) in the work for which God had called him. He was speaking to the intellectuals of the world. The laws of this city pronounced death upon anyone intro-ducing a foreign deity. Did that stop Paul? He was a Jewish tentmaker "whose bodily presence is weak and whose speech is of no account," but he spoke out in that classic and proud city of the ancient world.

It was in the marketplace at Athens that Socrates, "the wisest" of men, asked his immortal questions. Over in the nearby olive groves by the brook, Plato founded his academy. To the east was the Lyceum of Aristotle. Near at hand in the Agora were the garden of the Epicureans and the painted porch of the Stoics. Here was the home of the drama where the scholars spoke with pride the names of Aeschylus and Sophocles. Here spoke the orators of Greece. Here were his-torians like Thucydides and Xenaphon. In their Athenian temples the national spirit of Athens was deified in the mar-ble images of their heroes and soldiers, in the trophies of her victories, in her multifarious objects of interest. Here Paul introduced a foreign deity—God Almighty.

Here Paul preached:

The personality of God
The self-existence of God
The omnipotence of God
The unity of God
The reality of divine providence
The universality of divine providence
The efficiency of divine providence
The spirituality of divine worship
The nonexternality of divine worship
The unity of the human race
The brotherhood of the human race
The possibility of a true natural religion
The dignity of man
The dependence of man
The absurdity of idols and idol worship
The essential graciousness of God's dealings with the
  race of man
The duty of immediate repentance
The certainty of a day of judgment
The exaltation of Jesus Christ to the office of supreme
  judge
The reality of a future life.

Here Paul corrected the errors of:

Atheism, or the dogma that there is no God
Pantheism, or the theory that all is God
Materialism, or the notion that the world is eternal
Fatalism, or the superstition that no intelligence pre-
  sides over the universe, but all things come to pass
  either by necessity or chance
Polytheism, or the fancy that there are or can be many
  gods
Ritualism, or the imagination that God can be honored
  by purely external performances
Evolutionism, or the hypothesis that man is a product of
  force and of matter

Indifferentism, or the creed that man should seek after
nothing and no one higher than himself

Optimism, or the delusion that this is the best possible
world and man has no sin of which to repent

Unitarianism, or the tenet that Christ was an ordinary
member of the race

Annihilationism, or the belief that after death there is
nothing

Universalism, or the sentiment that all will be saved.

Talk about skill! Talk about mastering one's field! What
discipline!

The development of this skill required great industry,
and Paul had learned the wisdom of industry. He was always
engaged in some worthwhile pursuit. Because of his dili-
gence, God was pleased to open up to him doors of opportunity. As a result of the effective execution of his opportunity, God blessed his ministry and at the same time delivered him from fear and anxiety. "I know both how to be
abased and I know how to abound" (Philippians 4:12).

He was so busy he had no time for fear-producing, worry-
loaded thoughts!

Paul refused to worry even though he was imprisoned in
Rome. Read 2 Timothy 4:13. He makes request of Timothy to
bring the "books, but especially the parchments." Industry!
This mighty man of God remained industrious right to the
end.

Many people piously assert that they are bound "to wait
upon the Lord" and to "trust in the Lord" while they sit on
the stool of do-nothing, twiddle their thumbs, and piously
pretend to be waiting for the Lord's return. Now it is true that
we must "wait upon the Lord" and "trust in the Lord."
Nevertheless, the proof that we are waiting upon the Lord
and trusting in the Lord will be revealed in our "always
abounding in the work of the Lord" (1 Corinthians 15:58).

By industry I refer to activity with a worthwhile purpose
and toward a worthwhile goal. This is essential to the poise
that conquers worry since you cannot fasten your mind upon

two things at once. You cannot throw all your energies into God-glorifying activity while at the same time focusing your attention upon fear-producing thoughts.

Death is characterized by inaction, life by action. As death approaches, action decreases. It can also be proved that decreasing activity hastens death. Do you not know some people who were in good health until their retirement and then it seemed as though immediately their health began to break and death ran toward them like Mercury with wings at his heels?

There are some who would rationalize their idleness by their advanced years. Don't think to immunize yourself from the responsibility to industry simply because you are advanced in years.

Commodore Vanderbilt built most of his railroads when he was well over 70, making his hundreds of millions at an age when most men have retired.

Kant wrote some of his greatest philosophical works when he was past 70.

Goethe wrote the second part of *Faust* after he was 80 and Victor Hugo was still astounding the world with some of his finest writings after his eightieth birthday.

Tennyson was 83 when he wrote "Crossing the Bar."

Benjamin Franklin most helped his country after he was 60.

Palmerston was premier of England at 81, Gladstone at 83. Bismarck was vigorously administering the affairs of the German empire at 74. Christy was premier of Italy at 75.

Verdi wrote operas after he was 80.

Titian painted his incomparable "Battle of Lepanto" at 98, his "Last Supper" at 99.

Michelangelo was producing masterpieces in the field of sculpture at 89.

Monet was painting great masterpieces after 85.

I believe that one of the outstanding factors contributing to the longevity of Sir Winston Churchill and General Douglas MacArthur was the fact that they both knew and utilized the value of industry.

Men like these mentioned don't have time for anxiety. Worry is a time thief and they refuse to be robbed by it.

Norman Cousins, for years the celebrated editor of *Saturday Review*, believes there is a relationship between creativity and longevity. He illustrates his conviction with the experience he had in visiting two men who, at the time of his visits, were octogenarians—Pablo Casals and Albert Schweitzer. He tells about Pablo Casals just before his ninetieth birthday being assisted at about eight o'clock in the morning by his young wife, Marta, to the piano. Mr. Cousins said that watching Casals move, one was aware of his many infirmities—what appeared to be rheumatoid arthritis, emphysema, swollen hands, and clenched fingers. He was badly stooped, and his head pitched forward as he walked with a shuffle.

Then Mr. Cousins tells how Casals arranged himself at the piano and began to play the opening bars of Bach's *Wobltemperierte Klavier*. It appeared as though a miracle were taking place in front of Mr. Cousins' eyes. Casals' fingers slowly relaxed. His back straightened. He breathed more freely. He hummed as he played.

Then he plunged into a Brahms' concerto, and his fingers "now agile and powerful raced across the keyboard with dashing speed."

The older active octogenerarian, Albert Schweitzer, told Mr. Cousins, "I have no intention of dying so long as I can do things. And if I do things, there's no need to die. So I will live a long, long time." Schweitzer lived to be 95.

I concluded a long time ago that people who find joy in their work and who are committed to a life of productive industry enjoy the kind of poise conducive to good health and longevity. Furthermore, industry is consistent with God's will for each life.

19

Poise Through Stewardship

In talking about stewardship I am referring to material possessions, time, and talents.

No man has a right to expect blessings from God if he, through greed and covetousness, blocks the pathway down which God's blessings march.

God is the owner of all things. We are stewards. God knew that man would contest this fact and so He went to special pains to make His ownership clear in the opening chapters of the Bible. God's name is mentioned 14 times in the first 13 verses, 31 times in the first chapter, and 45 times in the first two chapters of Genesis.

God requires stewardship not because of His need, but rather because of our need. He has no need.

> For every beast of the forest is mine, and the cattle upon a thousand hills. . . . If I were hungry, I would not tell thee: for the world is mine, and the fulness thereof (Psalm 50:10,12).

> The silver is mine, and the gold is mine, saith the Lord of hosts (Haggai 2:8).

God has a threefold basis for demanding our stewardship. Read Isaiah 43:1:

> But now thus saith the Lord that created thee, O Jacob, and he that formed thee, O Israel, Fear not: for I have redeemed thee, I have called thee by thy name; thou art mine.

He created us, He redeemed us, and He sustains us.
It is impossible for a man to experience the poise that

conquers worry unless he possesses an awareness of the approval of God. Without the awareness of divine approval, man is plagued by feelings of guilt and consequent fears. He may be a Hottentot in Africa, or a man-eating savage from the South Sea Islands. He may be totally uncivilized; but as a result of that monitor God has placed in his breast, man knows that he is responsible to a higher power. Not until he comes to know this higher power—God Almighty—personally through the mediation of Jesus Christ is his guilt resolved and do his fears subside.

Many are foolishly trying to get victory over guilt and fear by the utilization of Freudian expressionism and catharsis, Gestalt formulas, positive thinking, and the like. However it is only God who banishes our fear and through the instrumentality of the Holy Spirit gives us the spirit "of power, and of love, and of a sound mind" (2 Timothy 1:7).

It is possible for a Christian to be out of fellowship with God and thus forfeit the poise that is dependent upon our awareness of His approval.

God has set forth certain principles which transcend the boundaries of time segments, geographical divisions, and race groups. One principle God set down was the principle regarding time which He made eloquently clear in the first chapter of the Bible: *One day out of seven belongs to Him.* This principle has never changed, though it has been disobeyed and denied and abused. God has never rescinded this requirement.

Another principle that transcends time is the principle regarding *the doctrine of substitutionary sacrifice as the only answer to man's sin.* When Abel offered an atoning sacrifice it was in response to this fundamental law—this unalterable principle. Hebrews 11:4 tells us that Abel offered the sacrifice "by faith," meaning that there had been a revelation from God concerning it. Now all sacrifices have had their fulfillment in Christ, "the Lamb of God which taketh away the sin of the world" (John 1:29).

The third fundamental law—unalterable principle—is that

relating to *the stewardship of material possessions.*

Attention! If you are inclined to get a little impatient with this emphasis on stewardship and turn over to the next chapter, I implore you to hear me out—or rather hear God's Word out. One out of every six verses of the four gospels has to do with the right and wrong use of material possessions and 16 of our Lord's 38 parables have to do with the right and wrong use of material possessions. Don't sin against yourself by ignoring this chapter. Suspend your judgment and "to thine own self be true." Surely more anxiety, worry, and divided-mindedness among Christians is caused by deficiency at this point than at any other.

In the Garden of Eden God kept to Himself the tree of knowledge of good and evil. This He did to remind Adam and Eve of their stewardship and of God's ownership. They were not to touch the fruit of that tree. It belonged to God in a special sense. True, everything belongs to God, but a certain proportion of that which He bestows upon us is to be set aside immediately and with no strings attached.

Is not the tenant farmer in the Midwest required to give back to the owner one-fourth of the corn crop? Is not the tenant farmer in the South required to give back to the land-owner one-third of the cotton crop? Since God is the owner of all things, is it not fair that we be required to give back to Him a proportion of that which He makes possible?

Remember verse 5 of our text in Philippians 4. The word *moderation* means "fairness" among other things. There is no poise without fairness and there is no fairness without stewardship of material possessions. This poise that brings peace is significantly dependent upon our obedience to stewardship opportunities.

The most impelling incentive to give is not to provide the church with financial resources. The child of God *pays* his tithe and *gives* offerings over and above the tithe "as the Lord hath prospered him":

1. In recognition of God's sovereign ownership:

But thou shalt remember the Lord thy God: for it

is he that giveth thee power to get wealth, that he may establish his covenant which he sware unto thy fathers, as it is this day (Deuteronomy 8:18).

What? know ye not that your body is the temple of the Holy Ghost which is in you, which ye have of God, and ye are not your own? For ye are bought with a price: therefore glorify God in your body, and in your spirit, which are God's (1 Corinthians 6:19,20).

2. In appreciative acknowledgment of redeeming grace:

For by grace are ye saved through faith; and that not of yourselves: it is the gift of God:
Not of works, lest any man should boast.
For we are his workmanship, created in Christ Jesus unto *good works*, which God hath before ordained *that we should walk in them* (Ephesians 2:8-10).

3. In surrender of life and talents to the Lord:

I beseech you therefore, brethren, by the mercies of God, that ye present your bodies a living sacrifice, holy, acceptable unto God, which is your reasonable service. And be not conformed to this world; but be ye transformed by the renewing of your mind, that ye may prove what is that good, and acceptable, and perfect, will of God (Romans 12:1,2).

When you prepare your tithe, you prepare for worship. In church as you put the money in the collection plate you are saying in substance, "This is a tangible expression of my total surrender to Thee. This money that I place in this plate represents my brains, my blood, my abilities—all of the blessings that have come from Thee, for I realize that

Every good gift and every perfect gift is from

above, and cometh down from the Father of lights,
with whom is no variableness, neither shadow of
turning (James 1:17).

"It is because of the health, because of the mental ability,
because of the friends, because of the various resources that
Thou hast given me that I am able to make a living. All that I
am and all that I have is Thine. My stewardship of material
possessions is but an expression of that fact."

The basis of our monetary responsibility is the tithe. Tithing is paying back to God ten percent of the increase. God
says that if you fail to pay that ten percent back into the
"storehouse" with faithful regularity you are a thief and a
robber.

There are those who would try to brainwash people into
believing that the responsibility of the tithe was only in force
during the days of the law—from the time of Moses to the
time of Christ. They will tell you that Malachi 3:10 has no
relevance for today because it is in the Old Testament. The
Lord must have known that such mischief would be attended.
Therefore He introduced the words of Malachi 3:6, "For I am
the Lord, I change not. . . ." After these words He calls Israel
back to His ordinances, to tithes and offerings, to the storehouse, and to His conditional promise of blessing. The New
Testament reaffirms these words of Malachi 3:6 by saying that
with God there is "no variableness, neither shadow of turning."

These same people who say that tithing was for those
under the law turn to Psalm 23 for comfort, to Psalm 32 for
guidance, to Job for wisdom and comfort in trials and tribula-
tions, to Elijah for a pattern of prayer, and to other Old
Testament passages for leadership.

To be consistent, these people who would throw out Malachi 3:10 ought also to throw out John 3:16 because it, too, was
spoken prior to the time that redemption was completed by
our Lord on the Cross of Calvary.

Tithing antedated the law. Abraham tithed. The law of the tithe is not an Israelite law. It is a fundamental and unalterable law of God. It is still in force. That is why tithing is commended by Jesus.

> Woe unto you, scribes and Pharisees, hypocrites: for *ye pay tithe* of mint and anise and cummin, and have omitted the weightier matters of the law, judgment, mercy, and faith: these ought ye to have done, and *not to leave the other undone* (Matthew 23:23).

Just as Abraham paid tithes to Melchizedek so we pay tithes to Christ. In Hebrews 7 this truth is made clear. The Son of God who liveth and abideth a priest continually after the order of Melchizedek "receiveth tithes"—receives them now! When paying tithes, Abraham acknowledged Melchizedek's sovereignty for he was a king-priest. Likewise today when one pays his tithe he acknowledges Christ as his Sovereign, his Lord. Refusal to pay the tithe is refusal to own Christ as Sovereign and as one's High Priest. Thus one makes Christ not only inferior to Melchizedek, but also inferior to the Levites, the priestly group of Old Testament times.

The tithe was incorporated in the law. This was done because it was a principle worthy of divine enforcement. God never repealed the fundamental law of tithing; grace has not annulled it; time has not altered it.

Tithing was commanded by Malachi.

> Will a man rob God? Yet ye have robbed me. But ye say, Wherein have we robbed thee? In tithes and offerings.
>
> Ye are cursed with a curse: for ye have robbed me, even this whole nation.
>
> Bring ye all the tithes into the storehouse, that there may be meat in mine house, and prove me now herewith, saith the Lord of hosts, if I will not open you the windows of heaven, and pour you out

a blessing, that there shall not be room enough to receive it.

And I will rebuke the devourer for your sakes, and he shall not destroy the fruits of your ground; neither shall your vine cast her fruit before the time in the field, saith the Lord of hosts.

And all nations shall call you blessed: for ye shall be a delightsome land, saith the Lord of hosts (Malachi 3:8-12).

In this command Malachi makes the practice of tithing essential to receiving blessings of a superior nature and to a degree and in a measure not otherwise promised.

This passage in Malachi teaches that when a man refuses to tithe he is: 1) guilty of robbing God, 2) subjected to a curse, and 3) denied the right of the blessings of God.

Grace does not abrogate the law. Grace fulfills the law—and goes much further than the most stringent demands of the law. Grace provides the dynamic necessary for fulfilling the law's mechanics. The law told man what to do, but failed to provide him with the capability to accomplish it. Grace provides the dynamic of the Holy Spirit whereby in the strength of God man fulfills the demands of the law—and much more.

Jesus said in Matthew 5:17-20:

Think not that I am come to destroy the law, or the prophets: I am not come to destroy, but to fulfill.

For verily I say unto you, Till heaven and earth pass, one jot or one title shall in no wise pass from the law, till all be fulfilled.

Whosoever therefore shall break one of these least commandments, and shall teach men so, he shall be called the least in the kingdom of heaven: but whosoever shall do and teach them, the same shall be called great in the kingdom of heaven.

For I say unto you, That except your righteousness shall exceed the righteousness of the scribes and Pharisees, ye shall in no case enter into the kingdom of heaven.

Already in this chapter it has been pointed out that Jesus commended the tithing of the Pharisees. In verse 20 of Matthew 5, the Lord tells us that our righteousness must *exceed* the righteousness of the scribes and Pharisees. Grace fulfills and amplifies instead of destroying and minimizing the law.

Proceed further in Matthew 5. The law says, "Thou shalt not kill." Jesus makes it clear that if a man hates his brother he is just as guilty as if he had murdered him. The law said, "Thou shalt not commit adultery." Jesus points out that under grace whosoever looks on a woman to lust after her has already violated the seventh commandment in his heart.

Carry this principle over in the matter of the stewardship of money. How can an enlightened child of God do less under grace than the Jew did under the law? The Jew gave offerings over and above his tithe, too. For instance, if you will study the Old Testament you will discover that the Temple and the equipage thereof were paid for by offerings over and above the tithes. There is always a question mark in my mind about the person who goes to extremes to prove that we are under no obligation to tithe. What is his motive?

In Leviticus 27:30 God makes it clear that "The tithe is the Lord's." Therefore we, as stewards, have absolutely no right to handle it as though it were ours. It must be placed where God says and when God says. Namely, in the storehouse on the Lord's day.

Jesus said, "Render therefore unto Caesar the things which are Caesar's; and unto God the things that are God's" (Matthew 22:21).

In other words, pay your taxes and pay your tithes. Your taxes belong to the government. The proof of this lies in the fact that they are deducted from your pay before you receive it. Your United States income tax is to be paid to the collector of Internal Revenue at a given location.

Suppose you owed the government an income tax of a

thousand dollars. Suppose that you made out your 1040 Form and attached a note to it in which you said:

> Dear Uncle Sam,
>
> You will notice that I owe you a thousand dollars. I am sending $100 to my local postmaster. He is one of your faithful servants and he is having a hard time financially. I am sending $100 to a U.S.O. down in South Carolina. They are doing a magnificent work boosting the morale of your own servicemen and they need help desperately. I am sending $100 to a nephew of mine who is a sailor with the Seventh Fleet. He is liable to get blown up any time and I think that he needs encouragement. After all, he is one of your faithful servicemen. Then I am sending $200 to the Veterans Administration. After all, they are loyally dedicated to carrying out your will. *But*, Uncle Sam, just to let you know my heart is in the right place, I am sending the remaining $500 to the collector of Internal Revenue in my area here.

"Absurd," you say. Why? Simply because no man would survive this miscarriage of responsibility with impunity.

Here is a man who owes God a tithe of a thousand dollars. But instead of accepting God's revelation that "The tithe is the Lord's" he says "The tithe is mine. My tithe!" Then, acting on that premise he high-handedly determines the distribution of that money which is not his in the first place. He will send $100 to a radio evangelist, another $100 to a Bible school, and another $100 to a missionary. The tithe is to go into the storehouse, which in this age is the church. *All the tithe is to go into the storehouse.*

Hear the Word of the Lord:

> Upon the first day of the week let every one of you lay by him in store, as God hath prospered him,

that there be no gatherings when I come (1 Corinthians 16:2).

Bring ye all the tithes into the storehouse, that there may be meat in mine house, and prove me now herewith, saith the Lord of hosts, if I will not open you the windows of heaven, and pour you out a blessing, that there shall not be room enough to receive it (Malachi 3:10).

The same word that is translated "store" in 1 Corinthians 16:2 is the word used in the Septuagint translation and translated "storehouse" in Malachi 3:10. In other words, it would be a correct translation of 1 Corinthians 16:2 to say, "Upon the first day of the week let every one of you lay by him in storehouse . . ."

These scriptural truths are set forth by one who doesn't pastor a local church. Rather, he leads up a para-church organization dependent upon the gifts of God's people.

Gifts over and above the tithe can be made to Christian causes. But "the tithe is the Lord's." The specific depository is the local church, and it is to be placed there undesignated.

In 1957, when the Lord led me to resign the pastorate to go into the field of evangelism, a dear friend who fought this truth said, "Haggai, now I reckon you will abandon this foolishness about storehouse tithing."

"My change in ministry doesn't mean a change in Scripture or commitment," I replied.

"Follow that notion, and in a year you will collapse for lack of support," he insisted.

Said I, "If this ministry is of God, He'll supply the need."

It was, and He has.

When a man refuses to storehouse tithe his money, he is repeating in kind—if not in degree—the sin of Adam and Eve. They took to themselves an authority that was not theirs in partaking of the forbidden fruit. That tree belonged to God, not to them. When a man does not tithe, he is taking to himself an authority that is not his in appropriating to himself money that belongs to God. How then can he expect peace? How can he expect victory over anxiety and freedom from worry? For God and God alone is the Author of peace.

Here is a man who will not honor God with the payment of the tithe. However, when his little child becomes critically ill, and the doctors say there is no hope apart from supernatural intervention, that same father will fall on his face before God and in substance will say, "O God, this is my child, bone of my bones, flesh of my flesh, blood of my blood. I hand him to Thee. Do what seems good in Thy sight. If it can please Thee, restore him to health and strength and to us." Such hypocrisy! He is willing to trust God with his own flesh and blood! Even this man who is not willing to trust God with his filthy silver and gold? Does he think more of his money than he does of his child? Do you see the hypocrisy of it, dear friend? How can God honor a man like this? How can God in justice bless a man like this who turns his back upon God when he so desires—yes, turns his back upon God every time he refuses to tithe.

Yet another illustration. You will remember the passage in Mark 12:41-44. Jesus sat over against the treasury and beheld how the people cast money into the treasury. You will remember, also, that a certain poor widow put in two mites. Jesus called His disciples together, and said, "This poor widow hath cast more in than all they which have cast into the treasury." How could He know? Perhaps they had put part of their tithe into a religious foundation, or some Bible college, or sent it to some radio evangelist. You say, they didn't have such things back then! That's true, but let me hasten to add, it is a fact of history that there were more depositories for the giving of alms in that day than there are today. The others could have said they had given much of the tithe to alms' depositories. Jesus judged their stewardship on the basis of what they put into the treasury of the house of God which today is our own literal, visible, local church.

Consider the process of bringing the tithe: 1)*Bring* the tithe. This couples tithing with worship. The two are inseparable. 2) Bring *all* the tithe. Don't deduct your doctor's bills, your transportation to and from work, your insurance policies, your gifts to the Red Cross, United Appeal Drive, and so forth. Bring a full 10 percent of your total increase. 3) Bring ye all the tithe into the *storehouse*. When this is done your responsibility ceases. Even when Paul was trying to get money together for Jerusalem, he didn't tell the Corinthian Christians to send their tithe there. He told them to put their tithe in their local church and then he urged the church itself to help out the church in Jerusalem.

Now notice the conditional promise of Malachi 3:10:

> And prove me now herewith, saith the Lord of hosts, if I will not open you the windows of heaven, and pour you out a blessing, that there shall not be room enough to receive it.

If I could not believe what God says about tithing, I could not believe what He says about anything. Strange it is that people will believe what He says about salvation, what He says about heaven, what He says about hell, what He says about baptism, what He says about soul-winning—yet they will not believe what He says about tithing and the stewardship of possessions.

I know a wealthy man who has set up a religious foundation. He allegedly puts ten percent of his earnings into that foundation and therefore considers himself a tither. However, he does not put the tithe where God says to put it. In addition to that manifest disobedience, one of his corporations borrows the money that is in the nonprofit religious foundation—borrows it at the rate of six percent. Therefore he has access to money on which he has to pay no tax—money that he uses to expand his business. You say, "Well, preacher, God is blessing him." Is He? The trouble is that too many people think only in terms of money when they think of God's opening the windows of heaven and pouring out blessings.

I know a man who made $40 million last year, but because

of an ulcerated stomach he can't eat a decent piece of meat. There are some men who would give all of their money if they could buy peace of mind, the respect of their children, the love of their wife.

Once again, let me remind you that from a selfish standpoint it would be to my advantage to preach that a person has a right to place his tithe where he wants inasmuch as on that basis additional money could be secured to undergird the responsibilities of our team. However, I know that God would not bless it. Sometime ago a dear friend of mine suggested that a group of businessmen give $10,000 a year out of their tithes to undergird this ministry God has given me. I thanked him for his generous proposal but said quite frankly, "You are barking up a tree where was never found a possum. I would no more be a party to accepting a part of a tithe of you businessmen—a tithe which is not yours, but which is God's—than I would be a party to taking a portion of your income tax—tax which is not yours, but which is Uncle Sam's."

You say, "What does this have to do with worry?" Plenty! If you went downtown and stole $100 from a merchant, would you have peace of mind? No. You would probably think that people were talking about you every time they looked at you. You would feel uncomfortable when you got in the vicinity of the business owned by the merchant whom you abused and to whom you were indebted.

In the fourth chapter of Philippians from which textual basis of our formula for victory over worry is found, Paul mentions the liberality of the Philippians. Is it not interesting that the Philippian church was the only church in which Paul found no doctrinal or ethical error? Read the fourth chapter and notice how he commends them for their liberality in the matter of monetary stewardship. Many people glibly quote verse 19: "But my God shall supply all your need according to his riches in glory by Christ Jesus." But may I suggest that the fulfillment of that promise is conditional upon a spirit akin to that expressed by the Philippians and recorded in the immediately preceding verses?

One of the reasons that many people worry is financial adversity—an adversity sometimes begotten of their own stewardship disobedience.

> Honor the Lord with thy substance, and with the
> first-fruits of all thine increase: So shall thy barns be
> filled with plenty, and thy presses shall burst out
> with new wine (Proverbs 3:9,10).

He wrote those words under the inspiration of the Holy Spirit of God.

Failure to tithe is incontrovertible evidence that the guilty party is more interested in himself than he is in the work of the Lord. One of the chief causes of anxiety and worry is self-centeredness.

> Where your treasure is, there will your heart be
> also (Matthew 6:21).

When your chief concern is not merely how to tithe, but how to give offerings—generous offerings over and above the tithe to the glory of God—you will experience a joy and a peace the world cannot define.

When a man refuses to tithe, he does so either from ignorance or covetousness. God's Word states that covetousness is idolatry.

> Mortify therefore your members which are upon
> the earth; fornication, uncleanness, inordinate af-
> fection, evil concupiscence, and covetousness,
> which is idolatry (Colossians 3:5).

Money becomes a tin god. Men resemble their gods; they assimilate what they conceive to be desirable. With money as your god there is no peace. But if Christ is the Lord of your life, the dominant dynamic of your experience, the over-mastering passion of your interests, you inevitably begin to resemble Him who "is our peace" (Ephesians 2:14). As a result of your fellowship with Him, you begin to experience that peace that only He can give.

> Peace I leave with you, my peace I give unto you; not as the world giveth, give I unto you. Let not your heart be troubled, neither let it be afraid (John 14:27).

Avail yourself of the blessings (including poise) that God promises to those who honor Him with their substance.

20

Poise Through Surrender

> Neither yield ye your members as instruments of
> unrighteousness unto sin: but yield yourselves
> unto God, as those that are alive from the dead, and
> your members as instruments of righteousness
> unto God (Romans 6:13).

Hear the words of Paul once again:

> But what things were gain to me, those I counted
> loss for Christ. Yea doubtless, and I count all things
> but loss for the excellency of the knowledge of
> Christ Jesus my Lord: for whom I have suffered the
> loss of all things, and do count them but dung, that
> I may win Christ (Philippians 3:7,8).

To be sure, the person who has totally surrendered himself
to Christ fulfills all the other contributory factors to poise that
have been mentioned. It may seem as though some of these
suggestions overlap, but I have put myself "on the stretch,"
as it were, to turn the diamond around and around at all
angles so that light may be flashed from every facet of it.

Certainly you have been impressed time after time when
you have listened to missionaries on furlough from a foreign
field. You have been impressed by the fact that they have
willingly forfeited economic affluence, wordly ease, the fellowship of relatives and friends here at home. They have a
serenity, a poise, that bespeaks a peace which cannot be
defined—"the peace of God that passeth all understanding"
(Philippians 4:7).

After hearing a returned missionary from China, a young
lady walked up to her and said, "I'd give the world to have
your experience."

"That," said the missionary, "is exactly what it cost me."

> He that findeth his life shall lose it: and he that
> loseth his life for my sake shall find it (Matthew
> 10:39).

Many times while in the pastorate and even on occasions since entering the field of evangelism, I have been approached by people who said, in substance, "I know that if I yield my life to the Lord He is going to make me preach and I don't want to do it." With some it wasn't preaching, but some other sphere of service. There are people who apparently are plagued with the misconception that if they surrender themselves to the Lord He will require of them that which they do not want. This is a trick of the devil. When you surrender yourself to the Lord you will want what the Lord wants for you. God's Word says,

> Delight thyself also in the Lord; and he shall give
> thee the desires of thine heart (Psalm 37:4).

> If ye abide in me, and my words abide in you, ye
> shall ask what ye will, and it shall be done unto you
> (John 15:7).

God's Word tells us that if we, as human parents, give good gifts to our children, how much more will our Heavenly Father give good things unto them that ask Him! Now suppose my little son had come to his mother and me and said, in substance, "Mom and Dad, I want to do everything that will make you happy. I know that you have had much more experience than I, and there are many mistakes that I can avoid by following your counsel and advice. I beg of you to guide me and direct me. To the best of my ability I will follow your suggestions." Can you imagine my wife and me then going into another room and in a confidential conference saying, "Now little John Edmund has put himself completely in our hands and at our mercy. Therefore let us do everything we can to make him as awkward and miserable and frustrated as possible." That's absurd. If we would not treat our own son that way, how much more true it is that our Heavenly Father would not treat us that way.

> If ye then, being evil, know how to give good gifts unto your children, how much more shall your Father which is in heaven give good things to them that ask him? (Matthew 7:11).

> Like as a father pitieth his children, so the Lord pitieth them that fear him (Psalm 103:13).

With surrender comes poise that conquers worry.

Lot pitched his tent toward Sodom. Too bad. Lot was a child of God. Second Peter 2:7,8 makes that clear. But Lot went his way instead of God's way. As a result of his disobedience he lost—lost dearly. The Lord told him to get out of Sodom. His married daughters, his sons-in-law, and his grandchildren would not leave with him. Parents may take their children to Sodom, but rarely will they ever take their children out of Sodom once they have been in Sodom for any period of time. Lot lost his wife. She was turned into a pillar of salt. He lost all his possessions, his position in the city, his prestige. He lost the respect of his two married daughters who in a cave got him drunk and then committed incest with him whereby he became the father of one son by each of his own daughters. Oh, the grief, the anxiety that would have been spared had Lot only surrendered himself to the Lord. He was robbed of the "desires of his heart" because he refused to "delight himself in the Lord."

Some time ago, in a distant city, a mother came to me requesting an interview. She was greatly distraught mentally and emotionally. The anguish of her heart was torturing her body. She had been under psychiatric care for more than four-and-a-half years, during which time she had been subjected to shock treatments. She was a professing Christian and gave every evidence of sincerely wanting to do the will of God.

After some brief but pertinent probing I asked her quite frankly if there were something which had taken place in her life, whether years ago or more recently, that was constantly preying on her mind. She said there was. It was a sin committed during the days of adolescence. I asked her if she had confessed it to the Lord. She assured me that she had.

I said, "I imagine, from my observation, that you have confessed it over and over and over—probably a thousand times—to the Lord. Is that right?"

She shook her head affirmatively.

I said, "You see, actually, you are making God a liar. You confessed that sin once. God promised you absolute forgiveness as we read in the words of 1 John 1:9—'If we confess our sins, he is faithful and just to forgive us our sins, and to cleanse us from all unrighteousness.' "

I said, "The reason you are going through this torture is simply that you have not surrendered yourself completely to the Lord. You do not trust Him. You are not willing to take Him at His Word. He has forgiven you, but you refuse to believe it. You refuse to forgive yourself. You are making the mistake of thinking that repentance is repining and that self-examination is brooding. Now then, simply take God at His Word. Surrender your life completely to Him. Surrender the limitations of your finite mind to the assurance of His immutable word. He has forgiven you. Now in complete surrender—*believe it*."

I am happy to say there seems to be abundant evidence that the Lord has corrected the situation. She is now enjoying the poise that comes with surrender.

There are businessmen all over the nation who, petrified by fear and paralyzed by anxiety over reverses in their business, could enjoy business success and even more—the peace that passes all understanding—if they would only surrender themselves to God and take Him as their partner.

There are many homes internally divorced where husband and wife live together under protest in an atmosphere of tension simply because they refuse to surrender to Jesus

Christ. It is trite, but it is nevertheless true that "If their home were built upon the Rock, Christ Jesus, it would not be headed for the rocks of chaos."

Here then is the secret of poise—surrender to Christ. Remember:

> I can do all things through Christ which strength-
> eneth me (Philippians 4:13).

He will strengthen us to observe the laws of self-control, relaxation, scheduling, stewardship, skill, industry, thought-control, and enthusiasm—all contributory factors in the mastery of poise which brings peace and conquers worry.

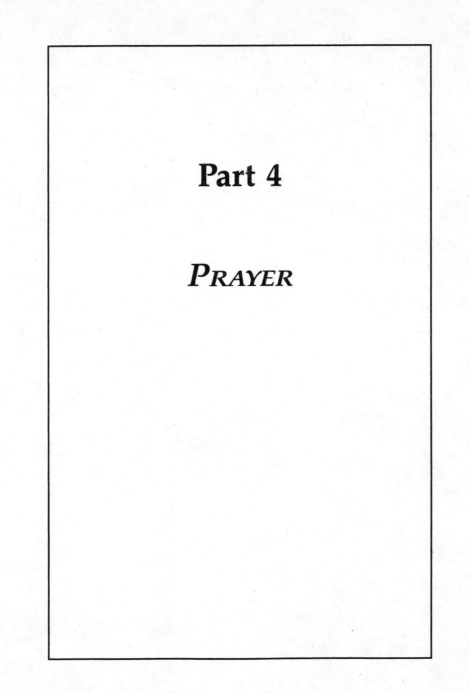

Part 4

PRAYER

21

Why Pray?

Paul's formula for victory over worry is Praise, Poise, and Prayer. Having discussed Praise and Poise, we now come to that leg of the tripod without which the other two legs of Praise and Poise cannot stand. That leg is prayer.

> Be careful for nothing; but in everything by prayer and supplication with thanksgiving let your requests be made known unto God (Philippians 4:6).

Peace is possible only to those who have related themselves to God through Christ—who is the Prince of Peace. The Bible declares:

> There is no peace, saith my God, to the wicked (Isaiah 57:21).

By "the wicked" is meant not only the guttersnipes, ne'er-do-wells, members of the riffraff of society. The wicked are those who, unrepentant of their sins, have either refused or neglected to come to the Son of God by faith. They have not received Him into their hearts.

Read very carefully, for what you are about to read is a staggering truth.

> And you hath he quickened, who were dead in trespasses and sins: Wherein in time past ye walked according to the course of this world, according to the prince of the power of the air, the spirit that now worketh in the children of disobedience (Ephesians 2:1,2).

God's Word here states that until you receive Jesus Christ as your Savior and Lord, you are "dead in trespasses and sins." As one who is dead in trespasses you are dead to God and to every quality inherent in His nature.

What are these qualities? Some of them are holiness, righteousness, love, truth, wisdom, justice, and power. As one who is dead to God you are therefore dead—and insensitive—to holiness, righteousness, love, truth, wisdom, justice, and power. Now pause just a moment and think what that means. To be sure, those who are dead in sin and therefore dead to God have set up standards. Unfortunately they are not God's standards. "Every man is a law unto himself." That explains marital discord, domestic strife, civil factiousness, labor-management antagonism, national crime, and international tensions.

As one dead in sin and therefore dead to God you are alive to Satan and to the qualities inherent in his nature. Some of these qualities are sin, hostility, error, folly, injustice, weakness, and fear. As a child of disobedience you are dominated and controlled by him. Read it again. He is "the spirit that now worketh in the children of disobedience."

Someone takes issue and says, "Well, I'm not a drunkard. I'm not a murderer. I'm not a sex libertine. I'm not an extortionist. I'm not a troublemaker. I'm not a thief. I'm not a blasphemer." Of course not. It is not to Satan's interests that everyone be a drunkard, a murderer, a sex libertine, an extortionist, a troublemaker, a thief, or a blasphemer.

He transforms himself as an angel of philosophic light, moral light, social-justice light, political light, and cultural light.

Until you come to Jesus Christ as a self-confessed sinner and by faith accept the salvation which He has provided, you are spiritually dead. Death means separation. Physical death means separation of the body from the personality. By peronality I refer to all of the unseen facets of man's being, including soul, spirit, mind, and heart. Spiritual death is separation of man in this life from God. Eternal death is the irremediable and unalterable separation of the total man from God forever.

Now, because you are spiritually dead, you are separated from God. Therefore you have no peace. Nor can you have any peace. You can use the power of positive thinking, resort to Gestalt psychology, adhere to Freudian suggestions, but it all will be to no avail. Your only hope is in Christ, the Prince of Peace, through whom you have access to God.

Life is union just as death is separation. Physical life is the union of the body and the personality. Spiritual life is synonymous with spiritual life.

When you receive the Lord Jesus Christ as your Savior you do not receive simply a new concept or a new creed, or a new formula for living. You receive a Person. It is "Christ in you" (Colossians 1:27). You receive a new nature.

> Whereby are given unto us exceeding great and precious promises: that by these ye might be *partakers of the divine nature*, having escaped the corruption that is in the world through lust (2 Peter 1:4).

Eternal life is the life of God in the soul of the believer. For the child of God, that which we call physical death is but a transition from life to life more abundant, from time to eternity, from the finite into the infinite. Therefore when one receives spiritual life he receives in kind, though not in degree, right here and now, everything that he will enjoy in heaven: communion with God, the favor of God, victory over sin, a transcendent love, divine motivation, and *peace*.

As mentioned, the formula for peace—victory over worry—is Praise, Poise, and Prayer. No unbeliever can have this perfect peace. The prayer of the unrighteous is an abomination before God (Proverbs 28:9).

God will not hear those who persist in unbelief.

> If I regard iniquity in my heart, the Lord will not hear me (Psalm 66:18).

The only way anyone can come to God is through Jesus Christ.

> Jesus saith unto him, I am the way, the truth, and
> the life: no man cometh unto the Father, but by me
> (John 14:6).

The blind man whom Christ healed in John 9 stated the truth—a truth that is refuted nowhere in God's Word—when he said:

> Now we know that God heareth not sinners; but
> if any man be a worshipper of God, and doeth his
> will, him he heareth (John 9:31).

Prayer is a family matter—a matter between God the Father, and born-again believers, His children.

Worry is a weakness of the flesh. You cannot conquer a weakness of the flesh in the energy of the flesh. It must be done in the power of God. Prayer gives you access to that power.

Prayer is fundamental because it makes available to you the divine dynamic whereby you master the mechanics leading to victory over worry. Prayer is essential to Praise. Prayer is essential to Poise. God shows us what we must do for victory. In response to prayer He channels to us through the indwelling Holy Spirit the ability to do what we ought to do—which is to obey His commandments.

Prayer raises us to God's level. It takes us into God's atmosphere. It brings us into communion and intimacy with God.

Prayer signifies dependence upon God. Without Him we can do nothing. With Him we can do everything. He is the source of our strength.

> I can do all things through Christ which strength-
> eneth me (Philippians 4:13).

He is the source of our resources.

> But my God shall supply all your need according
> to his riches in glory by Christ Jesus (Philippians
> 4:19).

The Grecian says, "Man, know thyself." The Roman says, "Man, rule thyself." The Chinese says, "Man, improve thyself." The Buddhist says, "Man, annihilate thyself." The Brahman says, "Man, submerge thyself in the universal sum of all." The Muslim says, "Man, submit thyself." The twentieth-century internationalist says, "Man, learn the art and practice the principles of peaceful coexistence." But Christ says, *"Without me you can do nothing"* (John 15:5).

Conversely, with Him we can do anything.

Prayer is the means whereby we make contact with God's strength and in Him overcome our weakness.

Only when we set aside our own strength will the Lord really become our strength.

Attempt to float. As long as you exercise your own efforts to keep up you will go down. Give yourself up to the water and it will immediately sweep under you with its waves and bear you up in its strength.

The Lord Himself is our strength. Don't pray, "Lord, give me strength," as though you are asking Him for a quality distinct from Himself. Rather say, "O Lord, be Thou my strength."

Listen to Ephesians 3:20:

> Now unto him that is able to do exceeding abundantly above all that we ask or think, according to *the power that worketh in us.*

Here again you have that word *energeo*. And the word translated power is the word *dunamis* from which we get the word *dynamic*. Just as Satan and his "powers of darkness" energize the unbeliever, so God energizes the obedient Christian. He becomes the divine dynamic whereby the believer conquers all things—including worry.

The same power that burnishes each star, points each blade of grass, hurls each wave upon the shore, formed the body of our Savior, raised Jesus from the dead, and will raise our bodies or transfigure them in the hour of glory, is the same power which is available to each obedient Christian. This power is made available through prayer.

This power is available only to those who are weak. God's helpfulness is meted out only to those who confess their helplessness.

> And he said unto me, My grace is sufficient for thee: for my strength is made perfect in weakness. Most gladly therefore will I rather glory in my infirmities, that the power of Christ may rest upon me. Therefore I take pleasure in infirmities, in reproaches, in necessities, in persecutions, in distresses for Christ's sake: for when I am weak, then am I strong (2 Corinthians 12:9,10).

Our strength lies in childlike helplessness. In your helplessness through prayer, cast yourself upon Him who is our strength. The very essence of the meaning of prayer is that you need help beyond your own strength.

The reason many of us do not pray is that we are too strong—strong in our own false, swaggering, blustering strength. We are strong in our own strength, the very heart of which is utter helplessness, emptiness, and weakness.

Worry is an intrusion into God's province. You are making yourself the father of the household instead of the child. You are setting yourself up as the master of God's kingdom, instead of the servant for whom the Master provides.

The basis of prayer is man's need and God's ability to meet that need. When one really prays he is confessing his utter helplessness. He is casting himself completely and wholly upon God. He is delighting himself in the Lord. Consequently the Lord grants unto him the desires of his heart.

Our needs are manifold. Our perplexities are multifarious and variegated. Don't worry. Instead, turn your care into a prayer. Follow the example of Paul who said, "I conferred not with flesh and blood" (Galatians 1:16). Conferring with flesh and blood about your worries instead of taking them to God is a fruitful cause for increased worry.

Years ago, while I was still in the pastorate, I concluded a Sunday night service with the benediction. Even before the choir's response had ended, an anxious woman rushed up to me and asked if I would talk with her child who was under conviction of sin and wanted to be saved.

It was my joy to see that keen and energetic youngster enter into peace with God through Christ. We had prayer together. As I rose to dismiss them, I realized that the mother was in agony, and she looked at me as if to say, "I am in such trouble. Can you help me?"

I asked her if she would like to speak with me. She grabbed the opportunity as a drowning man would grab a life belt. I asked the youngster to step into the next office for just a moment. Turning to the mother I said, "All right. Would you like to share with me the problem that is causing you this grief?" She burst into uncontrollable sobs. I assured her that having been pastor of a church of over three thousand members for several years I was now shockproof. I further reminded her that everything would be in strictest confidence.

Let me stop here long enough to tell you that this lady was one of the outstanding members of the church. She taught a Sunday school class, was prominent in the Training Union and in the Women's Missionary Society. She almost never missed a service. She tithed her money. She knew her Bible. If Gallup had taken a poll of the membership, I am sure this lady would have ranked among the most respected of all members.

Finally, she blurted out her story. I sat transfixed with astonishment as she told the most sordid story of duplicity and sin I ever had heard from a supposedly respectable woman.

Finally she nearly screamed out, "Preacher, have I committed the unpardonable sin?" It was my joy to assure her from God's Word that if she still desired to repent, God would receive her. I assured her in the words of Jesus who said, ". . . him that cometh to me I will in no wise cast out" (John 6:37b).

For 11 years she had been trying to win in her own strength the battle of life. Though not yet 40 she had already aged considerably. Her health was poor. She was under psychiatric care. Finally she came to Christ.

Today she is a charming, radiant Christian. Her health is fine. Her mind is free from personality-corroding, body-debilitating, mind-destroying worry.

It wasn't until she confessed her helplessness and cast herself wholly upon God that she received strength to live dynamically. Now, as a child of God, she has a prayer life by which she maintains communion with God and keeps un-clogged the channel through which His strength is released to her moment by moment and day by day.

Pray because prayer is essential to poise. Recall the story of Daniel in the lions' den. You remember that he had been hounded by the men who were bent upon his destruction. Nevertheless, he did not alter his habit one iota. There was no ruffling of his spirit. He continued to make his prayer unto God three times a day. He prayed in a spirit of deep humility, recognizing his absolute dependence upon God. Was this a sign of weakness? No! It was a sign of strength. To be sure, Daniel put his face in the dust before God, but he did not lose his courage before the wrath of Darius. He sobbed like a heartbroken child when he knelt before his God, but he faced without a quiver the jaws of the hungry lions. What poise!

There is a real efficiency in prayer. This fact ought also to induce a greater interest in prayer. Martin Luther was not talking through his hat when he said, "I have so much business I cannot get along without spending three hours daily in prayer." Prayer is efficient in that it saves time. It saves time by conditioning you for the day's activities and personal contacts. It saves time by conditioning those with whom you will associate. It saves time in that it makes available to you wisdom which in turn leads to quick and proper decisions.

> If any of you lack wisdom, let him ask of God,
> that giveth to all men liberally, and upbraideth not;
> and it shall be given him (James 1:5).

This of course leads to peace of mind. How many people there are who fret and mope around wasting precious time simply because they don't know what to do or how to do what they need to do. The Lord has promised them the needed wisdom, but they either refuse it or neglect to avail themselves of it. The resultant loss of peace and time is incalculable.

Let me digress here for just a moment. In chapter 23 stress is given to the importance of definite periods of prayer and waiting upon the Lord in prayer. You have just read the words of James 1:5. How ridiculous it is for the Christian to ask for wisdom and immediately terminate his prayer, taking leave of Him who is the Source of wisdom before He has had time to impart it. What would you think of a man who walked into your home and with apparent earnestness asked you a question, but turned around and walked out before you had time to answer it? Remember, prayer is not a one-way street. It is a two-way street.

Prayer is efficient because it puts you in touch with *infinite intelligence*. Prayer will dispel the fogs of human ignorance. It banishes the darkness of self-destructive errors in judgment. People of prayer, regardless of their academic limitations, are the recipients of a proper perspective and a keen understanding imparted to them by Him who is "the Truth."

Prayer is efficient in that it makes available to you the grace necessary to block out negative thoughts, distracting attitudes, and worries which torture the mind and deteriorate the body. Through prayer we cast

> . . . down imaginations, and every high thing that exalteth itself against the knowledge of God, and bringing into captivity every thought to the obedience of Christ (2 Corinthians 10:5).

When your thoughts are Christ's, they are not worry thoughts.

Prayer is efficient in that it enlists divine strength enabling you to effect the proper execution of your God-given responsibilities. While in the flesh upon this earth our Lord prayed before every great endeavor.

Prayer is efficient in that it can lead to the correction of circumstances that both consume time and saddle a person with destructive grief. Do you remember the prayer of Moses and Aaron on behalf of their sister Miriam who was suffering with leprosy? How would that story have ended had it not been for their prayer?

Prayer is efficient in that it leads to harmony. Read once again the first chapters of the Acts of the Apostles. How differently history would have been written had it not been for the prayer of the 120 in the upper room. The harmony that prevailed between them was one of the by-products of their prayer lives. We read concerning them, "and all that believed were together, and had all things common" (Acts 2:44). Worry cannot survive in an atmosphere of such harmony.

Prayer is efficient because it is productive of faith. And faith, of course, is the antidote to worry. Faith is acting in confidence upon the word of another. The one who is faithful in his prayer life acts in confidence upon God's Word. He goes to God with all his dilemmas, all of his assets and all of his liabilities. He acts in confidence upon God's Word which tells him that if he delights himself in the Lord, the Lord will give him the desires of his heart. He prays. God answers his prayer. The very answer is productive of greater faith—of a more eager and a more earnest disposition to act in confidence upon God's Word.

Prayer is efficient because it leads to inner security. The person who spends time regularly in prayer comes to know in his inmost soul that God's Word is true when He assures us, ". . . I will never leave thee, nor forsake thee" (Hebrews 13:5). The resulting inner assurance leads to much greater efficiency.

For instance, I know a man who always insisted on picking up the tab at the restaurant every time he and his friends were eating out. If he went to a ball game with ten or fifteen other folks, he insisted on paying the bill. He constantly gave away expensive gifts—gifts he simply could not afford. Why? His dreadful insecurity is the only answer I can conceive. He compensated for the lack of inner security in his mad effort to secure the fervent friendship of a host of people whose gracious responses to his generosity gave him a temporary sense of well-being.

When a man is properly related to God he has within himself all of the ingredients necessary to provide him with security, joy, and peace regardless of external conditions. This relationship is only maintained as a man spends time regularly with God.

Why pray? Pray because prayer is the means whereby you permit and invite God to so energize you that to His glory you live victoriously, overcoming the world, the flesh, and the devil.

Yes, pray because through prayer you enlist the power of the spirit of God to conquer the weakness of the flesh—*even worry*. When your thoughts are Christ's, they are not worry thoughts.

Pray, because through prayer you have opportunity to turn every care into a prayer.

22

How to Pray

Once again,

> Be careful for nothing; but in every thing by prayer and supplication with thanksgiving let your requests be made known unto God (Philippians 4:6).

In this verse, three different Greek words for prayer are introduced. The first word, translated "prayer," refers to a general offering up of wishes and desires to God. This word points to the frame of mind required in the petitioner—a mind of devotion. The word refers to unrestricted concourse between man and God. That which brings greatest glory to God and profit to you is the habit of prayer. We might call it the Prayer Mood or the Prayer Disposition.

The word translated "supplication" comes from a Greek word meaning "entreaty," a "seeking," "need," "indigence." It refers to an entreaty impelled by a great sense of need, an extreme want. In fact, the verb form of this word in the original means "to want." Therefore this word refers distinctly to the petitionary prayers that are expressive of personal need. This prayer is a special petition for the supply of wants, an act of solicitation.

The third word used and translated in the King James, "requests," refers to requests and even more strongly to demands.

Now the word translated in the King James as "prayer," includes adoration, thanksgiving, confession, and intercession.

The word translated "supplication" refers strictly to an entreaty to God to supply our needs and our wants. On the basis of the teaching of Philippians 4:6 it would be well for us to ponder several factors involved in effectual praying.

If you would have victory over worry, pray *intelligently.* "Let your requests be made known unto God." I heard of a certain man who spent six hours in prayer each day. Lest he should go to sleep when on board a boat, he stood upright and had a rope stretched across, so that he might lie against it. If he slept he would fall. His object was to keep on for six hours with what he called prayer. What sort of prayer was it? He kept on repeating, "There is no God, but God. There is no God, but God." He repeated the same thing over and over again. He did not plead with God to give him anything. Just as a witch repeats a charm, so he repeated certain words. That is not praying.

If you go on your knees and simply repeat a certain formula, you are speaking only words. You are not praying. Some people are criticized for using beads and fetishes to "say prayers." But there are many Protestants who just as definitely "say prayers." They do not pray. They repeat formulas. They say prayers as did the farmer who each night prayed, "O Lord, bless me, my wife, my son John, his wife, us four, no more. Amen." God does not hear you for your much speaking.

Even though on Mount Carmel the wild-eyed multitude cut themselves and chanted repetitiously, "O Baal, hear us!" they were not praying. Let your *requests* be made known unto God.

Get alone with God and tell Him what you want. Pour out your heart before Him. He does not care for high-flown language. Study the prayers of the Bible and you will be impressed that there was no formal phraseology, and there was no fixed and mechanical use of words. Go to God as you go to your mother, your father, or your friend.

Don't think that simply because you get on your knees for a spell every morning and every night that God is going to dissipate your worries. Pray intelligently. Tell Him your problem. Tell Him that you have sinned—that you have worried. Tell Him that you want victory over it. Be specific.

And that leads me to say if you would have victory over worry, pray *definitely*. In chapters 1 and 3 you learned what worry does to you physically. You also learned that worry is a sin. Therefore, as a worrier, you have a great need. Offer up supplications to the Lord—"entreaties expressive of your personal need that solicit God's answer for that need."

Indefinite praying is usually halfhearted praying. Indefinite praying is often insincere praying. It is usually a mere formality. There is no burden, no urgency, no overwhelming constraint in indefinite praying. Indefinite praying shows that one is not sure of the will of God. Therefore he knows not what to pray for. It often indicates that one is trusting in the *act* of praying rather than in the God who answers prayer.

The mind of man is so constituted that it cannot fasten its desires *intensely* upon numerous things at the same time. Jesus said,

> Therefore I say unto you, What things soever ye
> desire, when ye pray, believe that ye receive them,
> and ye shall have them (Mark 11:24).

Now it is impossible to desire strongly that which is not definite.

Your problem is worry. Pray definitely about this problem. Pray definitely that God will give you victory over your distrust of Him. Pray that God will forgive you for intruding into His own province by trying to carry on His business. Ask Him for the grace to cast all your cares upon Him.

In addition to all this, pray specifically concerning the problems causing your anxiety. If it is a wayward daughter, pray definitely and specifically for God's will to be done in her life and for God to give you the grace in the meantime to live triumphantly.

If it is financial difficulty, pray definitely that God will show you if you have been unwise in the handling of your money. If you have been unwise, ask Him to forgive you. Pray definitely that He will give you wisdom and grace to do what you can. Pray that He will miraculously do what you can't do.

Then rest in the truth of Psalm 37:25, "I have been young, and now am old; yet have I not seen the righteous forsaken, nor his seed begging bread."

If you are suffering from a nervous stomach pray definitely about it. Don't simply say, "Lord, take away my nervous stomach." Find out what are the causes of your condition. Be specific. Be definite. And then let your request be made known unto God. Or, as we could correctly translate it, "Make known your demands."

Every now and then I hear people say, "God heard my prayer, but He answered it a little differently than I was expecting." That is ridiculous. What would you think of me if I had five sons and I prayed, "Lord, save my five sons." A few days later my neighbor's five sons all went to church and professed faith in Jesus Christ. Supposing that I said, "Praise God; He answered my prayer. I prayed for the salvation of my five sons and He answered my prayer. He saved the five sons of my next-door neighbor." That is nonsense.

Pray definitely and expect a definite answer. Pray for bread. God will give you bread, not a stone. Pray for fish. God will give you a fish, not a serpent.

If you would have victory over worry, pray *importunately*. The word *importunate* means both "demanding" and "persistent." These qualities are consistent with the text. Remember, the word *requests* can be translated "demands." The tense used is the present imperative so that we might translate the words this way—"in everything by general concourse with God and specific entreaties arising out of peronal needs, with thanksgiving, let your demands be made known *perpetually* unto God."

You can make these demands because of your relationship with God through Christ. "But my God shall supply all your need according to his riches in glory by Christ Jesus" (Philippians 4:19).

He has promised to supply all your needs. You can demand the fulfillment of that promise with this warning, however. You are not to say, "Lord, supply all of my needs." Rather you are to specifically and definitely make known those needs one by one. And then pray persistently. Your cares are persistent. Therefore make your prayers persistent.

Pray to God and then pray again. If the Lord does not answer you the first time, be grateful that you have good reason for praying again. If He does not answer your requests the second time, thank Him that He loves you so much that He wants to hear your voice again. If He keeps you waiting until you have gone to Him seven times, say to yourself, "Now I know that I worship the God of Elijah, for Elijah's God let him go again seven times before the blessing was given."

Count it an honor to be permitted to wrestle in prayer even as Jacob wrestled with the angel during the long watches of the night. This is the way God develops His princes.

Jacob never would have been "Israel"—Prince with God—if he had received the blessing from the angel at the first asking. He kept on wrestling until he prevailed. Then he became a prince of God. Worry cannot exist with this kind of prayer.

Jesus taught us to pray all the way through the gospels. Two great illustrations He gave to us in the eleventh and in the eighteenth chapters of Luke.

The man who wanted to borrow bread at midnight is a striking example of the spirit Jesus desires to inculcate. The borrower was in dire need. He was terribly in earnest and would not take no for an answer. Jesus said when you pray be just as earnest and be just as persistent as this man was. You need the blessing of God much more than he needed his three loaves. You are seeking something that means more than bread, and just as the importunity of the borrower finally wins out, so the soul set upon finding God will command His attention and be heard.

God has no time for lukewarm pleas, for easygoing, half-hearted prayers. If the sense of need is not great, if you forget about the matter before the day is over, God will pay little heed to your prayer. If you have something vital at issue, if you are willing to give time and effort, and if you press your claim home to a finish, God will listen. The man who is willing to quit, or who can quit, is not in the condition of mind and heart to appreciate the favor of God. The soul who counts it the biggest privilege on earth to know God, who seeks for Him and His blessings as men seek for silver and gold, will not only be rewarded, but also will be conditioned to estimate rightly what has been received.

Jesus then adds:

> And I say unto you, Ask, and it shall be given you; seek, and ye shall find; knock, and it shall be opened unto you. For every one that asketh receiveth; and he that seeketh findeth; and to him that knocketh it shall be opened (Luke 11:9,10).

This is not the easy passage some people think it is. It does not mean that all you have to do is ask for something and receive it, or to knock and the door flies open. It refers to a life which is one continual search after God, a constant seeking, a daily asking, a habitual knocking.

This is the only antidote to worry which itself is perpetual. Let your prayer be perpetual. It means that you must desire that which lies behind the closed door intensely enough to knock with unshaken persistence. Jesus is here saying that to such knocking the door will open. To seeking of that sort will come the answer which makes life full and rich.

The parable found in the eighteenth chapter of Luke is still more striking, as it represents a case where the delayed answer is misunderstood. The petitioner is set forth in the figure of a poor widow seeking vindication and protection from an unjust judge. The judge is the perfect embodiment of heartless wickedness. No more complete portrait of utter depravity was ever drawn than Jesus sketched in that one terse sentence, "which feared not God, neither regarded man" (Luke 18:2). Just one stroke of the Master Artist's brush, and the cold, heartless man stands before us; one who regards not suffering humanity nor fears the coming judgment of God.

The feeble, insignificant petitioner was scorned. No heed was given, but Jesus said she continued to press her plea for justice until in absolute selfishness and for no other reason the judge granted the request.

> . . . Though I fear not God, nor regard man; Yet because this widow troubleth me, I will avenge her, lest by her continual coming she weary me (Luke 18:4b,5).

The argument is: If a man like that can be moved to do what means nothing to him, will not God hear the continual cry of His people He loves with a boundless compassion? There are long periods when prayers seem unanswered. There are long days of darkness, sometimes years of wearisome waiting, while countless petitions are sent to a heaven that seems deaf and empty. This is the time about which Jesus speaks. He says, "Cry on, God will hear. He is not heartless, neither has He forgotten."

This parable is for the time when faith has staggered and the heart has grown sick with waiting. Let us remember that the longest delay to us may be as the twinkling of an eye to the plans of God. Alexander Maclaren said years ago, "Heaven's clock does not beat in the same note with our little chronometers." Jesus teaches us to pray on. He says we must not quit. We must not doubt. God knows when to answer. He knows the best time and the most fitting place. We can, in all confidence, leave the question of *when* and *where* to Him. Of one thing we may be sure—*He will answer*. Worthy prayer does not become discouraged. It does not surrender. This is the power that defeats worry.

If you would conquer worry, *pray in faith*. Faith is acting in confidence upon the word of another. Faith in God is acting in confidence upon His Word. You were saved that way. It is also in this way you become mighty with God.

You develop faith as you meditate upon God's Word—the Bible.

> So then faith cometh by hearing, and hearing by

the word of God (Romans 10:17).

Prayer and the Word of God are inseparably connected. "Feasting" on the Word of God is productive of that faith without which prayer is useless.

Through the Word of God the Lord speaks to our hearts and conditions our hearts for prayer. In prayer we speak to Him in faith. So many times in the Scriptures we have passages indicating that the Lord spoke first, after which the one who heard the Word of the Lord spoke to Him in prayer. Read Jeremiah 1:4-6 as an example.

> Then the word of the Lord came unto me, saying, Before I formed thee in the belly I knew thee; and before thou camest forth out of the womb I sanctified thee, and I ordained thee a prophet unto the nations. Then said I, Ah, Lord God! behold, I cannot speak: for I am a child.

You remember also Daniel's great prayer. In the first year of the reign of King Darius we see Daniel reading the Word of God. He had in his hand the prophecy of Jeremiah in which the Lord had promised that the desolation of Jerusalem should last 70 years. After reading this prophetic promise, Daniel turned to the Lord. The reading of the Word of God led to prayer. The reading of God's Word was productive of the faith that made prayer effectual.

The German theologian Bengel had the reputation of being a great man of prayer, one who knew the secret of effectual prayer. One day a fellow believer watched him at the close of the day. He saw the old saint sitting before a large Bible, reading slowly, often stopping, meditating with the silent tears running down his cheeks. After reading and meditating a long time, Bengel closed the Book and began to speak to God in prayer. His heart had been prepared through the reading of the Word. Neglect of the daily reading of the Word of God and meditation on it soon results in neglected prayer as well.

The secret to earnest and effectual prayer—the prayer of faith—is faithful and diligent study of the Scriptures.

Faith is essential to effectual prayer. All real prayer has as its basis a firm faith in a God who reponds to the quest of the human soul.

> But without faith it is impossible to please him: for he that cometh to God must believe that he is, and that he is a rewarder of them that diligently seek him (Hebrews 11:6).

We come to God by our hearts and not by our intellects. The first condition of entering into His fellowship is a faith not only that God is, but that He will be found by the soul who honestly and persistently seeks for Him. God is not found by those who look for Him in the spirit of cold curiosity. He is not found by those who simply desire to extend the range of their intellectual conquest. This is the reason why many self-styled philosophers and many pseudoscientists have been unable to come to any clear conception of God. It was to men of this type that Zophar said,

> Canst thou by searching find out God? canst thou find out the Almighty unto perfection? (Job 11:7).

When a man says in the pride of his intellect, "I will now see if there be any God," he may turn his telescope upon the farthest heavens and count the myriad worlds that wander in the blue abyss. He may peer among the atoms and divide and subdivide the electrons, but the greatest thing in the universe will still be hidden from his eyes.

The laws of logic, the theories of philosophy, the investigation of chemistry and physics, all have their place and are of great value, but they are not milestones on the road into fellowship with God. The man who can say with the Hebrew psalmist, "My soul thirsteth for God, for the living God: when shall I come and appear before God?" (Psalm 42:2), is more nearly on the road to His presence. The humble man who with simple and sincere faith reaches out after God will find Him while the philosopher is groping in the shadows of his theories and the scientist is bewildered with the problems of his laboratory.

If you would enter into the prayer life that conquers care, spend some time each day with the Word of God. The time spent will be productive of faith that pleases God. This time spent will condition you for communion with God and as you commune with God you will develop ever more confidence in God and this glorious cycle will continue unabated as long as life shall last.

You worry. Here is God's Word that if you will utilize this formula of Praise, Poise, and Prayer He will give you peace. He also makes it clear that by prayer you will be given strength to offer praise and to manifest poise. As you pray you will become effective in prayer. Now believe this. Believe that He will give you precisely what He has promised to give you if you will meet the conditions. He will give you *peace*.

He cannot go back upon His promise. He is "the God, that cannot lie" (Titus 1:2).

Some of you pray, but you only say words. While you are asking God to give you victory over worry, you are at the very time worrying that you are not praying correctly. You are worrying that maybe you have not met all of the conditions. *Stop psychoanalyzing yourself.* Don't be a spiritual hypochondriac. *Get your mind off yourself and onto God. Spend enough time in your prayer thanking Him for what He has done and praising Him for who He is that you will be conditioned to pray intelligently, definitely, importunately, and in faith.*

As you pray, picture yourself a perfectly adjusted, dynamic, radiant personality living in the strength of God to the glory of God. This is certainly God's will for you. By faith, then, take God at His Word, lay hold upon Him in prayer, and become the personality to glorify Him and bring peace to your mind. You are what you think you are. Stop, therefore, insulting God. Recognize yourself as a redeemed soul. You are a child of the King. You are in league with the Creator of the universe. Recognize yourself as a potential recipient of qualities, attitudes, and resources that will glorify God and bless your fellowman as you live triumphantly over every worry and care.

If you would conquer worry, pray *privately*.

> But thou, when thou prayest, enter into thy closet, and when thou hast shut thy door, pray to thy Father which is in secret; and thy Father which seeth in secret shall reward thee openly (Matthew 6:6).

God deals with men face to face and heart to heart. You cannot have audience with a king and be engaged with the crowd at the same time. The matters between you and God are too sacred and personal to be laid bare to the eyes of the crowd. Furthermore, prayer calls for such concentration, such focalization, such rallying of all of our powers, that it demands the quiet of the inner chamber. When we pray we are going to share with God things which we would not for the very life of us share with the crowd. There are the secrets of our hearts to be talked over with Him. There are sins that need to be confessed to Him. There are yearnings and hungerings of our deepest souls to whisper into His ear about which we would not for anything speak to our dearest friend. Then God wants a real opportunity to speak to us. "The still, small voice" cannot be heard amidst jarring sounds, shattering voices, the hum of machinery, or the clamor of business.

Jesus did not mean that no man could pray unless in an empty and quiet room. He did mean that the door of mind and heart would shut out the world. The outside world must be locked away from the private transactions which take place there. "When thou hast shut thy door," when there is no one there but God and you, when you are all alone with Him, then pray.

It is so true that when we really pray, no one is there but God and ourselves. All else is outside. When we pray, our

dearest earthly friend is outside the door. He may be in the
same pew, in the same room, but he is outside the door. Every
business affair is without. Every allurement of the world is
without. All the silver that shines and the jewels that sparkle
are outside the locked door when we really pray. Not a dis-
traction, not an alien sound! How quiet it must be in there!
One can almost hear the beating of his own heart and the
rustle of his thoughts. That door is not made of steel or
lumber. It is the door of our will that closes and says to all the
world, "Out. Out. Out. I have great business at hand! I am
engaged with the Almighty. Keep out!"

I tell you, worry cannot abide when you are locked up with
God in the secret sanctuary of prayer.

If you would conquer worry, pray *thankfully*. This will lead
your mind to revert back to chapter 6 where the text says that
we are to pray and supplicate "with thanksgiving." The kind
of prayer that kills worry is a prayer that asks cheerfully,
joyfully, thankfully.

Pray, "Lord, I am in financial straits. I bless Thee for this
condition, and I ask Thee to supply all my needs." This is the
way to pray. "Lord, I am sick. I thank Thee for this affliction
for Thou hast promised that 'all things work together for
good to them that love the Lord.' Now heal me, I beseech
Thee—if it please Thee!" Or you will pray, "Lord, I am in great
trouble. I thank Thee for this trouble for I know that it contains a blessing even though the envelope is black-edged.
Now, Lord, give me grace as I pass through this trouble." This
kind of prayer kills worry.

If you would conquer worry, pray in *Jesus' name*.

> If ye shall ask any thing in my name, I will do it
> (John 14:14).

> And in that day ye shall ask me nothing. Verily,
> verily, I say unto you, Whatsoever ye shall ask the
> Father in my name, he will give it you. Hitherto
> have ye asked nothing in my name: ask, and ye
> shall receive, that your joy may be full. These

things have I spoken unto you in proverbs: but the time cometh, when I shall no more speak unto you in proverbs, but I shall shew you plainly of the Father. At that day ye shall ask in my name: and I say not unto you, that I will pray the Father for you: For the Father himself loveth you, because ye have loved me, and have believed that I came out from God (John 16:23-27).

Years ago I was involved in a four-car accident. Litigation proceedings began almost immediately. I needed help desperately. I needed the resources of the greatest accident lawyer in the country. His name was Weinstein. His fee was understandably large. So large that I, as a ministerial student, could not meet its demands. However, a dear friend of mine hearing of my need, came to see me. This friend was part owner of a large company in Chicago. He said, "Haggai, Weinstein is our lawyer. We retain him. Here, let me give you one of my cards." On the back of the card he scribbled a note of introduction to Weinstein. Weinstein saw me. He solved my legal problem. Why? Because of a fee I paid? Not at all. Because of the fee paid by my friend. He received me in the name of and on the merits of my friend.

The Lord Jesus Christ is my Friend "that sticketh closer than a brother." He paid the fee that I could not pay—the penalty of sin. He paid it with His own blood. In His name and on His merits I have access to God who alone can solve my problems.

Catch this insight. Grasp this concept. And you will be well on the way to the conquest of worry.

23

When to Pray

The tense used in Philippians 4:6 is present imperative. It carries the idea of durative action. Therefore we are being true to the meaning of the text when we translate Philippians 4:6, "Don't worry about anything whatever, but in all things by prayer and supplication with thanksgiving, let your requests be made known *perpetually* to God."

The present imperative tense is also used in the first part of the verse. In other words, Paul is saying, "Don't perpetually worry, but *perpetually* pray." *Let perpetual prayer take the place of perpetual care.*

Prayer is the Christian's breath. When breathing is obstructed, health is jeopardized. When the Christian permits any obstruction to his prayer life, his spiritual health is put in jeopardy.

Our little son breathed only once every two and a half minutes the first three hours he was in this world. Because of his deficient breathing only an inadequate supply of oxygen could reach the brain with the result that brain tissues were destroyed and body movement was impaired. Many Christians are suffering from spiritual cerebral palsy. An inadequate supply of the oxygen of prayer has destroyed spiritual fiber and impaired Christian effectiveness.

Breath is essential to life and health. The breath of prayer is essential to Christian well-being. When the Christian is praying he is breathing spiritually. Just as we must breathe ceaselessly, so we must pray ceaselessly.

The injunction of God's Word is that we "Pray without ceasing" (1 Thessalonians 5:17).

The trouble with many of us is that we pray when caught in the swirl of difficulty, oppression, and vicious circumstances. Then we think of Psalm 50:15:

> . . . call upon me in the day of trouble: I will
> deliver thee, and thou shalt glorify me.

The story is told of two Irishmen, Pat and Mike, who had narrowly escaped death on a sinking ship. They were floundering around in icy ocean waters on a couple of planks. Pat was addicted to the grossest profanity but he decided to repent of it if the Lord would come to his rescue. Mike thought his theology sound. Pat assumed the countenance of a Muslim at Mecca and began to pray. Just before arriving at the main thesis of his repentant prayer, Mike spotted a ship coming toward them. As delighted as Columbus when he first spotted the North American shore, Mike hollered, "Hold it, Pat. Don't commit yerself. Here's a ship." Pat immediately stopped praying! Isn't that the way many of us are? The only time we pray is when we are in a jam. As soon as things improve we forget God.

Spiritually speaking, most of us can much better afford adversity than prosperity. Like the Israelites of old, it seems that when our prosperity expands, our spirituality contracts. Like Mike, we call upon the Lord as long as things are precarious, but as soon as things improve we resort to our own resources. The Lord is but an escape mechanism for some.

The Christian's prayer life is one of incessant prayer. "Praying always," says Paul in Ephesians 6:18. That is, praying at all seasons and on all occasions. If you would conquer worry, you must always maintain a spirit of prayer. You must live in a prayerful disposition.

"Pray without ceasing." One of my theological professors, in discussing the meaning of 1 Thessalonians 5:17, told of an experience of some ministers. They had congregated early and were waiting for the Monday morning ministers' meeting. They were talking in the vestibule and this verse was mentioned. Discussion became spirited and the meaning of this verse evoked no small comment—and consternation. It wasn't long until they readily agreed that the verse puzzled them. How could one possibly pray without ceasing? A scrub woman about her work overheard them and said, "Excuse me, gentlemen. But it's all very simple." She then gave her interpretation of the verse in the form of a personal illustration.

She said, "I always pray. When I go to bed at night I thank the Lord for the joy of resting on His everlasting arms. When I awaken the next morning I ask Him to open my eyes that I may behold new and wondrous things out of His Word. When I bathe I ask Him to cleanse me from secret faults. When I dress I ask Him to clothe me with humility and love. When building the fire I ask Him to build the fire of love for souls in my heart. When I eat I ask Him to cause me to grow on the bread of His Word." On and on she continued explaining to those ministers the way in which she lived in the attitude of prayer. Prayer was her habit. They marveled. They grasped the truth. We are to "pray without ceasing."

In praying without ceasing, one's mind is stayed on Christ. One is constantly attuned to the will of God. While one may not be involved in deliberate and conscious contact with Him, one is nevertheless aware of His presence and one's life is regulated by His will. It is much the same as a mother who goes to sleep at night. The little baby is in the crib. The mother is sleeping. Even while sleeping, however, she is attuned to the baby's needs and wants. The slightest whimper of the baby arouses her from sleep. So it is in the life of the Christian who prays without ceasing. He is attuned to the will of God. God's slightest suggestion, command, or desire arouses the believer to obedience and action.

Isaiah says: "Thou wilt keep him in perfect peace, whose mind is stayed on thee: because he trusteth in thee" (Isaiah 26:3). When you pray without ceasing, you are "attuned" to God. When you live in an awareness of His will, your mind is "stayed" on Him. Now the truth is simply this: When your mind is stayed on Him, you have perfect peace. When you have perfect peace you don't have worry. If you would conquer worry, it is essential that you live in the atmosphere of prayer.

The pages of God's Word are replete with the names of those who prayed. All who had power with God and with men were people of prayer. Explain the poise of Daniel in the lions' den apart from the mighty prayer life he maintained.

Moses prayed until his face glistened with the glory of God.

The great example, of course, is our Lord. His whole life was a prayer. Before He did anything He prayed. After He did anything He prayed. He prayed morning, noon, and night. Sometimes He prayed all night. Whenever He was alone He prayed. Prayer was never off His lips and was never out of His heart. He was the incarnation of this truth, "Pray without ceasing."

Let me caution you against a prevalent mistake. There are those who say, "I always pray. When I am driving the car down the street I pray. When I go about my business I pray. I never spend great periods of time alone with God in prayer. I simply pray all the time in whatever I do." This is well and good. But it is also essential that one set apart a period each day when he can get alone with God and pray.

Charles Simeon devoted four hours each morning to prayer. Mr. Wesley spent two hours daily in prayer. It is said that John Fletcher stained the walls with the breath of his prayers. Sometimes he would pray all night. His whole life was a life of prayer. Said he, "I would not rise from my seat without lifting my heart to God."

Martin Luther said, "If I fail to spend three hours in prayer each morning, the devil gets the victory through the day. I have so much business I cannot get along without spending three hours daily in prayer." David Brainerd, the mighty missionary to the Indians, once said, "I love to be alone in my cottage where I can spend much time in prayer."

Adoniram Judson said, "Arrange thy affairs, if possible, so that thou canst leisurely devote two hours every day, not merely to devotional exercise, but to the very act of secret prayer and communion with God . . . to be resolute in His cause. Make all practical sacrifices to maintain it."

You may not have hours to devote to prayer. D. L. Moody never spent more than 15 minutes in prayer. But he prayed *often* and *about everything*. It is important that you have a definite time when you get alone with God every day. Not everyone can spend great periods of time. But surely there are few people, if any, who could not spend at least ten to 15 minutes in Bible study and 15 minutes in prayer daily.

Let me urge you to begin the day with your quiet time. I find that the more I commit myself to the Lord in the morning the less I have to confess to Him at night. We need food to strengthen us for the physical demands of our daily routine. Matthew 4:4 and 1 Peter 2:2 indicate that the Word of God is spiritual food.

> . . . It is written, Man shall not live by bread alone, but by every word that proceedeth out of the mouth of God (Matthew 4:4).

> As newborn babes, desire the sincere milk of the word, that ye may grow thereby (1 Peter 2:2).

If you would be strong, you must have spiritual food at the beginning of the day to sustain you through it. You are not likely to suffer great temptations while you are sleeping. The great strains and stresses will be encountered during the day. Of course it is well to spend some time with the Lord before going to bed at night. But let me urgently suggest that you make your personal devotions a matter of first concern in the morning. An old professor of mine had the motto, "No Bible, no breakfast. Speak to no one until you have spoken to God."

The effectiveness of your brief moments of prayer will be contingent upon these periods spent in prayer. Don't say you have no time. Some may have more money than others. Some may have more talent than others. But we are all on an even footing when it comes to time. We each have 60 seconds to each minute, 60 minutes to each hour, 24 hours to each day, seven days to each week, 52 weeks to each year.

As an evangelist, I was gone from home a great deal. There were occasions when on my way from one city to another, I could stop at my home for a few minutes. It delighted my heart, and my wife and son gave evidence that this delight was reciprocated. Suppose, however, that when I had a week off between meetings, I refused to go home. Suppose I had gone off to visit some friends instead. The next time I "bounced in" I would probably have "bounced out" just as fast. My family knew that I loved to be at home and that I spent every possible moment at home. This knowledge made even the briefest visits enjoyable to all of us.

So, too, our brief visits with the Lord bring mutual rejoicing if we are faithful in setting aside larger segments of time to commune with Him in deliberate and earnest intercession. Then "would our hearts condemn us not."

When to pray? Let us once again paraphrase Philippians 4:6, and hear—"Let your requests be made known *perpetually* unto God."

Remember, perpetual prayer is the answer to perpetual care.

24

For What to Pray

Be careful for nothing; but in *everything* by prayer and supplication with thanksgiving let your requests be made known unto God (Philippians 4:6).

Casting all your care upon him; for he careth for you (1 Peter 5:7).

Since you worry about everything, pray about everything. "In *everything* by prayer and supplication with thanksgiving let your requests be made known unto God." Peter tells us to cast *all* our care upon Him. Turn *every* care into a prayer.

You may pray about the smallest thing and about the greatest thing. Set no boundaries with respect to God's care. It is a wide-open field. You may pray for the fullness of the Holy Spirit. You may also pray for a new pair of shoes. Go to God about the food you eat, the water you drink, the clothing you wear.

Nothing is too small for Him to notice. Does He not attend the funeral of every sparrow? Has He not numbered the hairs of your head? Even the things you might consider big are little, yet important, to Him. Our entire earth is like a mere speck of sand on the beach of the great universe. If God is willing to consider this little speck, He would just as well stoop a little lower and consider our smallest problems.

You worry about the smallest things, do you not? Well, pray about the smallest things, since prayer is God's antidote to worry.

Read it again: "Casting *all* your care upon him, for he careth for you." The words translated *care* here are two distinct and different words in the original. The word *care* used in the first instance is the same word translated "anxious." It refers to the same word relating to worry, "to divide the mind." The

487

word *care* used in the second instance refers to God's solicitous interest in our highest good. Cast *all* your mind dividers, mind distracters, worries on Him for He is solicitous of your highest good. Cast them *all* on Him.

You know the old song by Tindley, "Take Your Burden to the Lord and Leave It There." The chorus goes,

> Leave it there, leave it there.
> Take your burden to the Lord and leave it there.
> If you trust and never doubt,
> He will surely lead you out.
> Take your burden to the Lord and leave it there.

The trouble with us is we pretend to take our burdens to the Lord, but we don't leave them with Him. We bring them back again.

Close friends of our family were living in Darlington, Maryland, in the early '40's. The husband and father was a classmate of my father during their school days. They had eight children. The mother, whom we affectionately called "Aunt Edith," was coming home from a neighbor's house one Saturday afternoon. As she came nearer she saw five of her youngest children huddled together in great concentration of interest and effort. As she came near, all the time trying to discover the center of attraction, she was aghast to see them playing with baby skunks. She screamed at the top of her voice, "Children, run!" *Each one grabbed a skunk and ran!* Isn't that what we often do? We have our little worries, our little problems—our little skunks. We take them to the Lord in prayer. He says, "Run." Instead of leaving them there, we grab the stinking little things and run.

No problem that I as a Christian have is too great or too insignificant for God's loving care. This is a thrilling thought that you will do well to ponder again and again.

A. T. Pierson, Bible teacher extraordinary, sat one day with George Muëller, the great Englishman of faith. Mr. Muëller was relating to Dr. Pierson some of the marvelous things God had done for the Faith Orphanage at Bristol. As Mr. Muëller talked he wrote, and Dr. Pierson noticed he was having difficulty with his pen point. In the midst of the conversation, Mr. Muëller seemed oblivious to the visitor. He bowed his head for a moment or two in prayer and then began writing again. Dr. Pierson said, "Mr. Muëller, what were you praying about just now?"

"Oh," said Mr. Muëller, "perhaps you didn't notice that I was having trouble with this pen point. I haven't another and this is an important letter, so I was asking the Lord to help me so that I could write it clearly."

"Dear me," said Dr. Pierson, "a man who trusts God for millions of pounds also prays about a scratchy pen point."

If Mr. Muëller had been like many of us, he would have become hot and bothered. Possibly he would have become a little exasperated with the man who sold him the pen or the company that made the pen. Perhaps he would have indulged in morbid reflection wondering why he didn't buy a pen of another make instead of the miserable pen that was giving him trouble. Or, if he had been like many of us, he may have in disgust thrown the pen down and discontinued the writing of the letter, with the result that his conscience would have bothered him later on for not having written. This would have added to the stress and anxiety. I draw your attention to this because I think it is one of the most lucid examples of the power of prayer in the seeming trivia of life.

Some there are who think we should pray only for problems of great magnitude. They consider it an insult to God and a waste of His time to pray for the so-called small things. It is here that we need the faith of a little child.

One day, many years ago, my father was replacing a burned-out bulb in the taillight of our old car. In replacing the lens he noticed he had lost a little screw in the tall grass. He had an urgent appointment for that night and not much time to spare. He searched and searched for the little screw, but to no avail. My younger brother Tom, then five or six years old, was playing next door with a friend. Finally, Dad called Tom and his friend over to contribute their help in finding the insignificant but essential little screw. When Dad told the children what he wanted Tom said, "Dad, have you prayed about it?"

My father replied, "No, I haven't, Tom."

Tom said, "Well, let's pray, Daddy." Tom prayed and said in substance, "Heavenly Father, Daddy has lost the screw that he needs for the taillight of his car. He can't find it and he needs it badly. Help us to find it. Thank You, Jesus. Amen."

Believe it or not, as soon as Tom had finished his prayer— so illustrative of the childlike faith that honors God—Dad put his hand down in the tall grass and retrieved the screw. Coincidence? Not at all! It was a distinct answer to prayer.

Possibly you read some years ago the article in *Reader's Digest* telling about the circumstances leading to Billy Graham's going on the air coast to coast. Many people had been after him to secure a coast-to-coast weekly broadcast. He had hesitated, saying that there were many other fine coast-to-coast broadcasts of the gospel. Also the finances were not available.

An increasing number of people insisted that for the glory of God and the profit of the people of America individually, as well as for America as a nation, it was imperative that Billy go on the air. Did Graham fret and stew and worry about whether or not he ought to go on? Did he let the decision upset him and thus reduce his effectiveness for Christ? Did he vacillate between the two possibilities? No. He simply took the issue to God in prayer.

Without publicizing the fact he put out a fleece as did Gideon. He prayed that if the Lord was leading him to broadcast the gospel coast-to-coast each week He would provide $25,000 within a specified time. As I recall, by the morning of the final day a little more than $23,000 had come in. Dr. Graham had set $25,000 as the figure. Did the fact that $25,000 in full had not come in upset him? Did he say, "Well, this is close enough"? Did he say, "My prayer is answered"? No. He had made his appeal to the Lord. He was honestly trying to know the will of God. His whole interest was the glory of God. If $24,995 had come in, Dr. Graham would not have gone on the radio. Before the day was over, however, the full $25,000 had come in and he knew the direction in which God was leading him.

Some of you say, "But really, some of the things that come to my mind are too insignificant to pray about." Do you really believe that? If you believe they are too insignificant to pray about, then why do you not believe they are too insignificant to worry about? Put this down: Anything big enough to worry about is big enough for you to pray about. Philippians 4:6 tells us in substance, "Don't worry about *anything* whatever; but in *everything* let your requests be made known unto God."

In this book is set down the biblical formula for victory over worry. If you are to have victory in putting this formula in operation, it is mandatory that you enlist the strength of Almighty God.

In your prayer ask God for the grace to enable you to rejoice, to control your feelings, regulating them according to His will, to count your many blessings. Ask Him to give you grace to respond to ingratitude with serenity. Call upon Him for the grace of becoming genuinely interested in other people.

By prayer call upon God to help you live in the consciousness of His nearness and therefore to display that poise which is the hallmark of the domination of the infinite God in the life of finite man.

Through prayer ask God to give you grace to "gird up the loins of your mind" so that you might have the mind of Christ.

> Let this mind be in you, which was also in Christ Jesus (Philippians 2:5).

Through prayer you will enlist divine help in the matter of self-control, in the matter of relaxation (resting in the Lord), in the matter of enthusiasm, in the matter of scheduling your day's activities, in the matter of your hobbies and sidelines, in the matter of living each day to the full by "redeeming the time," in the matter of the development of skill, in the matter of industry.

Through prayer spend time with God until you know His mind and do His will in the all-important matter of stewardship. Through the right kind of prayer life you will be strengthened to live the surrendered life so essential to the poise which conquers worry.

Through prayer you can duplicate the request of earnest men many years ago who, turning to Jesus said, "Teach us to pray."

The direct answers of God in response to your prayer give you strength to battle and conquer this vicious sin of worry. Apart from the blessings of prayer itself there is also a therapeutic value in the actual time and quiet spent before God.

Pray about everything. Turn every care into a prayer and *win over worry.*

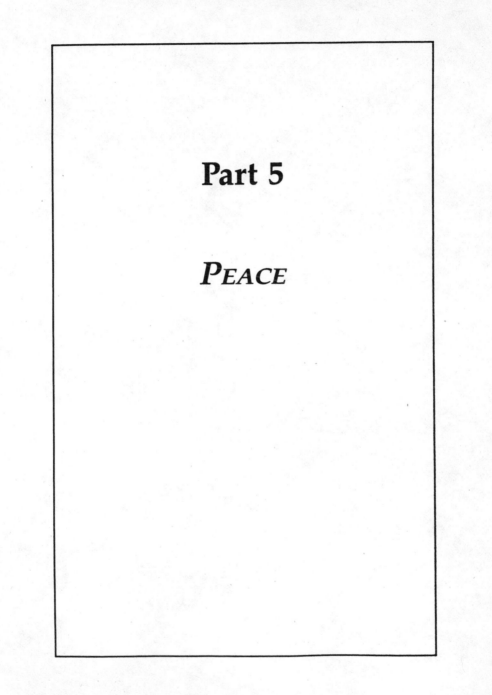

Part 5

PEACE

25

Perfect Peace

> And the peace of God, which passeth all understanding, shall keep your hearts and minds through Christ Jesus (Philippians 4:7).

Ponder my translation of verse 7:

> If you do this, then the peace of God, far more effective than any forethought or contrivance of man will keep watch over your hearts and your thoughts in Christ Jesus.

The word translated "peace" can also be translated "tranquility," "harmony," "concord," "security," "safety," "prosperity," and "felicity." Worry cannot survive in this kind of atmosphere. Just as worry means "divide the mind," so we might say that peace is "uniting the mind," fastening it upon worthwhile goals and stimulating it with worthwhile motives.

God is the Author of this peace. It is "the peace of God." And God is not the Author of confusion.

> For God is not the author of confusion, but of peace, as in all churches of the saints (1 Corinthians 14:33).

He is the Author of unity.

> Endeavoring to keep the unity of the Spirit in the bond of peace (Ephesians 4:3).

This is a genuine peace begotten of God. This is not the attitude of the man who takes everything lightly—who snaps his fingers, whistles, and sings. This fellow is a heedless, foolish, light-headed, and light-heeled person who for a little while may dance and sing. He simply postpones his sorrow. The day will come when he will give account. The day will come swiftly and with a vengeance.

This peace is far different than that attitude and disposition embraced by the stoic. The stoic braces his nerves. He will be shaken and moved by nothing. Run a knife into him. He feels the pain, but he will not show it. Despite all manner of rough knocks and blows in the rough and tumble world, he has set his teeth, and no expression will escape him to show that he feels or winces. This is not peace.

This peace is far different from that attitude and disposition embraced by the laughing epicurean who chortles out, "Let us eat, drink, and be merry for tomorrow we die." We are not steel-nerved stoics. We will live it up.

This peace is based upon fact. It is not a self-manufactured hallucination designed to color the facts. This peace is based upon the fact of God's all-sufficiency. It is also based upon our willingness to cast ourselves in self-confessed helplessness upon Him in response to which He lives through us His own life, bringing harmony, purpose, meaning, and poise to our lives.

Let me make a distinction between *peace with God* and the peace of God. Every child of God has peace with God.

> Therefore being justified by faith, we have peace with God through our Lord Jesus Christ (Romans 5:1).

But not every child of God has the peace of God. No one can enjoy the peace *of* God who does not have peace *with* God. On the other hand, it is possible, as witnessed by the experience of multitudes of Christians, to have peace *with* God and fail to appropriate the peace *of* God.

This peace *of* God has its foundation in the fact that God doeth all things well. It has its source in the fact that Jesus "will never leave thee nor forsake thee" (Hebrews 13:5).

Do you remember the story in Mark 4 of our Lord's trip across the Sea of Galilee? He was asleep in the bottom of the boat. The winds became furious. The waves sprang higher and higher in the air. Soon a tempestuous storm was raging. The little boat was perched perilously aloft the crest one moment only to be dashed into the darksome vortex the next. The terrified disciples cried out, "Lord, save us. We perish!" Jesus was asleep! What peace.

Jesus arose and subdued the storm, and then turned to the disciples and said, "Oh, ye of little faith. Why are ye so fearful?" I can hear them muttering "Little faith? Little faith? We are veteran seamen. We have never seen a storm like this, and you call it little faith!" Ah, yes. You see, Jesus didn't say, "Let us go out in the middle of the sea and get drowned." He said, "Let us pass over unto the other side" (Mark 4:35).

Now, dear friend, when you have invited Christ into your life and when you have turned the helm over to His control and when you have heard His words of assurance, "Thou art mine, I will never leave thee, nor forsake thee" (Hebrews 13:5), there is made available to you a peace the world cannot give and the world cannot take away.

Notice several points about the peace Christ can give:

1) *It is a peace that "passeth all understanding."* This may be interpreted in two ways.

First, it may be interpreted as too great for the poor grasp of our limited concepts. It is deeper, broader, sweeter, and more heavenly than the joyful Christian himself can explain. He enjoys what he cannot understand.

There is another sense in which the words *passeth all understanding* refer to superiority over human forethought or intellectual contrivance. Here is a man who has worries. He tries through the efforts of his own understanding to resolve his worries. He fails. He fails miserably. He may resort to stoicism or epicureanism or the power of positive thinking, but he fails.

This man comes to God's Word. He responds affirmatively to God's commands. Having entered into peace *with* God he now utilizes that formula which gives the peace of God: **Praise** plus **Poise** plus **Prayer** equals **Peace**. Perfect peace is his privileged possession. In this sense it passes understanding, in that it far exceeds in effectiveness all human contrivance and forethought.

2) *This peace is indestructible.* It "shall keep your hearts and minds through Christ Jesus." Paul here brings into union the conceptions of peace and of war, for he employs a distinctly military word to express the office of this divine peace. That word, translated "shall keep," is the same as the word translated in another of his letters, "kept . . . with a garrison" (2 Corinthians 11:32).

This peace of God takes upon itself militaristic functions. It garrisons the heart and mind. By *heart and mind* are not meant two different faculties, the emotional and the intellectual. Here, as is always the case in God's Word, *heart* means the whole inner man whether considered as thinking, willing, purposing, or effectuating any other inward and volitional functions. The word *mind* does not mean another part of man's nature. Rather it refers to the total products of the operations of the heart. The revised version renders it "thoughts" and that is correct if it be made to include emotions, affections, and purposes as well as thoughts in the more restricted sense. The peace of God garrisons and guards the whole man in the full scope of his manifold operations. This divine peace can be enjoyed in the midst of warfare.

This is an indestructible peace that guards and garrisons one against all care, anxiety, change, suffering, and conflict. It gives unalterable rest in God.

Deep in the bosom of the ocean beneath the region where winds howl and billows break there is calm, but the calm is not stagnation. Each drop in the fathomless abyss may be raised to the surface by the power of the sunbeams, expanded there by their heat, and sent on some beneficent mission across the world. Even so, deep in our hearts beneath the storm, beneath the raging winds and the lashing waves, this peace forms a central calm, a calm that is not stagnation.

"Drops" of this calm may be raised to the surface of our behavior by the power of the Son of Righteousness—Jesus Christ, the Light of the World—expanded there by the heat of the Holy Spirit and sent on beneficent service across the world.

3) *This peace is perpetual.* The tense used here is future indicative and the context makes it clear that it is the progressive future which means continuous and unabated action.

Stop perpetually worrying. Perpetually let your requests be made known unto God. And you have the assurance that perpetual peace will garrison and guard your mind and heart through Christ Jesus. What an antidote to worry!

The assurance of this peace is conditional upon no outside circumstance, for this peace is possible only through Christ. A life without Christ is the life without peace. Without Him you have excitement, worldly success, fulfilled dreams, fun, gratified passions, but never peace!

Mr. Horatio G. Spafford was a successful lawyer in Chicago and a member of the Fullerton Avenue Presbyterian Church in that city. In the financial crisis of 1873, he lost most of his property. In the stress and strain of the times, he prevailed on his wife and four daughters to take a trip to France—to get as far away from the scene of worry as possible. He booked passage for them on the *Ville de Havre.* They set sail November 15, 1873.

The trip was uneventful, and its hundreds of passengers were enjoying the indescribable uplift of an ocean voyage. That is, until the night of November 22.

Shortly after midnight the *Loch Earn,* bound for New York, collided with the *Ville de Havre.* In a few minutes, the French ocean liner sank beneath the waves. The *Loch Earn,* which was not damaged by the collision, rescued as many survivors as they could find. Of the 226 passengers on the *Ville de Havre,* only 87 survived.

Mrs. Spafford was among the survivors, but the four daughters perished. As soon as Mrs. Spafford reached land, she telegraphed from France to her husband: "Saved alone. Children lost. What shall I do?"

The Chicago attorney left immediately to join his wife and bring her back to Chicago. It was in the depths of their bereavement that he wrote his one and only hymn, "It Is Well With My Soul." The grief of his terrible loss and the peace he experienced as he and his wife submitted their lives to God's providential dealings, he describes in the four stanzas of the hymn.

Perhaps the words will take on new meaning for you as you ponder them:

> When peace, like a river, attendeth my way,
> When sorrow like sea billows roll;
> Whatever my lot,
> Thou hast taught me to say,
> "It is well, it is well with my soul."
>
> Though Satan should buffet, though trials
>   should come,
> Let this blest assurance control;
> That Christ has regarded my helpless estate,
> And hath shed His own blood for my soul.
>
> My sin—oh, the bliss of this glorious thought,
> My sin not in part, but the whole
> Is nailed to the cross and I bear it no more,
> Praise the Lord, praise the Lord, oh my soul!
>
> And, Lord, haste the day when the faith shall be
>   sight,
> The clouds be rolled back as a scroll;
> The trump shall resound and the Lord shall
>   descend,
> "Even so," it is well with my soul.

Christian friend, before you were saved you had no peace, did you? The Christless heart is like a troubled sea that cannot rest. There is no peace for it.

Now you are a Christian. The Lord has brought you peace with respect to your relationship with Himself and with respect to your outlook on eternity. However, if you are to enjoy the peace of God over daily worries and cares and anxieties, small though they be—"the little foxes spoil the vines"—you must fix your mind upon Him. "Looking unto Jesus" (Hebrews 12:2).

Keep your mind "stayed" on Him. This will enable you to fulfill the Bible formula of Praise, Poise, and Prayer.

Here is the glorious conclusion:

Praise plus **Poise** plus **Prayer**
equals **Perfect Peace!**

As Christ lives in you "your peace shall be as a river, and your righteousness as the waves of the sea."

Peace be with you.